D0821706

The Emergence
of Pakistan

CHAUDHRI MUHAMMAD ALI

The Emergence
of Pakistan

DS
480.83
A65
C. 2

Columbia University Press

New York & London 1967

Chaudhri Muhammad Ali served
as Prime Minister of Pakistan from 1955 to 1956.

Copyright © 1967 Columbia University Press
Library of Congress Catalog Card Number: 67-12535
Printed in the United States of America

To the memory of my brother
Dr. Ali Ahmad,
who urged me to write this book
but did not live to see it completed.

Preface

THIS BOOK is, in the main, an account of the events in the period 1946–48, immediately preceding and following the partition of British India and the creation of two independent sovereign states— Pakistan and the Union of India—on August 15, 1947. The introductory chapters describe the historical setting in which those events took place, and the social, economic, and political forces that shaped them. The last part of the book deals with the challenging problems which the newly born state of Pakistan had to face. Some of those issues are still alive, and I have in places briefly indicated developments beyond 1948.

Having been associated with the leaders of the Pakistan movement from 1946 onward and having taken an active part in the momentous events that led to the emergence of Pakistan, I have often been asked by friends in the past to write about them. In 1946 I was working as Financial Adviser, War and Supply, in the Government of India. When the Muslim League representatives joined the interim government of India and Liaquat Ali Khan became Finance Minister, my association with the Muslim League leaders became even closer. During the crucial days of partition I was one of the two members of the Steering Committee which was responsible to the Partition

Council for the immense administrative tasks involved in partition. My other colleague, H. M. Patel of the Indian Civil Service, represented India, while I represented Pakistan. The Partition Council was presided over by Lord Mountbatten, the Viceroy of India, and had as its members Sardar Vallabhbhai Patel and Rajendra Prashad from the Indian side, and Quaid-i-Azam Muhammad Ali Jinnah and Liaquat Ali Khan from the Pakistan side. On the establishment of Pakistan, I was appointed Secretary-General to the Government of Pakistan, with the duty of coordinating the work of the ministries. I also held the post of Cabinet Secretary.

I had thus an unusual opportunity to observe the movement of history in this part of the world at a critical time. But even though the facts narrated here were mostly in my personal experience, I have, wherever possible, cited documentary evidence from other sources. In particular, where the version of any incident given here differs from that put forward by Indian and British writers, I have taken care to quote from books which cannot be accused of bias against the Indian and British personalities involved. An example is provided by *Mission with Mountbatten*. The author, Alan Campbell-Johnson, was Press Attaché to Lord Mountbatten during his viceroyalty. Campbell-Johnson admired Mountbatten to the point of hero-worship and naturally presents him in the most favorable light. Or there is *Mahatma Gandhi: The Last Phase,* by Pyarelal, Gandhi's devoted follower and secretary. In dealing with the communal disturbances that form a prominent feature of the period under study, I have, in general, relied upon reports written by impartial British observers of the Indian scene. I mention this not to lessen my responsibility for the contents of this book but to indicate that I have tried as far as humanly possible to present an objective account. I should, however, be guilty of untruth if I were to claim an Olympian detachment. I have recorded the truth as I see it but I am deeply conscious that it is only a facet of the truth which I can see.

I gratefully acknowledge permission to quote from Abul Kalam Azad, *India Wins Freedom* (Calcutta, Orient Longmans, 1959); *Cabinet Mission and After,* ed. by Muhammad Ashraf (Lahore, Muhammad Ashraf, 1946); Alan Campbell-Johnson, *Mission with Mountbatten* (London, Robert Hale, 1953); John Connell, *Auchinleck* (London, Cassell, 1959); Lord Ismay, *Memoirs* (London, William

Heinemann, 1960; New York, Viking, 1960); Nicholas Mansergh, *Survey of British Commonwealth Affairs* (London, Oxford University Press, 1958); V. P. Menon, *The Story of the Integration of the Indian States* (Calcutta, Orient Longmans, 1956; New York, Macmillan, 1956) and *The Transfer of Power in India* (Calcutta, Orient Longmans, 1957; Princeton, N.J., Princeton University Press, 1957); Jawaharlal Nehru, *The Discovery of India* (Bombay, Asia Publishing House, 1961; New York, John Day, 1961); Kewal L. Panjabi, *The Indomitable Sardar: A Political Biography of Sardar Vallabhbhai Patel* (Bombay, Bharatiya Vidya Bhavan, 1962); Pyarelal, *Mahatma Gandhi: The Last Phase* (Ahmedabad, Navajivan, 1956); *Some Recent Speeches and Writings of Mr. Jinnah,* ed. by Jamil-ud-din Ahmad (Lahore, Muhammad Ashraf, 1952); *Speeches and Documents on the Indian Constitution, 1921–1947,* ed. by Sir Maurice Gwyer and A. Appadorai (London, Oxford University Press, 1957); Ian Stephens, *Pakistan* (London, Ernest Benn, 1963; New York, Frederick A. Praeger, 1963); and Sir Francis Tuker, *While Memory Serves* (London, Cassell, 1950).

MUHAMMAD ALI

Lahore
January, 1967

Contents

List of Maps

CHAPTER 1

Historical Background

THE ENCOUNTER between Hindu and Muslim cultures that began over a thousand years ago has profoundly influenced both. They have met at a thousand points, on battlefields and at festivals, around market places and in homes, on spiritual heights and in the lowlands of mundane affairs. They have learnt from each other, interacted with each other, and penetrated each other; their tongues have mixed to produce new and rich languages; in music and poetry, painting and architecture, in styles of dress, and in ways of living they have left their mark on each other. And yet they have remained distinct with an emphasis on their separateness. They have mixed but never fused; they have coexisted but have never become one. Hindu and Muslim families that have lived in the same neighborhood for generations can be distinguished at a glance from one another. The clothes, the food, the household utensils, the layout of homes, the manner of speech, the words of salutation, the postures, the gestures, everything about them will be different and will immediately point to their origin. These outer differences are only the reflection of an inner divergence. For among the varied social groups of mankind it is difficult to imagine a more striking contrast than that between Hindu and Muslim social organization and *Weltanschauung*.

The former is a closed society with a rigid hierarchical structure subdivided into thousands of castes. A caste system has been defined as "one whereby a society is divided into a number of self-contained and completely segregated units [castes] the mutual relations between which are ritually determined in a graded scale." [1] The accident of birth determines a man's status throughout life; but high or low birth is itself determined by what a man did in an earlier incarnation. "Observance of caste is equivalent to Dharma; that is, religious observance, righteousness, moral obligation." [2] The grossest social injustice is seen as ordained by a cosmic law, which squares up accounts over aeons. Since reincarnation may take the form of animals, this belief accounts partly for the sacredness attached to animal life. The principle of hierarchy applies here also. A cow is as sacred as the Brahmin, the highest caste of all.

The common people who remain entangled in the web of social life develop a spirit of intense loyalty to their caste, which regulates their diet, training, marriage, profession, and other social relations. From the earliest years of their lives they are conditioned to an intricate system of taboos, customs, and superstitions so that their entire psychic energy is irrevocably canalized into these channels. Since caste determines a man's profession, and since economic activity brings the various professions in economic relations with each other, these thousands of castes are integrated into an organic unity which is Hindu society as a whole. Such a system can make a claim upon men's loyalty only if they have been brought up in it from the time of their birth and are conditioned to accept its intricate patterns of relationship. The system in no way, by a single world view or set of beliefs, tries to appeal to an outsider. In fact, the outsider's status is also fixed by his birth. As someone born outside the fold of Hindu society he is in a literal sense an untouchable. It is not surprising, therefore, that Hinduism makes no effort to convert others. Outsiders may be attracted by the subtlety of its metaphysical thought, by the refinement of its psychological analysis, and by its exploration of the extreme possibilities of the human nervous system as demonstrated in various forms of Yoga, but they can never enter into the experience of feeling an intuitive unity with Hindu society.

Islam presents a radically different aspect of human thought and action. Its call is addressed to the whole of mankind, irrespective of color, race, tribe, and language. It summons all to submit to the One

God, the Ever-Living Creator and Sustainer of the universe to Whom each individual is accountable for his or her actions. Divine unity and human brotherhood are the essence of the teachings the Messengers of God have brought to men so that they may live in truth and justice. Birth confers no special status or privilege. In the earnest endeavor to establish a just social order on earth, Muslims are expected to exert themselves to the utmost and, if need be, to sacrifice life and property. In Islam there is thus a continual emphasis upon right belief and right action. If men live in ignorance and sin, they cannot throw the blame on an assumed incarnation of the past, but must accept responsibility for it here and hereafter.

These differences in world view and principles of social organization were powerfully reinforced by a difference in historical experience. Starting with Muhammad bin Qasim's invasion of Sind in A.D. 712 and ending with Ahmad Shah Abdali's victory over the Maratha confederacy in 1761, the Muslims came to the Indian subcontinent in waves of conquest. Even after the foundation of the Delhi Sultanate by Qutbuddin Aibak in 1206, these periodic attacks continued. The result was an expansion of Muslim power until it was supreme over the entire subcontinent. Inevitably this movement presented itself to Hindus and Muslims in diametrically opposed aspects. Kings and generals who were admired by Muslims as conquering heroes struck terror in the Hindu heart; and those who were ranged against the Muslim Empire appeared as rebels to the Muslims but as patriots in Hindu eyes.

When the British appeared on the scene, they saw that it would be to their own advantage to heighten these contrasts. There was even a deliberate attempt to rewrite Indian history, so as to show Muslims as oppressors and persecutors in order that the Hindus, who formed the bulk of the population, should have a more lively appreciation of the blessings of British rule.[3]

The Muslims who came to India with conquering armies, or in their wake, settled down in India. This, and the conversion of Hindus to Islam caused the population of India to undergo a gradual change. In course of time Muslims came to form one fourth of the total population. In the northwest and the northeast of the subcontinent they formed a majority, but in the center and the south only 15 to 5 percent of the population were Muslims. The spread of Islam in India owed little to the efforts of Muslim rulers. A modern British historian says, "The evidence of cooperation of Hindu officials with Muslim rulers from early days and of relations with Hindu chiefs is too strong to admit of the reign of terror which continuous forcible conversion would mean in a country like India. Forcible conversion happened, but exceptionally." [4] Rajendra Prasad, the first President of the Union of India, stated that "the attitude of the Muslim conquerors had, on the whole, been one of toleration." [5] Islam spread in India to the extent it did through the exertion and example of Muslim scholars and Sufis (mystics), who journeyed from one end of the land to the other and courted innumerable hardships and dangers in their endeavor to spread the light of truth.

The Muslims belonged to all walks of life. They were administrators, soldiers, teachers, landlords, peasants, artisans, and traders. They lived in the cities and in the country. Under Muslim rule it was natural that they should preponderate in the civil, judicial, and military administration. But the Hindus were not unrepresented in the administration. The revenue and financial administration, in particular, was almost entirely run by Hindus; they also served in the military, and Hindu generals led armies composed largely of Muslims. Trade continued to be mainly in Hindu hands. The feudal aristocracy included both Hindus and Muslims. There were a number of Hindu states under the suzerainty of the Muslim Empire. In the cities some localities would be predominantly Muslim and others Hindu, but quite often Hindu and Muslim households would be set up side by side.

Even so, the deeper causes of conflict between the two communities did not disappear. The Hindus tightened their caste and taboo regulations to reduce the area of contact with the Muslims. This was an automatic defense mechanism which preserved their social structure intact through many centuries of Muslim rule. Any article of food and drink touched by a Muslim became impure. There was no intermarriage between the two communities, except for a short time in Akbar's court. Dietary habits—one community was vegetarian and the other was not—stood in the way of free social intercourse. But the greatest obstacle was caste. "Caste: there was the iron curtain. . . . It was caste which divided the two communities for all time." [6]

But despite the closed character of their social organization the Hindus could not remain unaffected by Muslim culture. A number of movements sprang up within Hinduism which preached monotheism and emphasized devotion and good works for attaining salvation. Many of these movements stressed the unity of all religions—particularly of Hinduism in its purer forms and of Islam—and called upon men to follow the path of love. The style in which the Muslim nobility lived was widely imitated and influenced Hindu customs and manners. At the same time, the fine fabrics of Indian manufacture were used for garments worn by Muslims. Hindu painting and architecture influenced the arts brought by the Muslims from Persia, and a distinctive style evolved; a similar process took place in music and poetry. Gradually the intercourse of centuries led to the development of Urdu, which was the common language of Hindus and Muslims in the cities of upper India. Its basic vocabulary and syntax were Hindi, but it was embellished by Persian and Arabic words to form a new and flexible instrument of great adaptability and beauty.

The only deliberate effort at combining selected features of Islam and Hinduism was the ill-fated attempt of Akbar, the Mughul Emperor, to produce a synthetic religion for political and dynastic reasons. His death not only put an end to the scheme but produced a vigorous reaction, which reached its zenith under the last great Mughul Emperor, Aurangzeb. But even his untiring energy and severe austerity could not arrest the decline of morals or correct the habits of luxury into which the upper classes had fallen. The soft air and enervating climate of the Gangetic plain had sapped the vigor of their minds and bodies. Within a short time of Aurangzeb's death the imposing edifice of the Mughul Empire began to crack and crumble. The governors of outlying provinces became virtually autonomous and paid only lip loyalty to the central government, which was too weak and dissolute to exert any authority over them. The marauding Marathas reduced large parts of the empire to a state of anarchy.

Into this scene of confusion and decay entered a third party. "For a century and a half the English had been humble petitioners to the Mughul Emperors and their Viceroys." [7] But events turned in their favor about the middle of the eighteenth century, and for the next hundred years they were engaged in exploiting and undermining the empire of their erstwhile patrons. In this undertaking they employed all the weapons of diplomacy, force, and bluff, which they had used with such advantage in their trade with India. The Hindus, with whom they had long been connected through trade, were their natural allies in this struggle against the Muslims; when they finally won, the English used their power to crush the Muslims still further.

The struggle for freedom which led to the uprising of 1857 ended in disaster. The Mughul Empire was extinguished and British rule was established over the whole subcontinent. The Muslim nobility and middle classes were ruined, but the embers of discontent continued to smoulder. W. W. Hunter, writing in 1871, observed "The Musalmans of India are, and have been for many years, a source of chronic danger to the British Power in India. For some reason or other they have held aloof from our system, and the changes in which the more flexible Hindus have cheerfully acquiesced, are regarded by them as deep personal wrongs." [8]

The causes of discontent were many. Practically every measure taken by the British, from the battle of Plassey in 1757 till the end of the nineteenth century, affected Muslims for the worse. There was, first of all, the reservation of all higher civil, judicial, and military appointments for the British. In the heyday of their rule, Muslims had dominated but not monopolized the administration in the way the British now did. The social and economic position of the Muslims depended upon government employment; without it they had neither social status nor means of subsistence. The Hindus, who even under Muslim rule had held the lower rungs of the administration in large number, now proceeded to fill all the positions the British left open for Indians. As an Indian writer has said, "Hindus poured into official life with a joy which knew no bounds and hailed the British as their great benefactors." [9] To the caste-minded Hindu, discrimination against the outsider comes as naturally as the air he breathes. Pressed between the upper stone of British colonialism and the nether stone of Hindu exclusiveness, the Muslim was crushed out. "It is not that they must now take an equal chance with the Hindus in the race of life, but that, at least in Bengal, they have ceased to have a chance at all. In short, it is a people with great traditions and without a career." [10]

During Muslim rule, Persian had been the official language. The British did not make any changes until Macaulay wrote his celebrated "Minute on Education," which aimed at producing "a class of persons, Indian in blood and colour but English in taste, in opinion, in morals and intellect." In pursuance of this policy, it was declared, in 1835, that English would from now on be the language used in higher education, and that Persian would be replaced by English as the official language in government business and in the higher courts of law. To the Hindus it was the replacement of one foreign language by another, and they took to English readily. For the Muslims the decision was of infinitely greater consequence; to many it seemed a deliberate attempt to stamp out their culture and to pollute their religion. They kept aloof, and the result was that during 1880–81, though 36,686 Hindus studied in English high schools, only 363 Muslim pupils attended.[11]

The Code of Islam had been the law of the land during the many centuries of Muslim rule, although in matters of personal law each community was governed by its own provisions. Gradually this was replaced by Western legal institutions; the Indian Civil and Criminal Codes of Procedure and the Indian Penal Code came into force. Again, the effect was felt most acutely by the Muslims, both in jurisprudence and in judicial employment. As if to complete the ruin of the Muslim community, the British undertook a reexamination of rent free tenures that had been granted under Muslim rule, and of trusts and foundations for charitable and educational purposes. The large-scale confiscation that followed this examination brought greater revenues for the government, but in the process, the old aristocracy was impoverished, Muslim education was strangled, and the middle classes were turned into paupers. Too proud to cooperate with the victor, too sullen to adjust themselves to the new circumstances, too embittered to think objectively, too involved emotionally with the past to plan for the future, Muslim society in the decades following the events of 1857 presented a picture of desolation and decay.

Hindus, on the other hand, were forging ahead in all fields. Their rise as a landlord class had been facilitated by the 1793 Permanent Settlement of Bengal and they now formed a new aristocracy. Trade had been largely in their hands even under Muslim rule, and because they took avidly to English education, ways were opened for them to careers in law, engineering, medicine, teaching, and journalism. A new middle class arose, consisting almost entirely of Hindus, which assumed the leadership of the India that was taking shape under British rule. In 1878, "there were 3155 Hindus as against 57 Muslims holding graduate and post-graduate degrees." [12] Under the influence of English political ideas, nationalism became an increasingly powerful force and served to strengthen Hindu social cohesion.

In the darkest hour of its life in India, the Muslim community produced a great and courageous leader in Sir Syed Ahmad Khan. He saw with clear eyes the state into which the Muslims had fallen and the long and difficult ascent they had to undertake. He considered that the first essential step was to restore mutual trust between the British and the Muslim. Without it, any plan for the resurrection of Muslims would founder on the rock of opposition by the rulers and be drowned in the sea of popular misunderstanding. The next vital measure, he felt, was to reform the educational system, so as to impart modern knowledge to the Muslims and to prepare them for taking their due place in the new India. Sir Syed's twofold program, therefore, was modern education and cooperation with the government, and even in the face of intense opposition from conservative elements he persisted with it. He founded a scientific society for the promotion of knowledge, opened schools, started journals like the very influential *Tahzib-ul-Akhlaq,* gave a new tone and amplitude to Urdu literature, compiled and edited books of history, and promoted legislation. But his monumental achievement was the founding of the Mohammedan Anglo-Oriental College at Aligarh in 1877. He had wanted to build a university, but his wish could only be fulfilled some twenty-two years after his death, when the College grew into the Aligarh Muslim University. The college at Aligarh was more than an educational institution; it was the symbol of a broad movement affecting every phase of Muslim life—social, economic, political, literary, and religious. To carry the message of reform to the masses, Sir Syed organized the Muslim Educational Conference which held public meetings in various parts of the country. The greatest service these meetings did was to arouse a spirit of action and self-help. Schools and colleges modeled on Aligarh were opened in different places. Even the orthodox Ulama, or learned divines, who had denounced Sir Syed as an apostate, came to recognize his greatness. His precepts and example revived hope and self-confidence, showed new ways of organization and cooperative work, and opened the door to modern knowledge and economic progress.

Although Sir Syed devoted his life to work for the moral and material progress of Muslims, he was free from religious intolerance. He had a large circle of Hindu friends and worked in close cooperation with Hindu social workers. Aligarh College had Hindus on its faculty and was open to Hindu students. But, as a practical statesman, he could neither ignore Hindu characteristics nor lose sight of the differences in education and economic power between the two communities. He knew that Hindus were fifty years ahead of Muslims in education, and far in advance of them in the spheres of government, business, and the professions. When the Hindus started an agitation in 1867 for the replacement of Urdu, which was the common heritage of Hindus and Muslims, by Hindi written in the Devnagri script, Sir Syed realized for the first time that the two communities could not live together as a single nation. It was then that he made his prophetic remark: "I am convinced that the two communities will not sincerely cooperate in any work. Opposition and hatred between them, which is felt so little today, will in the future be seen to increase on account of the so-called educated classes." [13]

In 1885 the Indian National Congress was formed on the initiative of the retired British official, Allan Octavian Hume, and under the guidance of the Viceroy, Lord Dufferin. The Congress, which grew in time to be the most powerful political organization in India, was originally intended to provide a forum in which "Indian politicians should meet yearly and point out to the Government in what respects the administration was defective and how it could be improved." [14] Sir Syed advised Muslims not to join the Congress, and on the whole his advice was followed by the Muslim community for a considerable time. His views were not based on any differences with the Congress in its attitude toward the British government, since the Congress at that time was "absolutely unanimous in insisting on unswerving loyalty to the British Crown as the key-note of the Institution." [15] Nor were they based on opposition to democracy. In a letter to an English friend Sir Syed had written: "I have firm faith in Islam which teaches radical principles, is against personal rule and accepts neither limited monarchy nor hereditary government but approves of an elected President. Nor does Islam allow concentration of wealth." [16]

There were two reasons for his opposition. The first was connected with the composition and character of the Indian National Congress, which was mainly a Hindu body. The Hindus had advanced far enough in education, political consciousness, and wealth to dominate the Congress and to make it the vehicle for voicing demands which would suit them, but not necessarily the Muslims. At this time hardly any one envisaged a sovereign Indian parliament in the foreseeable future; the objective was gradual control over policy and administration by Indians within the framework provided by the British government. The main demands of the Congress were progressive Indianization of superior services and extension of representative institutions. The demand for the Indianization of higher ranks in the administration meant virtually their Hinduization, since Muslims were too backward, as far as English education was concerned, to receive their due share at that time. Sir Syed felt that Muslims should concentrate for a time on education and economic rehabilitation. Political agitation would divert their attention from these constructive tasks and perhaps revive British mistrust.

To anyone unacquainted with Eastern agrarian economy, the importance attached to government service will appear greatly exaggerated. Even today the peasant, and also the landlord and the trader, know through personal experience that the power of the administration to confer favors, withhold rights, inflict injury, and cause harassment is great. The revenue that has to be paid to the government forms a large proportion of the produce, and if drought or unseasonal rain or blight injures the crops, the burden may be intolerable. Where a system of canal irrigation exists, the officials who regulate the water supply exercise the powers of providence. Disputes over land, or distribution of water, or other village feuds, may mean lengthy litigation in which the parties are fair prey of the police and the subordinate judiciary. There is another, purely economic, reason for the competition to get into government service. In a static economy with a growing population, the economic opportunities available to the new generation are extremely limited. If a new educated class is growing up, it has practically no avenues open to it except those provided by government service.

The second reason for his opposition concerned the social and political difficulties which, as Sir Syed clearly foresaw, representative government would create, given the peculiar conditions of India. When, during Lord Ripon's viceroyalty, representative institutions were introduced in India, Sir Syed, though supporting the principle underlying them, had sounded a note of warning. In a speech in the legislative council in 1883 he had said:

In borrowing from England the system of representative institutions, it is of the greatest importance to remember those sociopolitical matters in which India is distinguishable from England. . . . India, a continent in itself is inhabited by vast populations of different races and different creeds: the rigour of religious institutions has kept even neighbours apart: the system of caste is still dominant and powerful. . . . The community of race and creed make the English people one and the same nation. . . . In a country like India, where caste distinctions still flourish, where there is no fusion of the various races, where religious distinctions are still violent, where education in its modern sense has not made an equal or proportionate progress among all the sections of the population, I am convinced that the introduction of the principle of election, pure and simple, for representation of various interests on the local boards and district councils would be attended with evils of greater significance than purely economic considerations. . . . The larger community would totally override the interests of the smaller community and the ignorant public would hold Government responsible for introducing measures which might make differences of race and creed more violent than ever.[17]

As long as effective power was in the hands of the British, conflicts between Hindus and Muslims were confined to cultural and social matters, but with the introduction of representative institutions, political questions came to occupy the center of attention. The devolution of political power was accompanied by many stresses and strains and brought dormant fears into the open. It brought new opportunities for cooperation between the two communities, but it also opened up new fields of conflict. If the two communities had been evenly matched in numbers, wealth, education, and influence, it might have been easier to find a solution. However that may be, the fact is the Muslims were greatly outdistanced by the Hindus in practically every field of social and economic endeavor, and the Hindus had come to regard this state of inequality as their birthright, due to them by virtue of their superior education, social status, and economic strength. They were determined to maintain and, if possible to improve, their position by means of political power. Prospects of democracy thus intensified the struggle between Hindus and Muslims. Democracy is rule by majority, but if the majority is fixed and hereditary, and also enjoys the privileges of superior education, greater economic and administrative power, control over the press, and talent and money for political organization, the minority is doomed forever to a position of subordination.

The first decade of the present century saw a clearer definition of the goal toward which India was moving. Until then, liberal voices in India and England had asserted, off and on, that India would ultimately attain self-government, but the day when England's trusteeship would end lay in a remote and indefinite future. Now new forces were in motion. The spell of European supremacy had been broken by the victory of Japan over Russia in 1905. Autocratic regimes in Turkey and Persia were crumbling. Asia was awakening from its long slumber.

The Minto-Morley reforms of 1909 accepted the principle of election, but maintained a majority of appointed members in the central legislature and in the provincial legislatures, except in Bengal, which had a slight majority of elected members. Election was to be held on the basis of separate electorates for Muslims and non-Muslims.

The demand for separate electorates had been put to the Viceroy Lord Minto in 1906 by a Muslim deputation led by the Agha Khan. In the address presented to the Viceroy, the deputation pointed out that

> the Mohammedans of India number, according to the census taken in the year 1901, over sixty-two million or between one-fifth and one-fourth of the total population of His Majesty's Indian dominions. . . . Under any system of representation, extended or limited, a community in itself more numerous than the entire population of any first class European power except Russia may justly lay claim to adequate recognition as an important factor in the State.

The deputation demanded that the representation of Muslims be

> commensurate not merely with their numerical strength but also with their political importance and the value of the contribution which they make to the defence of the empire. . . . It is most unlikely that the name of any Mohammedan candidate will ever be submitted for the approval of Government by the electoral bodies as now constituted unless he is in sympathy with the majority in all matters of importance.[18]

The Viceroy sympathized with the views of the deputation and expressed his conviction that "any electoral representation in India would be doomed to the mischievous failure which aimed at granting a personal enfranchisement regardless of the beliefs and traditions of the communities." [19]

Toward the end of 1906, the All-India Muslim League was formed in Dacca to protect political and other rights of the Indian Muslims.

The invitation to this historic meeting of Muslim leaders was issued by Nawab Salimullah Khan of Dacca. The Agha Khan was elected President of the League. Other Muslim associations had been formed in the past, but the All-India Muslim League assumed an importance far greater than those earlier organizations and was, in due course, recognized as the political body representing Indian Muslims.

The scheme of separate electorates aroused Hindu antagonism. In 1909 the Congress recorded its "disapproval of the creation of separate electorates on the basis of religion," and continued to reiterate its objection in later years.[20] Joint versus separate electorates became a major issue in Indian politics. The franchise was restricted, and since the Hindus were ahead of Muslims in wealth and education, the numerical majority of Hindus in the electorate was further enhanced. Few Muslims would be elected if the electorate were a joint one. Experience in the working of local self-government had shown that this apprehension was based on reality. In a joint electorate with reservation of seats for Muslims, only those Muslims would be returned whose "nationalism" was above suspicion in the eyes of Hindu voters. The slightest tinge of "communalism" would ruin the chances of a Muslim candidate; "communalism" in this context meant any endeavor to promote the welfare of the backward Muslim community.

The caste Hindus were in favor of a joint electorate, but the depressed classes of Hindus had everything to gain by separate electorates, which would bring their real representatives into the legislature and make their voices heard. In a joint electorate they had no chance against caste Hindus. But they were too low on the social scale, and too negligible a factor in the political life of the country, for the British government to pay any attention to their cause.

There were a few Muslim leaders, notably Muhammad Ali Jinnah, whose political convictions led them to support a joint electorate. Jinnah was an active lieutenant of Gopal Krishna Gokhale, the leader of the moderates within the Congress. The moderates believed in social reforms and gradual constitutional progress, and longed for the growth of supracommunal nationalism. There was a struggle for supremacy in the Congress between the extremists, whose leader was Bal Gangadhar Tilak, and the moderates. Tilak advocated the attainment of *swaraj,* or self-rule, through persistent agitation against the British government. He glorified Shivaji who had fought Aurangzeb and appealed to Hindu chauvinism. This divergence in basic attitudes and strategy of action continued for many years in various forms; the contestants changed, but the struggle continued to be essentially the same. The moderates appealed to the reason and mind of the educated middle class; the extremists to the sentiments and hearts of the Hindu masses.

There was a time when the issue hung in the balance and many Hindus and Muslims believed that a truly common nationalism was in the making. But with the growth of mass movements, reliance on specifically Hindu stimuli to action increased, and the fate of Indian nationalism was sealed. The outer aspect of Indian nationalism continued to be secular and noncommunal, but its inner spirit was informed by Hindu inspirations. It addressed its appeal to the patriotism of every citizen, Hindu or Muslim, but in any clash of interests the Hindu view prevailed.

The violent agitation to annul the partition of Bengal, which started in Bengal and spread to the rest of India, provides an early and significant illustration of this trend. In 1905, Viceroy Lord Curzon carried out, mainly for reasons of administrative efficiency, a readjustment of the boundaries of Bengal. This was an unwieldly province with a population of 78 million people. Curzon divided it, and by combining its eastern part with Assam, created a new province of Eastern Bengal and Assam, the bulk of whose population were Muslims. Bengal Hindus, who had thrived on the toil of the Muslim peasants of eastern Bengal, saw in this a threat to their cultural, economic, and political domination. Mass meetings and protest marches were held. A movement was launched for a boycott of Lancashire manufactures in favor of *swadeshi,* or Indian-made, cloth. There was an outburst of terrorist activity. Tilak and other Congress leaders took up the grievance and made it an all-India question. The Muslims, backward in education, political consciousness, and modern means of publicity, were too poorly organized to counter the movement. They relied upon the assurances given them by British officials and were soon disillusioned. The British government submitted to Hindu agitation, and in 1911 the provincial reorganization of 1905 was undone and the Muslims of eastern Bengal reverted to their previous position of subservience to the Hindus. A great "national" victory had been won.

When the First World War broke out a few years later, the

majority of the Indian peoples stood by the British. Indian princes vied with each other in demonstrations of loyalty to the Allied cause. A million men went to the battlefields, and there was a liberal flow of funds for the war effort. Toward the end, however, there were signs of discontent because of rising prices and coercion in recruitment.

The war period saw a *rapprochement* between the Muslim League and the Congress. Largely through the efforts of Jinnah, who was hailed the ambassador of Hindu-Muslim unity, an agreement on a scheme of constitutional reforms was reached between the Congress and the League at their annual sessions held in Lucknow in 1916. The agreement came to be known as the Lucknow Pact. It conceded separate electorates for Muslims and provided for provincial autonomy, election of four fifths of central and provincial councils, responsibility of the executive to the legislature with some reservations and a safeguard to the effect that no bill or resolution affecting a community should be proceeded with if three fourths of the representatives of that community were opposed to it. Under the Pact, the Muslim representation was fixed at 33⅓ percent of the Indian elected members for the central government; at 50 and 40 percent respectively for the provinces of the Punjab and Bengal, where the majority of the population was Muslim; and at 33⅓, 30, 25, 15, and 15 percent respectively for Bombay, United Provinces, Bihar, Central Provinces, and Madras. The Punjab and Bengal got less representation than their Muslim population warranted, whereas the other provinces, in which the Muslims were in a minority, received more. This arrangement has often been criticized by Muslim publicists on the ground that, while a higher percentage made no real difference to the position of Muslims in provinces where they were in a minority, they lost their majority in the Punjab and Bengal. Its great merit was that an agreed solution to constitutional questions had been found for the two major communities of Hindus and Muslims.

Wars are periods of rapid change. The British government felt it necessary to respond to Indian aspirations and on August 20, 1917, Edwin Montague, the Secretary of State for India, made an announcement of British policy in the House of Commons. Its key sentence was: "The policy of His Majesty's Government with which the Government of India are in complete accord, is that of the increasing association of Indians in every branch of the administration and the gradual development of self-governing institutions with a view to the progressive realisation of responsible government in India as an integral part of the British Empire."

In the middle of 1918 Montague and Lord Chelmsford, the Viceroy, published a joint "Report on Indian Constitutional Reforms," which formed the basis of the Government of India Act, 1919. This Act established legislative councils in the provinces with a system of dyarchy. Under this scheme anything relating to "law and order" was to be administered by executive councilors responsible to the governor; nation-building departments, such as education and agriculture, were to be in the charge of ministers responsible to the legislative councils. But before these constitutional reforms could be implemented, the whole subcontinent experienced a political storm of unprecedented severity that was to leave its mark on all subsequent events.

The match that ignited the great conflagration was security legislation passed in 1919 and known as the Rowlatt Acts. These Acts gave arbitrary powers of arrest and trial without jury to the government, and, naturally, aroused widespread indignation. A number of protest meetings were held all over the country. One such meeting, in Jallianwala Bagh in Amritsar, was drowned in blood by General Dyer who opened fire on the crowd without warning. Within a few minutes 379 persons were killed and over 1,200 wounded—unofficial estimates put the number of casualties still higher. Martial law was declared, and the citizens were subjected to innumerable humiliating indignities. Dyer's object was to intimidate the people by a demonstration of ruthless power. The results were exactly the opposite—quite unwittingly he had aroused a spirit of fierce resentment against the British raj.

Even so, the Congress, meeting in Amritsar in December, 1919, was prepared to work the Montague-Chelmsford reforms although it declared them "inadequate, unsatisfactory and disappointing." The agitation against the government might well have proceeded along old lines and not taken a revolutionary turn, had not an international event again stirred up feelings, and a supreme political strategist assumed control. The international event was the Treaty of Sèvres whose harsh terms made it clear that the victorious Allies were not content with the dismemberment of the Ottoman Empire, but were determined to destroy even the Turkish homeland. To Indian Muslims the Treaty appeared to be a deliberate attempt by the Christian

West to exterminate forever the political power of Islam as symbolized by the Khilafat, or caliphate. The dynamic leadership of the Ali brothers—Maulana Muhammad Ali and Shaukat Ali—Abul Kalam Azad, and other religious leaders stirred the deep disquiet of Muslim masses into the white-hot glow of intense emotion, which became reckless of all sacrifices. That more than eighteen thousand Muslims left hearth and home and migrated to Afghanistan in religious protest against British policy toward the caliphate indicates the temper of the time.

The political strategist who now assumed control of the situation was Mohandas Karamchand Gandhi. He had spent the greater part of his working life in South Africa, where he had fought against racial discrimination with the weapons of *Satyagraha*—literally, "holding on to truth"—and ahimsa, or nonviolence. The essence of the method was passive resistance to evil, and noncooperation with it without any thought of violence or hatred. The method had achieved a measure of success in South Africa. Gandhi returned to India in 1915; he was then a follower of Gokhale and by no means an extremist. He supported the British war effort and acted as a recruiting agent for some time. Although he took a leading part in organizing hartals, or strikes, against the Rowlatt Acts in 1919, he advocated acceptance of the Montague-Chelmsford reforms in the Amritsar session of the Congress held at the end of the year. But this was his last act of unreserved cooperation with the British.

He alone among the Hindu leaders had the vision to see that if he could use the tremendous energies aroused among Muslim masses by the Khilafat agitation to back the demand for *swaraj,* he would at one stroke bring about unity between the two great communities of Hindus and Muslims and convert the old constitutional struggle into a mass movement of the most revolutionary kind. Whether the Muslims won or lost on the Khilafat issue was immaterial to the cause of Indian independence; what mattered was the purpose the movement could be made to serve. He therefore advocated full support by the entire Indian nation of Muslim demands and outlined a program of action for the achievement of the dual objectives of Indian independence and the restoration of the caliphate.

The plan was to paralyze the administration by a complete boycott of British institutions and goods. Indians were to give up government service, renounce titles, boycott courts of law, walk out of schools and colleges, and take no part in the elections about to be held under the Montague-Chelmsford reforms. Nonviolence was an essential feature of the program. For Gandhi it was a matter of faith, for others of expediency; but all accepted it. Gandhi assured the people that if they carried out his program of "non-cooperation with the satanic government" in a united, disciplined, and nonviolent fashion, they would attain *swaraj* within a year. Gandhi's ascetic personality appealed tremendously to the religious sentiments of the Hindu masses. He assumed the garb of poverty and was known, and almost worshiped, as the Mahatma, or the great soul. In that garb and with that name he remained the undisputed master of the Congress political machine for the remaining twenty-eight years of his life. The enthusiasm of the Muslim masses had already been set on fire by the Khilafat committees which had been organized all over India; and the Congress, under Gandhi's leadership, adopted his program at a special session held in Calcutta, and reaffirmed it some months later at the Nagpur session in December, 1920. On this last occasion there was one lone dissenting voice—that of Jinnah—who had the courage to say what he thought, that Gandhi's methods would lead to disastrous confusion.[21]

The dramatic manner in which Gandhi espoused the cause of the caliphate and appealed for Hindu-Muslim unity as the essential prerequisite for *swaraj* made both Hindus and Muslims forget age-old animosities and suspicions. The fearless and dynamic leadership of the Ali brothers carried the message of unity everywhere. Touching scenes of amity and brotherhood between Hindus and Muslims were witnessed. The idea of *swaraj* took firm hold of the masses. The British, who until then had been regarded as superior beings, were now seen as sinful usurpers, and the foundations of British raj were shaken to the core. The army, the police, and all the other coercive apparatus of government lost their terror for the people; tens of thousands went to jail most cheerfully. Everything foreign was rejected; foreign cloth was burnt in bonfires, and khaddar, the coarse cloth made from handspun yarn, became the dress of even the most westernized sections of society. The charkha, or spinning wheel, became the symbol of Indian freedom. Gandhi himself practiced spinning every day. The economic consequences for Lancashire were obvious. What was not so obvious, but because of the limited supply of khaddar was nonetheless real, was the benefit to the Indian textile industry. Contributions from millowners, mostly Hindu, established a solid financial base for the Congress.

Muslims were foremost in this struggle and with religious zeal endeavored to carry out every part of the program. The Ulama pronounced service under the British government—both civil and military—to be forbidden by Islam. As part of the program for boycott of educational institutions recognized by the government the Ali brothers laid siege to the Muslim university at Aligarh. They did not succeed in closing it down, but a number of teachers and students broke away to found a rival, the Muslim National University, which was later transferred to Delhi and became known as the Jamia Millia Islamia. The Hindu university at Benaras, which was under the protective care of the orthodox Hindu leader Pandit Malaviya, did not undergo a similar ordeal.

Elections to the central and provincial legislatures, which were held in November, 1920, were boycotted by the Congress, but about a third of the electorate voted. The Unionist party in the Punjab, led by Sir Fazli Husain, and the Justice party of non-Brahmins in Madras formed stable ministries. The expected collapse of the administration did not come about because relatively few government servants resigned. But the movement continued in full swing throughout 1921, and the visit of the Prince of Wales in that year was boycotted. The tension between the government and the people was mounting.

On February 5, 1922, at Chauri Chaura, a village in the Forakhpur district, United Provinces, there was trouble between the police and a procession. The mob set fire to the police station and twenty-two policemen were burnt alive. It is not surprising that there was a break-down of discipline. What is astonishing is that the discipline held as long as it did. Gandhi was so upset by this act of violence that he immediately called off the movement and confessed that "there is not yet in India that non-violent and truthful atmosphere which alone can justify mass disobedience." [22] This sudden reversal produced bewilderment and dismay among the masses and the leaders. If the movement had been allowed to continue despite the Chauri Chaura incident, the British government, so the people felt, would have been compelled to make major concessions to Indian demands. The Ali brothers and many other leaders had already been arrested. Now

Gandhi was tried on a charge of sedition and sentenced to six years' imprisonment. With the movement in disarray and the leaders in jail, no one knew what to do.

The reaction among the Muslims was the strongest. They felt betrayed on the eve of victory. But still bigger shocks were in store for them. The caliphate, for which they had struggled so sincerely, was to receive its death blow, not at the hands of enemies but from a Muslim hero, Mustafa Kamal Ataturk. Under his leadership the Turks determined to make a new start as a modern nation and decided to unburden themselves of the load of the caliphate. However logical this decision might have been for the Turks, the Indian Muslims were stunned by it. The blood, the tears, and the sacrifices of the last few years were seen to have been in vain. They had been clutching at a form devoid of all substance; they had soared on wings of lofty sentiments; now they were brought back to earth with a thud.

Among the Hindus there was no corresponding feeling of having pursued an empty ideal. When Gandhi was arrested there was a setback, but Hindu leadership and Hindu masses emerged from the struggle with a new-found confidence in the power of political organization and disciplined courage. Independence had not been won, but it was only a matter of time before they would be masters of the subcontinent.

Gandhi and most of the other leaders were released from jail by 1924, but they stepped into a different world. The wild rapture of a revolutionary movement and the all-embracing spirit of Hindu-Muslim unity were things of the past. People were moving again within their traditionally narrow horizons. Old differences had quickly been brought up again. Some Hindu leaders started a movement for converting Muslims to Hinduism and this provided a new cause of bitterness and controversy. In the Punjab, Sir Fazli Husain's orders to reserve 40 percent of the seats for Muslims in some government colleges and provincial government services aroused a storm of controversy in the Hindu press. Over the next few years Hindu-Muslim riots occurred in a number of places. The political climate in the country was one of general apathy. Gandhi retired to his ashram, or hermitage, and devoted himself to spinning and problems of social reform.

On the question of immediate tactics there were differences in the Congress. The "no-changers" insisted upon a continued boycott of legislatures. Another group, organized as the Swarajya party under the leadership of C. R. Das and Motilal Nehru, advocated entry into legislative councils by contesting elections to them, and won their point. In C. R. Das the nation had discovered a great leader, a man of ample intellect and generous instincts. He was the only Hindu leader who was prepared to concede political power to the Muslims in the provinces where their majority justified it. In Bengal, he proposed, Muslims should get separate representation in the provincial council on a population basis, and 55 percent of government appointments should go to Muslims. This Bengal Pact, which was accepted by the Bengal Swarajya party in December, 1923, was rejected by the Congress next year. C. R. Das's death in the summer of 1925 removed the one Hindu leader who inspired unreserved confidence among the Muslims; never again was Hindu leadership to rise to his height.

In November, 1927, the British government appointed a commission under the chairmanship of Sir John Simon to report on India's future constitutional progress. Since the commission had no Indian member, it was boycotted by the Congress and by a section of the Muslim League led by Muhammad Ali Jinnah; another section of the latter organization, led by Sir Muhammad Shafi, cooperated with it. But it was felt, by leaders of both the Muslims and the Hindus, that a mere boycott was not enough, that it was necessary to take constructive action. An all-parties conference, which was convened in February, 1928, appointed a committee to determine the principles for India's constitution. The committee was presided over by Motilal Nehru, the leader of the Swarajya party.

The committee's report, known as the Nehru Report, demanded "full responsible government on the model of the constitutions of the self-governing Dominions." It recommended full provincial status for the North-West Frontier Province and Baluchistan and the separation of Sind from Bombay to form a new province. This was a concession to the Muslim point of view. On the other hand, the committee proposed the replacement of separate electorates by a joint electorate, but with reservation of seats, in proportion to its population, for the minority, who would also have the right to compete for additional seats. Only in the Punjab and Bengal were there to be no reservations of seats for any community. The result of this would have been to reduce the Muslim majority in these two provinces to a minority, since adult suffrage was as yet far off, and, on a franchise restricted by property and educational qualifications, Muslim voting strength would have been far below the Muslim proportion of the population (57 and 55 percent respectively). Hindu superiority in wealth and in strength of political organization, and their preponderance in the administration would have tilted the balance against the Muslims still further. The committee also proposed that the central government with its fixed Hindu majority, was to retain its powers over the provinces, as in the Montague-Chelmsford reforms, and was to be vested with residuary powers.

At the all-parties national convention held in Calcutta, in December, 1928, to consider the Nehru Report, Jinnah proposed three main amendments: one-third representation for the Muslims in the central legislature, Muslim representation in the Punjab and Bengal on the basis of population for ten years, and residuary powers for the provinces and not for the central government. "These amendments show," writes Dr. B. R. Ambedkar, "that the gulf between the Hindus and Muslims was not in any way a wide one. Yet there was no desire to bridge the same." [23] All three amendments, when put to the vote, were rejected by the Hindu majority.

The upshot was that, barring a few so-called nationalist Muslims, the Muslim community was united in opposition to the Nehru Report. An all-parties Muslim conference held in Delhi under the chairmanship of the Agha Khan in January, 1929, demanded the retention of separate electorates. The fourteen points, formulated by Jinnah, give a fair idea of the state of Muslim opinion at that time:

1. The form of the future constitution should be federal, with the residuary power vested in the provinces.

2. A uniform measure of autonomy shall be granted to all provinces.

3. All legislatures in the country and other elected bodies shall be constituted on the definite principle of adequate and effective representation of minorities in every province without reducing the majority in any province to a minority or even equality.

4. In the Central Legislature Muslim representation shall not be less than one third.

5. Representation of communal groups shall continue to be by separate electorates: provided that it shall be open to any commu-

nity, at any time, to abandon its separate electorate in favour of joint electorate.

6. Any territorial redistribution that might at any time be necessary shall not in any way affect the Muslim majority in the Punjab, Bengal and the North-West Frontier Province.

7. Full religious liberty, that is, liberty of belief, worship, and observance, propaganda, association, and education, shall be guaranteed to all communities.

8. No bill or resolution or any part thereof shall be passed in any legislature or any other elected body if three fourths of the members of any community in that particular body oppose it as being injurious to the interests of that community or in the alternative, such other method is devised as may be found feasible and practicable to deal with such cases.

9. Sind should be separated from the Bombay Presidency.

10. Reforms should be introduced in the North-West Frontier Province and Baluchistan on the same footing as in other provinces.

11. Provision should be made in the constitution giving Muslims an adequate share along with the other Indians in all the services of the State and in local self-governing bodies having due regard to the requirements of efficiency.

12. The constitution should embody adequate safeguards for the protection of Muslim culture and for the protection and promotion of Muslim education, language, religion, personal laws, and Muslim charitable institutions and for their due share in the grants-in-aid given by the State and by self-governing bodies.

13. No cabinet, either Central or Provincial, should be formed without there being at least one-third of Muslim Ministers.

14. No change shall be made in the constitution by the Central Legislature except with the concurrence of the States constituting the Indian Federation.

In retrospect it must astonish thoughtful Hindus that these reasonable and moderate demands were rejected by Hindu leaders.

In October, 1929, Viceroy Lord Irwin, after consultation with the Labour government, which was then in power in England, made a twofold declaration. The first part related to the constitution. He said: "I am authorized by His Majesty's Government to state clearly that in their judgement it is implicit in the declaration of 1917 that the natural issue of India's constitutional progress, as there contemplated is the attainment of Dominion Status." The second was the announcement of a Round Table conference at which the British government would meet representatives of British India and the princely states "for the purpose of seeking the greatest possible measure of agreement" on constitutional proposals. The statement gave general satisfaction since it defined both a goal and the procedure of advancing toward it.

Power would be transferred to Indian hands, but the question was, who among the Indians was to exercise that power. There were in fact two interconnected questions: the pace of the transfer of power and the distribution of that power among the Hindu and Muslim communities. These two questions were to dominate political discussion for nearly two decades, and what follows is largely a recital of the maneuvers and countermaneuvers of the three parties to this debate—the British, the Hindus, and the Muslims. It was obvious that if Hindus and Muslims could arrive at an agreement over the distribution of power between the two communities, they could present a unanimous demand to the British, who would then be forced to accelerate the transference of power. But such an agreement was never reached.

The year 1930 opened with a threat by the Congress of mass civil disobedience under Gandhi's personal command. The reason given was the failure of the British government to implement the Nehru Report during 1929; the abolition of the salt tax was made the focal point of the agitation.

The Muslims kept aloof. As Maulana Muhammad Ali put it: "We refuse to join Mr. Gandhi because his movement is not a movement for the complete independence of India but for making the seventy millions of Indian Musalmans dependents of Hindu Mahasabha [an extremist Hindu communal organization]." [24] Within a year Gandhi's movement had lost its momentum. The Viceroy now saw fit to negotiate with Gandhi to bring the whole thing to an end without bitterness. Under the Gandhi-Irwin Pact, a minor concession for the manufacture of salt in certain coastal areas was made, political prisoners were released, and the movement was called off. Actually, the government had won, but the psychological effect on the masses of Gandhi negotiating on equal terms with the Viceroy gave Gandhi the fruits of victory.

In December, 1930, the Muslim League held its annual session in Allahabad. The Muslim League at that time was not remarkable for its activity, and the session would have passed unnoticed but for the unusual fact that it was presided over by a poet who delivered an unusual address. Muhammad Iqbal is by common consent the greatest poet-philosopher that Muslim India has produced. In his presidential address, Iqbal surveyed the political scene and illumined it with philosophic insight. In striking words he indicated the goal toward which the conscious and unconscious strivings of the Muslim community were taking them.

> I would like to see the Punjab, North-West Frontier Province, Sind and Baluchistan amalgamated into a single state. Self-government within the British Empire or without the British Empire, the formation of a consolidated North-West Indian Muslim State appears to me to be the final destiny of the Muslims, at least of North-West India.[25]

The idea itself was not new. In 1920, Muhammad Abdul Qadir Bilgrami had advocated "the division of the sub-continent between the Hindus and Muslims even giving a list of the districts fundamentally not too different from the present boundaries of East and West Pakistan." [26] Three years later (in 1923), in his evidence before the Frontier Enquiry committee, Sardar Gul Muhammad Khan of Dera Ismail Khan had proposed a partition of India by which the Muslims were to get the area from Peshawar to Agra. In 1924, Lala Lajpat Rai, one of the founders of the Hindu Mahasabha, had suggested the partition of India between Hindus and Muslims. But these earlier tentative proposals had not received any attention. Now for the first time a person with high intellectual stature and prestige propounded a scheme for the establishment of a Muslim state from an authoritative platform. A new angle of vision had transformed the picture. Instead of looking upon themselves as a minority, desperately seeking safeguards for their cultural, economic, and political interests, Muslims saw themselves as a nation entitled to build a just social order on the basis of Islam in their own homeland.

Chaudhuri Rahmat Ali, a student at Cambridge, England, coined the word "Pakistan," in which P stands for the Punjab, A for Afghania (North-West Frontier Province), K for Kashmir, S for Sind, and TAN for Baluchistan. The word itself means "the land of the pure." It gave concise expression to Iqbal's idea and was both a symbol and a slogan. By a natural extension it applied to Bengal in the northeast as much as to the Muslim regions in the northwest.

Except for the Muslim youth, few paid attention to Iqbal's words at that time. All eyes were turned toward London where the first session of the Round Table conference began in November, 1930. During this and the subsequent sessions all efforts to settle the communal problem by mutual agreement among the representatives of the communities failed. Finally, in 1932, Prime Minister Ramsay MacDonald made what is called the Communal Award. Under it Muslims were allocated the following percentage of seats in various provincial legislatures on the basis of separate electorates.

Province	Muslim Percentage of Population	Percentage of Seats Reserved for Muslims
The Punjab	57	49
Bengal	55	48
Sind	71	57
North-West Frontier Province	92	72
Assam	34	31
The United Provinces	15	29
Bihar and Orissa	11	24
Bombay	9	17
Madras	8	13
The Central Provinces	5	14

In the central legislature, one third of the British Indian seats was reserved for Muslims. It was also decided to make Sind into a separate province. The Hindus denounced the Award; the Muslims acquiesced in it, not because it did justice to their position but because the two sides had not been able to reach an agreement on their own. The additional percentage given to Muslims in provinces in which they were in a minority was counterbalanced by the similar weightage given to non-Muslims in Muslim majority provinces. Nowhere was the Hindu majority reduced to a minority, but in the two key provinces, the Punjab and Bengal, the Award reduced the Muslim majority to a minority.

On Gandhi's return from London after the second Round Table

conference the Congress renewed the civil disobedience campaign. The new Viceroy, Lord Willingdon, struck hard. The movement collapsed within a few months and was formally called off in 1934.

The deliberations of the Round Table conference resulted in the Government of India Act, 1935, which provided for a "Federation of India," comprising both provinces and states. The provisions of the Act establishing the federal central government were not to go into operation until a specified number of rulers of states had signed Instruments of Accession. Since this did not come to pass, the central government continued to function in accordance with the 1919 Act, and only the part of the 1935 Act dealing with provincial governments went into operation. The provinces were given autonomy with respect to subjects delegated to them. Dyarchy had come to an end, and the provincial governments now had full responsibility. The provincial governors were, however, given the "special responsibility" of taking care of minorities, the civil services, and the prevention of any "grave menace" to peace or tranquillity. The enumeration of subjects delegated either to the central government or to the provinces was so exhaustive that the old controversy regarding residuary powers lost significance. The Act came into force on April 1, 1937.

Both the Congress and the Muslim League were critical of the Government of India Act, 1935, but decided to participate in the elections to be held under it during the first weeks of 1937. Their electoral programs were similar, and it was confidently expected that they would be able to cooperate in the provinces as they were already doing in the central assembly. The results of the elections and the elation they produced in the Congress camp shattered these hopes. The Congress won a great electoral victory; it obtained a majority in five provinces, and was able to form governments in seven out of eleven provinces after securing an informal assurance from the Viceroy that the governors would not ordinarily use their special powers.

The Muslim League did not do so well. The reason for this was that for a number of years it had been divided into factions. Jinnah, who in disgust at the state of Indian politics, had decided (in 1931) to settle for a time in England, was persuaded to return to India and take charge of the Muslim League a little more than a year before the elections. When he toured India in 1936, he found that local Muslim leaders who had entrenched themselves in the provinces were extremely reluctant to follow an all-India Muslim policy.

In the Punjab, Sir Fazli Husain had organized the Unionist party, which comprised Muslims and some Hindus and Sikhs. The Unionist party secured a majority in the elections under Fazli Husain's successor Sir Sikandar Hayat Khan.

In Bengal, Fazlul Haq had formed the Krishak Proja party and was able to head a coalition government which included the Muslim League and the Independent Scheduled caste group.

Sind was absorbed in the local game of factional politics, and the 35 Muslim members of the provincial assembly had been divided into four groups.

In the North-West Frontier Province, the Red Shirts led by Abdul Ghaffar Khan had aligned themselves with the Congress and had won 19 of the 50 seats in the provincial assembly. After the death of the first Chief Minister of the provincial government, Sir Abdul Qayyum Khan, a Congress coalition ministry came into existence under Dr. Khan Sahib, the brother of Abdul Ghaffar Khan.

Only in the provinces where the Muslims were in the minority was the Muslim League in a better position. In Assam it won a fair number of seats, and a coalition ministry under Sir Muhammad Saadullah was formed. Its greatest success was, however, in the United Provinces where it captured 29 seats, or about 80 percent of the seats it contested. No Muslim was elected from the United Provinces on the Congress ticket.[27]

In the discussions that preceded the 1935 Act, Muslims had demanded a statutory provision for the inclusion of Muslim representatives in the ministries, and had been reassured in general terms by Hindu and British statesmen. They expected that coalition ministries would be formed to include those who enjoyed the confidence of the Muslim community. The Congress, however, decided not to have a coalition with the Muslim League in those provinces in which the Congress had won a majority. In the United Provinces, the Congress leaders demanded as a price for the inclusion of members of the Muslim League in the cabinet that "the Muslim League group . . . shall cease to function as a separate group [and] the existing members of the Muslim League Party in the United Provinces Assembly shall become part of the Congress Party." [28] It is not surprising that the Muslim League refused to commit suicide and preferred to be in the opposition. All hopes of collaboration between the Congress and the League were at an end.

In provinces in which the Congress had a minority, it sought to divide the Muslims and to form coalition ministries controlled by or dependent on the Hindus. It succeeded in these designs in Assam and Sind. In the former, the Saadullah ministry fell and was replaced by a Congress coalition government. In the latter, a ministry was formed with Hindu support.

The Congress had for some years been claiming that it represented all Indians. There were a few Muslims in it, the most notable being Abul Kalam Azad, who led a group of Ulama, and Abdul Ghaffar Khan, the Red Shirt leader in the North-West Frontier Province; but this did not alter its character as a predominantly Hindu body. Of 143 members of the All-India Congress committee in 1936 only 6 were Muslims, three from the North-West Frontier Province, one from the United Provinces, and one from Bihar; the sixth was Abul Kalam Azad a former president of the Congress.[29] Now, flushed with victory, its leaders insisted that the Congress was the sole national organization, and even denied the existence of any other party. This was, in effect, an attempt to claim the right to be recognized as the sole inheritor of power from the British. Jawaharlal Nehru declared in March, 1937: "There are only two forces in India today, British imperialism and Indian nationalism as represented by the Congress." [30] Jinnah reminded him sharply that there was a third party to be reckoned with—the Muslims.

Discrimination against Muslims and other minorities had always been practiced by the Hindus. Now it became more open and flagrant. In Bombay, for instance, K. F. Nariman was the acknowledged leader of the local Congress party and should rightfully have become the Chief Minister of Bombay province. But he was a Parsi and was set aside by Vallabhbhai ("Sardar") Patel in favor of the Hindu G. B. Kher. Nariman appealed to the Congress Working Committee, to the Congress President, Nehru, to Gandhi himself, but all in vain. "Poor Nariman was heart-broken and his public life came to an end." [31]

Muslims were denied equality of opportunity and were deprived of their rightful place in the administration. Symbols of Hindu raj and Hindu culture were adopted in government institutions paid for by all taxpayers. *Vidya Mandirs,* Hindu temples of learning, were opened. Schools began the day by saluting the Congress flag, by singing the "Bande Matram," a notoriously anti-Muslim song, and by puja, or the worshiping, of Gandhi's portrait—a practice deeply obnoxious to Muslims. Insistence on the protection of cows took forms which inflicted economic injury upon the poorer Muslims and enforced submission to sentiments foreign to the Muslim mind. A systematic effort was made to replace Urdu, which was the common cultural heritage of Muslims and Hindus, with Hindi. Hindi received official patronage. Urdu schools were closed down or amalgamated with Hindi schools. In the heyday of Hindu-Muslim unity, Gandhi had often declared that both Urdu and Hindi were but a single language—Hindustani—which could be written equally well in the Persian or Devnagri script. He himself learned the Urdu script and advised everyone to learn both scripts. Now he moved to the position that Urdu, being written in the Quranic script, was the religious language of Muslims and that Hindi-Hindustani was the national language of India. Finally, even the word Hindustani was dropped and Hindi was proclaimed the national language.

The precedence of Hindu interests, which guided the policies of the Congress in administrative, educational, and cultural affairs manifested itself in the economic field also. For example, in the United Provinces and Bihar, where Muslims belonged to the landlord class, the Congress governments pressed forward with legislation for the security of land tenure and took credit for their progressive policies. But in Bengal, where the landlords were mostly Hindus, the Congress party opposed, to the point of bringing to a standstill, every effort at land reform. In the Punjab, where Hindu moneylenders were ruthlessly exploiting the peasantry,[32] the Congress party was bitterly hostile to legislation for the relief of rural indebtedness.

Muslims who lived in those provinces in which the majority was Hindu had obtained firsthand experience of Congress governments and now rallied to the League standard. The Punjab and Bengal Muslims also realized the danger Hindu domination posed for Muslims throughout India. The session of the Muslim League held in Lucknow in October, 1937, saw a closing of Muslim ranks. At this session the Punjab Premier, Sir Sikandar Hayat Khan, the Bengal Chief Minister, Moulvi Fazlul Haq, and the Chief Minister of Assam, Sir Muhammad Saadullah, pledged support to the Muslim League in all-India matters and accepted Jinnah, the President of the League, as their leader. From this point on the League made rapid progress and soon became a mass organization. Many branches of the League were established in every province. The Muslim League could now rightly claim to be the sole representative organization of Muslims in India.

The Congress tried to divide the Muslims and to disrupt the League by starting a Muslim mass-contact movement with the aim of winning Muslims over to the Congress camp. The Congress claimed to have the patronage and the power and if the Muslims wished to share in the spoils of office they should hasten to join it. However, this effort to lure the Muslims away from the League with prospects of material benefits had a boomerang effect and only served to strengthen the League.

There was increasingly bitter controversy between the League and the Congress. The League appointed a committee, under the chairmanship of the Raja of Pirpur, to inquire into Muslim grievances in the provinces ruled by the Congress party. The findings of the Pirpur Report established that Congress governments were trying by various means to impose Hindu culture upon the Muslims and discriminated against them. If the Muslims protested, they were branded as disturbers of the peace and the repressive machinery of government was set in motion against them. Other inquiries, such as the Shareef Report in Bihar, came to the same conclusion. Since governments run by the Congress party in the provinces were controlled by the top leaders of the Indian National Congress, these injustices could not be attributed to local lapses.

The opposition of Muslims to a federation of India hardened. A resolution passed by the Sind Muslim League conference at Karachi in October, 1938, declared that "the evolution of a single united India and united Indian nation inspired by common aspiration [was] impossible of realisation." The resolution recorded "its emphatic disapproval of the scheme of the All-India Federation as embodied in the Government of India Act, 1935" and recommended that the All-India Muslim League "devise a scheme of Constitution under which Muslims may attain full independence."

There was a widespread search for an alternative which would secure an honorable status for the Muslims in the future polity of India. The idea of Pakistan was gaining ground, but there were many who hesitated to go so far; instead, they wished to reorganize the subcontinent into a number of homogeneous zones loosely held together.

Of the many schemes produced, the most carefully worked-out was "A Confederacy of India," by Kifayat Ali, written under the pseudonym "A Punjabi." Others proposed that India be divided into several wholly independent and sovereign states. It is of some interest to note that the British statesman John Bright, in a speech in the House of Commons on June 24, 1858, had proposed dividing India into five presidencies each of which

> would have its finance, its taxation, its justice and its police department as well as its works and military departments, precisely the same as if it were a State having no connection with any other part of India and recognized only as a dependency of this country. . . . If at any future period the sovereignty of England should be withdrawn, we should leave so many Presidencies built up and firmly compacted together, each able to support its own independence and its own Government.[33]

CHAPTER 2

The Pakistan Resolution

AT THE OUTBREAK of the Second World War, the Viceroy, Lord Linlithgow, proclaimed India's entry into it without prior consultation with the Central Assembly or the main political parties. The subsequent negotiations of the Viceroy with Gandhi, Jinnah, and other leaders proved fruitless in persuading either the Congress or the Muslim League to lend unconditional support to the war effort. The British government wanted cooperation in the prosecution of the war, at the end of which it undertook to enter into consultations with representatives of the several communities, parties, and interests in India and with the Indian princes for a modification of the plan embodied in the Government of India Act, 1935. For the association of public opinion in India with the conduct of the war, the Viceroy proposed to establish a consultative group, representative of all major political parties and of the Indian princes, over which he would himself preside. Furthermore, the British government indicated its readiness for a still closer association with responsible Indian opinion by a temporary expansion of the Viceroy's executive council.

The Congress asked for a declaration of Indian independence, an immediate transfer of as much power as possible, and an agreement that the future constitution of India would be made by a constituent assembly elected on the basis of adult suffrage. It regarded the claims of minorities as irrelevant issues behind which the British were taking shelter, and held out the threat of civil disobedience if its demands were not met.

The Muslim League was equally desirous of attaining independence for the subcontinent, but made it clear that any future constitution must have the approval and consent of both Muslims and Hindus. It felt that the constituent assembly proposed by the Congress would, in Jinnah's words, be "a packed body, manoeuvred and managed by a Congress caucus." The League did not hinder participation in the war effort. In the Punjab and Bengal, whose chief ministers owed allegiance to the Muslim League, provincial governments cooperated with defense authorities, especially the Punjab, which was known as the sword-arm of India.

Negotiations with the Viceroy having failed, the Congress decided to withdraw its cooperation from the British government in the prosecution of the war. Ministries in eight provinces in which the Congress party was in power resigned, and governors assumed control of the administration. Thereupon Jinnah declared December 22, 1939, as a Day of Deliverance and Thanksgiving in token of relief from the "tyranny, oppression and injustice" of the Congress regime, and the Muslims celebrated the day with acclaim.

Three months later, the demand for the partition of India was formally put forward by the Muslim League; the stage was set for the struggle that culminated in the birth of Pakistan. In order to understand the course of subsequent events, it is necessary to review briefly the strength and weakness of each of the three main parties involved and their objectives.

The British were obviously the strongest in terms of economic, political, and military power, but they had been weakened by the First World War, and the Great Depression and the Second World War were to tax their strength still further. Their earlier memories of colonial exploitation in India had long been overlaid by a conscious sense of their mission to bring the benefits of parliamentary democracy and the rule of law to the peoples under their care. Theirs was not crude domination; it had a moral purpose. This may sound hypocritical to others, but the British had convinced themselves of its truth. The stages of constitutional advance were supposed to be determined by the fitness of the subject people; but as the growth of democratic institutions inside Great Britain had shown, this fitness could only be demonstrated by an organized struggle. Only those whose actions attested their will to freedom deserved to be free. With such adversaries the British were prepared to reach a settlement through a series of compromises. Although often accused of following a policy of "divide and rule," the British were inordinately proud of having given unity to the Indian subcontinent. If this administrative unity had not succeeded in producing cultural homogeneity or political harmony, the British felt that they were not to blame.

The Hindus, who formed three fourths of the population, were the next strongest. In wealth, education, political consciousness, and social cohesion they were far ahead of the Muslims and other minorities. Inevitably they identified their communal interests with Indian nationalism. Their social consciousness was shaped by the caste system, which made discrimination against outsiders a part of the natural order of things. Their control over the Indian press and news agencies was virtually complete. They had longer experience of political organization, and they had forged a political instrument of great power in the Indian National Congress. Their other parties, like the extremist Hindu Mahasabha or the moderate Liberal Federation, never acquired the same authority or representative character. In Gandhi they had an incomparable leader. He was, as he often said of himself a "Hindu of Hindus," the very quintessence of Hinduism. Everything about him, his dietary habits, his clothes, his sexual abstinence, his prayers, his *ashrams,* was widely publicized and continually reminded the Hindu masses, men and women, of his mahatmaic character. A revived and strengthened Hinduism was his life-long aim. His political activities for the attainment of Indian independence were a part of this wider objective. In his struggle against the British and other opponents, Gandhi used what he called "soul force" to bend the other party's will to his own. The essence of the method lay in being convinced of the rightness of one's cause and being prepared to undergo suffering in support of it. Everything that worked to the discomfiture of the opponent was permissible save physical violence. The British professed to be in India for the good of India; Gandhi took them at their word and proceeded to point out the discrepancy between word and deed. Even if he did not wholly succeed in making Englishmen feel hypocritical, he lowered their prestige in the eyes of Indians. If the British had used force ruthlessly, these tactics could not have succeeded; but they were not brutal enough to use terror as a method of government, and too prudent not to realize that their little island could not keep 400 million people indefinitely under its rule. In their own country they had a long tradition of freedom of speech and freedom of association, and they could not bring themselves to abrogate these freedoms completely. They allowed public meetings and processions to be held and usually repressed them only after they had largely achieved their purpose. Periodically they put their opponents in jail, but in such a manner as to make heroes of them. Gandhi took full advantage of these traits as well as of the British sensitiveness to economic loss. He was the greatest practitioner of the art of moral warfare the modern world has seen. His apparent meekness covered a clarity of vision, a shrewdness of wit, and a tenacity of will which was rare. His use of language was simple and subtle; its apparent simplicity covered pitfalls for the unwary and loopholes for escape from inconvenient commitments. Throughout the period dealt with here, he was the unquestioned master of the biggest and most powerful political machine in India. For instance, when, despite Gandhi's opposition, Subhas Chandra Bose was reelected President of the Congress in 1939, Gandhi made it impossible for him to continue in office and forced him to resign within a few months. Gandhi occupied the position of "permanent super-president," as Nehru put it, although he claimed to be not even an ordinary member of the Congress party. He could thus disclaim responsibility for the actions of the Congress whenever it was tactically desirable to do so. He used his sway over the masses to keep the Congress party in control. His campaigns for the boycott of foreign cloth benefited the, mainly Hindu, industrial and commercial interests. He was consequently able to draw large funds from business magnates to organize an army of political workers. His style of living proclaimed him to be a friend of the poor; his political campaigns made him a benefactor of the rich. He strove to remove the age-old curse of untouchability from Hindu society and to ameliorate the condition of the Depressed Classes. But when they were granted political rights by the British in the form of separate electorates, he staked his life by a fast unto death in order to deny them this elementary right; and Dr. Ambedkar, the Depressed Class leader, had to yield to what some called blackmail and others soul force. It is not surprising that Ambedkar called him "the greatest enemy the untouchables have ever had in India." [1]

Gandhi used all the weapons in his moral armory to cajole and intimidate the Muslims into accepting Hindu assurances of goodwill in place of constitutional guarantees. His humanitarianism is not in question; it was genuine and sincere. But he was determined that supreme political power in the Indian subcontinent should remain with the Hindus; and, as the Congress party grew in strength and discipline, that determination became more and more manifest.

The Muslims were the weakest of the three parties involved in the struggle. They numbered 100 million, but were only one fourth of the total population of the subcontinent. Except for areas in the northwest and the northeast they were in a minority everywhere. They had accepted English education much later than the Hindus, were inadequately represented in the administration, and fared even worse in trade and industry. In short, they were poor and backward. Their demand for fair representation in elective bodies or in the civil services was dubbed "communal" and "anti-national." Because they asked for a prior agreement on the sharing of power with Hindus, they were held up to obloquy for obstructing India's progress toward independence. They wanted freedom from British rule as much as the Hindus, but they felt that the common nationalism to which the Hindus beckoned them was an illusion and a snare. Behind it lay the ugly reality of Hindu domination which would deny them an equal place as citizens in the new social fabric. They had first-hand experience of Hindu discrimination against them in every field of endeavor.

Hindus regarded their interest in the Muslim world as extraterritorial sympathy and questioned their loyalty to India. The Muslims, therefore, found their minority status irksome and unbefitting their traditions of greatness.

A desire for a just social order is deeply ingrained in the minds of Muslims. But they could see no way of realizing it in the historical and geographical context in which they were placed. Even within their own society they were faced with un-Islamic class and caste distinctions. The feudal elements were strong and the middle class was weak. The former were time-serving, worldly men with an eye on personal interest. This weakness was also reflected in the Muslim political organization. The Muslim League had neither the cohesion nor the discipline of the Congress. "It could not hope, indeed, to fight the Congress on anything like equal terms. In organization, in machinery for publicity, in financial resources it was immeasurably poorer." [2] It was only when Muslims found a worthwhile goal in Pakistan, and were united behind their great leader Jinnah, that the Muslim League became an effective political organ of the masses and was able to fight the British on the one hand and the Hindus on the other.

Jinnah was in many ways the exact opposite of Gandhi. In manner and dress he was far removed from the popular leader of the masses; he never posed as a man of religion and was totally averse to any form of self-exhibitionism or to a histrionic exploitation of religious sentiments. His integrity was inviolable; office could not tempt him nor flattery corrupt him. Still less could threats or show of force intimidate him. His language was direct and precise; even a rigorous search would fail to find a second meaning. His occasional rudeness toward opponents sprang not from hauteur but from intolerance of humbug. Throughout the crucial period of the struggle he was the President of the Muslim League and openly exercised his responsibilities and powers as befitted the head of a political organization. He was a master of the art of political warfare, but he would have disdained to use "soul force" to demoralize an enemy or to resort to his inner voice to extricate himself from difficulties. In strength of will, in shrewdness of judgment, in clarity of vision and single-mindedness of purpose he was the equal, if not the superior, of Gandhi. The clash between these two personalities added drama to this period.

On March 23, 1940, at the historic session of the Muslim League held in Lahore, the resolution that came to be known as the Pakistan Resolution was passed. The resolution was moved by the Bengal Chief Minister, A. K. Fazlul Haq, and was seconded by Choudhry Khaliquzzaman and others. The resolution stated that

> no constitutional plan would be workable in this country or acceptable to Muslims unless it is designed on the following basic principle, namely, that geographically contiguous units are demarcated into regions which should be so constituted, with such territorial readjustments as may be necessary, that the areas in which the Muslims are numerically in a majority as in the north-western and eastern zones of India should be grouped to constitute independent States in which the constituent units shall be autonomous and sovereign. . . . Adequate, effective and mandatory safeguards should be specifically provided in the Constitution for minorities . . . for the protection of their religious, cultural, economic, political, administrative and other rights.

Jinnah's address on this occasion gave clear expression to the basic concept underlying the resolution. He said:

It has always been taken for granted mistakenly that the Musalmans are a minority. The Musalmans are not a minority. The Musalmans are a nation by any definition. . . . What the unitary government of India for 150 years has failed to achieve cannot be realised by the imposition of a central federal government. . . . except by means of armed force. . . . The problem in India is not of an inter-communal character but manifestly of an international one, and it must be treated as such. . . . The Hindus and Muslims belong . . . to two different civilizations which are based mainly on conflicting ideas and conceptions. . . . To yoke together two such nations under a single State, one as a numerical minority and the other as a majority, must lead to growing discontent and final destruction of any fabric that may be so built up for the government of such a State.[3]

This was the famous two-nation theory which aroused so much controversy. It was indignantly rejected by Congress leaders, although Savarkar, the President of the Hindu Mahasabha, had frequently referred to Hindus and Muslims as two nations.[4] A historically-minded Hindu has written, "The so-called two-nation theory was formulated long before Mr. Jinnah or the Muslim League: in truth, it was not a theory at all; it was a fact of history." [5]

The facts on which the two-nation theory was based were well-known to everyone including the British. The joint committee of Parliament on Indian constitutional reforms had stated in 1934:

India is inhabited by many races . . . often as distinct from one another in origin, tradition and manner of life as are the nations of Europe. Two-thirds of its inhabitants profess Hinduism . . . over 77 millions are followers of Islam, and the difference between the two is not only of religion in the stricter sense but also of law and culture. They may be said, indeed, to represent two distinct and separate civilizations.[6]

The British, partly for reasons of policy and partly from pride, were intent on maintaining the unity of India, which the joint committee described as "perhaps the greatest gift which British rule has conferred on India." [7] Behind that attractive phrase—the unity of India—lay the ugly reality of Hindu domination and exploitation. The Muslims saw no reason why they should sacrifice themselves for a British geopolitical concept. The use of the word "Nation" to describe the Indian Muslims brought their viewpoint nearer to the understanding of the British, whose own life had been organized for centuries around national concepts.

While the two-nation theory succeeded brilliantly in proving the need of a separate state for the Muslims, it did not solve wholly the minority problem in India. By separating Muslim majority areas from Hindu majority areas, minorities would be left on both sides, although greatly reduced in numbers. The Pakistan Resolution dealt with the issue and recommended effective and mandatory safeguards for the minorities in both Pakistan and Hindustan. Though the creation of Pakistan would not eliminate the problem of minorities, it would reduce the area of conflict between Hindus and Muslims and give each country an equal interest in the protection of the minorities within its borders.

There was another aspect of the Pakistan Resolution which caused misgivings. Instead of demanding the inclusion of the whole of the Punjab in the northwest and Bengal and Assam in the northeast, it delimited Pakistan to contiguous Muslim majority regions "with such territorial readjustments as may be necessary." This was understood by many to imply partition of the Punjab and Bengal and Assam. By leaving the boundaries vague the resolution invited criticism on the score of indefiniteness in the concept of Pakistan.

The reactions of the public to the Lahore resolution varied from community to community; Muslims responded to it enthusiastically and the Hindus condemned it roundly. If proof was needed of the truth of the two-nation theory, these diametrically opposed views provided it. The denunciations by Hindu leaders, who referred to partition as the "vivisection of Mother India," were calculated to arouse Hindu religious feelings. Gandhi called it a moral wrong and a sin to which he would never be a party. In fact, except for relatively short periods, the Indian subcontinent throughout its long history has never known a single centralized government. This being so, there could be no question of sacrilege in the suggestion that the subcontinent be divided into two sovereign states.

The hold which the idea of Pakistan rapidly gained over the imagination of the Muslim masses, and the phenomenal growth of the Muslim League in popularity and power, have puzzled many observers. In giving its allegiance to the Pakistan movement, the Muslim community was not merely seeking to escape the domination of the Hindu. What filled the masses with the urge for action was the desire to recreate a truly Islamic society in which the justice, the democratic equality, the freedom from want, and the devotion to social welfare that had characterized the earliest Muslim community should again prevail. It was the appeal of this ideal which transformed the Muslim League from a body representing the upper classes of Muslims into a mass organization. Only on this basis is it possible to explain the wholehearted participation of the Muslims of the minority provinces in the movement.

But even a great ideal may remain unrealized for lack of leadership. At this historic moment the Muslim community was fortunate in having as its leader Muhammad Ali Jinnah, whom Iqbal called "the only Muslim in India to-day to whom the community has a right to look for safe guidance through the storm which is coming to North-West India and perhaps to the whole of India." [8] Jinnah inspired unreserved confidence among the Muslims for his integrity, courage, statesmanship, and sincerity. He himself was aware of the weaknesses of Muslim leadership in the past. In a speech at Patna in December, 1938, he said: "Of the intelligentsia of the Muslims who were [in 1935] in the forefront of what is called political life, most—I do not say all—were careerists. They chose their place according to their convenience, either in the bureaucratic camp or in the other camp, that is the Congress camp." [9] Jinnah did not drive these men out of the Muslim League, but he knew their limitations and kept watch over them.

Jinnah himself was in the profoundest sympathy with the aspirations of the people. In a speech in Delhi in April, 1943, he visualized Pakistan as having "a people's government" and warned "landlords and capitalists who have flourished at our expense by a system which is so vicious, which is so wicked, which makes men so selfish that it is difficult to reason with them. . . . [not to forget] the lesson of Islam. . . . The constitution and the government will be what the people will decide." [10]

Those who rallied to his call and spread his message among the masses were the students, the idealistic youth, and the rising middle class. The students of the Aligarh Muslim University and other educational institutions were active workers in the cause of Pakistan. In the Punjab, which was being ruled by the feudal landlords of the Unionist party, the Muslim Students Federation under the leadership of Hamid Nizami played a significant part in changing the climate of opinion. A signal service was rendered by the Muslim newspapers in propagating the idea of Pakistan. The most prominent daily in English was the *Dawn;* in Urdu, *Nawai Waqt;* and in Bengali, *Azad.* The

Muslim newspapers were far fewer in numbers and had much smaller financial resources than the powerful Hindu press, but they battled valiantly in defense of the Muslim League and its policies.

A considerable section of the Ulama joined the struggle for Pakistan, and their influence over the masses was put to the service of the cause. Under the leadership of Maulana Shabbir Ahmad Usmani of Deoband, the Jamiatul Ulama-i-Islam consisting of Ulama in favor of Pakistan was organized in opposition to the Jamiatul Ulama-i-Hind—a body of Ulama aligned with the Congress.

As the Muslim League gathered strength, its President was able to impose discipline even on provincial premiers—at his behest they resigned from the National Defence Council. Toward the close of 1941, when Fazlul Haq, the Bengal Chief Minister, reorganized his cabinet in defiance of the League, he was, after a time, forced to resign. The motto of "Unity, Faith, and Discipline," which Jinnah gave to the League, became a living reality. For the first time since the days of British rule, the entire Muslim nation stood united in disciplined ranks behind Jinnah. He came to be known by the title of Quaid-i-Azam, or Great Leader, which was bestowed on him by a grateful people.

By April, 1940, the phase of the "phony war" was over. With the fall of France, England stood alone against the victorious arms of the Axis powers. In India the sudden revelation of British weakness produced shocked surprise, not unmingled with secret joy at their discomfiture and admiration for their courageous defiance. On August 8, 1940, the Viceroy, Lord Linlithgow, made an offer on behalf of the British government to expand the Executive Council immediately by including representatives of political parties, and to set up a War Advisory Council containing representatives of Indian states and of other interests. After the war, an Indian constitution-making body would be set up to devise a new constitution with due regard for the rights of the minorities. The British government made it clear that "they could not contemplate transfer of their present responsibilities for the peace and welfare of India to any system of government whose authority is directly denied by large and powerful elements in India's national life. Nor could they be parties to the coercion of such elements into submission to such a government." They hoped that cooperative endeavor for victory in war would "pave the way towards the attainment by India of that free and equal partnership in the British Commonwealth which remains the proclaimed and accepted goal of the Imperial Crown and of the British Parliament." [11]

Nothing came of the August offer. The Congress rejected it on the ground that its demand for a national government had not been met. At this time, C. Rajagopalachari made the "sporting offer" that the prime minister in the national government could be chosen from the Muslim League. This was an empty gesture. What the Congress wanted was to transfer power solely into its own hands. Gandhi, who was in undisputed control of the Congress, expressed this view with unusual candor:

> The British Government would not ask for a common agreement, if they recognised any one party to be strong enough to take delivery. . . . If [the Congress] does not weaken and has enough patience, it will develop sufficient strength to take delivery. It is an illusion created by ourselves that we must come to an agreement with all parties before we can make any progress.[12]

The Muslim League, while gratified at the assurance that no constitution would be adopted without its consent, could not accept the August offer since it promised inadequate representation to the Muslim League in the government. In brief, the British wanted to win the war first and transfer power afterwards; the Congress demanded power at once, and a Hindu-Muslim settlement afterwards; the Muslims insisted on a Hindu-Muslim settlement first. This pattern of behavior was to persist throughout the war.

In October, 1940, Gandhi launched his "individual civil disobedience" campaign under which selected individuals were to court arrest by making antiwar speeches; but neither the country nor the government took much notice of these acts of symbolic defiance. Orders for supplies and recruitment for war had provided a much needed stimulus to the Indian economy, in which unemployment and underemployment of resources had been endemic for many years before the war.

By March, 1942, it appeared to many in India that the Japanese could overrun India with the same ease with which they had conquered southeast Asia. Subhas Chandra Bose, who had escaped from India in 1940, was organizing the Indian National Army with Indian prisoners of war captured by the Japanese.

It was because of these circumstances that the British government sent a prominent member of the war cabinet, Sir Stafford Cripps, to

India with a draft declaration for discusson with Indian leaders. He arrived in Delhi on March 23, 1942, had discussions with Indian leaders, and departed a fortnight later without achieving anything. The draft declaration which Cripps brought with him promised a constituent assembly, consisting of elected representatives from the provinces and nominated representatives from the Indian states, immediately upon the cessation of hostilities. It also gave an undertaking on behalf of the British government to accept and implement the constitution framed by the constituent assembly, provided that any province or state would be free either to adhere or not to adhere to the new constitution. Meanwhile, the British government would retain control of the defense of India "as part of their world war effort [but invited the] immediate and effective participation of the leaders of the principal sections of the Indian people [in the] task of organizing to the full the military, moral and material resources of India." [13]

The Congress rejected the offer on the advice of Gandhi, who regarded it as "a post-dated cheque on a failing bank." The Muslim League also rejected it, because it did not concede Pakistan unequivocally. Of the Congress leaders only Rajagopalachari favored acceptance of the Cripps offer and the formation of a national front for prosecuting the war. He saw clearly that the main obstacle in the way of India's freedom and security was lack of agreement between the Congress and the Muslim League. Under his leadership the Congress members in the Madras legislature passed a resolution in April, 1942, recommending acceptance of Pakistan in principle. The leaders in control of the Congress party rejected the proposal and Rajagopalachari was driven into exile.

Gandhi now began to press for an immediate withdrawal of the British from India and the transfer of power to the Congress without a prior settlement with any other party. As he put it, "The presence of the British in India is an invitation to Japan to invade India. Their withdrawal removes the bait. Assume, however, that it does not; free India will be better able to cope with the invasion." [14]

These ideas were formally adopted by the All-India Congress committee meeting held at Bombay, on August 8, 1942, in the famous Quit India resolution, which demanded the "withdrawal of the British Power from India" and authorized "the starting of a mass struggle on non-violent lines on the widest possible scale." It stated that "such a widespread struggle would inevitably be under the leadership of

Gandhiji." Gandhi himself called it "open rebellion." Some days earlier he had declared that he did not want rioting as a direct result of the resolution, but that if in spite of precautions rioting occurred, it could not be helped. This time the government did not take long to act; Gandhi and other Congress leaders were arrested and Congress committees were declared to be unlawful associations. Gandhi's final message to members of the Congress was "Do or die." Widespread disorders soon broke out. Railways, post offices, telegraph and telephone systems, and police stations were attacked. By the end of November, 940 lives had been lost and property worth one million pounds sterling had been destroyed. Other political parties and the bulk of the population kept aloof.

The Muslim League saw in these actions an attempt "to coerce the British government into handing over power to a Hindu oligarchy." The Muslims were not a whit less insistent on the attainment of independence, but they felt that the purpose of the Congress was to bring about "the establishment of a Hindu Raj and to deal a death-blow to the Muslim goal of Pakistan." To Gandhi's slogan "Quit India," Jinnah replied with "Divide and Quit."

In February, 1943, Gandhi went on a twenty-one day fast. For a time it looked as if his life was in danger and great pressure was put on the Viceroy to release him unconditionally. Three members of the Viceroy's Executive Council resigned on this issue; but the government stood firm and Gandhi pulled through.

When Lord Wavell succeeded Lord Linlithgow as Viceroy in the fall of 1943, the tide of war was turning in favor of the Allies. India was the base for the South East Asia Command, and the strain of supplying the large military forces—American, British, and Indian—with provisions and equipment was telling on the Indian economy. The shortage of shipping, the fall in imports, the dislocation of the transport system by the heavy movement of men and material for the Burma front, the restricted supplies available for civilian consumption, and above all, the financing of the war effort in India by credit creation, led to a rapid rise in prices and serious inflationary pressures. The worst sufferer was Bengal, which was ravaged by a severe famine in 1943. Peasants who had been induced by high prices to sell rice died in millions; 1,873,749 persons, it was officially admitted, had died of starvation. The congestion of transportation delayed supplies; rationing was introduced tardily; and the central government did not intervene till a later stage, when Viceroy Lord Wavell gave personal attention to the problem.

In May, 1944, Gandhi was released on medical grounds. Soon afterward he wrote the Viceroy, offering renunciation of civil disobedience and "full cooperation in the war effort [by the Congress] if a declaration of immediate Indian independence is made and a national government responsible to the Central Assembly be formed." [15] During the earlier years of the war when the British were sustaining reverse after reverse, Gandhi had objected to Indian participation in the war, giving as his reason a fundamental religious principle, ahimsa (nonviolence). Now, with the sure prospect of Allied victory, ahimsa was conveniently laid aside; cooperation in the war effort was offered in order that the political goal, for which ahimsa and all the rest were means, could be gained!

The belief that the end of the war was in sight stimulated political activity; in response to a general public desire for a settlement of Hindu-Muslim differences, talks took place between Gandhi and Jinnah in September, 1944.

Gandhi's real concern, as he remarked to Rajagopalachari during the talks was "to prove from his [Jinnah's] own mouth that the whole of the Pakistan proposition is absurd." [16] Jinnah was in dead earnest and painstakingly explained the basis for the demand of Pakistan. "We maintain," he wrote to Gandhi, "that Muslims and Hindus are two major nations by any definition or test as a nation. We are a nation of a hundred million . . . we have our own distinctive outlook on life and of life. By all the canons of international law, we are a nation." He added that he was "convinced that the true welfare not only of the Muslims but of the rest of India lies in the division of India as proposed in the Lahore resolution." [17]

Gandhi, on the other hand, maintained that India was one nation and saw in the Pakistan resolution "nothing but ruin for the whole of India." If, however, Pakistan had to be conceded, the areas in which the Muslims were in an absolute majority should be demarcated by a commission approved by both the Congress and the League, and the wishes of all the adult inhabitants of these areas should be ascertained through a referendum. "If the vote is in favour of separation," Gandhi continued,

> these areas shall form a separate state as soon as possible after India is free from foreign domination. . . . There shall be a treaty of

separation which should also provide for the efficient and satisfactory administration of Foreign Affairs, Defence, Internal Communications, Customs, Commerce and the like, which must necessarily continue to be the matters of common interest between the contracting parties.[18]

This meant, in effect, that power over the whole of India should first be transferred to the Congress, which thereafter would allow Muslim majority areas that voted for separation to be constituted, not as an independent sovereign state, but as part of an Indian federation. In the process, the Punjab and Bengal, provinces with a Muslim majority, would be partitioned. Gandhi contended that his offer, gave "the substance of the Lahore resolution." Jinnah did not agree, and the talks broke down.

Soon after the end of the war in Europe, in May, 1945, Viceroy Lord Wavell decided to hold a political conference to which he invited Congress and League representatives, provincial premiers, and some other leaders. He proposed an interim central government in which all portfolios except that of war would be held by Indians. There was to be parity of representation between Muslims and caste Hindus. The conference began in Simla on June 25, and lasted till July 14, but it failed to achieve anything. There was a deadlock over the Muslim League's demand that all five Muslim members of the Executive Council should be taken from the League. The Viceroy said he was prepared to include four members of the Muslim League, but the fifth should be a Punjabi Muslim who did not belong to the League. Behind this apparently minor divergence of view lay a serious political dispute. When the Premier of the Punjab, Sir Sikandar Hayat, died in 1942, he was succeeded by Khizr Hayat Tiwana, who lacked the suppleness of his predecessor and soon fell out with Jinnah over the status of the Muslim League in the Punjab. In his stand against the Muslim League, Khizr Hayat Tiwana was supported by feudal Muslim elements, the Hindus and Sikhs of the Unionist party, and the British governor, Sir Bertrand Glancy. All of them ignored the rising influence of the League among the Muslim intelligentsia and masses of the Punjab. The landed interests, with their strong tradition of loyalty to the powers that be, were blind to the signs of the times. The Viceroy's insistence on a non-Leaguer from the Punjab was in accordance with the advice given him by British and Hindu officials to support Khizr Hayat Tiwana in his stand against the

League.[19] He was also supported by the Congress, which denied the League's claim to be the sole representative of Muslims.[20] When Jinnah stood firm, the conference broke up.

The Second World War came to an end with the surrender of Japan on August 15, 1945. The British general election at the end of July resulted in a large Labour majority. The Congress leaders, who had cultivated close relations with the leaders of the Labour party over the years, felt elated at this unexpected turn of events and immediately started exploiting their position of vantage. British policy had consistently favored the maintenance of India as a single administrative and political entity. Conservatives like Lord Linlithgow had emphasized it as much as had the soldier-statesman Lord Wavell. The Congress leaders expected even stronger support from the Labour party on this issue, which was dividing the Congress and the Muslim League.

The issue was put to the test at the general elections for the provincial and central legislatures in the winter of 1945–46. Both the Congress and the Muslim League exerted themselves to the utmost, for on the outcome of these elections depended the constitutional future of India. The results showed a decisive victory for Pakistan; the League won all the Muslim seats in the central assembly and 446 out of a total of 495 Muslim seats in the provincial assemblies. The Congress won a similar victory in the Hindu constituencies and came to power in all the provinces that had a Hindu majority. In Bengal, the Muslim League won 113 out of a total of 119 Muslim seats and was able to form a ministry with Husain Shaheed Suhrawardy as Chief Minister. In the Punjab, the Muslim League captured 79 out of 86 Muslim seats. In Sind, a Muslim League ministry was formed. Only in the North-West Frontier Province did the League fall short of a majority by winning only 17 out of a total of 36 Muslim seats, and the Congress formed a ministry under Dr. Khan Sahib.

The 1946 elections proved incontestably that the Muslim League alone represented the Muslims of India; but this only increased the hostility of the Congress toward it. Instead of recognizing the representative character of the Muslim League and coming to terms with it, the Congress persisted in its policy of dividing the Muslims and denying political power to the trusted representatives of the Muslim community, even in provinces where the Muslims were a majority. In this way the Congress deepened Muslim suspicion, intensified communal discord, and made an amicable settlement impossible.

The clearest illustration of its hostility to the Muslim League was seen in the Punjab. There the Unionist party, led by Khizr Hayat Tiwana, had been routed and the Muslim League had captured 79 out of 86 Muslim seats. The Muslim League was the biggest single party in a house of 175 members, but it did not command an absolute majority, because the Communal Award made in 1932 by the British government had reduced the Muslim majority in the Punjab to a minority. Apart from the rump of Unionists led by Khizr Hayat Tiwana, the other important groups in the Punjab were Akali Sikhs and Congress Hindus, who had always opposed the Unionists as reactionary agents of British imperialism. The League could only form a ministry with the help of some Hindus and Sikhs; but the maneuvers of the Congress and the shortsightedness of Sikh leaders made this impossible. Instead, Khizr Hayat Tiwana was persuaded by Abul Kalam Azad, the Congress President, and Baldev Singh to form an unstable ministry with the help of Congress Hindus and Akali Sikhs. The only object of this unprincipled combination was to keep the League out of power in the Punjab. Azad relates with pride and self-satisfaction how "through my endeavours the Muslim League had been isolated and the Congress, though it was a minority, had become the decisive factor in Punjab affairs." [21] Nehru felt that the participation of the Congress party in the Punjab government was not right, but Gandhi came out strongly in support of Azad and "held that there could be no better solution from the Congress point of view." [22]

By throwing in their lot with the Congress at this critical time, the Sikhs made a cardinal error. How and why they were induced to do so needs some explanation. The Sikh sect had been founded in the sixteenth century by Guru Nanak, a Hindu mystic, who under the influence of Islam had preached the unity of God and the brotherhood of man. But in course of time, like many other sects that have sprung from Hindu soil, the Sikhs had been reintegrated—although not completely, because of their distinctive style of hair and dress—into the social fabric of Hindu society with its network of castes and its invisible but immensely powerful economic sanctions against the outsider. Hindus and Sikhs dine with each other, and there is intermarriage; in a single family one brother may be a Hindu and another a Sikh. The turbulence of Sikhs during the troubles that beset the Mughul Empire in its decline brought them into conflict with authority and gave the sect an anti-Muslim bias. In the first half of the nineteenth century, Ranjit Singh carved out a Sikh kingdom in the Punjab, which, after his death, was lost to the British in 1849.

Although Sikhs were to be found all over India, their home was in the Punjab. They numbered five and a half millions and formed 13.2 percent of the population of the Punjab. In the Punjab assembly and in government service they were allowed 20 percent representation. They owned a high proportion of the most fertile land in the Punjab, particularly in the canal irrigated colonies of Lyallpur and Montgomery, and were well represented in the Indian army. In 1946 their leadership was in the hands of the impetuous Tara Singh, a Hindu converted to Sikhism, and his financial supporter, Baldev Singh, whose economic interests tied him to Hindu India.

The elections of 1946 had been fought on the issue of Pakistan, and the Muslims of the Punjab had given a clear verdict in its favor. The Hindus were opposed to Pakistan because it implied the partition of India. The position of Sikhs toward Pakistan had yet to be determined and would be decisive for the Punjab and the Sikhs. The Punjab districts were grouped into five divisions. In the west, Muslims were in an absolute majority in Rawalpindi and Multan divisions and in part of Lahore division. In the east, Hindus had a clear majority in Ambala division. In the central area, in Jullundur division and in part of Lahore division no community had a majority—the Sikhs held the balance between Hindus and Muslims.

If Pakistan ever came into being, it was likely that Ambala division, which had a clear Hindu majority, would be lopped off to form part of India. But this would not affect the essential unity of the Punjab because Ambala division was linguistically and culturally more akin to the contiguous Hindu areas of India. In fact, the original scheme for Pakistan, put forward by Iqbal in December, 1930, had contemplated the separation of Ambala division.

If, however, the Sikhs joined the Hindus in opposing Pakistan and refused to form a part of it, a fundamentally different problem would arise. The partition line would then run through the middle of the Punjab and cut the Sikh community into two more or less equal halves. The economic life of the Punjab, which depended upon the most extensive system of canal irrigation in India, would thus suffer terrible injury. It was in the obvious interest of both Sikhs and Muslims to preserve the unity of the Punjab, but this would only be possible if an agreement could be reached between the two communities whereby the Muslims guaranteed the legitimate rights of Sikhs as a minority, and the Sikhs accepted Pakistan with its corollary of Muslim rule. The Muslim League was prepared to guarantee special rights and privileges for the Sikh minority in Pakistan. Jinnah repeatedly offered them fair and generous treatment, but he could not alter the facts of demography and geography. Since the Sikhs were not in a majority in any district, he could not carve out a Sikh enclave, or Khalistan, as some Sikh leaders demanded, nor treat them in any other way but as a minority. Sikh leaders were invited to the convention of Muslim League legislators held in April, 1946; and though some of them attended, nothing came of these parleys, and the Sikhs cast their lot with the Congress. If the Sikh leaders had possessed the foresight and wisdom to compare the prospects for their community in Muslim Pakistan with those in Hindu India, they would have come to a different decision. In Pakistan they would have been the most important if not the largest minority; their position in the Pakistan army would have given them a decisive influence; they held the best lands in the rich colony districts; as sturdy farmers and good mechanics, they would have occupied an important position in the economic life of the country; and in the administrative services and in the legislature of Pakistan they would have enjoyed weightage. But the anti-Muslim traditions the Sikhs had inherited from Mughul days clouded their judgment.

By deciding to join Hindu India, the Sikhs virtually committed cultural suicide; for it is only a matter of time before their taboos against shaving and cutting their hair will disappear, leaving them indistinguishable from the Hindus. However, encouraged by the Hindus in their ambition to rule over the Punjab, they made their fateful decision. From that stage onward they were led step by step to side with the Hindus against the Muslims in the "war of succession" that lay ahead.

CHAPTER 3

The Cabinet Mission Plan

ON FEBRUARY 19, 1946, the British government announced its decision to send to India a special mission (the Cabinet Mission) consisting of three cabinet ministers, to seek in association with Viceroy Lord Wavell and in consultation with Indian leaders an agreement on constitutional issues. During the debate in the House of Commons on March 15 on the Cabinet Mission's visit to India, Prime Minister Attlee said:

> I am well aware that . . . I speak of a country containing congeries of races, religions and languages, and I know well the difficulties thereby created but these difficulties can only be overcome by Indians. We are mindful of the rights of the minorities. . . . On the other hand we cannot allow a minority to place a veto on the advance of a majority.

Attlee's words pleased the Congress and caused some misgivings in League circles. Jinnah gave the simile of the spider inviting a fly to its parlor: "If the fly refuses, it is said a veto is being exercised and the fly is intransigent." [1]

The Cabinet Mission, consisting of Lord Pethick-Lawrence, the

Secretary of State for India; Sir Stafford Cripps, the President of the Board of Trade; and Mr. A. V. Alexander, the First Lord of the Admiralty, arrived in New Delhi on March 24, 1946. The India they came to was full of expectations and unrest. Freedom was in sight, but the hands that reached out for it grappled with each other in conflict. Strife between the two major communities—Hindus and Muslims—was mounting. Economic uncertainty unsettled men's minds. During the war two and a half million men had been recruited and trained in the use of arms. The bulk of them were now awaiting demobilization and had to be reabsorbed into civil life. War orders had brought many new enterprises into being and had greatly expanded others; big fortunes had been made and had heightened the contrasts of lavish wealth and grueling poverty. The inflationary conditions that prevailed during the war strained the economy almost to breaking point; there had been fear of a flight from the currency at one time. Now there was the even more difficult task of readjustment to a lower level of economic activity. The specter of unemployment was rising.

In February, 1946, there was a mutiny in the Indian navy, though it was quickly suppressed. There were also strikes at air force stations, and disaffection was spreading in the army. The trial, in the Red Fort at Delhi, of some officers of the repatriated Indian National Army made heroes of those whom the British indicted as traitors, and both the Congress and the Muslim League came to their defense. These events made British military authorities wonder whether they could rely for long on the discipline and loyalty of the Indian armed forces. During the war the number of Indian commissioned officers had been greatly increased, and the character of the force had been permanently changed. The preponderance of British officers in the Indian army could not now be restored. The need for manpower during the war had compelled military authorities to widen the field of recruitment to the south, beyond the traditional martial classes of the north. The latter were largely Muslims and Sikhs; the former were Hindus. At the end of the war it was impossible to revert to the earlier position.

In the Indian civil administration, the British element had been seriously attenuated by the stoppage of recruitment during the war. The civil and military administration at the end of the war was predominantly Hindu. The Hindu educated classes, including those in the administration, were in sympathy with the Congress, which also had the support of Hindu masses. It was against this social and economic background that the political drama was being played.

The most active member of the Cabinet Mission was Sir Stafford Cripps, and he was in pronounced sympathy with the Congress. The Mission conducted individual negotiations with the top leaders— Gandhi, Jinnah, and others—and early in May, 1946, arranged a joint conference in Simla in which the Congress was represented by the Congress President, Abul Kalam Azad, and by Jawaharlal Nehru, Vallabhbhai Patel, and Abdul Ghaffar Khan; the Muslim League was represented by the League President, Muhammad Ali Jinnah, and by Liaquat Ali Khan, Nawab Muhammad Ismail, and Abdur Rab Nishtar. Gandhi was also in Simla, but he did not formally attend the conference. The stands taken by the Congress and by the Muslim League conformed, with slight adjustments, to the established pattern.

The Congress wanted a single constituent assembly to draw up a constitution for "an all-India Federal Government and Legislature dealing with Foreign Affairs, Defence, Communications, Fundamental Rights, Currency, Customs, and Planning as well as such other subjects as, on closer scrutiny, may be found to be intimately allied to them," including the power to raise revenues by taxation and to "take remedial action in cases of breakdown of the constitution and in grave public emergencies." The remaining powers were to be vested in provinces or units. "Groups of provinces may be formed and such groups may determine the Provincial subjects which they desire to take in common." Major communal issues would require the consent of a majority of the representatives of the community concerned.[2]

On April 9, 1946, a convention of Muslim League legislators— Central and Provincial—in Delhi had passed a resolution demanding that the six provinces of Bengal and Assam in the northeast and the Punjab, North-West Frontier Province, Sind and Baluchistan in the northwest be constituted into a sovereign independent state of Pakistan, and that two separate constitution-making bodies be set up by the peoples of Pakistan and Hindustan for the purpose of framing their respective constitutions. In keeping with this resolution, the Muslim League, in its negotiations with the Cabinet Mission, proposed two constitution-making bodies, one for the six provinces in the Pakistan group and the other for the group of six Hindu provinces. However, by way of an offer, the Muslim League was prepared to accept a joint meeting of the two constitution-making bodies, provided there was parity of representation between the two groups of Hindu and Muslim provinces in the central government and no decision on any controversial matter was made unless accepted by a three-fourths majority vote. It was also stipulated that the central government should have no power of taxation.[3]

Neither party could accept the proposals of the other. The fundamental issue was whether there should be one sovereign state for the whole subcontinent or two independent states. Either solution involved the presence of minorities, and both the Congress and the Muslim League agreed that minorities should receive adequate constitutional protection. Indeed, this was their only common ground. The mediation of the Cabinet Mission could not bridge the gulf between them.

On May 16, the Cabinet Mission and the Viceroy published a statement containing their own solution of the constitutional problem. The focal point of their plan was the preservation of the single state, which the British had labored to build up. (For the distribution of British provinces and Indian states before the transfer of power, see Map I.) On administrative, economic, and military grounds they rejected the proposal for two independent sovereign states. The Mission could see no justification for including within a sovereign Pakistan those districts of the Punjab, Bengal, and Assam in which the population was predominantly non-Muslim. On the other hand, a smaller sovereign Pakistan confined to the Muslim majority areas alone was regarded by the Muslim League as quite impracticable. The Mission saw, however, the force of the Muslim apprehension that their culture and political and social life might become submerged in a purely unitary India dominated by the Hindus. These considerations led them to formulate a three-tier constitutional plan.

First, there should be a Union of India embracing both British India and the states, which should deal with the subjects of foreign affairs, defense, and communications and have the power to raise the necessary finances. Major communal issues would be decided by a majority of the representatives of each of the two major communities as well as by a majority of all members present and voting.

Second, there should be three groups of provinces; section A comprising the six Hindu majority provinces; section B, the provinces of

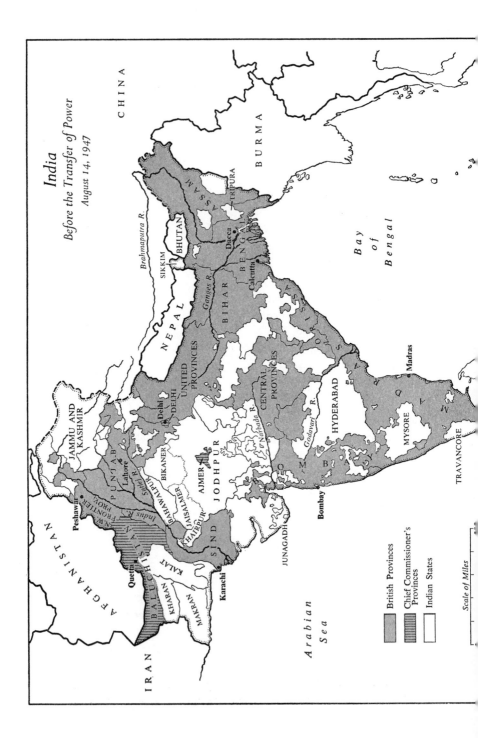

India

Before the Transfer of Power
August 14, 1947

British Provinces

Chief Commissioner's
Provinces

Indian States

Scale of Miles

CHINA

BURMA

Bay
of
Bengal

Arabian
Sea

IRAN

AFGHANISTAN

NEPAL

BHUTAN

SIKKIM

JAMMU AND
KASHMIR

Brahmaputra R.

Ganges R.

ASSAM

TRIPURA

BENGAL

Dacca

Calcutta

BIHAR

UNITED
PROVINCES

Delhi
DELHI

Peshawar

NORTHWEST
FRONTIER
PROV.

PUNJAB

Lahore

Indus R.

Sutlej R.

Chenab R.

BIKANER

BAHAWALPUR

JAISALMER

AJMER

JODHPUR

SIND

Karachi

KHAIRPUR

BALUCHISTAN

Quetta

KALAT

KHARAN

MAKRAN

JUNAGADH

Bombay

B O M B A Y

CENTRAL
PROVINCES

Narbada R.

Godavari R.

HYDERABAD

MYSORE

Madras

M A D R A S

TRAVANCORE

the Punjab, North-West Frontier Province, Sind, and Baluchistan; and section C, the provinces of Bengal and Assam.

Third, the provinces and the states should be the basic units. All subjects other than the Union subjects and all residuary powers would vest in the provinces; the states would retain all subjects and powers other than those ceded to the Union.

The plan also proposed that in the constituent assembly each province should have seats in proportion to its population, roughly in the ratio of one to a million. The representatives allotted to each of the three communities—General or Hindus, Muslims, and Sikhs—were to be elected by the members of that community in the provincial legislative assembly.

Each of the three sections (A, B, and C) of the constituent assembly should settle the constitutions for the provinces included in each section and also decide whether any group constitution should be set up for those provinces. However, the new legislature of any province should be free after the first general election under the new constitution to opt out of the group.

The Mission stated that they attached the greatest importance "to the setting up at once of an interim government in which all portfolios, including that of War Member, will be held by Indian leaders having the full confidence of the people." [4] The statement of the Cabinet Mission thus included both a long-term plan for constitution-making and a short-term plan for an interim central government. The statement was further elucidated in broadcasts by Lord Pethick-Lawrence and the Viceroy and in a statement by Sir Stafford Cripps. The Mission also held a press conference on May 17.

Gandhi "applied his legal mind" to the statement of May 16 and left it in tatters. He maintained that the Cabinet Mission plan was "an appeal and an advice" and that the constituent assembly, as a sovereign body, could vary the plan, for example, by adding to the jurisdiction of the central government or by abolishing the distinction between Muslims and non-Muslims! Similarly, he said, the provinces were free from the start to join a group or not; "the freedom to opt out is an additional safeguard." Subject to these "interpretations," which completely vitiated the whole scheme, "it is the best document the British Government could have produced in the circumstances." [5] Lord Pethick-Lawrence, whose approach to Gandhi was that of a disciple from the materialistic West to a guru in the spiritually advanced East, has nowhere recorded his reaction to this piece of Gandhian sophistry, but it can perhaps be imagined. He was learning something about Gandhi's "experiments with truth." When Gandhi, at about this time, twisted Cripps's words about Indian states to mean something different, even Lord Pethick-Lawrence was moved to the feeble protest, "You are misinterpreting what Sir Stafford said." [6]

The Congress Working Committee in its resolution of May 24 dutifully followed the line indicated by Gandhi, and demanded a transfer of power to a Hindu dominated legislature. It recognized no limitation on the authority of the constituent assembly, with its fixed Hindu majority, to alter the Cabinet Mission plan in any way it liked, and interpreted away the groups which, along with a limited central government, were the only concessions to the Muslim point of view.

In a letter to Lord Pethick-Lawrence, the Congress President expressed the fear that since the Punjab in section B and Bengal in section C would play a dominating role, they might frame a provincial constitution entirely against the wishes of the North-West Frontier Province and Assam, and might even lay down rules nullifying the provision for a province to opt out of a group. [7] Obviously he was apprehensive about the role of the Punjab and Bengal Muslims, but they were in a minority in their respective sections. Even the total Muslim representation, as the Cabinet Mission statement pointed out, was only 62.07 percent in section B, and 51.69 percent in section C. With such slender majorities it was hardly possible for the Muslims, even if they were so minded, to ride rough-shod over the educated and well-knit non-Muslims. The truth is that the Congress was not prepared to trust Muslims with political power anywhere, but expected them to put their faith in a constituent assembly dominated by the Hindus.

On May 22, 1946, Jinnah issued a statement on the Cabinet Mission plan in which he regretted that the "Mission should have negatived the Muslim demand for the establishment of a complete sovereign state of Pakistan," and raised a number of points regarding various aspects of the plan. But, he said, he did not wish to anticipate the decision of the Muslim League Council, which would meet shortly in Delhi and take decisions after a thorough and dispassionate examination of the May 16 statement.

The Cabinet Mission felt it necessary to issue a further statement

on May 25. In it they stated in clear and firm language the meaning
and purpose of their plan.

> Since the Indian leaders, after prolonged discussion, failed to arrive
> at an agreement, the Delegation put forward their recommendations
> as the nearest approach to reconciling the views of the two main
> parties. The scheme stands as a whole and can only succeed if it is
> accepted and worked in a spirit of cooperation. . . . The authority
> and the functions of the Constituent Assembly, and the procedure
> which it is intended to follow are clear from the Cabinet Delega-
> tion's statement. . . . The interpretation put by the Congress reso-
> lution on paragraph 15 of the Statement to the effect that the
> provinces can in the first instance make the choice whether or not
> to belong to the section in which they are placed does not accord
> with the Delegation's intentions. . . . The grouping of the prov-
> inces . . . is an essential feature of the scheme and can only be
> modified by agreement between the parties. The right to opt out of
> the groups after the constitution-making has been completed will be
> exercised by the people themselves, since at the first election under
> the new provincial constitution this question of opting out will ob-
> viously be a major issue and all those entitled to vote under the new
> franchise will be able to take their share in a truly democratic deci-
> sion.

The statement also made it clear that "the present constitution must
continue during the interim period; and the interim Government cannot therefore be made legally responsible to the central legislature."

The Muslim League Council met early in June and deliberated for
three days. Quite clearly the British government was determined not
to accept two independent sovereign states. For years Muslims had
seen their destiny in Pakistan; now it seemed to elude their grasp.
Many felt deeply disappointed; others consoled themselves with the
hope that the scheme would ultimately result in the establishment of a
sovereign Pakistan. Within the framework of a single state for the
whole subcontinent, the plan presented by the Cabinet Mission was
better than any previously worked out. It did not concede Pakistan,
but it gave Muslims in their majority areas reasonable control over
their political, cultural, social, and economic interests. But whether
even this plan, which fell short of the Muslim demand, would survive
the attacks of the Congress was not absolutely sure.

Gandhi was still claiming the right to make the Cabinet Mission's
statement mean what he wanted it to mean, irrespective of what its
authors said it meant. He was inciting Assam to keep out of section
C, and the North-West Frontier Province and the Sikhs in the Punjab

not to send representatives to section B. Assam and the North-West Frontier Province had Congress ministries; the Sikhs, who were being wooed by the Hindus, and pampered by the British for their contribution to the defense of the Empire, were in a truculent mood. The final reactions of the Congress were not known, but the main demand for a single state having been conceded, the Congress was unlikely to reject the plan. In keeping with its past policy—to deny Muslims any share in political power—it engaged in pressure tactics against the British combined with sentimental appeals to the statesmen of the Labour party.

The Congress had not, however, succeeded in its efforts to swing the Cabinet Mission into compliance with its wholly invalid interpretation of the May 16 statement. The Cabinet Mission's statement of May 25 allayed fears and misgivings on this score. An even firmer guarantee of the British government's resolve to hold the scales even was provided by the letter the Viceroy wrote to Jinnah on June 4.

> You asked me yesterday to give you an assurance about the action that would be taken if one party accepted the scheme in the Cabinet Delegation's statement of May 16 and the other refused. I can give you on behalf of the Cabinet Delegation my personal assurance that we do not propose to make any discrimination in the treatment of either party and that we shall go ahead with the plan laid down so far as circumstances permit if either party accepts but we hope that both will accept.[8]

The assurance of the Cabinet Mission and of the Viceroy played a decisive role in determining the final attitude of the Muslim League leaders.

The Muslim League Council, after weighing the pros and cons, decided on June 6 to accept the Cabinet Mission plan, both the long-term plan and the short-term plan. The Council affirmed that the Muslim League would join the constitution-making body. With regard to the proposed interim government, it authorized its President to negotiate with the Viceroy and to take such decisions and actions as he deemed fit and proper. It reserved the right to revise its policy if the course of events so required.[9]

Jinnah was often accused by Congress leaders of never making a positive commitment. He, it was alleged, let others make the first move, consolidated his gains and then put forward a bigger demand. At this historic moment, the Muslim League under his leadership took the courageous and far-reaching decision of accepting the Cabinet Mission plan while the Congress was still quibbling about it. In the last analysis it was an act of faith—faith that the prospect of freedom would touch the hearts of Hindu leaders with a little generosity of spirit and make them ready to live in partnership with Muslims without grasping for total power, faith in British honor and sense of fair play and above all, faith that the Muslims, given reasonable equality of opportunity in public life, would grow in greatness and power to a position worthy of their traditions and their culture. Jinnah, in particular, felt that his life-long endeavor for the freedom of the subcontinent and for a fair settlement of Hindu-Muslim relations was about to find fulfillment. The "wise and statesmanlike" decision of the Muslim League, as the British press described it, brought relief to the country at large. At last, it appeared, the Hindu-Muslim differences had been amicably resolved and independence was in sight.

As events showed, the optimism was premature and shortlived. Negotiations for the formation of the interim government proved difficult beyond expectation. Nothing else shows so clearly the hollowness of the repeated statements made by Gandhi and other Congress leaders that if freedom were won, they would not care to whom the power went. On May 25, Abul Kalam Azad, the Congress President, sought from the Viceroy an assurance about the status and the responsibility of the interim government and stated that if these "two basic questions" were satisfactorily solved, "the other details regarding the composition of the Interim Cabinet" would present no difficulty at all. The Viceroy in his letter of May 30 gave the assurance that "His Majesty's Government would treat the new interim Government with the same close consultation and consideration as a Dominion Government [and would] give to the Indian Government the greatest possible freedom in the exercise of the day-to-day administration of the country." [10] Having got this assurance the Congress leaders started haggling about the composition of the interim cabinet and made it the cardinal issue. The Viceroy had led Jinnah to understand that there would be twelve portfolios, five Congress, five League, one Sikh, and one Indian Christian or Anglo-Indian; this had been an important element in bringing about the acceptance of the Cabinet Mission plan by the League. The Congress refused to accept this arrangement. Nehru saw the Viceroy on June 12 and proposed that there should be fifteen members in the interim cabinet, five Congress (all Hindus), four Muslim League, one non-League Muslim, one non-Congress Hindu, one Congress Scheduled Caste Hindu, one Indian Christian, one Sikh, and one woman, to be nominated by the Congress. The Viceroy could not agree to this unfair distribution. The question of parity between the Congress and the League in the interim cabinet now became an "insuperable obstacle," to quote the Congress President.[11] In order to appease the Congress, the Viceroy proposed that there should be thirteen members, six Congress (including a member of the Scheduled Caste), five Muslim League, and two representatives of the minorities. He added "I do not see how this can be called parity. Nor is there parity between Hindus and Muslims, there being six Hindus to five Muslims." Even this was not acceptable to the Congress since it smacked of parity between caste Hindus and Muslims. The Congress President, in his letter to the Viceroy dated June 16, admitted that the Congress had accepted parity between the caste Hindus and Muslims at the Simla conference in July, 1945, but went on to say, "Now conditions have entirely changed and we have to consider the question in another context, that of approaching independence and the Constituent Assembly." [12]

The real obstacle, it now became clear, was that Congress desired total authority in the new India. The Hindus must be in absolute control; political power must not be shared with Muslims. In a letter to Cripps at this time Gandhi wrote, "If you have courage you will do what I suggested from the very beginning. . . . You will have to choose between the two—the Muslim League and the Congress, both your creations." [13]

The Cabinet Mission and the Viceroy decided to issue a statement setting forth their own proposals for the formation of a strong and representative interim government. Their statement of June 16 announced the names of fourteen persons to whom the Viceroy was issuing invitations to serve as members of the interim cabinet. Six were members of the Congress, including a Scheduled Caste representative; five were members of the Muslim League; there was one Sikh, one Indian Christian, and one Parsi. The list included the names of Nehru and Jinnah, although the latter had told the Viceroy he would not accept any office so long as he was President of the Muslim League. To placate the Congress, the statement gave the assurance that "this composition of the Interim Government is in no way to be taken as a precedent for the solution of any other commu-

nal question. It is an expedient put forward to solve the present difficulty and to obtain the best available Coalition Government." The
statement had a ring of finality about it. It affirmed, in paragraph 8,
that "In the event of the two major parties or either of them proving
unwilling to join in the setting up of a Coalition Government on the
above lines, it is the intention of the Viceroy to proceed with the formation of an Interim Government which will be as representative as
possible of those willing to accept the Statement of May 16th." [14]

A week of furious political activity followed a war of nerves directed against the Cabinet Mission and the Viceroy, by the Congress
leaders, the Hindu officials, and the Hindu-controlled press. The air
was thick with rumors. A storm was raised over the correspondence
between the Viceroy and Jinnah, which had leaked out to the press,
about the filling of Muslim vacancies in the cabinet with members of
the Muslim League only. Gandhi threatened to leave Delhi unless a
nationalist Muslim was included in the interim cabinet, although the
Cabinet Mission had a written assurance from Azad, the Congress
President, that the Working Committee would not insist on that. [15]
Gandhi hinted darkly at turning the constituent assembly into a rebel
body. Cripps came running to Gandhi, who again demanded that the
Cabinet Mission "must choose between the one or the other party,
not attempt an amalgam." [16]

Within six days the Cabinet Mission capitulated. On June 22,
Sudhir Ghosh, a friend of Cripps, reported to Gandhi that he had
seen Cripps, who had told him that if the Congress declined to accept
office, the Cabinet Mission "did not feel that the League by itself
could be entrusted with it," but before deciding to entrust it solely
to the Congress, they would have to return to London for personal
discussion. After seeing Cripps again, Sudhir Ghosh, on the morning of June 24, passed on to Gandhi the gist of his talk with Cripps,
who

> had told him that they [the Cabinet Mission] had decided that if the
> Congress accepted the long term plan and rejected the short term
> proposal, all that the Cabinet Mission had done under the 16th June
> declaration for the formation of an Interim Government would be
> scrapped and a de novo attempt made for the same. They invited
> Bapu [Gandhi] and Sardar [Vallabhbhai Patel] to meet them. They
> seem to have made up their mind to clear up the mess created by
> the assurances given to Jinnah by Lord Wavell. [17]

It is pertinent to remark that these assurances—no discrimination in
the treatment of either party and proceeding with the formation of the

interim government even if either of the two major parties proved unwilling to join it—had been given on the authority of the Cabinet
Mission themselves.

Gandhi, accompanied by Sardar Patel and Sudhir Ghosh, immediately went to meet the Cabinet Mission. Patel had already had a talk
with Lord Pethick-Lawrence, who in his anxiety to win over "the
strong man of the Congress" to the new plan, had been searching for
him since early morning. Since this was Gandhi's day of silence he
communicated by writing notes. "I understood," he wrote, "that you
propose to scrap the whole plan of Interim Government as it had
gone up to now and consider the situation de novo." Having obtained
a confirmation of this understanding, Gandhi and Patel returned to
inform the Congress Working Committee.[18] In keeping with the understanding reached between Gandhi and the Cabinet Mission, the
Congress President sent a letter to the Viceroy on June 25 rejecting
the interim government proposal and accepting the long-term plan
while "adhering to our views" regarding it.[19]

The views to which the Congress adhered were totally destructive
of those elements in the plan which had made it acceptable to the
Muslim League; namely, a central government with limited powers
and the provincial groups. Without those elements, which were an
integral part of the scheme, it was not the Cabinet Mission plan but
the Congress plan for a Hindu-dominated sovereign constituent assembly free to make any kind of constitution for the whole subcontinent.
The Cabinet Mission in their statement of May 25 had categorically
stated that "the scheme stands as a whole and can only succeed if it is
accepted and worked in a spirit of cooperation" and that the interpretation of the Congress resolution (of May 24) "does not accord with
the Delegation's intentions." Incredible as it may seem, the Cabinet
Mission now decided that the Congress President's letter (of June
25), which rejected one part of the statement of May 16—the short-
term plan—and gave an invalid acceptance of the other part—the
long-term plan—constituted an acceptance of the statement. The
truth was that Muslim League alone had accepted the statement of
May 16 in its entirety—the long-term plan as well as the short-term
plan—and had done this in good faith. But the Cabinet Mission put
the Congress and the League on a par and declared that both had
accepted the statement of May 16 and were qualified to enter the
interim government.

Immediately following the rejection by the Congress of the short-term plan, the Muslim League passed a resolution agreeing to join the interim government on the basis of the Cabinet Mission's statement of June 16. In terms of that statement the Viceroy should have called upon the Muslim League to form the government along with others "willing to accept the Statement of May 16th." But despite Jinnah's insistent reminders to the Cabinet Mission and the Viceroy to honor their undertakings, the Viceroy formed a caretaker government of permanent officials in order to have "a short interval before proceeding with further negotiations for the formation of an Interim Government." Jinnah's comment was: "I maintain that the Cabinet Mission and Viceroy have gone back on their word within ten days of the publication of their final proposals in not implementing the statement of 16 June and I fully endorse what has been put so well—'Statesmen should not eat their words.'" [20]

Having eaten his words once, a statesman might acquire facility in the art; practice makes perfect. What the Cabinet Mission had done with their undertakings regarding the short-term plan, they proceeded to do with the long-term plan as well. Elections for the constituent assembly were fixed for early July, and under the rules issued by the Viceroy's Reforms Office, candidates had to declare that they would be "willing to serve as representatives of the Province for the purposes of paragraph 19 of the Statement" of May 16. This was the paragraph dealing with the formation of groups and for Gandhi it was a "drop of poison." When, at the crucial meeting with the Cabinet Mission on June 24, Gandhi had obtained their confirmation to the scrapping of the short-term plan, he had asked them to amend also the long-term plan in a vital way by not binding members of the constituent assembly to make a constitution in terms of paragraph 19. Gandhi was apprehensive that they might resist his proposal, but they exceeded his expectations and made the change he wanted. The revised pledge merely required members to cooperate in framing a new constitution for India. Encouraged by this, he wanted to turn the screw harder. He wanted power to enforce the decisions of the constituent assembly and, therefore, advised the Congress Working Committee "not to accept the long-term proposition without its being connected with the Interim Government." The Working Committee, however, felt that sufficient gains had been secured for the time being.

Pyarelal, Gandhi's faithful secretary, has recorded that this marked the beginning of a

cleavage between Gandhiji and some of his closest colleagues.
. . . Practically all the important resolutions and drafts of the
Working Committee were first conceived in Gandhiji's brain and
subsequently adopted or adapted by the Working Committee.
. . . [Gandhiji's] insistence on being left alone to settle directly
with the Muslim League after the British had quitted, even if it
meant civil war . . . his readiness to face chaos and anarchy in
preference to peace imposed by British arms, not only remained unchanged, they stiffened as time went by. The members of the Working Committee with their purely political approach, felt out of their
depth in these uncharted waters.[21]

It was a sight to make angels weep to see the apostle of ahimsa—who
had preached nonviolence to all the world as the highest religious
principle, who had advised England in its hour of deadly peril not to
oppose Hitler with arms—thirsting "to settle directly with the Muslim
League after the British had quitted even if it meant civil war." Nonviolence, then, was a weapon for use only against the well-armed
British; against the numerically smaller and weaker Muslims war was
to be waged.

Incidentally, this episode shows clearly the distribution of power
within the Congress. As Congress President, Abul Kalam Azad was
the chief negotiator with the Cabinet Mission on behalf of the Congress. He also believed sincerely in the Cabinet Mission plan and was
anxious to see it implemented. But when it came to a crucial decision,
the Cabinet Mission ignored him and, behind his back, made a deal
with Gandhi and Patel. The Congress Working Committee merely
stamped its approval on the deal. Abul Kalam Azad was the most
eminent of the "nationalist" Muslims associated with the Congress.
The Congress made use of his influence with the Jamiatul Ulama-
i-Hind for its own purposes, and paraded him as proof that it was a
noncommunal organization. But neither he nor the other "nationalist" Muslims counted for much in the inner counsels of the Congress.
Patel's caustic remark about there being "only one true nationalist
Muslim—Jawaharlal [Nehru]," [22] indicates the esteem in which they
were held by the strong man of the Congress.

The Cabinet Mission departed from India on June 29, 1946, and
left behind them a legacy of discord and bitterness. Their pattern of
behavior—a brave effort at doing "justice" followed by an abject retreat in the face of Congress threats—was to exhibit itself again and
again in the conduct of Indian affairs by the Labour party. In a way,
the result of this first clash of wills between the Cabinet Mission and

the Congress leadership was decisive. Having lost this battle, the Labour government never regained its nerve. Each retreat left it weaker until, in the end, it lost all power of initiative and did the bidding of the Congress while making desperate efforts to save appearances. As the British historian Percival Spear says, "The British could only argue and persuade; they could no longer command." [23] No doubt the Labour party had in it men of courage and idealism, Ernest Bevin and Philip Noel-Baker, for instance, but the views that finally prevailed in Indian affairs were those of Sir Stafford Cripps and Prime Minister Attlee.

Early in July, 1946, Jawaharlal Nehru took the place of Abul Kalam Azad as Congress President. The choice, as usual, was Gandhi's. Vallabhbhai Patel was deeply disappointed since it was clear that whoever became Congress President would soon head the interim government and be the first prime minister of free India. As Gandhi explained later, "Jawaharlal, a Harrow boy, a Cambridge graduate and a barrister is wanted to carry on the negotiations with Englishmen." [24] On July 10 the new Congress President held a press conference in Bombay in which he said that the Congress would enter the constituent assembly "completely unfettered by agreements and free to meet all situations as they arise." In reply to a question if this meant that the Cabinet Mission plan could be modified, Nehru stated emphatically "The Congress had agreed only to participate in the Constituent Assembly and regarded itself free to change or modify the Cabinet Mission Plan as it thought best." [25] He declared, "the big probability is, from any approach to the question, there will be no grouping" because, he explained, section A (the Hindu majority provinces) would be opposed to it, and the North-West Frontier Province would oppose it in section B, as would Assam in section C. He envisaged a much stronger central government than that proposed in the Cabinet Mission plan. The central government would control foreign affairs, defense, and communications, and these would be broadly interpreted to include industries necessary for their support, foreign trade policy, currency and credit, loans and taxing power. The central government would also have the authority to settle interprovincial disputes and to deal with administrative or economic breakdowns. "The scope of the Centre," he concluded, "even though limited, inevitably grows, because it cannot exist otherwise." [26]

Nehru's Canadian biographer, Michael Brecher, writes that

"Nehru's remarks certainly cleared the air of confusion and hypocrisy. At the same time they destroyed the facade of agreement which the Cabinet Mission tried to maintain." [27] Jinnah immediately pointed out that Nehru's statement was "a complete repudiation of the basic form upon which the long-term scheme rests," and suggested that the British government should, in the forthcoming parliamentary debate, "remove the impression that the Congress has accepted the long-term scheme." The British government, however, chose not to do so. Speaking in the House of Lords on July 18, Lord Pethick-Lawrence said:

> I should perhaps say a few words regarding some of the recent reports from India as to the intentions of the parties in joining the Constituent Assembly. We saw both parties shortly before we left India and they said to us quite categorically that it was their intention to go into the Assembly with the object of making it work. Of course, they are at perfect liberty to advance their own views of what should or should not be the basis of a future constitution. . . . But having agreed to the statement of 16 May and the Constituent Assembly, elected in accordance with that statement, they cannot, of course, go outside the terms of what has been agreed. To do so would not be fair to other parties who come in and it is on the basis of that agreed procedure that His Majesty's Government have said they will accept the decisions of the Constituent Assembly.

On the same day Sir Stafford Cripps, speaking in the House of Commons, expressed similar sentiments in almost identical language. Cripps tried to justify the strange behavior of the Cabinet Mission by putting a construction on paragraph 8 of the statement of June 16, which the plain sense of its words could not bear; his close association in India with the masters of the art of "interpretation" had not been in vain. He said that "Mr. Jinnah was anxious to enter the Coalition Government as laid down in the statement of 16th June, but as paragraph 8 of that statement made the setting up of such a government dependent upon acceptance by both parties, it was impossible to proceed upon that basis when one party—and that the major party—had stated its unwillingness to accept." [28] No more eloquent commentary on these words can be given than the text of paragraph 8 quoted earlier (p. 63).[29]

It was against the background of these events that the Muslim League Council met in Bombay in the last week of July. In his speech to the Council, Jinnah retraced the course of negotiations with the Cabinet Mission, and showed how the Muslim League had "made concession after concession . . . because of our extreme anxiety for an amicable and peaceful settlement which will lead not only Hindus and Muslims but also other communities inhabiting this sub-continent to the achievement of freedom"; how the League "is the only party that has emerged from these negotiations with honour and clean hands"; how the Congress had "done the greatest harm to the peoples of India by its pettifogging, higgling attitude [and had] no other consideration except to down the Muslim League"; how "throughout these negotiations the Cabinet Mission were under terror and threats of the Congress"; how the Cabinet Mission, by treating the invalid acceptance by the Congress of only the long-term plan as a genuine acceptance, "went back on their plighted word" with regard to the interim government, and "to-day are cowed down and paralysed." The Congress President, Jawaharlal Nehru, he continued, had "made it quite clear that the Congress was committed to nothing [and was] not bound by paragraph 15 or paragraph 19 of the State Paper" of May 16, and that beyond the "pious expression" of the Secretary of State that Indian parties could not go outside the terms of the plan because that would not be fair to other parties, "there is no effective check or remedy provided in the event of the Congress, which happens to have a brute majority in the Constituent Assembly, taking any decision which is ultra vires and incompetent of the Assembly."

Jinnah's strongest words were reserved for Sir Stafford Cripps, "that ingenious juggler of words [who had put] a fantastic and dishonest construction" on paragraph 8 of the statement of June 16 to evade the formation of the interim government. "All these prove clearly beyond a shadow of doubt that the only solution of India's problem is Pakistan. I feel we have exhausted all reasons. It is no use looking to any other source for help or assistance. There is no tribunal to which we can go. The only tribunal is the Muslim nation." In his concluding speech to the Council, Jinnah said, "The League, throughout the negotiations, was moved by a sense of fair play and sacrificed the full sovereign state of Pakistan at the altar of the Congress for securing the independence of the whole of India. They voluntarily delegated three subjects to the Union, and by doing so did not commit a mistake. It was the highest order of statesmanship that the League displayed by making concessions. . . . But this has been treated with defiance and contempt." [30]

When the resolution withdrawing acceptance of the Cabinet Mission plan was put before the League Council on July 29, there was not a single dissenting voice. The last paragraph of the resolution noted that

> The scheme cannot succeed unless it is worked in a spirit of cooperation. The attitude of the Congress clearly shows that these conditions precedent for the successful working of the constitution-making body do not exist. This fact, taken together with the policy of the British Government of sacrificing the interests of the Muslim nation and some other weaker sections of the peoples of India, particularly the Scheduled Castes, to appease the Congress and the way in which they have been going back on their oral and written solemn pledges and assurances given from time to time to the Muslims, leave no doubt that in these circumstances the participation of the Muslims in the proposed constitution-making machinery is fraught with danger and the Council, therefore, hereby withdraws its acceptance of the Cabinet Mission's proposals which was communicated to the Secretary of the State for India by the President of the Muslim League on 6th June, 1946.[31]

The Council also passed another resolution which read, in part, "The time has come for the Muslim nation to resort to direct action to achieve Pakistan and to get rid of the present slavery under the British and contemplated future Caste Hindu domination," and gave instructions for the preparation of a "programme of direct action . . . to organize the Muslims for the coming struggle to be launched as and when necessary." Furthermore, "as a protest against and in token of their deep resentment of the attitude of the British," the Council called upon Muslims to renounce the titles "conferred upon them by the Alien Government." [32]

At a press conference on July 31, Jinnah made it clear that direct action was not a declaration of war against anybody. He said that the Muslim League alone had scrupulously kept itself within the constitutional orbit and had been following constitutional methods. During the negotiations which led to the Cabinet Mission plan, the Muslim League had found the British government to be

> under the spell of the sword of Damocles . . . [fearing] that if the Congress [were] not appeased or satisfied, it would launch a struggle . . . a thousand times worse than 1942. . . . The British have machine-guns and can interpret what they say as they like. . . . The Congress, armed to the teeth with another kind of weapon . . . is not to be trifled with. We, therefore, are now forced for our self-defence and self-preservation to say good-bye to constitutional methods and we have decided . . . to prepare and resort to direct action as and when the time may come to launch it.[33]

In short, the Muslim League was to forge sanctions of the same sort as the Congress, which had practiced direct action for a quarter of a century.

The Congress took this as a challenge to itself. Speaking at a public meeting, Sardar Patel said that the threatened direct action by the League, if it was real, was not aimed at the British but at the Congress because the British had already made it clear that they had no intention of staying in India.[34] The general reaction among the Hindus was that the resolutions of the Muslim League were bluff and bluster. The Hindus knew that the Muslim masses were with the League, but, they reasoned, if an army is only as good as its officers, a political organization cannot be better in its powers of cohesion and resistance than the bulk of its leadership. Jinnah apart, it was argued by the opponents of the League, its leadership in the higher ranks consisted for the most part of moderates with a feudal background of subservience to authority, or of well-to-do middle-aged men who could not be expected to stand the rigors of a prolonged civil disobedience campaign. These men, the Hindus felt, had never been through the fire of battle and could not be compared with the Congress veterans in capacity for sacrifice and discipline. Their gesture of giving up British titles on the eve of the British departure could convince no one since it involved no real sacrifice. It was maintained, not altogether unjustly, that the younger elements in the newly rising middle class who were fired with idealism and a sincere belief in Pakistan were largely unrepresented in the Muslim League hierarchy and wielded little influence; and that unlike the Congress, the Muslim League lacked the financial means of maintaining an army of political workers and their families in or out of jail. Thus, the Hindus sought, by means of ridicule, abuse, and threats to intimidate the Muslims. Inevitably relations between the two communities deteriorated.

Only rarely was the voice of sanity heard. As Sir Chimanlal Setalvad, a leader of the Liberal Federation, pointed out, there had not been "sufficient realisation of the importance of the first decision of the League to agree to a common Centre, however restricted, and to enter into the Constituent Assembly to frame a constitution for one united India." He called upon the Congress to "reassure the League that there is no intention to disavow any part of the scheme in the State paper."[35] The distinguished British journalist, Sir Arthur Moore, former editor of the *Statesman* of Calcutta, commented that the Muslim League alone had accepted the long-term and the short-term plan. . . . No glimmer of thanks or gratitude reached them. Our concern is that by going back on the statement of 16 June we let down those who trusted us . . . the British press had to represent the Cabinet Mission as a success and to conceal the wrong done to the Muslims. We have produced a situation in which civil war is an obvious possibility.[36]

By the end of July, elections to the constituent assembly were held. The Muslim League won 95 percent of the Muslim seats and the Congress captured as high a proportion of the general (non-Muslim) seats. There was a Congress government in Assam; and the Assam assembly though electing representatives to the constituent assembly instructed them not to take part in section C from the very start. The sixty million members of the Scheduled Castes felt greatly perturbed at the result of the elections. Their true representatives had been kept out of provincial assemblies by the votes of Caste Hindus under the Poona Pact and, since provincial assemblies formed the electoral college for the constituent assembly, they were excluded from the latter as well. As Dr. Ambedkar, leader of the Scheduled Caste Federation explained, "In the primary elections wherever held in the country, no Congressman won against the Federation candidate. But in the general elections the candidates selected by their community were rejected and 'stooges' and 'tools' of another party came on top because of Caste Hindu votes." The Muslim League sympathized with these down-trodden people and espoused their cause; but the Congress stuck to the Poona Pact, which Dr. Ambedkar had accepted under pressure of Gandhi's fast unto death and which, according to him, had "resulted in the political disenfranchisement of the very people [Scheduled Castes] in whose interest it was made." [37]

The Sikhs protested against the Group system and at first held aloof from the elections to the constituent assembly. The Sikh leaders' objection, that the formation of section B implied Muslim majority domination from which Sikh areas could not opt out, had been instigated by Gandhi who continually played upon Sikh fears. How insubstantial this objection was can be seen from the fact that there was not a single district in the Punjab in which the Sikhs were in a majority. In section B the Sikhs would have been entitled to 4 out of 35 seats as against 4 out of 28 seats in the Punjab. The formation of section B would thus have made little difference to their minority status. The British were anxious to give the most sympathetic consideration to Sikh claims but, as Sir Stafford Cripps explained in the House of Commons on July 18,

> the difficulty arises, not from anyone's underestimate of the importance of the Sikh community but from the inescapable geographical facts of the situation. What they demand is some special treatment analogous to that given to the Muslims. The Sikhs, however, are a much smaller community, 5½ against 90 millions, and moreover are not geographically situated so that any area as yet devised . . . can be carved out in which they would find themselves in a majority.

Jinnah had time and again assured the Sikhs that their rights would be fully safeguarded and their claims dealt with generously, but neither he nor any one else could alter their minority status.

The Congress, which wanted an ally against the Muslim League, passed a resolution "assuring the Sikhs that the Congress would give them all possible support in removing their legitimate grievances." [38] In response to the appeal of the Congress, the Sikhs decided to accept the statement of May 16 and to elect their representatives to the constituent assembly. An alliance was formed between the Congress and the Sikhs; the latter did not know it, but they were to be used as a cat's paw against the Muslims, and after having been so used they were to discover with bitter disillusionment the true worth of Congress promises. When the Sikh agitation for a Punjabi-speaking province within the Union of India was ruthlessly put down by Nehru's government in 1961, Tara Singh ruefully had to admit that the Sikh proposal for an independent Sikh state in 1946 had been incited by the Congress as a counterblast to the Muslim demand for Pakistan.[39] But it is for a Sikh historian to narrate how Baldev Singh died a broken-hearted man and how Tara Singh undertook a "fast unto death" against Hindu domination and barely escaped with his life.

On July 22, Lord Wavell resumed his effort to form the interim government and wrote to Nehru and Jinnah proposing a cabinet of fourteen members, six to be nominated by the Congress (including one Scheduled Caste representative), five by the Muslim League, and three representatives of minorities, who were to be nominated by the Viceroy. Neither party would have the right to object to the names submitted by the other, provided the Viceroy accepted them. The Congress and the Muslim League would each have an equitable share of the most important portfolios. The Viceroy reiterated the assurance about the status of the interim government given in his letter of

May 30 to Abul Kalam Azad, and added that he "would welcome a convention, if freely offered by the Congress, that major communal issues can only be decided by the assent of both the major parties." [40]

Nehru wrote back expressing his dissatisfaction with the Viceroy's assurance about the status of the interim government, and said the Congress wanted independence of action for the interim government, with the Viceroy acting only as a constitutional head; therefore he was wholly unable to cooperate in the formation of a government on the lines suggested by the Viceroy. Jinnah sent his reply on July 31. He pointed out the many ways in which the present proposal was detrimental to the Muslim League as compared with the original proposal for the formation of the interim government and concluded that there was no chance of the Muslim League Working Committee accepting it.

Upon receiving these replies the Viceroy sent for Nehru, but not for Jinnah, to have a personal discussion. On August 6, with the concurrence of the British government, he invited Nehru to form the interim government, leaving it to him to consider whether he should first discuss the proposals for the formation of the government with Jinnah. To Jinnah the Viceroy wrote that he had decided to invite the Congress to make proposals for an interim government and hoped that the Muslim League would join if the Congress made a reasonable offer of a coalition. On August 8, the Congress Working Committee, meeting at Gandhi's ashram in Wardha, accepted the Viceroy's invitation. Nehru made an approach to Jinnah but, as might have been expected, it led nowhere.

To keep the Muslim League out of the interim government answered the Congress's purpose of not sharing power with the chosen representatives of the Muslims, since "nationalist" Muslims and other stooges could always be found for cabinet appointments. But a constituent assembly in which 95 percent of elected Muslim representatives did not participate would be so pronouncedly Hindu in composition that it would be difficult to keep up the pretense of its being a national organization qualified to draw up a constitution for the whole of India, including Muslim majority provinces. It was therefore necessary to lure the Muslim League into the constituent assembly or, at any rate, to make its abstention appear as willful intransigence. Some Congress leaders felt that Nehru's frank disclosure of their intentions had been a tactical mistake; the Viceroy also was unhappy about it.

To soothe these susceptibilities the Congress Working Committee at Wardha resorted to another display of verbal acrobatics. It passed a resolution, on August 10, in which, in answer to the criticism of the Muslim League that the Congress acceptance of the statement of May 16 was conditional, the Committee asserted that they "accepted the scheme in its entirety [but] interpreted it so as to resolve the inconsistencies contained in it and fill the omissions in accordance with the principles laid down in that Statement." The resolution affirmed that "each province has the right to decide whether to join a group or not," and emphasized "the sovereign character of the Constituent Assembly [which] will naturally function within the internal limitations . . . inherent in its task." [41]

Jinnah subjected the resolution to a searching analysis and pointed out that it was "only a repetition of the Congress stand taken . . . from the very beginning, only put in different language and phraseology [and that, therefore,] the so-called acceptance [by the Congress] was in fact a rejection." [42]

August 16 had been fixed by the Muslim League as "Direct Action Day." Two days before, Jinnah issued a statement to the press explaining that the day was

> for the purpose of explaining to the Muslim public all over India the resolutions that were passed by the Council of the All-India Muslim League on the 29th July at Bombay . . . and not for the purpose of resorting to direct action in any form or shape; therefore, I enjoin upon the Muslims to carry out the instructions and abide by them strictly and conduct themselves peacefully and in a disciplined manner and not to play into the hands of the enemies. [43]

The day passed off peacefully all over India except in Calcutta, which was the scene of an unprecedented Hindu-Muslim riot that came to be known as the Great Calcutta Killing. Although Bengal was a Muslim majority province, its capital, Calcutta, had a predominantly Hindu population, only 24 percent being Muslims. At that time a Muslim League ministry was in power and Husain Shaheed Suhrawardy was the Chief Minister. According to Lt. General Sir Francis Tuker, who was General Officer Commanding-in-Chief, Eastern Command,

> For the first half of August, speeches of public men of both Congress and Muslim League at large meetings in Calcutta were inflammatory and violent in their character, all directed against the opposite community. On the 15th August, an acid debate took place

in the Bengal Assembly when the Bengal government had announced its decision to make the 16th August, Direct Action Day, a public holiday. The debate showed how bitterly the Hindus resented this order. One of the causes for their resentment was that, up till now, the Congress had more or less possessed monopoly rights for imposing and enforcing hartals paralysing the whole of Calcutta's transport . . . they thus strongly resented the prospect of any other competitor, especially so formidable a bidder as the Muslim League, entering this highly coveted field of political exploitation.[44]

The meeting of August 16, at which Suhrawardy gave an address, passed off without incident, but

> at 4.15 p.m. Fortress H.Q. sent out the codeword "Red" to indicate that there were incidents all over Calcutta. . . . February's killings had shocked us all but this was different: it was unbridled savagery . . . let loose. . . . On one night alone some four hundred and fifty corpses were cleared from the streets by the three British battalions. . . . By the 22nd August . . . Calcutta was quiet.[45]

Ian Stephens, editor of the *Statesman* of Calcutta, wrote:

> Perhaps during the first day's fighting, and certainly during the second and third, Muslim losses were the worst. . . . What decisively tipped the scales . . . was perhaps not the massive retaliatory Hindu onslaughts but the intervention during the second afternoon of the Sikhs, who had in the main held aloof on August 16th. . . . The present writer recalls watching hordes of them . . . join the fray on the Hindus' side in the city's smoke-shrouded northern slums.[46]

The Calcutta riot has been the subject of much polemical writing. The above comments by responsible Britishers present an objective picture of what actually happened. The tragedy of Hindu-Muslim riots had often been witnessed in the subcontinent, but the Calcutta killing was on an unprecedented scale. It aroused horror and revulsion in every sane man. Jinnah unreservedly condemned the acts of violence and deeply sympathized with those who had suffered.

On August 24, the Viceroy announced the names of the members of the interim government who would take office on September 2. Nehru had wanted to fill all the five Muslim seats with non-League Muslims but the Viceroy, who was still hoping that the Muslim League might come in, appointed only three, leaving two vacancies. The Viceroy then went to Calcutta; what he saw there convinced him that unless agreement could be reached between the Congress and the Muslim League no communal harmony was possible and the country would soon be plunged into civil war.

In an effort to bring about a settlement, the Viceroy met Gandhi and Nehru on August 27. In the Viceroy's view, what stood in the way of concord between the Congress and the Muslim League was the way the Congress interpreted grouping in sections, and he wanted this point cleared before the constituent assembly was summoned. He asked them to agree to a declaration in the following terms:

> The Congress are prepared in the interest of communal harmony to accept the intention of the statement of 16th May that Provinces cannot exercise any option affecting their membership of the sections or of the groups if formed until the decision contemplated in Para 19 (viii) of the statement of the 16th May is taken by the new legislature after the new constitutional arrangements have come into operation and the first general elections have been held.[47]

Gandhi and Nehru refused to agree to this formula, which was clearly in accord with the Cabinet Mission's statement of May 16. The Congress leaders went on harping on their own untenable interpretation, and instead of treating the Cabinet Mission plan as a political agreement freely arrived at, started referring to it as a legal statute, the opposing interpretations of which should be referred to the federal court for a judicial pronouncement. A law suit would have exacerbated feelings still further and made an amicable agreement between the two parties almost impossible. For the judgment could in its turn be "interpreted" and converted into a fresh battleground; Gandhi's infinite ingenuity, which had raised these legal issues, would no doubt have been equal to the task. "Gandhi," wrote V. P. Menon, "went into legalistic arguments about the interpretation of the Mission's statement, but the Viceroy asserted that he was a plain man and not a lawyer; he knew perfectly well what the Mission meant, and compulsory grouping was the whole crux of the plan." [48]

This was lèse majesté. Gandhi immediately cabled a message to His Majesty's government in London that the Viceroy was "unnerved owing to the Bengal tragedy" and needed to be assisted by "an abler and legal mind," otherwise "the repetition of the Bengal tragedy [was] a certainty." Obviously Mahatmas are made of sterner stuff! To the Viceroy he wrote on August 28: "Your language last evening was minatory. As representative of the King you cannot afford to be a military man only, nor to ignore the law, much less the law of your own making. You should be assisted, if necessary, by a legal mind enjoying your full confidence." And he thereupon presented the entire Congress position on the interim government and the invidious effect of continuing British presence. Gandhi asked the Viceroy to cable the whole text of his letter to the British cabinet, which the Viceroy dutifully did. Prime Minister Attlee was perturbed and remarked that "if in Gandhi's judgment the situation is such that the Viceroy needs the assistance of a mind abler than his own and if Gandhi thinks that otherwise a repetition of the Calcutta tragedy is not only possible or probable but certain, then that is a matter which must be taken seriously." [49] Lord Pethick-Lawrence was, however, of the view that the Congress, who were now in a powerful position, should make some concession to the Muslim League.

From now on Lord Wavell was a marked man. The Congress pulled all the strings in London it could, and finally succeeded in getting him dismissed some months later. Gandhi turned against Lord Wavell not merely because of the latter's impatience with legal hair-splitting or his soldierly repugnance to unnecessary bloodshed, but because of his determination to settle the differences between the Congress and the Muslim League. Why could the Viceroy not see that an agreement was not wanted and that power had to be given to one or the other; since it could not be the League, the Congress alone must have it. Once in the saddle, no one would be able to dislodge the Congress. The armed forces were predominantly Hindu and Sikh; the civil administration almost entirely Hindu. The British were losing their grip and could not continue in India much longer. They desperately needed all their manpower for the task of reconstructing their war-torn economy in the United Kingdom and, anyhow, were reluctant to use British troops for the thankless task of keeping warring Hindus and Muslims apart. If, by threats and constant digs at their good faith, the British could be made to withdraw, leaving the Congress in command, the Congress would know how to deal with these troublesome Muslims. Jinnah was incorruptible, but there were many Muslim leaders who could be won over once they saw that the Congress alone disposed of all power and patronage. If division in Muslim ranks did not do the job, they could be put down even if it meant a civil war. The final result could not be in doubt since the Hindus would have numbers, economic power, armed forces, civil administration, organizational strength, and control over publicity and communication.

It is only against this background that one can understand Gandhi's insistence on the inclusion of "nationalist" Muslims in the cabinet, his persistent opposition to a coalition of the Congress and the Muslim League, his many maneuvers for obstructing an agreed solution of constitutional issues, and his war of nerves against the British cabinet and the Viceroy. There was a time when Gandhi used to place Hindu-Muslim unity prior to independence, but then it had been a means to an end. That phase had passed long ago, and although, occasionally, he still paid homage to it as an amiable sentiment, it was no longer a political necessity, but rather an obstacle to Hindu hegemony.

Nehru and the rest of the cabinet were sworn in on September 2. Nehru was designated Vice-President of the Executive Council. Everything was going well from the Congress point of view except that the Viceroy was still trying to bring about a settlement with the Muslim League. He felt that if the intentions of the Congress were what Gandhi's letter of August 28 suggested, "the result of its being in power could only be a state of virtual civil war in many parts of India." [50] In the Viceroy's view, it was essential to adhere to the statement of May 16 as a whole, since the Cabinet Mission had never intended constitution-making on a one-party basis. He saw Jinnah on September 16 and again on September 25. Jinnah said that the League had accepted the statement of May 16 in good faith, but the Congress had not. "The only good thing in it," he added, "was the provision for sections and grouping, and the only guarantee for the successful working of the scheme was that it should be implemented with honour and good will." [51] The question of the Muslim League going into the constituent assembly would have to be referred to the All-India Muslim League Council, while the Working Committee of the League could take a decision about the interim government. There the main stumbling block was that the Congress insisted on the inclusion of a "nationalist" Muslim. When Lord Wavell saw Gandhi the next day and suggested he waive the right to nominate one, Gandhi replied "One may waive a right, one cannot waive a duty," meaning that the Congress owed it to the nationalist Muslims. When the Viceroy stressed the need for bringing in the Muslim League, Gandhi answered "Let Jinnah seek an interview with Pandit Nehru and come to an honourable understanding." Gandhi was prepared to drop the constituent assembly if no agreement could be reached but, "no matter what happened, the National Government, having been once summoned, should continue to function." [52]

The Viceroy, however, continued his efforts for a settlement by personal discussions and correspondence with Jinnah and Nehru. The final result was that there would be fourteen ministers in the interim government, six nominees of the Congress, including one Scheduled Caste representative; five of the Muslim League; one Sikh; one Indian Christian; and one Parsi. Each party was free to nominate its representatives. Except that minority representatives were to be given a share of major portfolios, there would be an equal distribution of the most important portfolios between the Congress and the Muslim League. A Muslim League minister would be nominated vice-chairman of the coordination committee of the cabinet. About the long-term plan, the Viceroy stated, "since the basis for participation in the Cabinet is, of course, acceptance of the statement of 16 May, I assume that the League Council will meet at a very early date to reconsider its Bombay resolution." [53] Jinnah replied that he was prepared to call a meeting of the Muslim League Council to reverse its decision as soon as he was satisfied that the statement of May 16 would be observed.

On October 14, 1946, Jinnah nominated Liaquat Ali Khan, I. I. Chundrigar, Abdur Rab Nishtar, Ghazanfar Ali Khan, and Jogendra Nath Mandal to the cabinet, on behalf of the Muslim League. Mandal was a Scheduled Caste representative and was a minister in the Muslim League ministry of Bengal. His inclusion was deeply resented by the Congress. The insistence of the Congress to include among their nominees a Muslim from outside the League was made with the intention of weakening the League's claim of being the sole representative organization of the Muslims. By including Mandal in its quota, the Muslim League was able to demonstrate that the claim of the Congress to represent all Indians was not tenable even with regard to Scheduled Caste Hindus, let alone other communities. Gandhi was unhappy, and indicated that the League's entry into the cabinet had not been "straight." What troubled him and other Congress leaders was that the League had come into the government in its own right and not by favor of the Congress or on Congress conditions. Indeed, it was a remarkable feat of statesmanship by Jinnah that he succeeded in bringing the Muslim League into the interim government without losing self-respect or surrendering any point of principle. On October 15, a press statement announced the reconstitution of the

Executive Council. The distribution of portfolios was to be settled later.

While talks for the inclusion of Muslim League representatives in the interim government were under way, an episode occurred that left no mark on the political situation but pointed to a noticeable change in the relationship between Gandhi and the rest of the Congress hierarchy. In the first week of October, the Nawab of Bhopal, who was on friendly terms with Gandhi, came to Delhi at Gandhi's suggestion and entered into negotiations for a rapprochement between the Congress and the Muslim League. A meeting was arranged between Gandhi and Jinnah, and a formula to provide a basis of cooperation between the Congress and the League was worked out and agreed to by Gandhi and Jinnah. It read:

> The Congress does not challenge and accepts that the Muslim League now is the authoritative representative organization of an overwhelming majority of the Muslims of India. As such and in accordance with democratic principles they alone have today an unquestionable right to represent the Muslims of India. But the Congress cannot agree that any restriction or limitation should be put upon the Congress to choose such representatives as they think proper from amongst the members of the Congress as their representatives.[54]

When this formula was seen by Nehru and Patel, they and the rest of the Congress Working Committee demurred. Gandhi was taken to task, and Nehru wrote to Jinnah on October 8, "As I have told you, my colleagues and I did not accept the formula agreed to by Gandhiji and you." [55] It was maintained that there was another paragraph in the formula, namely, "It is understood that all the ministers of the Interim Government will work as a team for the good of the whole of India and will never invoke the intervention of the Governor-General in any case." But in actual fact, the formula as signed by Gandhi and Jinnah did not contain this paragraph, which had still to be further examined and discussed.

This was the first time in over a quarter of a century that the Congress Working Committee challenged the authority of Gandhi and repudiated his pledged word. And in this Nehru, Patel, and other members of the Working Committee were wrong. Gandhi was head and shoulders above them in intellectual power and political foresight, and his gamut of movement far exceeded their limited range of action and emotion. His severest onslaughts against political opponents were usually clothed in the language of love; his self-control was so great that he could pass in a moment from war to peace. Gandhi had tried his hardest not to let the Muslim League share power with the Congress, but his recent interviews with Lord Wavell had convinced him of the Viceroy's determination to bring the League into the interim government. Was it not better, therefore, that the League should come in through the goodwill of the Congress and not through the favor of the Viceroy? Where strife had failed, could not loving kindness prevail? Why not recognize the League and try to break down its guards of suspicion and mistrust? The Congress Working Committee, however, had become fixed in the habit of opposing the Muslim League and lacked the suppleness of mind and the flexible strategy of the Master.

It was freely said in Congress circles at the time, that the old man was suffering from the infirmity of wishing to go down in history as a second Buddha. Gandhi put on sackcloth and ashes, and at his prayer meeting he said that "he felt impelled to tell them of the error committed by him three days ago. He was thoroughly ashamed of it. While his mind had been relieved of a burden through confession it would take a long time for him to regain confidence." [56] Now that the ship of the Congress was safely anchored in the harbor of state, the pilot who had guided its course through the uncharted seas of mass movement and civil disobedience without foundering on the rocks of uncontrolled violence or passive despair was quietly dropped. Gandhi himself sensed that he was not wanted and soon withdrew to remote Noakhali in East Bengal, where communal disturbance had taken place as an after-effect of the Great Calcutta Killing. Never again was he to exercise supreme authority over the Congress. The men in power, Nehru and Patel, now occupied the center of the stage and, although they continued to pay homage to Gandhi, felt themselves capable of taking vital decisions without consulting him or even caring to inform him.

CHAPTER 4

The Interim Government

THE MUSLIM LEAGUE entered the interim government against the wishes of the Congress. The conditions of possible cooperation had been destroyed by the Congress leadership through its arrogant assumption of superiority, its claim to a monopoly of patriotism, and its continual efforts to break the will and to kill the self-respect of any other organization.

It was an uneasy partnership from the start, and battle was joined over the allocation of portfolios. The Viceroy had promised an equitable distribution of major portfolios and had "urged that one of the three senior portfolios—External Affairs, Defence and Home Affairs—be transferred to the League. Nehru refused on the specious grounds that this would have an unsettling effect on the country. In the face of Wavell's persistence he threatened to resign." [1] The External Affairs portfolio had been assigned to Nehru, the Home portfolio to Patel, and the Defence portfolio had been given to Baldev Singh. The League wanted the Home or the Defence portfolio. Patel, who aimed to be in control of internal security forces during the "war of succession," vehemently opposed the suggestion and said that "he would rather leave the Government than give up the Home Department." [2] Baldev Singh stuck equally doggedly to the Defence portfolio.

Because of the special position of Sikhs in the Indian army, and the alliance which was being forged between the Congress and the Sikhs against the League, the Congress supported him. Then the Congress leaders hit upon the idea of offering the Finance portfolio to the Muslim League. It was argued that "because of the technical nature of the subject, the League would refuse the offer. If this happened, the Congress would lose nothing. If on the other hand the League nominee accepted the Finance portfolio, he would soon make a fool of himself. . . . Either way Congress would stand to gain." [3] With these noble sentiments Patel agreed and gave the proposal his strong support. The Viceroy was informed that the Congress would offer Finance to the Muslim League.

In June, 1946, when the formation of the interim government first seemed likely, Quaid-i-Azam Jinnah had consulted me on the subject of portfolios for the League. He himself was strongly inclined toward Home and Defence. I expressed the view that law and order and the police were provincial subjects over which the central government could exercise little control. The Congress provinces would not heed a Muslim League Home Minister; and the Muslim League provincial governments would not need his guidance. I said it would be certainly worthwhile to have the Defence portfolio, but if the League wanted to influence the policies of government in every department, it should take charge of Finance. I had not succeeded then in convincing him of the strategic importance of Finance, but now events practically forced the Finance portfolio upon the League. When I was sent for again, I repeated my advice even more emphatically. Liaquat Ali Khan who, as the chief representative of the Muslim League in the cabinet, would have had to take the Finance portfolio felt extremely hesitant. I placed my services at his disposal and assured him and the Quaid-i-Azam of a successful outcome. The proposal was accepted and Liaquat Ali Khan became Finance Minister. From this time on I was to work as unofficial adviser to the Muslim League bloc in the cabinet. This was nothing unusual, since many of the senior Hindu officials were acting in a similar capacity for the Congress bloc. According to Azad, the "Congress soon realised that it had committed a great blunder in handing over Finance to the Muslim League." [4]

The other portfolios entrusted to the Muslim League were Commerce, to I. I. Chundrigar; Communications, Post and Air, to Abdur Rab Nishtar; Health, to Ghazanfar Ali Khan; and Legislative, to

Jogendra Nath Mandal. The remaining portfolios in the reconstituted cabinet were held by Jawaharlal Nehru (External Affairs and Commonwealth Relations), Vallabhbhai Patel (Home and Information and Broadcasting), Rajendra Prasad (Food and Agriculture), C. Rajagopalachari (Education and Arts), Asif Ali (Transport and Railways), Jagjiwan Ram (Labour). Asif Ali was soon replaced by Abul Kalam Azad, who took over the portfolio of Education and Arts, while Transport and Railways was transferred to Rajagopalachari. These were the six Congress representatives including the Scheduled Caste member, Jagjiwan Ram. The representatives of other minorities were Baldev Singh (Sikh), who held the portfolio of Defence; John Matthai (Indian Christian), who was entrusted with Industries and Supplies; and Bhabha (Parsi), who had charge of Works, Mines and Power.

The Congress, while full of mistrust and hostility toward the League, wanted Nehru to be recognized as the leader of the entire cabinet. This the League refused to accept. At a press conference Liaquat Ali Khan made it clear that Nehru was "nobody else's leader except of the Congress bloc in the Government." [5] Though denying collective or joint responsibility in its constitutional sense, he made it clear that the Muslim League ministers would work in harmony and cooperation with their colleagues, in the interests not merely of Muslims but of all the peoples of India.

Harmony and cooperation were certainly needed, for communal disturbances were spreading. In the second week of October, trouble broke out in some areas of Noakhali and Tippera districts of East Bengal where Muslims were in a majority. By the end of the month the situation was under control. The conclusion reached by the Governor (Sir Frederick Burrows), after inspection of the area, was that there had been no general rising of Muslims against Hindus; but, he reported, "the disturbances have been caused by a body of hooligans who have exploited the existing communal feeling and who . . . are temporarily joined in each locality by belligerent Muslim roughs." [6] Lt. General Sir Francis Tuker, the General Officer Commanding-in-Chief, Eastern Command, estimated that the total number "killed in this episode was well under three hundred. Terrible and deliberately false stories were blown all over the world by a hysterical Hindu Press, and these stories did infinite harm in India by kindling in Bihar and the United Provinces the Hindu desire for revenge." [7]

In the first week of November, a planned massacre of Muslims in Bihar began.

> Of all the terrible doings of 1946 this fearful carnage was the most shocking. Its most dastardly side was that great mobs of Hindus turned suddenly, but with every preparation for the deed, upon the few Muslims who had lived and whose forefathers had lived in amity and trust all their lives among these very Hindu neighbours. . . . The number of Muslim dead, men, women and children, in this short, savage killing was about seven thousand to eight thousand.[8]

Congress and Muslim League leaders alike condemned the violence in scathing terms, and exhorted the people to restore peace and to avoid reprisals. The Viceroy and four ministers of the central government, Nehru, Patel, Liaquat Ali Khan, and Nishtar visited Calcutta and Bihar. "Pandit Nehru and Sardar Nishtar, who stayed there for some days, made vigorous and effective speeches, neither of them hesitating to condemn the members of his own community who had brought disgrace upon it in Bihar and Bengal." [9]

Gandhi was still in Calcutta on his way to Noakhali when news of the Bihar massacre reached him. Despite earnest appeals to him from Muslim Congressmen of Bihar to visit the province and exert his immense influence on the murder-bent Hindu majority, he contented himself with issuing an appeal to Bihar and proceeded to Noakhali where he spent the next four months giving solace to Hindu refugees and rehabilitating them in their homes. Peace had been restored in Noakhali by the time he set out for it, on November 6, but Bihar was on fire. A Muslim leader of Bihar had this comment to make on Gandhi's activities in Noakhali. "Why . . . Mr. Gandhi indefinitely prolonged his stay in Noakhali and . . . adopted a comical walking tour of at the most two or three miles a day is a question . . . not easy to answer." [10]

When Gandhi was finally persuaded to visit Bihar in March, 1947, his eyes were opened. The Congress ministry in the province was evasive and unrepentant. General Tuker recorded that "what most struck our officers at this time was how calmly these Hindu Ministers took the awful tales, mostly true, of atrocities. They could not, it seemed, be shocked." [11] They professed to have done all they could, but when Gandhi pointed out that no commission of enquiry had been appointed to date, the Chief Minister, Sri Krishna Sinha, expressed the fear that the Muslim League would make political capital out of it.

Gandhi, like other Hindus, had always believed in the popular image of the mild Hindu who was by instinct and tradition non-aggressive. On the other hand, the Muslim was, in Hindu eyes, by diet and upbringing inclined to violence. In any communal disturbance Hindu leaders invariably put the blame on Muslims. Now the image of the mild Hindu lay shattered beyond repair. The evidence of Bihar was too strong for anyone to retain illusions. Appropriately, the chapter on Gandhi's visit to Bihar in Pyarelal's book, *Mahatma Gandhi: The Last Phase,* has the title "The Veil Lifted." In it he says that the "Bihar disturbances of 1946 finally shattered the dream of an undivided India." [12] And they also shattered Gandhi's inherited belief in the innate pacifism of the Hindu. From this time on there was a noticeable change in him. Previously, in any communal conflict his chief concern had been to save Hindus; now, he was anxious to protect Muslims also. While still striving for the political supremacy of Hindus over the whole of India, he made sincere efforts to avert bloodshed. His humanitarian impulse was stirred to its depths; and he was to pay for it with his life.

The Bihar butchery was followed a few days later in November by another massacre of Muslims, at Garhmuktesar in the United Provinces, where a Hindu fair is held annually. A number of Muslim stall-holders at the fair who were quietly plying their trade were suddenly set upon. "Practically every Muslim man, woman and child" wrote Tuker,

> was murdered with appalling cruelty. . . . Someone quickly clamped down on this massacre a strong, impenetrable screen of censorship through which nothing could reach the outside world. The provincial government, willingly helped by its Indian administrators, soft-pedalled these outrages committed by Hindus, and the Hindu papers purposely emphasised the far smaller acts of retaliation by Muslims in the area of the disturbances, in order to cover up the misdeeds of their Hindu co-religionists. . . . Pandit Pant, Prime Minister of the United Provinces, later announced in Council that there would be a judicial enquiry into the affair. None was held.[13]

Tension was mounting all over India. The strains and stresses of the situation were reflected in continuing friction between the Congress and Muslim League blocs in the central government. On every

major issue there were separate consultations within each bloc. The
Muslim League ministers—able men who competently managed their
own portfolios—were determined to maintain their independence of
judgment and not to give recognition in any shape or form to Nehru's
pretensions to being the de facto Prime Minister. As Jinnah
pointed out, Nehru was merely "the Member for External Affairs in
the Viceroy's Executive Council."

In the second half of October, Nehru paid a visit to the North-
West Frontier Province and Tribal Areas in his capacity as minister
for External Affairs. There was a Congress ministry in the North-
West Frontier Province under Dr. Khan Sahib and Nehru felt sure of
a warm reception. The reception he got was warm indeed, but in a
very different sense, for he was greeted with black flags and worse.
During 1946 a big change had taken place in the climate of opinion
in the North-West Frontier Province, and the majority of Muslims
had turned to the League. Abdul Ghaffar Khan, the Red Shirt leader,
still had a considerable following, but he was losing his hold on the
people. Abul Kalam Azad who attributed this change to the miser-
liness of the Khan brothers—Dr. Khan Sahib and Abdul Ghaffar
Khan—wrote, "During the General Elections, Congress placed large
amounts at their disposal, but the Khan brothers spent as little as
possible out of these funds. Many candidates lost in the elections because they did not receive sufficient or timely help. Later, when they
came to know that the funds were lying idle, these men became bitter
enemies of the Khans." [14] Even the Hindus were tired of seeing their
money disappear into the coffers of the Red Shirt leader, but his
greed, niggardliness, and nepotism—the Muslim ministers in the
province were related to him by birth or marriage—are only part of
the explanation. The real causes lie deeper. The Muslims in the North-
West Frontier Province formed 92 percent of the population. The local Hindus could pose no threat to them, and they were chiefly concerned with fighting British rule. The Tribal Areas just across the settled districts were almost wholly Muslim and were fiercely jealous of
their freedom. The British had led many campaigns to subjugate them
but had never succeeded. As long as this state of affairs lasted, the
constitutional struggle in the rest of India had little significance for
the people in this area, but with the impending departure of the British a radically new situation arose. If Hindu designs succeeded,
Hindus would be the successors of the British throughout the subcon-

tinent and would exercise all the powers of the British. Instead of British raj there would be Hindu raj. Jawaharlal Nehru's visit to the North-West Frontier Province was a visible reminder of this change of rulers, and the people of the Province reacted accordingly. "He found everywhere a large section of the people against him. . . . In some places his car was stoned and Jawaharlal was once hit on the forehead. Dr. Khan Sahib and his colleagues seemed so completely helpless that Jawaharlal took the situation into his own hands." [15]

The constituent assembly was provisionally scheduled to meet on December 9. The Congress was pressing the Viceroy to summon the assembly and to ensure the attendance of the Muslim League; and, if the Muslim League refused to come into the constituent assembly, to turn the Muslim League ministers out of the interim government. The Congress was still insisting on its own untenable interpretation of the statement of May 16. Without a genuine agreement between the Congress and the Muslim League on the grouping of provinces and on the procedure to be followed in the constituent assembly and in its sections, it was futile to convene the assembly, and even dangerous, since its acrimonious debates would add fuel to the fire of communal discord raging in the country. When the Viceroy wrote to Jinnah on the subject in November, the latter pointed out that the Congress had never accepted the statement of May 16 and drew attention to recent actions of Congress leaders nullifying their so-called acceptance. Nehru had written to Gopinath Barodoloi, the Chief Minister of Assam, that "a Province must decide both about grouping and its own constitution [and] in no event are [we] going to agree to a province like Assam being forced against its will to do anything." On October 23, Gandhi had again refused to accept the Cabinet Mission's interpretation of their own plan, saying that "no law-giver can give an authoritative interpretation of his own law." Jinnah felt that in the "highly surcharged and explosive atmosphere [created by] the mass organised and planned massacre of Muslims in various parts of Bihar [it was] neither advisable nor possible" to convene the constituent assembly, and that all energies should be concentrated on restoring peace and order and on rehabilitating the refugees.[16]

When, despite this advice, the Viceroy and the British government decided to summon the constituent assembly on December 9, Jinnah called it a "blunder of very grave and serious character." He charged the Viceroy with "playing into the hands of the Congress

[and] appeasing them in complete disregard of the Muslim League and other organisations and elements in the national life of the country," and stated that no representative of the Muslim League would participate in the constituent assembly.[17] Thereupon the Viceroy told Liaquat Ali Khan that unless the League attended the constituent assembly, its representatives could not remain in the interim government; to which Liaquat Ali Khan replied that they would rather go out of the government than come into the constituent assembly without a clear agreement on the fundamentals of the statement of May 16. The Viceroy was merely echoing the demand of the Congress for pressing the League to attend the constituent assembly or to quit the government. V. P. Menon summed up the situation in the following words:

> Everything ultimately rested on agreement between the parties concerned. The Congress could not make a constitution for the whole of India without the Muslim League; nor could the League force a constitution on Assam, or any other province in sections B and C, against the consent of the Congress. The alternative to agreement was civil war, which was likely to be disastrous for the Muslims and would break up the Indian Army. Nor could the British remain on indefinitely in India until the parties reached agreement.[18]

The British government decided to make one final effort at bringing about agreement on the basis of the statement of May 16, and invited the Viceroy, two representatives of the Congress, two of the League, and one of the Sikh community to London. Nehru at first refused but was persuaded to go. On December 2, Lord Wavell together with Nehru, Jinnah, Liaquat Ali Khan, and Baldev Singh arrived in England; discussions with the British government lasted four days.

The main differences between the Congress and the Muslim League were about the powers of the constituent assembly and the grouping of provinces. Jinnah maintained that the constituent assembly had no authority to change the structure of the plan and that the grouping of provinces was an essential part of the plan; the provinces must in the beginning join the group, but could, after the first election under the new constitution, opt out. It was on the basis of distribution of powers between the central government, the groups, and the provinces that the Muslim League had been persuaded to accept the plan. The Cabinet Mission had themselves interpreted their statement of May 16 in the same way as the Muslim League did.

The British cabinet found that all their efforts to persuade Nehru to accept the plain meaning of the statement of May 16 were in vain. They sought legal advice which confirmed the Cabinet Mission's interpretation of the disputed paragraph 19 of the statement. The Muslim League agreed with the Cabinet Mission's interpretation but the Congress did not. The deadlock was complete. On December 6, the British government issued a statement which affirmed that

> the Cabinet Mission have throughout maintained the view that the decisions of the Sections should, in the absence of agreement to the contrary, be taken by a simple majority vote of the representatives in the Sections. This view has been accepted by the Muslim League, but the Congress have put forward a different view. They have asserted that the true meaning of the statement, read as a whole, is that the Provinces have the right to decide both as to grouping and as to their own constitution. His Majesty's Government have had legal advice, which confirms that the Statement of May 16 means what the Cabinet Mission have always stated was their intention. This part of the Statement as so interpreted must therefore be considered as an essential part of the scheme of May 16 for enabling the Indian people to formulate a constitution which His Majesty's Government would be prepared to submit to Parliament. It should therefore be accepted by all parties in the Constituent Assembly.[19]

The statement urged the Congress to accept the view of the Cabinet Mission in order that the Muslim League could reconsider its attitude. The concluding paragraph of the statement of December 6 declared that "there has never been any prospect of success for the Constituent Assembly except on this basis of an agreed procedure. Should a constitution come to be framed by a Constituent Assembly in which a large section of the Indian population had not been represented, His Majesty's Government could not of course contemplate —as the Congress have stated they would not contemplate—forcing such a constitution upon any unwilling parts of the country." [20]

The statement of December 6 by the British government, like the earlier Statement of May 25 by the Cabinet Mission, produced no change in the attitude of the Congress. Nehru and Baldev Singh returned to India to take part in the constituent assembly. Jinnah and Liaquat Ali Khan stayed on for some time in England. At a press conference in London on December 14, Jinnah stated that if the Congress unequivocally accepted the British government's interpretation of the statement of May 16, he would call the Muslim League Council to reconsider the matter.[21] In a speech in London he showed that

Pakistan would have a population bigger than most states in the world and yet leave the Hindus with control over three quarters of the Indian subcontinent. "The only objection [to Pakistan] is that the Hindus want the whole. If the whole is [given] them, then we are reduced to nothing but a minority. Therefore, the problem is—is Britain going to stand [by] with its bayonets and hand over authority to the Hindu majority? If that happens, you will have lost every cent of honour, integrity and fair play." [22]

With the failure of the London conference, relations between the Muslim League and the Congress in the interim government deteriorated still further. The leaders of both sides were too urbane to engage in open hostilities in the cabinet, but there was a hardening of attitudes. Mistrust and suspicion grew and were fed by misunderstandings about how the Finance department functioned.

In every government demands for expenditure far exceed resources. The treasury or the finance department, which has to scrutinize schemes for new expenditure, is by the very nature of its task unpopular with other departments. Almost everywhere it is looked upon as an undesirable obstruction to the smooth operation of Parkinson's Law for the growth of bureaucratic organizations. A finance minister may win the respect but not the affection of his colleagues. A popular finance minister is likely to be a bad finance minister. Even if a neutral person like Dr. John Matthai had continued as Finance Minister, he would, in course of time, have incurred the displeasure of his colleagues to some extent. But when Congress proposals were turned down by the Finance department presided over by Liaquat Ali Khan, the irritation was greatly intensified and directed against the Muslim League.

The Congress ministers were suspicious and saw special malice even in the normal functioning of the Finance department; at the same time the discomfiture of his Congress colleagues gave confidence and comfort to the Finance Minister. The man who most resented the work of the Finance department was Patel. He was in charge of the Home department and he had hoped thereby to exercise control over the law and order machinery of the entire country. He was dictatorial by temperament and could brook no opposition. Abul Kalam Azad wrote:

When Liaquat Ali became the Finance Member, he obtained possession of the key to Government. Every proposal of every Department was subject to scrutiny by his Department. In addition he had the power of veto. . . . Sardar Patel had been very anxious about retaining the Home Membership. Now he realized that he had played into the hands of the League by offering it Finance. Whatever proposal he made was either rejected or modified beyond recognition by Liaquat Ali. . . . Internal dissensions broke out within the Government and went on increasing.[23]

The picture is somewhat overdrawn, but it portrays the sentiments of Congress ministers; and it is true that the power and responsibility that reside in the Finance department were exercised without fear or favor. Merely because a proposal had the powerful backing of Nehru or Patel was no reason for accepting it. Its rejection might produce bad blood in the cabinet, but that could not be helped.

Nehru suspected that there was, what he called, a mental alliance between the League and senior British officials. This was a figment of his imagination. British officials were trying to serve both the Congress and League ministers with equal fidelity. They knew that the days of British raj in India were numbered and they were anxious to part on good terms, particularly with the Hindu Congress which as the strongest party would inevitably be in control of the greater part if not the whole of the subcontinent. Nor was there any truth in Nehru's allegation that the League was the King's party in the government. As Liaquat Ali Khan pointed out, the League bloc never once invoked the Viceroy's special powers nor asked for his or the British government's intervention in any matter. In his petulant way Nehru threatened to resign more than once; Patel who was a realist differed from him. When the quarrel was carried to Gandhi, Patel defended himself by writing to Gandhi: "The charge that I want to stick to office is a pure concoction. Only, I was opposed to Jawaharlal's hurling idle threats of resigning from the Interim Government. . . . Repetition of empty threats has lost us the Viceroy's respect and now he regards our threats of resignation as nothing but bluff." [24]

The constituent assembly opened on December 9, but the Muslim League members did not attend it. Rajendra Prasad was elected President. Nehru moved the Objectives Resolution which envisaged an independent sovereign republic comprising autonomous units with residuary powers. The rules of procedure approved by the constituent assembly provided that the assembly should not be dissolved except by a resolution of the assembly itself passed by at least two thirds of its members. In a speech in Benares on December 15, Nehru said that "whatever form of Constitution we may decide in the Constituent Assembly will become the Constitution of free India—whether Britain accepts it or not. . . . We cannot and will not tolerate any outside interference." [25] When the constituent assembly met again on January 20, 1947, the Objectives Resolution was passed, and Nehru asserted that though the assembly would welcome the League representatives at any time no work would be held up in future whether any one came or not.

On December 22 the Congress Working Committee passed a resolution in which it reiterated its acceptance of its own untenable interpretation of the Cabinet Mission plan. It criticized the British government's statement of December 6 as a variation of the Cabinet Mission's statement of May 16; and declared that a reference to the Federal Court had become purposeless in view of the pronouncements of the British government.[26] The All-India Congress Committee passed a resolution on January 6, 1947, endorsing the statement of the Working Committee of December 22. The resolution went on to say that the All-India Congress Committee

> appreciates the difficulties placed in the way of some provinces, notably Assam, Baluchistan, Sind and the North-West Frontier Province and the Sikhs in the Punjab, by the British Cabinet scheme of 16 May 1946 and more especially by the interpretation put upon it by the British Government in their statement of December 6, 1946. . . . [and agrees] to advise action in accordance with the interpretation of the British Government in regard to the procedure to be followed in the sections.

It immediately qualified this acceptance by the following reservation:

> It must be clearly understood, however, that this must not involve any compulsion of a province and that the rights of the Sikhs in the Punjab should not be jeopardised. In the event of any attempt at such compulsion, a province or part of a province has the right to take such action as may be deemed necessary in order to give effect to the wishes of the people concerned.[27]

"This reservation," as the London *Economist* of January 11, 1947, observed, "practically nullifies the so-called acceptance. . . . The purpose of the Congress majority seems to have been to convince the British Government and public of its reasonableness rather than to reach agreement with the Muslim League."

The Working Committee of the Muslim League met toward the end of January, 1947 in Karachi and took stock of the reactions of the Congress to the British government's statement of December 6, and of the activities of the constituent assembly. In its resolution of January 31, the Working Committee carried out a detailed analysis of the Congress Working Committee's resolution of December 22 and the All-India Congress Committee's resolution of January 6, 1947. It pointed out that since these Congress resolutions conferred the right of veto within the sections on a province or even on a part of a province, as well as on the Sikhs in the Punjab, they completely nullified the so-called acceptance by the Congress of the Cabinet Mission plan. There was indeed a glaring inconsistency in the attitude of the Congress. It claimed that the constituent assembly had the right to make a constitution for all the provinces, but denied the right of the sections of the constituent assembly to make a constitution for the provinces included in them. The League Working Committee declared

> This All-India Congress Committee resolution is no more than a dishonest trick and a jugglery of words by which Congress has again attempted to deceive the British Government and the Muslim League and public opinion in general. The question at issue was a very simple one. What was required was a straight and honest answer . . . whether the Congress honestly and sincerely agreed to the proposals of May 16 as clarified by His Majesty's Government on December 6, 1946 and whether it was prepared to honourably abide by them.

The League resolution also criticized the proceedings of the constituent assembly and declared that, since the Objectives Resolution went beyond the Cabinet Mission's statement of May 16, it was "illegal, ultra vires and not competent to the Constituent Assembly to adopt." There was no warrant or justification for the rules of procedure passed by the constituent assembly by means of which it assumed control of the sections. The resolution concluded that the Congress, "by rejecting this final appeal of His Majesty's Government [and by having] converted the Constituent Assembly into a body of its own conception has destroyed all fundamentals of the Statement of May 16 and every possibility of compromise on the basis of the Cabinet Mission's constitutional plan." Finally, the League Working Committee called upon the British government "to decide that the constitutional plan formulated by the Cabinet Mission, as announced on May 16, has failed" and to dissolve the constituent assembly.[28]

The Congress bloc in the interim government retorted by demanding of the Viceroy that he should dismiss the Muslim League ministers. When the Viceroy communicated this demand to Liaquat Ali Khan, the latter pointed out that if the basis of participation in the interim government was acceptance of the statement of May 16, which neither the Congress nor the Sikhs had done, they had no greater right to be represented in the interim government than the Muslim League. The Muslim League was the only party that had genuinely accepted the Cabinet Mission plan. If the Congress even now accepted the plan without any reservations, the League would reconsider its position, but not otherwise. The Viceroy himself believed that the Congress had not accepted the plan. The British government knew it also, but they did not dare to ask the Congress for an unequivocal acceptance, as the Viceroy suggested, and the Congress continued to exert pressure to get the Muslim League out of the interim government. Nehru again wrote to the Viceroy demanding the resignation of the League ministers, and Patel threatened openly that if the Muslim League representatives remained in the interim government, the Congress would withdraw from it.

The British government was in a quandary. To accept the demand of the Congress for the expulsion of the League from the interim government would have ended all possibility of agreement and of a peaceful transfer of power. On the other hand, to have dismissed the constituent assembly, as demanded by the Muslim League, would have brought about an immediate conflict with the Congress. The British could neither reconcile the two antagonists nor impose their own solution.

The number of British officers in the administration and the armed forces had been so greatly reduced that they could not hope to remain in control for long. In the Superior Civil Services the number had come down to 1,600 from 2,942 in 1935. The steel frame of the Indian Civil Service had only 500 British officers left. Recruitment had been suspended during the war and it was politically impossible to resume it. In the Indian armed forces the number of British officers had dropped from 11,000 to 4,000. In January, 1947, the Parliamentary Under-Secretary for India came to Delhi to discuss the question of compensation for British civil and military officers who might be retired as a result of constitutional changes. Units of the British army stationed in India were being withdrawn for demobilization in order to meet the demands of manpower in the United Kingdom for economic reconstruction.

The war had also brought about another important change in the status of India which had been a debtor country before the war but was now a creditor country. The enormous supply of men and materials from India for the war effort of the United Kingdom had built up sterling balances that stood at £1,200 million. These could be repaid by the United Kingdom only over a period of years out of trade surpluses. England did not need political control over India for purposes of commerce; it would be in India's interest to maintain trade with her. A British treasury mission under the leadership of Sir Wilfred Eady came to Delhi from Whitehall to negotiate a scaling down of the sterling balances. According to a British financial commentator, British opinion ranged from outright repudiation in lieu of independence to a compromise for repaying between one third and one half of the total. He stated flatly: "The fact that the balances represent incontestable legal obligations counts for nothing in the eyes of the overwhelming majority of the British people." [29] The demand for a scaling down of sterling balances was resisted by the Finance Minister, Liaquat Ali Khan, who rightly pointed out that

> we not only bore our full share of our war burdens under the financial settlement, which was freely agreed to between His Majesty's Government and the then Government of India but also had to strain ourselves to assist the United Kingdom and her allies in various ways. Our own share of burdens for which we are making no claim, was enormous and can stand favourable comparison with those borne by the richer nations. I cannot believe that any fair-minded person will wish to deny to a people so poor and backward as we, what is justly due to us and is so greatly needed for raising us from our appallingly miserable condition.[30]

All in all, the relationship between India and England had greatly changed. The British had neither the manpower nor the financial resources to reestablish their power and prestige in India. Their efforts to bring the two main parties together in a united India of their conception had failed. Under the circumstances the Viceroy, Lord Wavell, came to the conclusion, as he reported in a letter to King George VI, that "it would be better for the interests both of ourselves and of India to remove our control as soon as possible and to leave Indians to determine their own future. . . . I recommended the withdrawal of British control by stages, beginning with the south of India. . . . The date I recommended for the final transfer of power was March 31st, 1948." [31] Though the British government did not approve Lord Wavell's plan of phased withdrawal, they accepted his basic assumption that British rule could not be maintained on its existing basis beyond the summer of 1948.

On February 20, 1947, Prime Minister Attlee made a historic statement in the House of Commons; he announced the definite intention of the British government "to take the necessary steps to effect the transference of power to responsible Indian hands by a date not later than June, 1948." The statement affirmed the British government's

> desire to hand over their responsibility to authorities established by a constitution approved by all parties in India in accordance with the Cabinet Mission Plan. . . . If . . . such a constitution would not have been worked out by a fully representative Constituent Assembly [before June, 1948] His Majesty's Government will have to consider to whom the powers of the Central Government in British India should be handed over, on the due date, whether as a whole to some form of Central Government for British India or in some areas to the existing Provincial Governments, or in such other way as may seem most reasonable and in the best interests of the Indian people.[32]

The Prime Minister also announced that Lord Wavell would be replaced as Viceroy in March by Lord Mountbatten. The reasons for this change were not disclosed, but there are good grounds for the view that it was Congress wire-pulling in London that led to Wavell's virtual dismissal. The Congress had never forgiven him for bringing the Muslim League into the interim government on equal terms with the Congress. At his first interview with the next Viceroy, Lord Mountbatten, "Nehru ran through his interpretation of the major developments from the period of the Cabinet Mission onwards. Mountbatten considered it was substantially accurate and tallied with information he had gathered in London. In Nehru's view, Wavell had made one serious blunder in inviting the Muslim League into the Interim Government instead of waiting a little longer for them to ask to be brought in." [33] Abul Kalam Azad has recorded that Nehru and his other colleagues were against Lord Wavell. The lesson was not lost upon his successor.

Explaining the background to the decision for a final transfer of power by June, 1948, Sir Stafford Cripps described in the House of Commons the alternatives before the British government:

> Those alternatives [are] fundamentally two . . . first, we could attempt to strengthen British control in India . . . to maintain for as long as might be necessary our administrative responsibility while awaiting an agreement amongst the Indian communities. Such a policy would [mean] . . . we should remain in India for at least fifteen to twenty years, because for any substantially shorter period we should not be able to reorganise the Services on a stable and sound basis. . . . The second alternative [is] . . . to persuade the Indians to come together, while at the same time warning them that there was a limit of time during which we were prepared to maintain our responsibility while awaiting their agreement. . . . We [rule] out the first alternative, as both undesirable and impracticable.[34]

There was indeed no other alternative to Indian independence. All parties in India were agreed on it, they only differed on whether there should be one independent state or two. World opinion, particularly public opinion in the United States, during and after the Second World War had been exerting steady pressure upon the British to relinquish power in India. In bowing to the inevitable willingly and gracefully, the British government showed great political wisdom. By setting a definite date for the transfer of power, they rid themselves of the charge of wishing to prolong their hold on the country by exploiting differences between the major communities in India. On the contrary, they showed that they hoped the shock produced by their impending departure would bring the two main parties together by the very urgency of the need for agreement.

The Conservative opposition was highly critical of the decision by the Labour government to withdraw from India by June, 1948. Their main charge was that fifteen months was too short a period for dealing with the difficult questions of framing a constitution or constitutions, transferring power to one or more authorities, and settling the varied and complex issues of services, defense, finance, trade, communications, and a host of other matters. Winston Churchill concluded his speech with the words: "Let us not add—by shameful flight, by a premature hurried scuttle—at least, let us not add to the pangs of sorrow so many of us feel, the taint and smear of shame." [35] However, as a former Viceroy, Lord Halifax, had pointed out, no better alternative was in sight; and Attlee's statement of February 20, 1947, was approved by Parliament.

The announcement was, on the whole, well received in India. Both the Congress and the Muslim League welcomed the British decision to leave by June, 1948. Both criticized the vagueness with which the authorities to whom power was to be transferred were referred to. This vagueness, which for want of agreement between the two parties was inevitable, aroused the hopes and fears of both. The Congress leaders were still grasping for power over the whole subcontinent, but not without misgivings that the whole would elude their grasp. In that eventuality they wanted to keep as much as they could, and their minds were, therefore, turning toward a partition of the Punjab and Bengal. When Nehru saw the Viceroy on February 21, he argued that since "His Majesty's Government had recognized that they could not contemplate forcing an unwelcome constitution upon unwilling parts of the country; it was only logical that large minorities inside a province, such as the Hindus in Bengal and the Hindus and Sikhs in the Punjab, could also not be compelled into an unacceptable constitution." [36]

Partition was thus looming large on the horizon, but the League could not be certain that it would be the final solution. The uncertainty arose partly from the attitude of the British and their strong predilection for an undivided India and partly from the political situation in the Muslim majority provinces, particularly the key province of the Punjab.

Although the Muslim League had won 79 out of 86 Muslim seats in the Punjab in the 1946 elections, it had been cheated of the fruits of victory by a combination of Congress Hindus, Akali Sikhs, and the rump of Muslim Unionists led by Khizr Hayat Tiwana. As Penderel Moon, a British civilian serving in the Punjab at that time noted, "This unnatural and unholy alliance seemed to have been designed, with the connivance of the British Governor, simply to keep them [the Muslims] from power." [37]

Khizr Hayat Tiwana's unstable ministry was dominated by Hindus and Sikhs and was highly unpopular with the Muslims. It relied on force to keep it going. Penderel Moon recorded the views of two of Khizr Hayat Tiwana's henchmen—one of them a minister in the government—"We have a danda (or stick) in our hand," they kept repeating, "and mustn't give it up." [38] On January 24, 1947, they decided to use this stick and declared the Muslim League's National Guards an unlawful body. To keep up appearances, Rashtriya

Swayam Sewak Sangh, a militant Hindu organization, was also declared unlawful, but no action was taken either against the Congress volunteers or the Sikhs who, as everyone knew, were busy collecting arms. Somewhat earlier, orders prohibiting meetings and processions had been issued with the object of thwarting Muslim political activity.

The Muslim League met this challenge with alacrity and decided to start an all-out nonviolent mass struggle. "We are courting arrest," declared the Khan of Mamdot who was the President of the Punjab Muslim League, "to vindicate civil liberties in the Punjab, where an unrepresentative Ministry, in order to keep itself in power, is resorting to most objectionable methods to gag popular liberties." [39] Ian Stephens, who was editor of the *Statesman* at that time, gave a graphic description of the movement.

> The intention, in fact, was to make the Punjab the first formal testing-ground for the League's "direct action" resolution passed during the previous July. The struggle proved well organized. With mocking exactitude it mirrored the techniques used by the Congress party for its recurrent "civil disobedience" campaigns waged against the British since the 1920's. Thousands of enthusiastic Muslim demonstrators had to be arrested, women as well as men, who offered themselves for imprisonment willingly, seeking martyrdom. Jails quickly became overfull. Resort was had to the device of arresting leading persons only, and removing the rest in lorries to distant places and decanting them there to find their way home as best they could; this perhaps attracted attention to the movement all the more.[40]

A novel feature of the movement was the prominent part taken in it by women, veiled and unveiled. It was the first time that Muslim women came out in hundreds of thousands to fight for political rights and freedom. Their processions were tear-gassed and many of them suffered imprisonment for defying the ban on meetings. They picketed and demonstrated in front of the Women's Jail in Lahore where many of their political coworkers were imprisoned. One heroic girl braved many injuries to hoist the Muslim League flag on the building of the Punjab government secretariat in Lahore.

The campaign was in full swing when the British government's announcement of February 20 offered Khizr Hayat Tiwana a way out of an untenable situation. On February 26, the Punjab government came to a compromise with the Muslim League: the ban on meetings was withdrawn, and those arrested in connection with the agitation were released; the League on its side agreed to call off the civil disobedience movement. On March 2, Khizr Hayat Tiwana resigned. In the statement he issued on this occasion he said that Prime Minister Attlee's announcement required that parties in the province should be brought face to face with realities, and continued: "It is now incumbent on me to leave the field clear for the Muslim League to come to such arrangements vis-à-vis the other parties as it might consider in the best interests of the Muslims and the Province." [41]

But in the mounting communal tension, to which Khizr Hayat Tiwana's own action in becoming a tool of Hindu and Sikh interests and ambitions had made a notable contribution, no settlement was possible. The Governor invited the Khan of Mamdot, the leader of the Muslim League in the Punjab, to form a ministry. This was a purely formal move. The Muslim majority in the Punjab had been reduced to a minority under the Communal Award, and no government could be formed without the participation of non-Muslims. The Hindus and Sikhs were totally opposed to a Muslim League government. On March 5, Governor Sir Evan Jenkins took direct charge of the administration, under section 93 of the Government of India Act, 1935.

The Hindu and Sikh leaders now started making inflammatory speeches inciting their followers to violence. The fiery Sikh leader, Tara Singh, raised the slogan "Pakistan Murdabad" (death to Pakistan!) and brandishing a sword shouted, "Raj karega Khalsa, aqi rahe na koi" (the Sikhs will rule, no resister will remain).[42] In a speech at a mass rally he called upon the Hindus and Sikhs to be ready for action. "If we can snatch the Government from Britishers," he declared, "no one can stop us from snatching the Government from the Muslims. . . . Finish the Muslim League." [43] Penderel Moon wrote, "This foolhardy bravado brought at once its own nemesis. It touched off violent communal rioting throughout the province in which Hindus and Sikhs were far the worst sufferers." [44]

There were Muslim League ministries in Bengal and Sind, but in the North-West Frontier Province a Congress ministry under Dr. Khan Sahib was still functioning, although with rapidly diminishing popular support. The demonstrations organized by the Muslim League against the ministry in the North-West Frontier Province led to large-scale arrests; Khan Abdul Qayyum Khan and the highly respected and influential Pir of Manki Sharif were among the arrested, but the tide of popular support for the Muslim League was running too strong to be checked by force. "As in the Punjab," wrote Ian Stephens, "feminist activity was in evidence which startled those knowing how strict Purdah had been on the Frontier till very recently. . . . The rural areas were also affected. . . . Tonga-load after tonga-load of hefty Pathan peasants, handcuffed to constables, [were] borne off stolid but determined down the Mardan-Peshawar road to prison, after attending village demonstrations for the League. Clearly the campaign had good discipline and substantial public backing." [45] In Assam the Congress ministry's campaign to evict Bengali Muslim immigrants who had settled on vacant land led to a civil disobedience movement by the Muslim League.

CHAPTER 5

Poor Man's Budget

ON FEBRUARY 28, 1947, Liaquat Ali Khan presented to the central assembly his budget for the fiscal year April, 1947, to March, 1948. This was the first budget made by a non-British Finance Minister in undivided India; it was also the last and the most controversial. It led to the severest cabinet crisis of the interim government and produced consequences far beyond its impact on the financial and economic life of the country.

During the Second World War, India was the base for the Allied armed forces in South East Asia and an enormous quantity of stores was procured and supplied from India for the maintenance of these forces. Although the liability for the bulk of this expenditure was that of the United Kingdom, the rupees required for these purchases had to be found by the Government of India, who did so largely by inflating the currency. Money was also being pumped into the Indian economy by the pay of Indian personnel in the armed forces whose number had risen to two and one-half millions. The American forces stationed in or based on India from 1942 onward were also supplied by India on Reverse Lease-Lend. Difficulties of shipping made it necessary to meet civil and military needs, as far as was possible, from local sources. Imports, whether for military purposes or for civil consumption, were reduced to a minimum. One of the consequences was the Bengal famine of 1943, which took a toll of nearly two million lives. The strain on the economy of India was so great that in the beginning of 1945 the Government of India sent an official mission to the United Kingdom to seek a reduction in the volume of procurement from India for the armed forces, since what was left for the civil economy was inadequate, and prices were rising sharply. Distribution and price controls were only partially effective. Black markets flourished everywhere. The administration, swollen by temporary recruitment during the war, deteriorated in honesty and efficiency. There was large-scale evasion of taxes. Under these conditions, big war-time profits were inevitable, and Indian businessmen (who were for the most part Hindus) took full advantage of them. These profits were made at the expense of the poverty-stricken masses of India. The salaried and wage-earning classes faced serious hardship from the continuous rise in prices. Although the bigger farmers reaped the benefit of higher prices for farm products, the peasantry and landless laborers suffered greatly. The purchasing power of the rupee was a fraction of what it had been before the war. The normal expenditure on civil and military administration had gone up many times. The financial settlement for the division of war expenditure between India and the United Kingdom came to an end on March 31, 1947. All defense expenditure incurred thereafter for India would be an Indian liability, as in prewar days. Defense expenditure for the next year was estimated at Rs. 1,887 million, as against Rs. 450 million before the war. Inflationary conditions still prevailed and to rely upon deficit financing would aggravate them. An even more important factor was the universal desire for the economic betterment of the common man and social justice. To satisfy this "revolution of rising expectations," the government needed resources that could only come from the richer sections of society.

In his budget speech, the Finance Minister explained that the budgetary position for the following year at the then existing level of taxation would, after providing for an expenditure of Rs. 1,887 million on defense and Rs. 1,392 million on the civil administration, leave a deficit of Rs. 485 million. After describing the state of the economy and dealing with problems relating to sterling balances, postwar planning and development, the Finance Minister made proposals for the nationalization of the Reserve Bank and for control of speculation on the stock market and on the commodity and bullion exchanges. He then proceeded to lay before the central assembly his budget proposals. He explained that these were related not to purely financial purposes, but to certain social objectives which

> must be kept prominently in view by all those who have the good of the countless millions of this sub-continent at heart. . . . India is a land of glaring contrasts and disparities. . . . The conditions created by the last war served to accentuate these disparities; the rich became richer and the poor poorer. This meant the concentration of wealth in fewer and fewer hands and, inevitably, the use of that wealth for the purpose of tightening the stranglehold of Big Money over the economic life of the country as a whole by the acquisition of businesses, companies, public utilities, and the press. A set of conditions in which the few are able to wield such vast power over the many can hardly be regarded as anything but a negation of the principles of social justice. And although I am not one of those who consider the abolition of private property and the complete equalization of incomes as the only remedy for these ills, I do believe in the Quranic injunction that wealth should not be allowed to circulate only among the wealthy, and the stern warning given against accumulations of wealth in the hands of individuals. It is against this background that my budget proposals have been formulated although I am afraid I cannot claim that they represent anything more than the first stage of a policy of social justice and development which it will require years to bring to full fruition.

The first proposal in the implementation of the policy indicated by the Finance Minister was the setting up of a Commission to investigate the accumulation of wealth arising from tax evasion.

Of the taxation proposals the first two involved loss of revenue. One proposal abolished the salt tax and the other raised the minimum exemption limit for income tax from Rs. 2,000 to Rs. 2,500. Agitation against the salt tax had a long history; it was a flat rate tax upon a necessity of life and was regressive because the poor man payed as much as the rich man. Gandhi had launched his civil disobedience campaign of 1930 on the salt tax issue, but had not succeeded in having the tax abolished, except for a few coastal areas. The Muslim League Finance Minister now accomplished what the Congress leader had struggled for.

Since these proposals involved a loss of revenue of Rs. 85 million, the gap between the revenue and expenditure rose to Rs. 570 million. The Finance Minister had come to the conclusion that the greater part of this gap should be filled by direct taxation; accordingly, he proposed new or increased taxation, which was designed to yield Rs.

440 million, of which Rs. 40 million would go to the provinces as their share.

His most important proposal was to levy a special income tax of 25 percent on business profits exceeding Rs. 100,000. The excess profits tax that had been in force during the war had been abolished a year earlier, but inflationary conditions continued to prevail and fears of postwar depression did not materialize. The consensus of informed opinion in the country was that the abolition of the excess profits tax had been premature. The business profits tax, which the Finance Minister proposed to levy, was much more simple to operate and fairer in its incidence than the excess profits tax. It also embraced professions and vocations that had been exempt from the excess profits tax. The expected yield of the tax was estimated at Rs. 300 million.

The next proposal was a graduated tax on capital gains exceeding Rs. 5,000 which would yield Rs. 35 million. Large capital gains had been made in recent years, but they were outside the scope of the Income Tax Act. The tax structure in India until now had been modeled on that of the United Kingdom, which did not tax capital gains. Other proposals were for raising the corporation tax from one anna to two annas (yielding Rs. 40 million); lowering the point at which the maximum rate of supertax was reached (yielding Rs. 25 million); and raising the export duty on tea from two annas per pound to four annas per pound (yielding Rs. 40 million).

These proposals would still leave a deficit of Rs. 170 million, apart from the additional expenditure that might result from the recommendations of the Central Pay Commission. The Finance Minister concluded:

> Transition from war to peace presents the economy of every country with problems of great magnitude and difficulty. In our case there is, superimposed on these problems, the still greater problem of the transfer of power from British to Indian hands. . . . But if we tackle it with wisdom and courage and arrive at a peaceful, just and honourable settlement, we will have succeeded in ensuring the future progress and happiness of the peoples of this vast subcontinent.

These proposals were greeted with enthusiastic approval by all sections of the central assembly. The phrases "first national budget," "poor man's budget" were on the lips of many a member of the Congress and were echoed in the press. But this phase of felicitation did not last long, and Liaquat Ali Khan soon learnt the truth of Burke's dictum: "To tax and to please, no more than to love and be wise, is not given to men." A storm of opposition was raised by capitalists (who happened to be mostly Hindus). The budget proposals hit them in their most sensitive spot—their pockets. Worse still, they came to look on the budget as a deliberate attempt by the Muslim League Finance Minister to ruin them. A tremendous hue and cry was raised. The British planters who were affected by the higher duty on tea also joined the chorus. There was panic among the rich. Almost every stock exchange in the country suspended business.

The Congress party was financed by Hindu capitalists, who, in turn, had benefited greatly from the Congress movement for a boycott of foreign goods. Hindu propaganda presented the Congress as deriving its strength from the masses of India, and carefully hid the fact that the base of its power was in the money contributed by capitalists. Without the financial help of the capitalists, the Congress could not have become such a massive organization, and without the support of the Congress the Hindu businessmen could not have made such big profits. The capitalists were now outraged to find that a cabinet in which the Congress party predominated had approved proposals of this kind.

Patel had raised funds for the Congress, and these businessmen had turned over millions of rupees to him. They rushed to him now with accusations that he had betrayed them. How could the Congress leaders, they cried in anguish, have agreed to proposals of a kind that hit their own financial supporters the hardest? Patel saw the whole Congress organization threatened with financial starvation. He had been smarting under the control of the Finance department for quite some time, but this was a deadly blow. He, therefore, placed himself in a position of intractable opposition to Liaquat Ali Khan's proposals and wanted them to be withdrawn. But Liaquat Ali Khan stood firm. Never in the past had the budget proposals of the Finance Minister been repudiated by the cabinet after having been presented to the assembly.

With some honorable exceptions, the Hindu press rallied to the support of Hindu capitalists. The very men who had praised the proposals now condemned them roundly. The entire posture of the Congress as a socialist organization dedicated to the welfare of the masses was exposed to view as never before. It was forced to come out in its true colors of supporter of big business. On the other hand, the Muslim League, which had been regarded as a reactionary body of landlords and other similar elements, was shown to be working for social justice and an egalitarian society. The proposals were not revolutionary, but they were a first step toward the creation of a juster social order. A new dimension was thus added to the struggle between Hindus and Muslims. The Hindu capitalist class felt that if the Muslims had any share in political power in India, they would inevitably be on the side of social reform, equality of opportunity, and less inequality in the distribution of wealth and income. This sudden reversal of the roles of the Congress and the Muslim League surprised and confused many people. Hindu publicists refused to credit the Muslim League with sincerity of purpose and, instead, saw in the budget proposals a design for destroying the economic power of Hindus.

In the past, the Finance Minister had discussed his budget proposals in detail only with the Viceroy. After he had secured the approval of the Viceroy he submitted them to his colleagues only on the morning of the day on which he was to present them before the assembly. This convention had been adopted to prevent leakage. The cabinet approval of budget proposals was, therefore, a rather formal affair. In 1947, the Viceroy asked the Finance Minister to discuss his budget proposals in the presence of Nehru. At Nehru's suggestion, Matthai was also present. Matthai was an economist of great experience, had been economic adviser to the Government of India and subsequently a director of the great firm, Tatas. In the interim government he had held the Finance portfolio before the Muslim League came in. The budget proposals had thus been discussed by Liaquat Ali Khan with the Viceroy, Nehru, and Matthai, who had approved them; they were subsequently put before the cabinet according to normal procedure.

The first reaction of the cabinet to the proposals was favorable. Abul Kalam Azad wrote "it was the declared policy of Congress that economic inequalities should be removed and a capitalist society gradually replaced by one of a socialist pattern. . . . We were all anxious that there should be increasing equalization of wealth and that all tax-evaders should be brought to book. We were therefore not against Liaquat Ali's proposal in principle." [1] The cabinet approved the budget without a single voice of dissent.

But when the capitalists set up a howl, there were stormy scenes in the cabinet. "Sardar Patel and Sri Rajagopalachari in particular were violently opposed to his budget, for they felt that Liaquat Ali was more concerned to harass industrialists and businessmen than to serve the interests of the country . . . that his main motive was to harm the members of the business community, the majority of whom were Hindus." [2] Outside pressures were also being built up. The Federation of Chambers of Commerce and Industry launched a bitter attack on the budget proposals and even went so far as to prepare an alternate budget. Sober opinion in the country, however, realized that the tax proposals of the Finance Minister were sound and would reduce inequalities of income. C. N. Vakil, professor of economics, Bombay University, commenting on the budget, wrote:

> The poor man was made to pay for the war in the form of continuously rising prices by inflationary methods—a process which, incidentally, helped the rich to become richer. Not only [that], but a class of new rich also came into existence. . . . Some of the methods of evasion of the payment of taxes and encouragement of black markets became so common that they were considered as almost natural. . . . The poorer sections of the community and, particularly, the middle classes were being gradually squeezed out.[3]

Liaquat Ali Khan was accused of having driven a wedge between the right wing of the Congress and the left wing with his budget proposals, and communal motives were freely attributed to him. But as the weekly *Indian Finance* pointed out, "It is inevitable that any system of taxation should impose more burdens on the majority community than on the minority; and if one community should have a higher proportion of the rich than the other, it can hardly be an argument for the Finance Member desisting from the measures which he should have proposed even with perfect freedom from communal bias." [4]

After his return from London in December, 1946, Liaquat Ali Khan inquired of me if I had any suggestions to make for the next budget. I asked him whether he wanted to present a conventional budget or a budget that would break new ground and have social and economic objectives. He preferred the latter course, and some days later I submitted to him the proposal for setting up a commission that would investigate the accumulation of wealth during the war and also the main taxation proposals. The credit for working them up and integrating them into the budgetary structure goes to the Principal Secretary, Sir Cyril Jones, and other senior officials of the Finance department. When the proposals were attacked by the British and the Hindu moneyed interests, these men stood by them not merely out of loyalty to their political chief but out of a genuine conviction that the proposals were soundly conceived and were an improvement over previous budgets, which had been concerned only with raising enough revenue to cover the costs of a law and order administration and to which ideas of social needs and economic development had been foreign.

When the bills incorporating the proposals were referred to the select committee, the Congress members, including those known for their leftist views, took an uncompromising attitude of opposition. No agreement could be reached in the select committee. The Finance Minister, while defending the proposals stoutly, had throughout shown a reasonable attitude and was prepared to accept a compromise which would retain the essential features of the proposals but soften their effect. Finally, an agreement was reached. Announcing the terms of the compromise in the assembly on March 25, 1947, Liaquat Ali Khan stated that "in its anxiety to get the support of all sections of the House for the budget proposals the Government would be willing to accept amendments even in the Bills as reported upon by the Select Committee." The amendments were:

> With regard to abatement as provided for in the Business Profits Tax Bill, instead of six and five per cent., a uniform figure of six per cent. would be acceptable. With regard to the rate of tax instead of 25 per cent. a rate of 16⅔ per cent. would be acceptable to Government. As regards the Capital Gains Tax, Government would be willing to accept an amendment to exclude personal effects from capital gains.

When a crystal particle is introduced into a supercharged solution, it precipitates crystallization. Liaquat Ali Khan's budget played some such role in the supercharged political situation of India. The undeclared civil war between Hindus and Muslims being waged in various parts of the country, the dissensions in the cabinet between the Congress and Muslim League blocs, and the Congress irritation over the policies of the Finance department had strained nerves to the breaking point. On top of all this came Liaquat Ali Khan's budget and the bitter battles inside and outside the cabinet to which it gave rise. Hindu capitalists pointed out to Patel that a united India with poverty-stricken Muslims, who would constantly demand, in the name of social justice, a share in the wealth of the Hindus, would be a nightmare; the sooner they were separated from Hindus the better.

Patel was psychologically prepared for a parting of the ways and, with his usual determination, promptly set about it. Abul Kalam Azad wrote: "Among Congressmen the greatest supporter of partition was Sardar Patel . . . [who] threw his weight in favour of partition out of irritation and injured vanity. He found himself frustrated at every step . . . by Liaquat Ali Khan as Finance Minister. . . . He was also convinced that the new State of Pakistan was not viable and could not last." [5] On March 4, only three days after the battle of the budget started, Patel wrote to a friend in Bombay, "If the League insists on Pakistan, the only alternative is the division of the Punjab and Bengal. . . . A strong Centre with the whole of India—except Eastern Bengal and a part of the Punjab, Sind and Baluchistan—enjoying full autonomy under the Centre will be so powerful that the remaining portions will eventually come in." [6] Patel's biographer wrote: "With his uncanny foresight Sardar [Patel] came to the fateful decision that unless the country was partitioned, chaos and anarchy would spread throughout the land. The Congress Working Committee took a realistic view and agreed with him." [7] On March 8, the Congress Working Committee passed a resolution which, after referring to the scenes of violence witnessed in India during the past seven months, continued: "The tragic events have demonstrated that there can be no settlement of the problem in the Punjab by violence and coercion and that no arrangement based on coercion can last. Therefore it is necessary to find a way which amounts to the least compulsion. This would necessitate division of the Punjab into two provinces, so that the predominantly Muslim part may be separated from the predominantly non-Muslim part." [8] The Congress President explained that a similar partition was contemplated for Bengal also.

This resolution was the first unmistakable indication of a fundamental change in Congress thinking. It was widely interpreted in the country as acceptance by the Congress of the partition of India. Indeed, it could have no other logical consequence. If the Hindus could not tolerate a Muslim majority even in the provinces of the Punjab and Bengal, it was idle to expect the Muslims to submit to a Hindu majority throughout the subcontinent. There were only five provinces in which the Muslims were in a majority—the North-West Frontier

Province, Sind, Baluchistan, the Punjab, and Bengal. The first three had relatively small populations, and the Hindu minority was not only numerically weak but was scattered all over the province. In the big provinces—the Punjab and Bengal—on the other hand, the non-Muslims formed over 40 percent of the population. In the Punjab, the non-Muslims were in a majority in the eastern part of the province and in Bengal in the western part. The Congress resolution of March 8 demanding the separation of the predominantly non-Muslim areas was a precursor of the partition of India. Nehru made this abundantly clear when, in a speech to the All-India States' People's Conference on April 18, he declared: "The Congress has recently on practical considerations passed a resolution accepting the division of the country." Some days later he said, "The Muslim League can have Pakistan if they want it but on the condition that they do not take away other parts of India which do not wish to join Pakistan." [9]

It is worth noting that Gandhi, who was in Bihar at this time, saw the resolution on the partition of the Punjab for the first time in the newspapers. According to Pyarelal's account, Gandhi "had not been consulted or even forewarned. 'I think I do not know the reason behind the Working Committee resolution,' he wrote to Pandit Nehru on 20th March. 'I can not understand it,' he wrote to Sardar Patel." And Pyarelal goes on to ask in wonder: "What had made the Congress High Command to whom the very idea of partition was anathema, forsake the ideal of undivided India for which they and the Congress had toiled and sacrificed without even a formal reference to their erstwhile oracle?" But to these questions neither Gandhi nor his faithful secretary were ever to receive a frank answer from Nehru or Patel.[10]

Another resolution passed by the Congress Working Committee at this time welcomed the British government's statement of February 20, 1947, and demanded that the interim government should be recognized in practice "as a Dominion Government with effective control over the Services and administration and the Viceroy and Governor-General functioning as the constitutional head of the Government. The Central Government must necessarily function as a Cabinet with full authority and responsibility." In other words, the Congress majority in the cabinet should rule and the Viceroy, functioning as a constitutional head, should give effect to the decisions of the majority. The Working Committee reiterated its so-called acceptance of the Cabinet Mission plan and invited the Muslim League afresh to join the constituent assembly. It declared that "the Constitution framed by the Constituent Assembly will apply only to those areas which accept it. It must also be understood that any Province or part of Province which accepts the Constitution and desires to join the Union can not be prevented from doing so. Thus there must be no compulsion either way." Finally, the resolution invited "the All-India Muslim League to nominate representatives to meet representatives of the Congress in order to consider the situation that has arisen and to devise means to meet it." [11]

As the Congress leaders well knew, there was no chance of the Muslim League coming into the constituent assembly except in the unlikely event that the Congress reversed its policy and accepted the Cabinet Mission plan in a spirit of sincerity and goodwill. Nehru forwarded these resolutions to the Viceroy, Lord Wavell, on March 9, and wrote that if the Muslim League did not come into the constituent assembly, the division of the Punjab and Bengal would become inevitable.[12] The die was cast; the partition of India had become inevitable.

CHAPTER 6

Mountbatten's Mission

LORD MOUNTBATTEN, the last Governor-General and Viceroy of India, arrived in Delhi on March 22, 1947. He came charged with the mission to make a peaceful transfer of power from British to Indian hands by June, 1948. "It is a mission," Prime Minister Attlee said in Parliament, "not as has been suggested of betrayal on our part, it is a mission of fulfilment." This gave Mountbatten an immediate and vast advantage over all his predecessors. Because they were not backed by an unequivocal declaration of this kind, they could not be trusted to fulfill the aspirations of the peoples of the Indian subcontinent.

He was no stranger to India, for he had been Supreme Commander of Allied forces in South East Asia during the Second World War and had paid visits to India, then the base for operations. He was descended from royalty and was intensely conscious of his blue blood. Vigorous of mind and body, strikingly handsome, he was at the height of his powers and energy at forty-six. He had an abundance of natural charm and used it to full effect. In his undertakings he was greatly assisted by the social graces of Lady Mountbatten. He was a wonderful talker and could hold his own in argument with anyone. In persistence, resilience, and resourcefulness he had few equals. He had a flair for publicity and paid more attention to the cultivation of public relations than most politicians. Because of his overflowing vitality, he never looked tired or frustrated. He carried with him a magnetic force of which the keynote was self-confidence. He was resolved to break any impasse, whatever the pains to himself and the cost to others. These great gifts were matched by an equally great vanity. He desired glory too avidly to have that inner poise which gives integrity to the human spirit.

The instructions given to Mountbatten were set out in a letter from Prime Minister Attlee:

> It is the definite objective of His Majesty's Government to obtain a unitary Government for British India and the Indian States, if possible within the British Commonwealth, through the medium of a Constituent Assembly, set up and run in accordance with the Cabinet Mission's plan, and you should do the utmost in your power to persuade all Parties to work together to this end. . . . Since, however, this plan can only become operative in respect of British India by agreement between the major Parties, there can be no question of compelling either major Party to accept it. If by October 1 you consider that there is no prospect of reaching a settlement on the basis of a unitary government for British India, either with or without the cooperation of the Indian States, you should report to His Majesty's Government on the steps which you consider should be taken for the handing over of power on the due date. . . . You should aim at 1 June 1948 as the effective date for the transfer of power. . . . There should be the fullest cooperation with the Indian leaders in all steps that are taken as to the withdrawal of British power. . . . You should take every opportunity of stressing the importance of ensuring that the transfer of power is effected with full regard to the defence requirements of India. In the first place you will impress upon the Indian leaders the great importance of avoiding any breach in the continuity of the Indian Army and of maintaining the organization of defence on an all Indian basis. Secondly you will point out the need for continued collaboration in the security of the Indian Ocean area for which provision might be made in an agreement between the two countries. At a suitable date His Majesty's Government would be ready to send military and other experts to India to assist in discussing the terms of such an agreement.[1]

The letter deserves careful study as it is the policy directive of the British government to the last Viceroy of India. When it was written in March, 1947, the British government knew, from firsthand experience, that every effort to persuade the Congress to abide by the Cabinet Mission's plan had failed, and that the Congress plan for a strong unitary government without any grouping of provinces was wholly unacceptable to the Muslim League. If, even at this hour, the British government was still intent on securing a unitary government for India and was reluctant to outline a clear alternative—the only alternative being partition—the reasons lay partly in calculated British interests and partly in the bias of the Labour party.

In the words of a British historian, the Labour party's "political bias, its belief in centralization and planning, its concept of a socialist state, all predisposed its leaders in favour of the aspirations of the left wing of the Congress, and made them if not antipathetic, at least allergic to Muslim League demands for partition and a separate Muslim state." [2]

British interests pointed in the same direction. The British could not maintain their rule in India without an expenditure of manpower and money that the state of their economy at the end of the Second World War forbade. But it would be wrong to assume that since they were relinquishing power in India, they had no interests of their own to serve. In fact, they had world-wide interests in which the India of the future was not an unimportant factor. Inevitably their own interests would take precedence over those of the Indian peoples and parties. If they could transfer power to a unitary government with the consent of the Indian leaders, their objective of keeping the new India within the British Commonwealth was likely to be gained. Politically and economically this was of great importance to a nation that sets a high value on continuity of tradition and an even higher one on profitable trade.

The defense requirements of the British Empire could best be met by maintaining the Indian army intact. During the two world wars, the Indian army had played a vital role in defending British interests in the Middle East and in South East Asia. It was, in fact, the main instrument of power in the hands of the British in the Indian Ocean area; its dismemberment would leave a power gap the British, with their depleted resources, would find hard to fill. This accounts for the emphasis in Attlee's letter upon "the great importance of avoiding any breach in the continuity of the Indian Army and of maintaining the organization of defence on an all Indian basis." British military opinion recoiled in horror from the prospect of splitting the Indian armed forces; it was regarded as militarily unsound and administratively impracticable.

Partition, which was opposed by the powerful majority community, would jeopardize each one of these British interests. It would deeply offend the Hindu Congress leaders, who might then break all connections with the British. Pakistan, as the weaker party, might be willing and perhaps anxious to be within the Commonwealth, but this would make relations with Hindustan even worse. And if both were outside the Commonwealth, the brightest jewel in the British Crown would be gone; the loss to Britain's world position and prestige would be incalculable. Trade would suffer and economic cooperation in the solution of such difficult issues as sterling balances would not be easy to secure. Politically, economically, and militarily, partition would create awkward problems for the British and weaken their position in the East.

Another set of problems was created by the choice of June, 1948, as the effective date for the transfer of power. The fifteen months from March, 1947, to June, 1948, was too short a period for the innumerable political, constitutional, and administrative decisions involved. Was it going to be, in the words of Winston Churchill, a "shameful flight" and a "hurried scuttle," the consequences of which would fall wholly on the peoples of India? If so, whose would be the responsibility? These are questions which every historian dealing with these events must answer.

There was yet another problem to which no clear solution was in sight. While the British had fostered the growth of democratic institution in British India, they had preserved and protected autocracy in the Indian states. This protection could last only so long as they retained power in British India. The transfer of power had to be complete in the entire subcontinent, or it would lose all grace and breed fresh mistrust. But that created the difficult problem of the relationship between the successor authority, or authorities, on the one hand and the Indian states on the other. Could democracy and autocracy be fitted into a single constitutional structure?

The British government looked to the new Viceroy to find solutions to these complex problems. Above all, they wanted the solution to safeguard British political, economic, and military interests without the expenditure of more British resources in men or money. They had neither the will nor the power to impose a solution on India, and had no desire to risk their own interests for the sake of justice. They were not in search of a new policy; the policy of the transfer of power by June, 1948, was set. The question was how to execute that policy in a manner which would, if possible, promote British interests and, in any case, not prejudice them. That is why the British government looked to a new personality for the achievement of its purpose—a personality more supple and pliable than the last Viceroy. In essence his role was that of mediator between the Congress and the Muslim League who also had to arrive at some sort of adjustment with the rulers of the Indian states. But the mediator was not a disinterested party.

"His primary aim," wrote Alan Campbell-Johnson, the Press Attaché to Lord Mountbatten during his viceroyalty, "is to achieve a solution which inspires sufficient good feeling to enable the Indian parties to remain within the Commonwealth structure from the out-set." [3] His success in his own eyes, and in the eyes of the British government, would be measured by the extent to which he achieved this primary aim. Those who appointed him had, on personal and policy grounds, a heavy bias toward the stronger of the two main Indian parties—the Congress—and were keen to win its goodwill. Mountbatten was aware of this preference and was himself inclined the same way. In any case, he was too shrewd and ambitious to follow any other course. But there was an apparent conflict between the objective of the Congress party and Mountbatten's primary aim. The Congress had, through the Objectives Resolution adopted by the constituent assembly, committed itself to making the Indian Union an independent sovereign Republic. The Commonwealth at that time consisted of self-governing Dominions and Dependencies under the British Crown and had no constitutional room for a Republic. To persuade the Congress to remain within the Commonwealth was for Mountbatten the problem of problems.

When Mountbatten arrived in India, League ministries were functioning in Bengal and Sind. The Punjab was under the rule of its British governor. The Congress was in power in all other provinces including the North-West Frontier Province and Assam. In the latter two provinces the Muslim League had launched civil disobedience movements against the provincial governments and, particularly in the North-West Frontier Province, the ministry was holding on by the skin of its teeth. In the interim central government, the Congress and Muslim League blocs were at loggerheads.

There was communal tension all over the country. Fights were breaking out sporadically, and Bombay and other places had fairly heavy casualties several times. The Punjab, in particular, was seething with communal passions. The Sikhs were busy collecting arms and preparing for revenge. Since the Punjab supplied a high proportion of soldiers for the Indian army—48 percent before the war—it was feared that communal clashes in the Punjab countryside might put an unbearable strain on the cohesion and discipline of army units containing Punjabi Muslims and Sikhs.

The constituent assembly was continuing with its work. The Muslim League's boycott of it was in full force despite Congress efforts to divide its ranks. "Our general outlook at present," wrote Nehru to Gandhi on February 24, 1947, "is to approach privately some of the Muslim leaders to try to induce them to come into the Constituent Assembly." [4] Sikhs and Hindus from the Punjab and Bengal, and representatives of the Congress ministries in the North-West Frontier Province and Assam were participating in the work of the assembly. The constituent assembly went about its work in complete disregard of the Cabinet Mission plan. It did not divide into sections and had no intention to form groups. The various committees it had appointed proceeded in the same spirit. Thus the Union Powers Committee recommended not only a wide interpretation of the subjects of foreign affairs, defense, and communications, which the plan had allotted to the central government, but also added fourteen other subjects as inevitably coming within the powers of the central government, and another eight subjects, because they were essential to ensure uniform standards of trade and commerce throughout the Union.[5]

But whatever doubts might have lingered in the minds of the authors of the Cabinet Mission plan about the fate of the plan should have been removed by the Congress resolution of March 8, 1947, on the partition of the Punjab and implicitly of Bengal and, therefore, of the whole subcontinent. In their statement of May 16, 1946, the Cabinet Mission had examined "the question of a separate and fully independent sovereign State of Pakistan . . . [which] would comprise two areas; one in the north-west consisting of the Provinces of the Punjab, Sind, North-West Frontier, and British Baluchistan; the other in the north-east consisting of the Provinces of Bengal and Assam."

After pointing out that the non-Muslim minority would be 37.93 percent of the population in the northwest area and 48.31 percent in the northeast area, the Cabinet Mission had stated that they could not "see any justification for including within a sovereign Pakistan those districts of the Punjab and of Bengal and Assam in which the population is predominantly non-Muslim. Every argument that can be used in favour of Pakistan, can equally in our view be used in favour of the exclusion of the non-Muslim areas from Pakistan. . . . [But] such a Pakistan is regarded by the Muslim League as quite impracticable. . . . We ourselves are also convinced that any solution which involves a radical partition of the Punjab and Bengal, as this would do, would be contrary to the wishes and interests of a very large proportion of the inhabitants of these Provinces." After adding further administrative, economic, and military considerations the Cabinet Mission concluded: "We are therefore unable to advise the British Government that the power which at present resides in British hands should be handed over to two entirely separate sovereign States."

On the other hand, the Cabinet Mission were fully aware of the "very real Muslim apprehensions that their culture and political and social life might become submerged in a purely unitary India in which the Hindus with their greatly superior numbers must be a dominant element." They, therefore, suggested a compromise—the Cabinet Mission plan. Lacking mutual acceptance by the Congress and the Muslim League, it had failed; and the field was left open to partition as a solution of the constitutional problem.

According to the Muslim League's resolution of 1940, generally known as the Pakistan Resolution, Pakistan would comprise geographically contiguous "areas in which the Muslims are numerically in a majority as in the north-western and eastern zones of India . . . with such territorial readjustments as may be necessary." Both the Hindus and the British as well as many Muslims had drawn the conclusion that the Pakistan Resolution implied a readjustment of the boundaries of the Punjab, Bengal, and Assam. The extent of the re-adjustment might be open to argument but the principle had been conceded. The Congress demand for the partition of the Punjab and Bengal, however distasteful it might be to the Muslims of these provinces, had behind it the logic of the Pakistan Resolution.

The attitude of the Congress, in effect, was that it would rather concede a truncated Pakistan than work the Cabinet Mission plan as conceived by its authors. Some Congress leaders hoped that the League, confronted with a truncated Pakistan would accept the Cabinet Mission plan as modified by the Congress, but this was wishful thinking. If the choice were between a truncated Pakistan and a genuine Cabinet Mission plan, the League could choose the latter, but as the choice lay between a truncated Pakistan and the Congress's concept of a unitary India, a truncated Pakistan was preferable. In short, as of March, 1947, a truncated Pakistan was mutually acceptable to the Congress and the League, although neither relished it.

Thus, by the time Mountbatten took charge as Viceroy and Governor-General of India, the issue of partition had been settled. There were big problems ahead, but they were related to the time, manner, and extent of partition and not to the principle of partition.

A wide gulf separated the Congress from the League standpoint on all these questions. To the Muslim League, the demand for the division of the subcontinent between two sovereign independent states—Hindustan and Pakistan—was a just demand that trespassed on the rights of neither Hindus nor Muslims, but gave to each its due share. Minorities would still remain in each of these states; they would be entitled to receive equal rights as citizens and adequate protection for their culture. Partition was conceived as a division of property between two brothers, to be carried out in a peaceful and fair manner, with due deliberation and without hurt or detriment to either party. The last task of the departing rulers of India, in Muslim eyes, was to ensure fair play between the two brothers, one of whom was weaker than the other, so that the transfer of power took place in peace and justice. This alone would confer nobility on the departure of the British after a rule of nearly two centuries during which Britain had risen to greatness and wealth.

The Congress, however, had accepted partition in anger and in anguish. The Hindus felt frustrated at being deprived of dominion over the whole of the subcontinent just when the prize was almost within their grasp. They had cast themselves for the role of a "great power" in the style of nineteenth-century great powers. In September, 1946, when he took office as Minister for External Affairs in the interim government, Nehru had declared: "There are only four Great Powers in the world—USA, USSR, China and India." The United Kingdom did not appear in the list, presumably because the new India was conceived as the successor of the British in the East. Earlier still, in his book, *The Discovery of India* (1945), Nehru had proclaimed: "The Pacific is likely to take the place of the Atlantic in the future as a nerve centre of the world. Though not directly a

Pacific state, India will inevitably exercise an important influence there. India will also develop as the centre of economic and political activity in the Indian Ocean area, in South East Asia and right up to the Middle East. Her position gives an economic and strategic importance in a part of the world which is going to develop rapidly in the future. If there is a regional grouping of the countries bordering on the Indian Ocean on either side of India—Iran, Iraq, Afghanistan, India, Ceylon, Burma, Malaya, Siam, Java, etc.—present day minority problems will disappear or at any rate will have to be considered in an entirely different context. . . . For the small national state is doomed. It may survive as a culturally autonomous area but not as an independent political unit." [6] And yet this grand theorist of a new imperialism had been forced to accept Pakistan as an independent political unit and as a solution of present-day minority problems. Such unpleasant realities hurt Congress pride and awakened a spirit of vengefulness.

General Tuker noted

the vindictive attitude of the majority of Hindus [at this time] . . . . In effect they said "Well, if the Muslims want Pakistan, let them damned well have it and with a vengeance. We shall shear every possible inch off their territory so as to make it look silly and to ensure that it is not a viable country and when they have got what's left we'll ensure that it can't be worked economically." [7]

A speech that Sardar Patel delivered in the constituent assembly in November, 1949, fully bears out Tuker's impression. Although delivered more than two years after these events, it still breathed a spirit of vengeance. In the course of this speech Patel said: "I agreed to partition as a last resort, when we should have lost all. . . . Mr. Jinnah did not want a truncated Pakistan but he had to swallow it. I made a further condition that in two months' time power should be transferred." [8]

The acceptance by Congress of partition was a tactical move, but the strategic goal—to rule over the entire subcontinent—remained unaltered. To ensure the success of this goal it was necessary that:

1. Hindustan or the Indian Union should be recognized as the only successor to the British government in India; Pakistan would be treated as certain territories that had seceded.
2. The areas to be included in Pakistan should be as small as possible

and confined to East Bengal, West Punjab, Sind, and Baluchistan and should exclude the North-West Frontier Province. Pakistan should, if possible, be encircled strategically.

3. Pakistan should be subjected to the maximum handicaps by being denied time and resources—civil and military, manpower and material—to establish and consolidate itself.

4. Whatever could be done to make Pakistan unviable should be done. (The Congress leaders were convinced that Pakistan could not last for long; their aim and endeavor was to hasten the collapse of its economy.)

5. The Indian states should be incorporated in the Indian Union.

To achieve these objectives, the Congress leaders needed the help of the British who still had control over the civil administration and the armed forces. What the Congress wanted above all was an immediate transfer of power to itself. Attlee's government had been willing enough to do what the Congress wanted, but it was felt that the British government's representative in India, Lord Wavell, had not quite played the game by bringing the Muslim League into the interim government. Now a new viceroy had come and it remained to be seen how he would behave. As things turned out, he exceeded the expectations of Congress leaders and won an everlasting name for himself in the annals of the new India. He was too enamored of success to risk annoying the powerful men who had had his predecessor virtually dismissed. And in subtlety of intellect he was no match for the Hindu leaders who were so imbued with the spirit of Kautilya, the author of the famed book on statecraft *Arthashastra,* that Machiavelli appears a crude and clumsy blusterer in comparison.

Mountbatten brought with him from England a carefully selected staff, including such distinguished men as Lord Ismay, who had been Winston Churchill's Personal Military Adviser during the Second World War; and Sir Eric Miéville, who had been Private Secretary to Lord Willingdon and, later, Assistant Private Secretary to King George VI. They were his principal advisers on the military and civil side, and Lord Ismay acted as chief of staff for the whole team. Alan Campbell-Johnson came as Press Attaché, Captain Brockman as Personal Secretary, and Colonel Erskine Crim as Conference Secretary. George Abell, a British officer of the Indian Civil Service who was already Private Secretary to the Viceroy, and V. P. Menon, a

Hindu official who was Constitutional Adviser to the Governor-General completed his entourage.

It was Mountbatten's practice to hold frequent informal meetings with members of his staff at which all questions were discussed with the utmost freedom and without any mental reservations. V. P. Menon was, at first, occasionally and, soon, invariably invited to take part in these staff meetings. It was known to Mountbatten, and indeed to all, that V. P. Menon was, to use Campbell-Johnson's phrase, "the trusted confidant of Vallabhbhai Patel," [9] who was thereby not only kept informed of the inner councils of the Viceroy, but was able to influence the Viceroy's policies through his mouthpiece. If a Muslim officer had been in V. P. Menon's position and was known to maintain a liaison with Jinnah, no Viceroy could have tolerated it without laying himself open to the charge of partisanship; in any case, the Congress would have made it impossible for such an officer to continue in that position.

Lord Mountbatten's first task was to make the acquaintance of the great political antagonists—the leaders of the Congress and of the Muslim League—and he succeeded in a short time in winning their confidence and admiration. That men like Gandhi, Nehru, and Patel on the one hand, and Jinnah and Liaquat Ali Khan on the other, should all be captivated by this glamorous scion of royalty who had come to liquidate the British Empire in India was an astonishing phenomenon; and yet this seemingly impossible feat was performed by Lord Mountbatten. Gandhi was charmed by Mountbatten and Nehru was more than charmed by Lord and Lady Mountbatten. Nehru's biographer, Michael Brecher, writes that "Mountbatten's most notable triumph in the sphere of personal relations was an intimate bond of friendship with Nehru. Other Congress leaders, including Gandhi and Patel were well-disposed to the Governor-General. But with Nehru there developed a relationship of mutual trust, respect, admiration and affection which is rare among statesman and unprecedented in the annals of British Raj. . . . As for Lady Mountbatten it can only be surmised that she helped to fill a void in Nehru's life." [10] Even a man with the cold dignity and reserve of Jinnah spoke in unusually warm terms about Mountbatten. That Mountbatten did not reciprocate Jinnah's sentiments is clear to any one who has read Campbell-Johnson's book *Mission with Mountbatten*; but Jinnah was unaware of it. Campbell-Johnson has left a record of the planning and the thought that went into the seemingly unpremeditated charm exercised by Mountbatten upon these diverse personalities; but Mountbatten had one other weapon of which Campbell-Johnson was, perhaps, not aware.

In the well-founded belief that political opponents of such long standing as the leaders of the Congress and the Muslim League would not exchange notes, he won the confidence of both by denouncing the one to the other. At the very time when he was wooing Congress leaders day and night, he was portraying them to Jinnah as unreasonable men whom it was exceedingly difficult to persuade into accepting any fair terms. These words naturally found a sympathetic response in Jinnah's mind. It is not difficult to imagine the terms in which Mountbatten must have described Jinnah to the Congress leaders; even his staff were told that a dinner engagement with Jinnah was put off by a day because "Mountbatten felt he could not sustain another session with him to-day." [11] Nevertheless, the technique worked. Both the Congress and the Muslim League leaders felt that here was a man who had political and psychological insight, understood human character and motives, was frank enough to point out difficulties in the way, and made a sincere effort to remove them. In any case this voluble man of keen perception and quick understanding was a welcome contrast to his predecessor with his awkward silences and stony reticence.

Having completed this first task successfully and having settled a few outstanding problems, such as the controversy over the budget proposals and the Indian National Army trials, Mountbatten plunged with characteristic energy into discussions with Indian leaders on the constitutional problems. Gandhi came out with a variant of the plan he had put to the Cabinet Mission: Entrust responsibility for the whole of India to the Muslim League alone, and, if that was not possible, hand it over to the Congress alone. He knew full well that the British government would never agree to entrust the Muslim League alone with power to rule over India with its overwhelming Hindu majority. His offer to the Muslim League was only an opening gambit for the real objective of gaining unshared power for the Hindu Congress over the whole of India. This time his offer to the Muslim League to form the government was embellished with a conditional assurance of support by the Congress majority.

Gandhi's plan was considered by Nehru and some other members of the Congress Working Committee, but as Gandhi wrote to Mount-batten on April 11, 1947: "I could not convince them of the correct-ness of my plan. . . . Thus I have to ask you to omit me from your consideration." [12] Those who might attribute this difference between Gandhi on the one hand, and Nehru and Patel on the other, to the inability of practical Congress politicians to rise to the heights of Gandhian idealism, should read the memorandum in which Gandhi set out the implications of his plan.[13] After numerous conditions, such as the partition of the Punjab and Bengal, the exclusion of the North-West Frontier Province from the Pakistan zone, and participa-tion by the League in the constitutent assembly, Gandhi wrote:

> Subject to the foregoing, the Congress pledges itself to give full co-operation to the Muslim League Cabinet if it is formed and never to use the Congress majority against the League with the sole purpose of defeating the League. On the contrary every measure will be con-sidered on its merits and receive full cooperation from the Congress members wherever a particular measure is provably in the interest of the whole of India.

The judge of whether a measure was provably in the interest of the whole of India would, of course, be the Hindu majority.

It is hardly surprising that when Gandhi's plan was discussed at Mountbatten's staff meeting it "was described as an old kite flown without disguise." [14] Jinnah pointed out that "Gandhi's position was mischievous because it entailed authority without responsibility." [15] The trouble with Gandhi's plan was not that it conceded too much to the Muslim League, but that it conceded nothing at all and could not, therefore, lead to a settlement. Nehru and Patel were by now con-vinced that the only way to exercise real power in the central govern-ment was to throw out the Muslim League by conceding a truncated Pakistan to them—the more truncated the better, and the sooner the better.

Mountbatten's discussions with Jinnah, which followed those with Gandhi, were remarkable for the way in which he succeeded in winning Jinnah's confidence. At the end of the second interview on April 7, Mountbatten remarked to his staff, "Jinnah can negotiate with me but my decision goes." [16] The main reason for Jinnah's trust in Mountbatten was the belief he had at this time that Mountbatten would endeavor to carry out partition in a fair and impartial man-ner. Mountbatten himself was constantly emphasizing that "his mandate was impartiality." [17] Jinnah knew that even though the Congress had accepted partition, it would do its utmost to mutilate and injure Pakistan. He realized that the Punjab and Bengal would have to be partitioned—note his remark that "a moth-eaten Pakistan would be better than no Pakistan at all." [18] But that made the manner and method of partition all the more important. The British had a vital role to play in the execution of the partition plan. If they held the scales even between the Congress and the Muslim League, Pakistan might be saved from the worst depredations of the Congress.

One result of Mountbatten's discussions with Gandhi and Jinnah was an appeal to the peoples of India for peace, issued on April 14 over the joint signatures of the two leaders. The appeal produced some effect, although not a lasting one, but it certainly enhanced Mountbatten's prestige and provided public evidence of his skillful diplomacy.

The directive given to Mountbatten by the British government required him to make efforts for a unitary government in accordance with the Cabinet Mission plan. But the Cabinet Mission plan had been mangled by the Congress months before, and was unacceptable to the Muslim League in that form. Mountbatten knew that his predecessor had broken himself by his well-intentioned endeavors to make the Congress accept the plan in conformity with the intentions of the Cabinet Mission and the British government. The discussions with Congress and Muslim League leaders during the first fortnight convinced Mountbatten of the futility of insisting on the Cabinet Mission plan. Although he toyed with the idea that he might "get Congress to accept the Cabinet Mission Plan in full and then confront Jinnah with coming in or accepting a truncated Pakistan," [19] he never actually made such an attempt. An alternative to which he gave some thought was that the representatives of Pakistan and Hindustan should come together on a basis of parity in a central government that would deal with external affairs, defense, and communications.[20] This alternative also never got beyond the stage of discussion at his staff meetings. What he was really groping for was a solution that would enable both Pakistan and the Indian Union to remain within the Commonwealth.

CHAPTER 7

The Making
of the Partition Plan

BY THE middle of April, 1947, Mountbatten had worked out a partition plan, the principles of which were that if partition came, it should be the responsibility of the Indians; provinces should have the right to determine their own future; Bengal and the Punjab should be partitioned; Sylhet district in Assam should have the option to join East Bengal; and there should be general elections in North-West Frontier Province. The plan was discussed at a conference of provincial governors on April 15 and 16. The governors "all agreed on two points. First that a quick decision was of great importance; and secondly, that a united India was now out of the question. No one liked the idea of Partition, but no one could suggest how it could be avoided." [1]

The Hindus and Sikhs were insisting on a partition of the Punjab. The Sikhs by this time were so taken in by Congress leaders that they were blind to their true interests. When the Sikh deputation saw Mountbatten he pointed out to them that the partition of the Punjab they were demanding would divide their small community into two; but they were adamant. They were busy collecting arms and were bent on producing chaos. Baldev Singh, the Defence Minister, was reported to be the treasurer of the Sikhs' appeal fund. Baldev Singh denied the allegation, but, as Campbell-Johnson remarks, the fund was "undoubtedly being subscribed for warlike and unconstitutional purposes." [2]

At the governors' conference,

> Jenkins [the Governor of the Punjab] gave a lucid analysis of the implications of Punjab partition, showing just how the Moslem versus non-Moslem issue was complicated by Sikh and Hindu Jat claims. Tyson [Secretary to the Governor of Bengal] similarly examined the prospects for Bengal, if under partition. East Bengal, he felt, would become a rural slum. There were some twenty-five million Hindus in Bengal—forty-five per cent of the population—and they all wanted to be absorbed into Hindustan. The concept of East Bengal was unacceptable to many local Moslems. The relationship between Jinnah and the present Moslem Premier of Bengal, Suhrawardy, was far from cordial. Suhrawardy [was] frightened of partition and [was] ready to play with the Hindus.[3]

The situation in the North-West Frontier Province was complicated by the fact that although the province was overwhelmingly Muslim and the bulk of the Muslims now supported the League, there was a Congress ministry in the province; and the Congress laid claim to it. The Muslim League was waging a successful campaign against the ministry whose position was getting more and more untenable. If, as demanded by the Muslim League and recommended by the governor, fresh elections were to be held, the Congress ministry was sure to be defeated. The Congress was, therefore, opposed to elections and had, indeed, given "notice that the whole Congress attitude towards the British Government's plan might change if there was any tampering with the Frontier Ministry." [4] To ascertain the true position, Mountbatten paid a visit to the province toward the end of April. The Muslim League demonstrations he saw there, and the discussions he had with the Governor, Sir Olaf Caroe; the Chief Minister, Dr. Khan Sahib and his colleagues; with tribal Maliks; and with the Muslim League leaders, Khan Abdul Qayyum Khan, and the Pir of Manki Sharif, who were specially released from jail for the occasion, convinced him that a reference to the people was necessary to decide the conflicting claims of the Congress and the Muslim League.

An essential part of any plan for partition was a plan for the division of the armed forces. A sovereign state without armed forces under its own control was an impossibility. Although the partition of the country was, by April, 1947, a foregone conclusion, and the British were to hand over power by June, 1948, no preparations for a partition of the Indian armed forces had been made—not even a study of the question had been made. The Commander-in-Chief, Field Marshal Sir Claude Auchinleck, and, indeed, the whole body of British military officers were so proud of the Indian army they had built up with devotion and skill that the idea of splitting it was abhorrent to them. Though time was pressing, nobody was taking cognizance of the problem. The advantages of delay would accrue wholly to the Congress, because it would inherit the capital at New Delhi and the civil and military administration of the Government of India, including control over the armed forces. The Muslim League would be the loser. Liaquat Ali Khan, therefore, addressed a letter to the Viceroy suggesting a reorganization of the armed forces so that they could be readily divided between Pakistan and the Indian Union at the appropriate time. When Mountbatten read this letter at his staff meeting on April 8,

> Ismay stressed that to take any action on Liaquat's letter would be to prejudice the political issue. Until and unless the Viceroy reported otherwise to His Majesty's Government, the Cabinet Mission Plan held the field, and that Plan envisaged one National Army. Mountbatten agreed that there could be no splitting of the Indian Army before the withdrawal of the British, for two reasons. "The mechanics won't permit it, and I won't." [5]

Both Mountbatten and Ismay knew by this time that the Cabinet Mission plan was dead and that partition was inevitable. But since it was in the British interest to maintain the Indian army intact, they refused to face the consequences of partition in the military sphere. If, as Mountbatten insisted, there could be no splitting of the Indian army before the British withdrawal, to which authority would control over it be transferred by the departing British, and how would its partition be carried out subsequently? Liaquat Ali Khan had not asked for an actual division of the armed forces; he had merely drawn attention to the need for preparatory action. He restated his proposal in a memorandum under the heading, "Preparation of Plan for the Partition of the Indian Armed Forces":

> In order that the constitutional issue should not be prejudged it is necessary to devise a course of action which should not be to the advantage or prejudice of either political party. This neutral position would be obtained by reorganizing the Armed Forces in such a

manner that they can be split up when a decision on the partition of the country is taken. An essential preliminary is the preparation of a plan by the Commander-in-Chief and his staff for the partition of the Armed Forces. This will necessarily take some weeks and if taken in hand immediately should be ready by about the time that a decision on the main constitutional issue is reached. The time limit set by His Majesty's Government demands that no time should be lost in preparing such a plan which will in no way interfere either with the present political negotiations or the present status of the Armed Forces.

Liaquat Ali Khan's proposal was opposed by the Commander-in-Chief, Field Marshal Auchinleck, who stated that "The Armed Forces of India, as they now stand, cannot be split up into two parts each of which will form a self-contained Armed Force." When Liaquat Ali Khan pointed out that that was precisely the reason why he had suggested that the armed forces be reorganized, the Commander-in-Chief replied, "Any such drastic reorganization would have to be carried out in stages over a period of several years, and during this period there would be no cohesive Armed Force capable of dealing with any serious defensive operations on the North-West Frontier." Thus, even the preparation of a plan for the partition of the armed forces did not find favor with the Commander-in-Chief, who claimed: "As it is likely that any rumour concerning a proposal to divide the Armed Forces would have an immediate and unsettling effect on the morale of the Muslim soldiers, ratings and airmen, it is urged that this matter should not be discussed except on the highest level." [6] Baldev Singh, the Defence Minister and mouthpiece of the Congress bloc, fully supported the stand taken by the Commander-in-Chief—the Congress had everything to gain by inaction. Baldev Singh wrote that he was "strongly of the view that the time is not opportune to discuss the proposal" of the Finance Minister. This was on April 20, two days after Nehru had publicly stated at Gwalior that the "Congress have recently on practical considerations passed a resolution accepting the division of the country." The whole country was ringing with discussions of partition, but the Defence Minister and the Commander-in-Chief insisted that a consideration of its logical corollary—the division of armed forces—even in the secret discussions of the Defence Committee of India was inopportune.

When the question came up before the Defence Committee on April 25, Liaquat Ali Khan urged that there should be a plan in readiness to go ahead with separation if Pakistan was accepted, and Baldev Singh affirmed that any division of the armed forces must follow the political decision in favor of Pakistan. Auchinleck pointed out that his paper had been written to explain the practical difficulties and was not intended in any way to influence the decision for or against Pakistan. Although Mountbatten agreed that "there must be a plan because when Pakistan is announced it will be imperative at once to let the Armed Forces know where they stand," all that he would accept was a small high-level committee to determine the problems that would have to be tackled. He insisted that he bore personal responsibility for law and order until he could hand it over to one or more responsible authorities. He continued,

> While I bear that responsibility I have, in the last resort, the use of British troops to fall back on. After 1 June 1948 there will be no British troops. But the need for reliable and impartial armed forces may still exist. By unduly hastening the process of separation we may defeat our own ends and produce a situation in which the Armed Forces may be semi-organized and not reliable. Much as I should like to see the separation completed, I must emphasise my own doubts as to the possibility of achieving this in the time available, without weakening the Armed Forces. This I cannot possibly accept while I am responsible for law and order.[7]

These views reflected the British desire to evade or postpone the partition of the Indian armed forces. But whether one agrees with them or not, there is no doubt on one point, namely, that as of April 25, 1947, when this discussion was held, the accepted date for the transfer of power was June 1, 1948. The partition plan Mountbatten was on the point of sending to the British government for approval had been prepared on the basis of that date. Indeed, Mountbatten was opposed to unduly hastening the process of separation, and he regarded the time available till then as inadequate for carrying out the task of partition. How and why that date was changed to August 15, 1947, resulting in terrible cost of human lives and in untold misery, is the tragic story that will now be told.

On April 26, Mountbatten "decided to send Ismay and George Abell back to London with the first draft of the Plan, to hammer it out clause by clause with the Government and officials concerned." [8] The text of the draft plan which Ismay took to London had not been shown to the Congress and the Muslim League, but its general terms were known to them. Under this plan "The Indian peninsula was to be partitioned into two independent sovereign States, one predominantly Hindu, to be called India, and the other predominantly Moslem, to be called Pakistan. The Provinces of the Punjab and Bengal were also to be partitioned." [9]

The Congress Working Committee that met on May 1 formally accepted partition, and Nehru wrote to the Viceroy "In regard to the proposals which, I presume, Lord Ismay is carrying with him to London, our Committee are prepared to accept the principle of partition, based on self-determination applied to definitely ascertained areas. This involves the partition of Bengal and the Punjab. . . . Any proposal to put an end to a duly constituted Provincial Government having a large majority at its command, and to hold elections as a result of terrorism must be considered a surrender and must be resisted." [10] The last sentence referred to the part of the plan dealing with the North-West Frontier Province. Therefore, except in regard to that province, where the Congress was opposed to the proposal to ascertain the wishes of the people, Mountbatten's partition plan, with June 1, 1948, as the date for the transfer of power, was acceptable to the Congress.

But what was not known was whether both the Indian Union and Pakistan would be in the Commonwealth. That Pakistan was willing, Mountbatten already knew since Jinnah had disclosed it to him as early as April 12, 1947. The Congress stood committed to the resolution of the constituent assembly in favor of a sovereign independent Republic, which implied leaving the Commonwealth. Krishna Menon, "one of Nehru's closest friends to whom he [had] given a roving commission at this critical time," was, however, trying to find a formula for "common citizenship" between India and Britain that would avoid Dominion Status.[11] The Congress was worried and afraid that Pakistan would come to occupy a position of vantage over the Indian Union. Campbell-Johnson recorded on April 26,

> The Commonwealth issue is looming large. There has been a fair indication of Patel's policy on this subject in the leading article of to-day's *Hindustan Times*. Ismay drew attention to the relevant extract, which runs as follows: "If there is a settlement between the Congress and the League as a result of which the Muslim majority areas are allowed to constitute themselves into separate sovereign States, we have no doubt that Union will not stand in the way of

Britain establishing contacts with those States. It must be clearly understood, however, that the Indian Union will consider it a hostile act if there is any attempt by Britain to conclude any treaty or alliance involving military or political clauses." [12]

Faced with this attitude of the Congress, "Mountbatten came down heavily against the concept of allowing only a part to remain in [the Commonwealth], with the consequent risk of Britain being involved in the support of one Indian sovereign State against another." [13] As already stated, Mountbatten's primary aim was to achieve a solution that would keep both the Indian Union and Pakistan within the Commonwealth. Soon he was to be shown a way of gaining this coveted objective.

After Ismay's departure for London to obtain the approval of the British government to the partition plan, Mountbatten went up to Simla for a short rest. V. P. Menon, who accompanied Mountbatten to Simla, put it to him that Congress would accept Dominion Status in return for a very early transfer of power. Menon had been canvassing this idea with Patel for quite some time on the ground that by this means the Congress would win the friendship of Britain and the support of British officers, civil and military, in the Indian administration. On May 1 Menon had conveyed to Mountbatten through Miéville that "Patel might be ready to accept an offer of Dominion Status for the time being." [14] Now, in Simla, he had an opportunity of putting Patel's condition for accepting Dominion Status directly to Mountbatten. The condition was that power should be transferred in two months.[15] Gandhi's secretary, Pyarelal, has given substantially the same version. He writes that in the second half of April, 1947, it was put to Patel, that "if the Congress could accept Dominion Status as an ad interim arrangement, it would be possible to anticipate the date of the British withdrawal. It would, further, take away from the Muslim League its bargaining power with the British. The argument, it seems, went home. On the 1st May the Viceroy's secretary reported that the Sardar [Patel] was now ready to accept an offer of Dominion Status for the time being." [16]

Mountbatten, whose primary aim was to bring the Indian Union also into the Commonwealth, jumped at the proposition put forward by V. P. Menon. He had been searching for a solution; now, suddenly, through the good offices of V. P. Menon he saw the way, and felt properly grateful. In a letter to Menon he wrote:

It was indeed fortunate that you were Reforms Commissioner on my Staff, and that thus we were brought together into close association with one another at a very early stage, for *you were the first person I met who entirely agreed with the idea of Dominion status, and you found the solution which I had not thought of, of making it acceptable by a very early transfer of power. History must always rate that decision very high, and I owe it to your advice; advice given in the teeth of considerable opposition from other advisers.*[17]

Mountbatten's other advisers, all of them British, were, of course, in favor of the Indian Union remaining in the Commonwealth, but some of them doubted if an extremely hurried scuttle was not too high a price to pay for it. Mountbatten, however, plunged into the deal with his usual vigor.

Things now moved quickly. On May 7, at Mountbatten's staff meeting V. P. Menon "confirmed both Patel's and Nehru's positive approach to the subject and the need for dropping the terms 'King-Emperor' and 'Empire' to which so many Indians objected." [18] The next day Nehru and Krishna Menon arrived in Simla and stayed with the Viceroy as his guests. Krishna Menon said that "Nehru is attracted to the concept, if only because it may give Mountbatten opportunity to bring his influence to bear on the more recalcitrant Princes." [19]

On May 10, Mountbatten held a conference attended by Nehru, Miéville, and V. P. Menon to discuss the new plan. According to V. P. Menon,

> The broad outlines were that the Muslim majority areas should be separated from India and that the transfer of power should be to two central Governments, India and Pakistan, on the basis of Dominion Status, each having its own Governor-General. . . . The Viceroy remarked that whereas it seemed to him that it would be a fairly easy matter . . . to transfer power at a very early date on a Dominion Status basis to the Union of India, there would for some time to come be no authorities in Pakistan to whom power could be transferred. I assured him that this problem would not present any insuperable difficulty and that we could find a solution. Nehru . . . said that it was very desirable that there should be a transfer of power as soon as possible on a Dominion Status basis.[20]

It will be noticed that there is no difference between the plan discussed at this conference and the partition plan taken by Ismay to London except an earlier transfer of power on the basis of Dominion Status.

Mountbatten was too experienced an administrator to be unaware of the immense difficulties that Pakistan would have to face under this new plan for a very early transfer of power. "What are we doing?" he asked. "Administratively it is the difference between putting up a permanent building, a nissen hut or a tent. As far as Pakistan is concerned we are putting up a tent. We can do no more." [21] The injustice to Pakistan, however, weighed little with him against the grand object of bringing the Indian Union into the British Commonwealth of which, he said, "The value to the United Kingdom both in terms of world prestige and strategy would be enormous." [22]

Within the subcontinent, the advantages of this hurried transfer of power would accrue wholly to the Indian Union and the disadvantages to Pakistan. The former was inheriting the administrative machinery of the Government of India, practically intact. All the departments of government as well as army, air force, and naval headquarters were located in the capital at New Delhi. The number of Muslim officers, civil and military, was small, and their disappearance would make little difference. Within the two months stipulated by Patel and accepted by Mountbatten it would be impossible to carry out an orderly division of the administrative machinery and of the armed forces or to complete the innumerable tasks involved in setting up the governments of Pakistan and of the partitioned provinces of the Punjab and Bengal. The Indian Union would virtually be the successor state to British India. Pakistan would be in the position of territories that had seceded from the parent country and would start with enormous handicaps, without an organized administration, without armed forces, without records, without equipment or military stores. It is difficult to imagine conditions more calculated to bring about a breakdown in Pakistan.

The cost in human life and misery of this deal between Mountbatten and the Congress leaders was incalculable. Winston Churchill called the transfer of power within fifteen months a "shameful flight" and "a hurried scuttle." What epithet can adequately describe the same operation being carried out in two months? Its appalling consequences in rivers of blood and the uprooting of millions lay in the future and may not have been apparent to the actors in this tragedy. But what could be seen clearly was that the immense administrative difficulties inherent in the transfer of power and in partition would be multiplied to such an extent as to be virtually beyond control. There could be no planned and orderly transition so far as Pakistan was concerned—but what did that matter? Both the Indian Union and Pakistan would be within the Commonwealth; the primary aim of British diplomacy would be achieved. A spirit of vengefulness filled the breast of Hindu leadership at this time; to mutilate and injure the nascent Pakistan so as to make its existence impossible seems to have been the ruling passion that made it blind to all considerations of humanity and justice.

Ismay and others have been at pains to cover up this secret bargain. Thus Ismay wrote that before leaving England he thought fifteen months to be too short a time for the transfer of power, but after reaching India he was convinced it was too long. The reasons he gave for this change of mind were the inordinate growth of communal bitterness, the deterioration in the administration, the disputes in the interim government, and Nehru's threat to resign unless other arrangements were made in the very near future.[23] All these considerations had played their part in convincing the British and the Indian parties that partition was inevitable; and a decision for partition had been reached with the consent of the Congress and the Muslim League. But to implement that decision in an orderly fashion was bound to take time. The partition plan that Ismay took with him to London was drawn up after paying heed to all the factors enumerated by Ismay; and it provided for the transfer of power on June 1, 1948.

The change to an earlier date was made for none of the reasons given by Ismay; it was the price paid to the Congress for agreeing to stay within the Commonwealth. The record on this point is clear beyond doubt. For this one gain to themselves, the British were prepared to pay any price—at the expense of Pakistan.

On the same day (May 10) that Mountbatten had his conference with Nehru, the partition plan as amended by the British government was returned to him from London. An announcement was made for a conference on May 17 with Nehru, Patel, Jinnah, Liaquat Ali Khan, and Baldev Singh at which the plan approved by the British government would be presented to them. Mountbatten, however, had a "hunch" that he should show it to Nehru in advance of the other leaders and did so that same evening. Nehru reacted against it vehemently. The next morning he sent a note to Mountbatten attacking the proposals in the plan mainly on the ground that "starting with the rejection of an Indian Union as the successor to power, they invited the claims of large numbers of successor States who would be

permitted to unite if they so wished into two or more States. . . .
The inevitable consequence of the proposals would be to invite the
Balkanisation of India." [24] He also objected to the procedure to be
followed for ascertaining the wishes of the people in Baluchistan and
the North-West Frontier Province, but the gravamen of his complaint
was that the amendments by the British government had not pre-
served the concept of India as a continuing entity. In Campbell-
Johnson's words, "he really [wanted] it to be fully established that
India and the Constituent Assembly [were] the successors to and
Pakistan and the Muslim League the seceders from, British India." [25]

Mountbatten was completely shaken and asked V. P. Menon to
prepare an alternative draft plan immediately. The revised plan was
shown to Nehru and after acceptance by him was communicated to
London for the approval of the British government. After a frenzied
exchange of telegrams with London informing them of "this volte-
face" on the part of Mountbatten, conference with the Indian leaders
was postponed to June 2.

Mountbatten's reactions to this episode are typical of the man. He
told his staff that without the "hunch" that he should show the plan
to Nehru, "Dickie Mountbatten would have been finished and could
have packed his bag. [He and his staff] would have looked complete
fools with the Government at home, having led them up the garden to
believe that Nehru would accept the Plan. . . . Most of his staff,
with natural caution, had been against his running over the Plan with
Nehru, but by following his hunch rather than their advice he had
probably saved the day." [26] After a night's rest, he regained his
resilience and remarked that he had been "able to establish his own
integrity with the Indian leaders." [27] At no time does it seem to have
occurred to Mountbatten that his behavior, in showing the plan to
only one of the two Indian parties concerned and amending it to suit
the wishes of that party, was not befitting a British Viceroy "whose
mandate," as he had himself often reiterated, "was impartiality." [28]
What struck him was that he had saved his career from ruin, and had
been "able to establish his own integrity with the Indian leaders."
Perhaps it was his curious concept of integrity that endeared him to
the Congress leaders. V. P. Menon, who was keeping Patel informed
of the developments in Simla, wrote that Patel "was delighted by the
turn of events. He assured me that there would be no difficulty in the
Congress accepting Dominion Status." [29]

Meanwhile V. P. Menon, having won "the complete confidence" [30] of Mountbatten, was not slow to take advantage of his exceptional position. He maintained that it was "more than possible that Jinnah would not accept the Plan in the draft announcement," and persuaded Mountbatten to obtain the approval of the British government for an alternative plan for "demission of power under the present constitution. It would not in the last resort require the agreement of Indian leaders. Provincial subjects would be demitted to existing Provincial Governments and Central subjects to the existing Central Government; but it would put the Moslems under the Hindu majority." [31] This Demission plan, for which Mountbatten sought and obtained the approval of the British government, was, in essence, the same scheme for which Gandhi had long been agitating and which Patel advocated publicly at that time. In a press statement issued on May 9, 1947, Patel said

> There would be peace in the country within a week if power were transferred to the Central Government as it now stands. The Viceroy should stand out and let the Interim Government function. Lacking interference by a third party to whom either side could appeal, the Congress and the Muslim League would settle their differences at once. If there are conflicts in the Cabinet over any question, the majority would rule. [32]

The purpose of the Demission plan was to hold the sword of Damocles over the Muslim League. The conditions under which partition was being carried out were being made as unfavorable to Pakistan as possible. If the Muslim League should find these conditions intolerable, they would be faced with the worse alternative of being placed in the power of the Hindus. The contrast between Wavell and Mountbatten must be noted. Less than three months before the date of Mountbatten's Demission plan, Wavell had written a letter to King George VI in which he outlined possible courses of action if the Cabinet Mission plan broke down. One of the courses was "to support the majority party i.e., the Congress in establishing their control over India." Wavell's comment was: "I did not think that this policy was a just or honourable one, in view of our pledges to the Minorities and to the Indian States; we might not be able to protect them any longer but it would be wrong to help the Congress to suppress them, which is what this policy would amount to." [33] It is easy to see why the Congress leaders were against Wavell and lauded Mountbatten.

The British government, somewhat puzzled by the revisions in the plan, summoned Mountbatten to London for consultation. Before leaving he asked V. P. Menon to draw up Heads of Agreement to be shown to the Indian leaders for their acceptance. With the Congress this was a mere formality since the plan on which these Heads of Agreement were based had already been approved by Nehru in draft. The Heads of Agreement were:

(a) That the leaders agree to the procedure laid down for ascertaining the wishes of the people whether there should be a division of India or not;

(b) That in the event of the decision being taken that there should only be one central authority in India, power should be transferred to the existing Constituent Assembly on a Dominion Status basis;

(c) That in the event of a decision that there should be two sovereign States in India, the central Government of each State should take over power in responsibility to their respective Constituent Assemblies, again on a Dominion Status basis;

(d) That the transfer of power in either case should be on the basis of the Government of India Act of 1935, modified to conform to the Dominion Status position;

(e) That the Governor-General should be common to both the Dominions and that the present Governor-General should be reappointed;

(f) That a Commission should be appointed for the demarcation of boundaries in the event of a decision in favour of partition;

(g) That the Governors of the provinces should be appointed on the recommendation of the respective central Governments;

(h) In the event of two Dominions coming into being, the Armed Forces in India should be divided between them. The units would be allocated according to the territorial basis of recruitment and would be under the control of the respective Governments. In the case of mixed units, the separation and redistribution should be entrusted to a Committee consisting of Field Marshal Sir Claude Auchinleck and the Chiefs of the General Staff of the two Dominions, under the supervision of a Council consisting of the Governor-General and the two Defence Ministers. This Council would automatically cease to exist as soon as the process of division was completed.

The point (e) deserves special notice. The proposal that Mountbatten should be the common Governor-General of both the Dominions was in a way a corollary of the decision to transfer power within two months, since it was obvious that all the processes of partition could not be completed within that time. Such a provision would have been unnecessary if the original date of June 1, 1948, had been allowed to stand.

The Viceroy wanted a written acceptance of the plan from the Congress and the Muslim League. Nehru, on behalf of the Congress, wrote that the Congress accepted the plan, generally, but that its acceptance was strictly subject to the other parties agreeing to it as a final settlement and to no further claims being put forward. The Congress agreed that if during the interim period there were to be two states, the Governor-General should be common to both. Nehru added that the Congress would be happy if Lord Mountbatten would continue in office and would help them with his advice and experience.[34]

When Mountbatten discussed the plan with Jinnah and Liaquat Ali Khan, he impressed upon them the imperative need for speed. Previous plans, he maintained, had been wrecked by prolonged wrangling and the time taken for second thoughts. If the opportunity for establishing Pakistan that now offered itself were not immediately grasped, it would never recur. The Congress leaders would find a thousand loopholes through which to wriggle out of their commitments. Bold and swift action was required, otherwise all would be lost. These were impressive arguments, although he who advanced them did so for other reasons. Be that as it may, Jinnah and Liaquat Ali Khan, who had till then no reason to doubt Mountbatten's impartiality, and who did not need to be reminded of the devious ways of the Congress, generally accepted the plan as outlined by Mountbatten—including a very early transfer of power. But despite the eloquent persuasion of Mountbatten, Jinnah refused to give his consent in writing. Mountbatten then held out the threat of the Demission plan, which would place the Muslims at the mercy of the Hindus. Campbell-Johnson recorded Jinnah's reaction in the following words:

> Jinnah had apparently been very calm, and had said simply that he could not stop such a step in any event. In some respects this may well turn out to be the most delicate and decisive moment for Mountbatten's and Jinnah's diplomacy. Mountbatten felt that Jinnah's reaction was both abnormal and disturbing. It was certainly shrewd. The *ballon d'essai* has gone up and come down again, providing only the evidence that Jinnah has a very steady nerve. Mountbatten feels that Jinnah is well aware of his potency as a martyr butchered by the British on the Congress altar.[35]

Those of Jinnah's Muslim detractors, who regard him only as an able advocate who pleaded the Muslim case in the court of British justice, would do well to study this episode carefully. They might then perhaps gain some idea of the measure of his greatness as a statesman. There never was, and in the nature of things never could be, a court of justice—British or Indian—to decide the political destiny of the peoples of India. There was, instead, a struggle of world importance in which three nations were involved—the British, the Hindus, and the Muslims. As in all such struggles, the wisdom, the courage, and the strength of will of the leaders, and their ability to rally their respective nations behind them was tested to the full. That the contest in India did not break out into a full-fledged war does not alter the essential character of the struggle. War, as Clausewitz pointed out, is the continuation of politics by other means, and its aim still is to bend the will of the opponent. Except for Jinnah, there was no Muslim leader at that time whom blandishment might not have won or pressures would not have bent. And the pressures were tremendous; they threatened the very existence of Muslims as a political entity. Of many of these other leaders it is not unfair to say that in their moderation and urbanity they could hardly understand and barely tolerate the intransigent and unbending posture of Jinnah. And, yet, without these qualities he could never have won the battle for Pakistan. The first sign of weakness in him or of a willingness to compromise would have sent scores of these other men to the other camp. They stood by Jinnah because he had the Muslim masses behind him. There were plenty of Muslim leaders of the second rank who were willing to make sacrifices or bear personal suffering. These qualities are not uncommon; they are necessary but not sufficient for the achievement of great national goals. When, however, the burdens of a whole nation press on the soul of a statesman whose nerve and judgment may make or mar its future, the need arises for leadership of the highest order.

It is necessary at this stage to give an account of Gandhi's activities, for, although he had removed himself from the scene of negotiations for the transfer of power, he was, as yet, an immense political force and was working day and night for his chosen end of establishing Hindu dominion over the whole subcontinent. His speeches at his daily prayer meetings presented partition as a moral evil with which others could compromise, but not the votary of truth and nonviolence. To apply moral judgments uncritically to group conflicts violates the first of all moral values—truth. Every national group tends to identify its interest with the Good. Gandhi carried this identification further than any modern statesman. He regarded his passion for rule by the Hindu majority over the whole subcontinent as absolutely good. Any movement that thwarted his desire, as the Pakistan movement for self-determination by the Muslims in their majority areas did, he called evil. It did not occur to him to ask in what way his desire was morally right, and the desire of the Muslims to govern themselves in areas in which they were in a majority morally wrong.

It is obvious that two large and distinct human groups have an equal right to self-government in their own homelands. For a relatively small minority scattered all over the country self-rule is impracticable. But the Muslims were a hundred million strong and were in a clear majority in large and contiguous territories. The fact that a foreign race had ruled over both Hindus and Muslims for a century and a half did not make them one nation. The test of nationhood must be sought in the consciousness of the people, their culture, their beliefs, and their sense of identity with each other. That the Muslims were a distinct cultural group no one denied. What Hindus like Gandhi contended was that they were not a separate nation, and they pointed to many customs and traits they shared with Hindus. The concept of "nation" was borrowed from the West and signified a group which had or deserved the right of political self-determination.

Among Muslims, political consciousness in the modern sense was of slower growth than among the Hindus who had taken to Western education fifty years ahead of Muslims. Hindu social cohesion, rooted as it was in a system of taboos nurtured from earliest childhood, was a powerful force with marked antipathy to outside groups. These two factors—greater political consciousness and stronger internal cohesion—fortified Hindu ambitions to rule over India exclusively and made them strangers to the need for give and take. As Western education spread among Muslims, they gradually caught up with the Hindus in political consciousness. To ask at what point they became a nation is about as meaningful as wanting to know the precise moment when a boy becomes a man. There was a period of growth, and during this period Muslims were again and again surprised and pained by Hindu rejection of their moderate demands. This helped to arouse and intensify their sense of separate nationhood, but it simultaneously increased Hindu hostility, which in turn reacted upon the Muslims. This process might have been halted and reversed in its earlier stages by sensitive and far-seeing statesmanship on the part of the Hindu majority; but Hindu leadership failed to avail itself of the many opportunities for mutual accommodation that were offered it during the last fifty years of British rule. On the contrary, it turned each one of those opportunities into an occasion for demonstrating the incompatibility of Hindu and Muslim interests. That Gandhi, or any other Hindu leader, did not harm the individual Muslim, or actually served him with loving care, was irrelevant to the political issue. It could not justify the exercise of political power over Muslims any more than the services rendered by British medical or educational missionaries could justify British imperialism. And even as the efforts of British apologists to present British rule over India as inspired by idealistic and altruistic motives failed to impress Indians, Gandhi's endeavors to clothe Hindu ambitions in terms of love and unity could not win Muslim hearts. He had some admirers and partisans among the Muslims, but the more he praised them, the more they were looked upon as traitors to their own community.

The man upon whom Gandhi at this time focused the limelight was Abdul Ghaffar Khan, the Red Shirt leader of the North-West Frontier Province, whom he fondly called Badshah Khan. Abul Kalam Azad, who till a year ago had been much publicized as the Congress President, was now in the background, and Abdul Ghaffar Khan filled the stage as the most prominent "nationalist" Muslim. It was Gandhi's aim to detach the North-West Frontier Province from Pakistan. He knew that the Congress ministry in that province was tottering and the Muslim League was daily gaining strength. Thus, with the majority of the people on the side of Pakistan and the ministry on the side of Hindustan, was produced what Ismay called a "bastard situation" that could not last long. Although Congress leaders claimed the North-West Frontier Province for the Indian Union, and although its representatives were in the constituent assembly, yet it appeared inevitable that a reference to the people would be made. In a straight contest between Hindustan versus Pakistan, the verdict of the people, who were 92 percent Muslims, would be in favor of Pakistan. Gandhi, therefore, conceived the idea of Pakhtoonistan or an independent North-West Frontier Province.

It might, at first sight, appear strange that the apostle of Indian unity to whom the demand for Pakistan appeared as a vivisection of mother India should advocate the establishment of still another independent state. But this was only a tactical move in a larger strategy aimed at reducing the territories of Pakistan and encircling it. Later, when Congress plans with regard to the state of Jammu and Kashmir would materialize, it would be possible to bring the North-West Frontier Province, which was contiguous with Kashmir, back into the Indian Union. For the moment, Gandhi's attention was centered on the scheme for Pakhtoonistan and on Badshah Khan, to whom he made the most touching references at his daily prayer meetings. Pyarelal recorded an incident showing the kind of sentiments that Gandhi was trying to nourish. On May 6, Abdul Ghaffar Khan sadly remarked: "Before long we shall become aliens in Hindustan. The end of our long fight for freedom will be to pass under the domination of Pakistan—away from Bapu [Gandhi], away from India, away from all of you. Who knows what the future holds for us?" When Gandhiji heard of this, he said, "Verily Badshah Khan is a fakir. Independence will come but the brave Pathan will lose his. They are faced with a grim prospect. But Badshah is a man of God." [36]

This "fakir," or "man without property," was one of the richest landlords of the North-West Frontier Province. He was looking forward, with the help of Congress, to perpetuate family rule in that province where the Chief Minister Dr. Khan Sahib was his brother and the other Muslim minister was related to him by marriage. Gandhi's fond epithet "Badshah," or King, was an oblique encouragement of the ambitions entertained by this "man of God." The brave Pathans, who would have enjoyed the blessings of freedom in a Hindu-dominated India were supposed to lose independence in Muslim Pakistan!

At the same time Gandhi was also striving to avert a referendum in the North-West Frontier Province. On May 8, he wrote to Mountbatten, "Referendum at this stage in the Frontier (or any Province for that matter) is a dangerous thing in itself. You have to deal with the material that faces you. In any case nothing should or can be done over Dr. Khan Sahib's head." [37] In the same letter he reverted to his favorite theme that power should be handed over to the Congress alone.

When he wrote this letter Gandhi was on his way to Calcutta. The movement for independent Bengal that had started there had possibilities that could be exploited to break up Pakistan. H. S. Suhrawardy, the Chief Minister of Bengal, had floated a plan for a Sovereign United Bengal with the support of Sarat Chandra Bose, the brother of Subhas Chandra Bose. The British governor was also in favor of it. For two hundred years the wealth of Bengal had poured into Calcutta, which was the second largest city in the British Empire and the capital of the province and its main port. Jute, the major commercial crop of Bengal, was grown mostly in East Bengal, but all the jute mills were in or around Calcutta. A united Bengal would keep the jute growing areas and the jute industry together in a single political entity, and was, therefore, supported by the Europeans who had a big stake in jute.

In Calcutta Gandhi met Sarat Chandra Bose, Suhrawardy, and other leaders, including Abul Hashim, the secretary of the Bengal Muslim League. The last, "to Gandhiji's agreeable surprise, based his case for a United Bengal on the ground of 'common language, common culture and common history that united the Hindus and Muslims of Bengal alike.' " [38] Gandhi insisted that in United Bengal *"every act of the Government must carry with it the cooperation of at least two-thirds of the Hindu minority in the executive and the legislature."* [39] This demand is the final answer to the endless propaganda by Gandhi, Nehru, and other Hindu publicists against the two-nation theory of Jinnah. In Bengal the Muslims had a bare majority of 55 percent. The Hindus were far more advanced educationally, economically, and politically. And yet, on behalf of this strong minority of nearly 45 percent, Gandhi asked for political safeguards of a kind he would never accept for Muslims in India. Much milder demands by Muslims had been refused by Hindu leaders, including Gandhi. The condition he suggested would have put the entire power of government in the hands of the minority and could only be justified on the basis of disparate interests of Hindus and Muslims. But paradoxically enough, Gandhi also wanted an admission by the Muslim League that Bengal had a common culture. As Pyarelal proceeds to elaborate,

> Since recognition of the fundamental unity of the people of Bengal, whether Hindus or Muslims, constituted the basis of Suhrawardy's proposal and since the Bengal Muslims were numerically preponderant in Pakistan, as envisaged by the Muslim League, repudiation of the two-nation theory in action by the Bengal Muslim League, with Jinnah's concurrence and consent, would leave nothing of the Pakistan plan based on that theory.[40]

At a conference on May 20, which was attended by Sarat Chandra Bose and other Hindu leaders and by Suhrawardy and some Muslim representatives, a tentative agreement for a sovereign united Bengal was drawn up,[41] but nothing came of it ultimately. There was a strong section of Hindus, led by the Hindu Mahasabha leader Dr. Shyamaprasad Mukherji, which was resolutely opposed to the scheme for a united Bengal. As early as April 4 the executive committee of the Bengal provincial congress had passed a resolution that

> If His Majesty's Government contemplate handing over its power to the existing Government of Bengal, which is determined on the formation of Bengal into a separate sovereign State . . . such portions of Bengal as are desirous of remaining within the Union of India should be allowed to remain so and be formed into a separate Province within the Union of India.[42]

The Assam congress took fright at the prospect of Assam being cut off from India if Bengal became a separate sovereign state. Both Nehru and Patel were against the proposal,[43] and Mountbatten revised the partition plan "to take away any option for independence either for Bengal or for any other Province." [44]

In the face of Gandhi's incessant propaganda for Hindu rule over the whole subcontinent, and his efforts to break up Pakistan even before it was formed, the Muslim League had to adopt an even stronger tone in its demand for Pakistan. Jinnah denounced the partition of the provinces of Bengal and the Punjab and reiterated the demand for a full-fledged Pakistan. During the course of an interview with a Reuters' correspondent on May 22, he answered in the affirmative a question on the need for a corridor to link East and West Pakistan. This reply caused a furore in the Indian press. Gandhi was becoming more and more violent in his campaign against Pakistan; on May 31, addressing his prayer meeting, he said: "Even if the whole of India burns, we shall not concede Pakistan." [45] Strange language indeed for the apostle of peace and nonviolence!

CHAPTER 8

The Partition Plan

H A V I N G obtained the acceptance of the Indian leaders to an outline of the revised partition plan, including an early date for the transfer of power, Mountbatten left for London on May 18, 1947, accompanied by V. P. Menon. The British Cabinet approved the plan, and Mountbatten on his return to Delhi put it to a conference of seven leaders—Nehru, Patel, Kripalani (then President of the Congress), Jinnah, Liaquat Ali Khan, Abdur Rab Nishtar, and Baldev Singh—on June 2. The plan had been cast in the form of a statement to be issued by His Majesty's Government on June 3, 1947.

The main thesis of the plan was that power should be transferred in accordance with the wishes of the Indian people themselves. Since no agreement had been reached among Indian political parties, the British government had, after full consultation with political leaders in India, devised a practical method for ascertaining the wishes of the people. The existing constituent assembly would continue to function. But, since it was clear that any constitution framed by that assembly could not apply to the parts of the country unwilling to accept it, a procedure was prescribed for ascertaining whether such parts of the country wished their constitution to be framed by the existing constituent assembly or wanted "a new and separate Constituent Assembly consisting of those areas which decided not to participate in the existing Constituent Assembly. When this has been done, it will be possible to determine the authority or authorities to whom power should be transferred."

In the Punjab, Bengal, and Sind the decision was left to the provincial assemblies. The Punjab and Bengal assemblies were to meet in two parts, one representing the Muslim majority districts and the other the rest of the province. The members of the two parts of each legislative assembly sitting separately would be empowered to vote whether or not the province should be partitioned. If a simple majority of either part decided in favor of partition, it would take place, and each part would decide which constituent assembly it would join. But in order that "the representatives of each part should know in advance which Constituent Assembly the province as a whole would join in the event of the two parts subsequently deciding to remain united," there was provision for a meeting of all members of the legislative assembly (except Europeans) to decide the issue as to which constituent assembly the province would join if it remained undivided. The boundaries of the two parts would be provisional until a boundary commission, appointed by the Governor-General in consultation with those concerned, should demarcate the final boundaries on the basis of an ascertainment of the contiguous majority areas of Muslims and non-Muslims and after having taken other factors into account.

If the Punjab decided on partition, a referendum would be held in the North-West Frontier Province to determine which constituent assembly it would join. There was a Congress ministry in this province, and two of the three provincial representatives were taking part in the existing constituent assembly. But because of the geographical position of the province and other considerations, it was necessary to give the province an opportunity to reconsider its position. Similarly, if it was decided that Bengal should be partitioned, a referendum would be held in the district of Sylhet, in Assam, to determine whether this predominantly Muslim district should join with contiguous East Bengal. In either case the referendum would be held under the aegis of the Governor-General and in consultation with the provincial government concerned. Means were also to be taken to ascertain the wishes of British Baluchistan. The plan provided that agreements with the tribes of the North-West Frontier Province would have to be negotiated by the appropriate successor authority. In regard to states, the policy contained in the Cabinet Mission memorandum of May 12, 1946, remained unchanged.

The plan concluded by stating that since the major political parties had repeatedly emphasized their desire for

> the earliest possible transfer of power in India. . . . [His Majesty's Government were] willing to anticipate the date of June 1948 [and would] introduce legislation during the current session for the transfer of power this year on a Dominion Status basis to one or two successor authorities according to the decisions taken as a result of this announcement. This will be without prejudice to the right of the Indian Constituent Assemblies to decide in due course whether or not the part of India in respect of which they have authority will remain within the British Commonwealth.[1]

In presenting the plan to the conference of seven leaders on June 2, Mountbatten said that "during the past five years he had taken part in a number of momentous meetings at which the fate of the war had been decided, but he could frankly remember no decisions reached likely to have such an important influence on world history as those which were to be taken at this meeting." Having made a last formal reference to the Cabinet Mission plan, which everybody knew was dead, he proceeded to point to the inevitability of partition in view of the attitudes of the Muslim League and the Congress, and emphasized the necessity for the utmost speed. He was

> at pains to stress the backing of the British Conservative Opposition. . . . With characteristic finesse, he introduced the new Paragraph 20 of the Plan under its heading "Immediate transfer of power," and defended the resulting Dominion Status not from the imputation of Britain's desire to retain a foothold beyond her time but from the possible charge of quitting on her obligations. Therefore, he said, it was abundantly clear that British assistance should not be withdrawn prematurely if it was still required.[2]

Nehru, in deference to whose views the plan had been recast, found it easy to indicate that the Congress would accept the plan. Jinnah said he would submit the plan to the Muslim League Council, which would meet a week later. Mountbatten pressed him for an immediate decision, but all that Jinnah could promise was that he would go to his masters, the people, with the sincere desire to persuade them to accept it.

Since it had been arranged that the British government would announce the plan in the House of Commons on June 3, Mountbatten asked for the reactions of the Congress and Muslim League Working Committees and of the Sikhs by midnight of June 2. He also secured the agreement of Nehru, Jinnah, and Baldev Singh to follow him with broadcasts to the people over the All-India Radio next evening.

The Congress Working Committee met the same day. According to Abul Kalam Azad, Gandhi spoke in favor of partition at this meeting.[3] The letter which Kripalani sent to the Viceroy, on behalf of the Congress Working Committee, accepted the plan, subject to "acceptance of the proposals by the Muslim League and a clear understanding that no further claims will be put forward." [4] Two more points were raised by the Congress. One was that in case the Indian Union decided to go out of the Commonwealth Pakistan should not be allowed to remain in it. The other was that in the North-West Frontier Province "the proposed referendum should provide for the people voting for independence and subsequent decision as to their relation with the rest of India." [5] The first point was a clearly inadmissible attempt to subordinate the foreign policy of Pakistan to that of India. On the second point Mountbatten reported to His Majesty's Government: "I pointed out to Nehru that since it was at Nehru's own request that I had dropped the original proposal to vote for Pakistan, Hindustan or independence, they could hardly expect me to reintroduce it at this stage." [6]

The Congress President also expressed concern for the Sikhs, saying that the plan "would result in injury to them unless great care were taken and their peculiar position in the Punjab were fully appreciated." [7] On behalf of the Sikhs, Baldev Singh wanted "instructions to the Boundary Commission included in the printed plan and wished them to take Sikh interests more fully into consideration." [8] For the present Mountbatten waived this point aside, although, as will be seen subsequently, the award of the boundary commission was influenced by these considerations.

Jinnah saw Mountbatten in the evening. Ismay, who was present at the interview, reports that Jinnah

> was in one of his difficult moods. After describing the plan as scandalous, he said that he himself would support it and do his best to get the Moslem League Council to do likewise, but he could not commit them in advance. After a good deal of "horse trading," the most that the Viceroy could squeeze out of him was an admission that Mr. Attlee might safely be advised that he could go ahead with his announcement about the plan to the House of Commons on the following day.[9]

The conference was resumed on the morning of June 3, and Mountbatten was able to announce the written acceptance of the Congress and the Sikhs. On behalf of the Muslim League he said: "Mr. Jinnah has given me assurances which I have accepted and which satisfy me." Jinnah kept silent and nodded his head in assent. At this meeting Mountbatten circulated a thirty-page memorandum on "The Administrative Consequences of Partition."

Attlee announced the plan in the House of Commons on June 3, 1947. It received the guarded approval of the opposition; they as well as the statesmen of the British Dominions of Canada, Australia, and New Zealand found satisfaction in the fact that both the Indian Union and Pakistan would remain in the Commonwealth. Winston Churchill observed

> It appears that the two conditions foreseen at the time of the Cripps Mission have been fulfilled . . . agreement between the Indian parties and . . . a period of Dominion status in which India or any part of it may freely decide whether to remain in the Commonwealth or not. If . . . these two conditions [are proved] to have been maintained, then . . . all parties in this House are equally pledged by the offer and the declaration that we have made.[10]

In the evening there were broadcasts by Mountbatten, Nehru, Jinnah, and Baldev Singh. Mountbatten said that it had been his firm opinion that "with a reasonable measure of goodwill between the communities a unified India would be by far the best solution." To his great regret it had been "impossible to obtain agreement on the Cabinet Mission Plan or any other plan that would preserve the unity of India. But there can be no question of coercing any large areas in which one community has a majority to live against their will under a Government in which another community has a majority. And the only alternative to coercion is Partition." The Muslim League had demanded the partition of India, and the Congress had used the same argument for demanding, in that event, the partition of certain provinces. "In fact neither side proved willing to leave a substantial area in which their community have a majority under the Government of the other." He sympathized with the Sikhs who were so distributed that the "partition of the Punjab, which they themselves desire can not avoid splitting them to a greater or lesser extent. The exact degree of the split will be left to the Boundary Commission on which they will of course be represented." [11]

Nehru said that the British government's announcement envisaged, on the one hand, the possibility of certain areas seceding from India and, on the other, it promised a big advance toward complete independence. "It is with no joy in my heart that I commend these proposals," he continued, "though I have no doubt in my mind that this is the right course. . . . We are little men serving great causes but because the cause is great some of that greatness falls upon us also." He expressed his deep appreciation of the labors of Mountbatten.

Jinnah said, "The Plan does not meet, in some important respects, our point of view and we can not say or feel that we are satisfied or that we agree with some of the matters dealt with by the Plan. It is for us now to consider whether the plan . . . should be accepted by us as a compromise or a settlement." He added that a final decision could only be taken by the Council of the All-India Muslim League. He paid a glowing tribute to Mountbatten: "The Viceroy has battled against various forces very bravely, and the impression that he has left on my mind is that he was actuated by a high sense of fairness and impartiality. It is up to us now to make his task less difficult, and help him . . . fulfil his mission of the transfer of power to the peoples of India in a peaceful and orderly manner." Then, in view of the forthcoming referendum in the North-West Frontier Province, he called upon the Muslim League of the province to withdraw the movement of civil disobedience. He concluded by appealing most earnestly to all to maintain peace and order.[12]

Baldev Singh, who followed, saw the plan not as a compromise; he preferred to call it a settlement. "It does not please everybody, not the Sikh community anyway but it is certainly something worthwhile. Let us take it at that." [13]

On June 4, Mountbatten held a press conference at which, according to all accounts, he gave a masterly performance. He said that at every stage and every step of the development of the June 3 plan he had worked hand in hand with Indian leaders, and that the plan came as no shock and no surprise to them. He emphasized the absolute determination of every responsible leader to maintain peace and avoid bloodshed, and said that the interim government was unanimous in its decision not to tolerate any more violence.

All the leaders, Mountbatten went on to say, had wanted speed in the actual transfer of power, but power could not be transferred unless the successor governments had a constitution, "One of the Governments was not even in being nor was it certain it was coming into being. The other Government would take time in framing their Constitution." The Government of India Act, 1935, suitably modified, provided the obvious answer but, as he explained, "Independence through Dominion Status is complete and the different administrations are at liberty to opt out of the Commonwealth whenever they please." In answer to a question he said: "We won't allow any separate part of India to come into the Commonwealth. But if the whole of India decides to break into two independent States, they could both come in." In reply to a question whether each Dominion would have full responsibility for its own defense, the Viceroy said that each state would be wholly and solely responsible for its own defense. He added "The process of partition of forces, if it is to be done in a way that will not cause the collapse of the morale and the disintegration of the army, must be done in an orderly and well-disciplined manner. When the partition has taken place, the States are absolutely at liberty to get together and have a combined plan for the defence of India or to make their own separate plans."

Referring to the position of the Sikhs, Mountbatten said he found that "It was mainly at the request of the Sikh community that the Congress had put forward the resolution on the partition of the Punjab . . . but when I . . . studied the distribution of the Sikh population . . . I was astounded to find that the plan which they had produced divided their community into two almost equal parts. I have spent a great deal of time both out here and in England in seeing whether there was any solution which would keep the Sikh community more together. . . . I have not found that solution."

Of the boundary commission he said: "It shall have representatives of all the parties. So far as it is humanly possible there will be no interference or dictation by the British Government."

In reply to a question on the need for a referendum in the North-West Frontier Province, Mountbatten explained that of all the provinces in India, the minority community enjoyed the heaviest weightage in the North-West Frontier Province. Though the minorities in that province represented only about 5 percent of the population, they had been given twelve seats out of a total of fifty in the assembly. Hence, the plan provided that the Viceroy, in consultation with the provincial government, should arrange for a referendum of the whole body of voters to the assembly. When asked why the voters had not been given the alternative to opt for independence, the Viceroy said that if the Congress and the Muslim League agreed upon it, he too would agree.

At the end of the press conference, Mountbatten said that he had the assurance of the British government, in agreement with the opposition, that they would rush through the necessary Act of Parliament for Indian independence within two months.[14] He announced that the transfer of power would take place on about August 15, 1947.

Mountbatten had been worried that Gandhi might oppose the plan, but after a meeting with Mountbatten, Gandhi said: "The British Government is not responsible for partition. The Viceroy has no hand in it. In fact he is as opposed to division as Congress itself. But if both of us, Hindus and Muslims, cannot agree on anything else, then the Viceroy is left with no choice." It was, he added, on the basis of the plan that agreement could be reached.[15] In fact, Gandhi had accepted partition, in principle, weeks ago but had been opposing it in public for tactical reasons. Abul Kalam Azad has left on record that soon after Gandhi's first meeting with Mountbatten on March 31, Patel

> was closeted with him [Gandhi] for over two hours. What happened during this meeting I [Abul Kalam Azad] do not know. But when I met Gandhiji again, I received the greatest shock of my life, for I found that he too had changed. He was still not openly in favour of partition but he no longer spoke so vehemently against it. What surprised and shocked me even more was that he began to repeat the arguments which Sardar Patel had already used.[16]

On June 9, the Council of the All-India Muslim League met in Delhi and passed a resolution in favor of the plan. The Council gave Jinnah full authority "to accept the fundamental principles of the plan as a compromise" and to take all necessary steps and decisions in connection with it.

A joint conference of Sikh organizations welcomed the division of the Punjab, but was of the considered view that no partition of the province that did not preserve the solidarity and integrity of the Sikh community would be acceptable to the Sikhs.

On June 14, the All-India Congress Committee passed a resolution accepting the plan, although it regretted "the secession of some parts of the country." Govind Ballabh Pant moved the resolution. Abul Kalam Azad and some others opposed it. Azad's distress is understandable; he was the only Congress leader who genuinely supported the Cabinet Mission plan. "But it was Patel who delivered the keynote address. He used the analogy of a diseased body and argued that if one limb was poisoned it must be removed quickly lest the entire organism suffer irreparably. The speech was typical of the man— pointed, brutally frank, unemotional." [17] Gandhi threw his support in favor of the resolution and it was carried by 157 votes to 29 with 32 abstentions.

The immediate effect of the announcement of the plan and its ac- ceptance by the main political parties was to still controversy and bring about a semblance of calm. At last the great issues that had dominated the Indian political scene for decades and had aroused such strong passions were settled. Among Muslims there was a sense of fulfillment at having achieved Pakistan. It might be truncated—no one realized quite to what extent—but it would at least be their own, and they would be free to build a just social order. For the 40 million Muslims left in India there were fraternal feelings and deep solici- tude. Both they and their more fortunate brethren in Pakistan had known that they would inevitably be left behind in India; yet they had willingly and cheerfully rallied to the support of the movement for Pakistan, had made great sacrifices in its cause, and had earned the enmity of the Hindu majority in whose midst they would have to live. It was an astonishing phenomenon, only possible among a people possessed of a profound feeling of brotherhood.

The Hindus, on the other hand, felt that Pakistan had been ex- torted from them in the face of their opposition, and they were re- solved to retrieve these lost territories. The All-India Congress Committee in its resolution accepting partition stated: "Geography and the mountains and the seas fashioned India as she is, and no human agency can change that shape or come in the way of her final destiny. Economic circumstances and the insistent demands of inter- national affairs make the unity of India still more necessary." [18] The Hindu Mahasabha was more frank and said: "India is one and indivisible and there will never be peace unless and until the sepa- rated areas are brought back into the Indian Union and made integral parts thereof." [19]

A still more dangerous trend was at work. Referring to the state of feeling among Congress leaders at the time of the passing of the All- India Congress Committee resolution, Abul Kalam Azad wrote:

All hearts were heavy at the idea of partition. Hardly anyone could accept the resolution without mental reservations. . . . What was worse was the kind of insidious communal propaganda which was gaining ground. It was being openly said in certain circles that the Hindus in Pakistan need have no fear as there would be 45 millions of Muslims in India and if there was any oppression of Hindus in Pakistan, the Muslims in India would have to bear the consequences. In the meeting of the All-India Congress Committee the members from Sind opposed the resolution vehemently. They were given all kinds of assurances. Though not on the public platform, in private discussion they were even told by some people that if they suffered any disability or indignity in Pakistan, India would retaliate on the Muslims in India.[20]

Azad did not specify what circles were advocating this theory of hostages, but it is not difficult to surmise that he was referring to Patel, Kripalani (who was from Sind), and other aggressively anti-Muslim leaders. There were some among the Muslims, too, who subscribed to the theory of mutual hostages. It was foolish and irresponsible talk, since, considerations of morality and humanity apart, Muslims in India were three times as numerous as non-Muslims in Pakistan. Jinnah himself, on every suitable occasion, emphasized that the non-Muslim minority would have equal rights as citizens of Pakistan and would be entitled to the full protection of the law.

By far the worst and most destructive sentiments were prevalent among the Sikhs. They had insisted on the partition of the Punjab but now were seething with anger at the consequences of their own demand. On the surface they were quiet, and many people were misled when Baldev Singh called the partition plan a settlement, not a compromise as Jinnah had suggested. But the calm was deceptive and intentionally so. The Sikh leaders were working feverishly on a scheme for bringing their community together and regaining their lost integrity. Their scheme was madly nihilistic and it was to bring immense suffering upon the people of the Punjab, including the Sikhs.

The plan accepted by the two main political parties and by the Sikhs conceded the principle of partition to the Muslim League but almost everything else, including the time and manner of its implementation, to the Hindu Congress. This was not surprising since the plan had been drafted by a Hindu official, V. P. Menon, under the instructions of Nehru, and had been approved by the latter in draft. The Muslim League's concept of partition had been the division of India between two successor authorities in a fair and impartial manner. The Congress view was that certain areas had seceded from the parent body, which was the only true successor of British power. This difference in points of view between the Congress and the League affected the administrative implementation of the partition plan at many a point.

Pakistan had to prove its claim to each of its territories by a positive vote. Even the predominantly Muslim provinces of Sind and Baluchistan, whose representatives were not taking part in the constituent assembly, had to give a fresh verdict in favor of Pakistan. No such test was imposed on the Hindu majority provinces. The results, of course, would not have been any different, in either case.

But the most serious handicap for Pakistan was in the time allowed for the implementation of the plan—seventy-two days. V. P. Menon after noting the acceptance of the plan said: "Acceptance was one thing; its implementation was a different matter altogether. Here was a task which normally should have taken years to accomplish but which had to be compressed into the short space of a few weeks." [21] And who, it may be asked, was responsible for this compression with all its tragic consequences, the loss of millions of lives and untold suffering? Those who had bargained for a very early transfer of power—Mountbatten and Nehru and Patel and V. P. Menon himself!

CHAPTER 9

Problems of Partition

THE TIME from June 3, 1947, when the partition plan was announced, to August 15, 1947, the date of the transfer of power to the two new Dominions—the Union of India and Pakistan—was seventy-two days in all. It took some days to sort out the major problems and to set up the machinery of partition; the effective period of work was just the two months stipulated by Sardar Patel. Within this period a host of problems had to be solved and innumerable administrative tasks had to be undertaken and completed. The problems were far more numerous and onerous for Pakistan than for the Dominion of India. The Government of India in Delhi was a going concern, which would continue to function much the same as before, except that it would cease to exercise jurisdiction over the areas which were to form Pakistan. The number of British and Muslim officials who might leave its service was not big enough to call for a major reorganization. The diplomatic and trade missions that had been established abroad were taken over by the Union of India. The system of currency and banking, together with other economic and financial institutions, was operating on an all-India basis and its control remained in the hands of the Government of India. The Indian railways, ports, posts, and telegraphs linked the various parts of the subcontinent in a unified system of communications controlled from Delhi. Almost all the industrial installations and research institutions of the Government of India were situated in the territories of the Indian Union. Central government archives and records were in Delhi and the Imperial Library was in Calcutta. Army, air force, and navy headquarters were in Delhi near the Department of Defence. All ordnance factories and nearly all military store depots were located in the Indian Dominion. The reorganization and division of the armed forces presented India with far fewer problems than Pakistan.

For Pakistan by far the most important task was to devise an administrative machinery capable of performing all the functions of a modern government, and to establish this government in a new capital. Elections to a new constituent assembly had to be held and a new federal court had to be set up. Personnel, reference books, equipment had to be divided, and records and current files to be split up or duplicated. Arrangements for the separate collection of central government revenues had to be made to provide the financial resources for running the administration. Since partition was to take place in the middle of the fiscal year, which ran from April to March, there arose budgetary and accounting complications that had to be resolved. Then there were questions relating to currency and exchange. Pakistan had to have its own currency, but it was physically impossible to print new notes and mint new coins by August 15. Interim arrangements had to be made until Pakistan could set up its own currency authority with its own notes and coins. Trade and economic controls presented another set of problems. If India and Pakistan were immediately to embark on divergent policies, economic activity in both countries might suffer injury. A proper trade agreement between the two countries would take time to prepare. Meanwhile, temporary agreements for the movement of commodities and for setting up tariffs and economic controls were necessary.

The share of each Dominion in the assets and liabilities of the undivided Government of India had to be determined. Different categories of assets had to be examined separately and divided on an equitable basis. For instance, the allocation of fixed assets like railway and telegraph lines could only be done on a territorial basis; military stores had to be divided on the basis of army units allocated to each Dominion. For the apportionment of assets like cash balances and foreign exchange and the net liability of the government a different formula was required.

The provinces had yet to cast their vote for or against Pakistan. In particular, the referendum in the North-West Frontier Province and in Sylhet needed careful organization and intensive political work. After the provinces had voted, the vitally important problem of the boundary between India and Pakistan would arise. In the two partitioned provinces, Bengal and the Punjab, new provincial governments would have to be organized.

The relationship between the Indian states and the two Dominions had also to be determined. It was a task fraught with dangerous possibilities.

These great changes had to find their constitutional formulation in parliamentary legislation and in adaptations of the Government of India Act, 1935, to provide the interim constitutions of the two new Dominions.

This brief and by no means complete outline of major problems is enough to show that partition and the transfer of power made the most strenuous demands on the energies of political leaders and officials. These varied problems had to be undertaken simultaneously, although logically some should have preceded others. In theory, the immense administrative tasks of dividing assets and liabilities, the civil services and the armed forces, should have followed the verdict of the provinces and the passage of parliamentary legislation, since only then would the issue of partition and the establishment of two new Dominions have been finally and formally decided. But this would have wasted precious time. After acceptance of the June 3 plan by the Congress, the Muslim League, and the Sikhs, partition was a foregone conclusion. Immediate steps were therefore taken to set up the administrative machinery of partition both in the central government and in the Punjab and Bengal. Every day, indeed every hour, counted. To emphasize the urgency, Mountbatten devised a tear-off calendar which showed in bold letters the number of days left to prepare for the transfer of power. Such a calendar was placed on the table of each official dealing with the problems of partition. A prodigious amount of work was put through. All exerted themselves to the utmost. Officers and staff worked, literally, day and night. It was a race against time, which seemed to be moving faster and faster every moment. A report or a statistical return, which normally would have taken weeks to compile, had to be prepared in a day or two, and the staff of a whole office would work twenty-four hours or more at a stretch to get it ready in time. Then it was discussed with the other side, and as often as not had to be revised. Immediate orders had to issue for giving effect to the decision and a watch kept over its implementation. A delay in one field might upset the timetable in another interlinked field and slow down progress everywhere. The consequences of delay would be far more serious for Pakistan which would be so much the less equipped by August 15. I was in the thick of the work; yet, looking back, I am astonished that so much was accomplished in so short a time.

In the account that follows, each main topic is dealt with separately, but it should be borne in mind that these separate strands were inextricably intertwined in time and in fact.

The event of first importance was, of course, the vote of the provinces.

Both in the Punjab and in Bengal, the same pattern of voting was followed. After the majority in the provincial assembly voted in favor of joining a new constituent assembly, separate meetings of representatives of the Muslim majority districts and non-Muslim majority districts were held. The representatives of the latter voted by a majority for a partition of the province, and the former also by a majority against it. Since the vote of either group for partition was decisive, partition was declared. East Punjab and West Bengal decided to join the constituent assembly of the Indian Union; West Punjab and East Bengal decided to join the new constituent assembly of Pakistan. Elections to the Pakistan constituent assembly from East Bengal and West Punjab were held in due course.

The Sind legislative assembly decided by a majority to join the constituent assembly of Pakistan.

For Baluchistan, the Viceroy decided to entrust the responsibility to the Shahi Jirga and the nonofficial members of the Quetta municipality; they decided unanimously to join the constituent assembly of Pakistan.

In Sylhet the referendum was won for Pakistan by a majority of votes—239,619 to 184,041—and the district was incorporated into East Bengal.

The referendum in the North-West Frontier Province was the subject of a stormy controversy. It was to be held under the aegis of the Governor-General in consultation with the provincial government. The Chief Minister, Dr. Khan Sahib, and his brother, Abdul Ghaffar Khan, the Red Shirt leader, were with the Congress, and strongly opposed the Muslim League. They were now in a quandary because the referendum was sure to result in a verdict for Pakistan. According to Abul Kalam Azad, when the partition plan came up for discussion in the Congress Working Committee on June 2, and Gandhi spoke in favor of it, Abdul Ghaffar Khan "was completely stunned." When, after some time, he was able to speak, he said again and again that it would be an act of treachery if the Congress came to terms with the Muslim League over partition and deserted the Red Shirts. He reminded the Working Committee of his past services to the Congress and appealed to them to save him from his enemies. Dr. Khan Sahib also joined the committee meeting. He had been told by Lord Mountbatten about the plan for a referendum in the North-West Frontier Province and had been asked if he had any objection to it. The two brothers did not want a referendum but could not refuse it, because to do so would be to admit that they did not have the support of a majority in the North-West Frontier Province. On their return to the Province, they raised the slogan of independence for the North-West Frontier Province.[1]

The slogan of an independent frontier state or Pakhtoonistan had been provided for the Khan brothers by Gandhi. Behind this demand was the far-reaching strategy of reabsorbing the Province at a later stage after contiguity with it had been gained through the state of Jammu and Kashmir. For, as Mountbatten reported to the British government in June, 1947: "Nehru quite openly admitted that the NWFP [North-West Frontier Province] could not possibly stand by itself. . . . Nehru spoke about Khan Sahib wishing to join the Union of India at a subsequent stage." [2]

Gandhi employed all the weapons in his armory to detach the North-West Frontier Province from Pakistan; but the facts of geography, the logic of the situation, and the will of the people were too strong for him. The first shot fired was the demand by the Congress Working Committee that the voters' choice should be widened to include independence. Mountbatten, however, pointed out that the original partition plan had been revised at Nehru's instance to exclude the option of independence for any province.[3]

Having been defeated in this, Gandhi tried, on the ground of fear of violence, to avert the referendum for the time being, and thus to avoid a definite decision in favor of Pakistan. On June 7, he wrote to Nehru, charging him with being largely responsible for the situation in regard to the referendum. In reply, Nehru wrote a long note:

> The British Government and the Viceroy are definitely committed to this referendum. Some of us are also more or less committed. . . . The question of referendum, therefore, appears to be a settled one and it is not quite clear how we can get out of it. For the Viceroy it is still more difficult. Any change in the plan . . . may even lead to conflict on a big scale.

This is typical of Nehru. He never fully committed himself, and had no compunction in trying to get out of any undertaking; unfortunately it was not quite clear to him how he and the Congress could get out of the commitment for a referendum in the North-West Frontier Province. Nehru explained that in order to ensure peaceful conditions the referendum "should be organised by British military officers to be imported from outside"; the provincial government would be closely associated with arrangements for it, and there was not much chance of "any big violent conflict." [4]

About the same time, Gandhi asked Mountbatten to persuade Jinnah to go to the North-West Frontier Province, in order to put the case for Pakistan to the leaders and the people there, so that a referendum could be avoided, and the risk of bloodshed removed. When Jinnah agreed, provided the Congress "undertake that they will not interfere with the people of the Frontier," Gandhi wrote back that he could not "ask the Congress to commit harakiri." [5] Since Jinnah had not taken the bait, or in Gandhian parlance, had refused to "woo" Abdul Ghaffar Khan, his brother, and his other colleagues, Gandhi asked Abdul Ghaffar Khan to "approach and woo the League instead." On June 18, Abdul Ghaffar Khan saw Jinnah but nothing came of it. Indeed, nothing could come of it because Abdul Ghaffar Khan made no secret of his being totally opposed to Pakistan. One of his conditions to Jinnah was that "in case Pakistan, after independence, decided to stay under British domination, the Pathans in the Settled Districts or in the Tribal areas should have the power to opt out of such a Dominion and form a separate independent State." [6] But he was quite content that the North-West Frontier Province should be a part of the Indian Union which also was going to be a Dominion in the British Commonwealth!

On June 21, the Congress committee in the North-West Frontier

Province and the Khudai Khidmatgars, or Red Shirts, passed a resolution that "a free Pathan State of all Pakhtoons be established." [7]
The Afghan government also took a hand in the campaign waged by
Gandhi and Abdul Ghaffar Khan for Pakhtoonistan. There were reports of Congress emissaries having approached the Afghan government, who sent notes to the British and Indian governments, demanding that the areas west of the river Indus, which were inhabited by
Afghans, should be given the right to decide whether their future
should lie with India, Afghanistan, or be independent. Lord Listo-
well, who had replaced Lord Pethick-Lawrence as Secretary of State
for India, stated categorically that "Afghanistan has no right to interfere, as they are trying to interfere, in the rights of the North-West
Frontier Province." [8]

But neither the efforts of Gandhi and Abdul Ghaffar Khan, nor
those of the Afghan government, were of any avail against the declared will of the people of the North-West Frontier Province. On
June 29, Gandhi wrote to Mountbatten: "Badshah Khan [Abdul
Ghaffar Khan] writes . . . that he had failed in his move for a free
Pathanistan [Pakhtoonistan] therefore, the referendum would go on
without any interference by his followers, the latter abstaining from
voting either way. He fully realises that in this case the Frontier
would probably go to Pakistan." [9] Gandhi was still hoping that the
boycott of the referendum by the Congress and the Red Shirts would
be effective. On July 5, he wrote to Abdul Ghaffar Khan: "Boycott
would certainly result in a legal victory for Pakistanis but it would be
a moral defeat, if without the slightest fear of violence from your
side, the bulk of the Pathans refrained in a dignified manner from
participating in the referendum." [10] Even these hopes were doomed
to failure.

The Muslim League of the North-West Frontier Province had
called off the civil disobedience movement on June 3 in response to
Quaid-i-Azam Jinnah's broadcast that evening. It was in the obvious
interest of the Muslim League that conditions in the province, before
and during the referendum, should be peaceful. Abdul Qayyum
Khan, the Pir of Manki Sharif, and other leaders threw themselves
heart and soul into the campaign for the referendum. Muslim students from Aligarh University and other colleges played a notable
part in carrying the message of Pakistan to every village. There was a
danger that the Red Shirts might create disturbances. An agitation

was being carried on by the Red Shirts to persuade people not to vote, and Mountbatten wrote to Gandhi that "any action of this sort is likely to lead to the very violence you and I are anxious to avoid." [11]

At the insistence of the Congress, the Governor of the North-West Frontier Province, Sir Olaf Caroe, was replaced by Lt. General Sir Rob Lockhart. Under Referendum Commissioner Brigadier J. B. Booth, forty British officers of the Indian army, with experience of the North-West Frontier Province, were put in charge of the referendum, and 50,000 troops were concentrated in the province to help the police keep order. The referendum, which was held from July 6 to 17, was peaceful. There were 289,244 votes for Pakistan against 2,874 for India. The votes cast for Pakistan were 51 percent of the total electorate. But since all the voters never turn up in any election, a fairer idea of the result is gained if the fact is taken into consideration that only 65 percent of the electorate had voted in 1946, and that on this basis, 78 percent had voted for Pakistan. Thus each of the territories which were to comprise Pakistan—East Bengal, Sylhet, West Punjab, Sind, Baluchistan, and the North-West Frontier Province gave a positive vote for inclusion in Pakistan.

A major task was the reorganization of the interim government. During the seventy-two days the energies of the Indian government were concentrated on the problems of partition. The normal work of administration came virtually to a standstill. Soon after the announcement of the June 3 plan, the cabinet agreed that no orders would be passed by any department that might adversely affect or embarrass either of the successor governments and that a list of all decisions taken by the ministers would be placed before the cabinet each week for its information. A few weeks later, the latter decision was revised and all departments were asked to send a list of the decisions taken during the day to the Private Secretary of the Viceroy every evening. Restrictions were imposed on higher appointments. Decisions on important matters were to be taken only with the approval of the cabinet. On July 19, after the Indian Independence Act was passed, the cabinet was reconstituted into two separate groups representing the two successor governments of India and Pakistan. Each group was responsible for the administration of all portfolios of its Dominion. In matters of common concern the two cabinets met under the chairmanship of the Viceroy. Each department of government was split into two departments—an Indian department, staffed by those who had opted for India, and a Pakistan department, manned by those who had chosen to serve in Pakistan.

Another important factor was the machinery of partition. A committee of cabinet was formed to consider the memorandum on The Administrative Consequences of Partition that had been presented by Mountbatten to the conference of leaders on June 3. The committee was presided over by the Viceroy, and had as its members Sardar Patel and Rajendra Prasad from the Congress, and Liaquat Ali Khan and Abdur Rab Nishtar representing the League. On June 27, after the provinces had voted in favor of partition, the committee was replaced by the Partition Council. The Viceroy was chairman of the Council. Sardar Patel and Rajendra Prasad, with Rajagopalachari as alternate member, represented the Congress. In view of the vital importance of the issues that had to be decided by the Partition Council, Jinnah decided to be on the Council. Pakistan was represented by the Quaid-i-Azam and Liaquat Ali Khan, with Abdur Rab Nishtar as alternate member.

The Partition Council worked through a Steering Committee of two officials—H. M. Patel of the Indian Civil Service on behalf of India, and I representing Pakistan. A partition secretariat, with the members of the Steering Committee as its two secretaries, was established. To assist the Steering Committee, ten expert committees, each dealing with an important group of subjects, were set up. One expert committee dealt with organization, records, and personnel; another with assets and liabilities; a third with central revenues; a fourth with contracts; then came currency and exchange; budget and accounts; economic relations (controls and trade); domicile; and foreign relations; finally, there was the Armed Forces Reconstitution Committee. A large number of departmental committees assisted the expert committees. For example, the expert committee on organization, records, and personnel had 20 departmental committees, and that for assets and liabilities had 21. A departmental committee dealt with one or two Departments such as Agriculture, Industries, Commerce, Railways, Works. The committees were composed of equal numbers of Muslim and non-Muslim officials of the Government of India. The former represented Pakistan, and the latter India. On the Armed Forces Reconstitution Committee and its subcommittees, however, there were a number of British officers. The committees were given full powers to settle their own procedure, to examine official witnesses and records, and generally to obtain any information necessary to complete their work within a specified time. The work of partition was given absolute priority over all other work.

The Steering Committee's function was to make sure that concrete proposals were evolved on time by the expert committees, that these proposals dovetailed into each other and formed a comprehensive whole, that recommendations were submitted to the Partition Council for decision in a suitable form, and that the decisions reached were implemented. The Steering Committee was also asked to provide day-to-day advice, guidance, and direction to the expert committees and was required to keep in close touch with the Partition Council. The Steering Committee played a key role in the work of partition. On the one hand it maintained intimate and continuous liaison with the expert committees and the departmental committees and was able to smooth out difficulties before they had time to harden. On the other hand, by working as secretaries to the Partition Council, the members of the Steering Committee acquired a first hand knowledge of the way in which the Partition Council was likely to react to a proposal. Of course, each member of the Steering Committee was in close contact with the political leaders of his own side. The Steering Committee could thus move with a sure step in an arena bristling with controversies. For the great political debates of the last few years had left their mark on the administration. What might at first sight appear as purely administrative or financial matters were often charged with hidden political meaning and, hence, were liable to arouse an emotional storm.

The committees began their work in the third week of June and were expected to submit their reports within a month. Every effort was made to present to the Partition Council agreed recommendations for their decision. The committees were able to reach agreement in their recommendations over a considerable area, and the Steering Committee, which considered the reports in the first instance was successful in reaching agreement on the bulk of unsettled points.

This was possible only because H. M. Patel and I reached an understanding at the very outset to be completely frank with each other. We knew each other well enough to realize that open diplomacy offered the best chances of success. There were large areas where the interests of the two Dominions clashed, but the conflict could be resolved sooner by bringing it out into the open than by skirting around it. The advantages and disadvantages of any proposal for India and Pakistan were, therefore, freely discussed between us. The fact that negotiations ranged over a wide field was a help rather than a hindrance, since it facilitated give and take. H. M. Patel was burdened with a large number of senior Hindu officials who met each morning to advise him. Although the advisers were agreed as to the objective, which was to secure India's interest at Pakistan's expense, they were by no means agreed as to the methods to be used to achieve it, and that caused some confusion. Since the number of senior Muslim officers was far smaller, I had a much freer hand, which was an advantage. The knowledge I had gained (during eleven years of service in the Finance department) of how the other departments of the Government of India—civil and military—functioned stood me in good stead. On all major issues I consulted the Quaid-i-Azam and Liaquat Ali Khan or other ministers concerned, such as Abdur Rab Nishtar or Ghulam Muhammad on financial questions because he had been designated as the future Finance Minister of Pakistan. The confidence they placed in my judgment helped me immensely in the speedy transaction of business. Time, it is needless to repeat, was of the essence, at any rate as far as Pakistan was concerned. A deadlock could seldom hurt India, which was in possession of almost everything.

On his side H. M. Patel enjoyed the confidence of Sardar Patel. When H. M. Patel and I failed to agree, the Partition Council was, in general, equally divided and acrimonious debates would ensue. Sardar Patel was blunt to the point of incivility; the Quaid-i-Azam had a great facility for producing the incisive phrase. Sparks would fly and at times tempers would rise.

The differences were further reduced by the Partition Council. Mountbatten, who made a superb chairman, was determined not to let a deadlock develop, and used his ingenuity and resourcefulness to keep things moving. It will suffice to give one example of his technique. Pakistan was deficient in printing presses; Karachi, which had been selected as the capital of Pakistan, had no modern press. On the other hand, India had many first class printing presses. The Government of India itself owned a printing press in Delhi and another in

Simla, which was not put to much use. No modern government can function without a printing press. Pakistan representatives suggested that the Government of India press at Simla should be transferred to Karachi. This was opposed by the Indian representatives. When the matter came up before the Partition Council, Sardar Patel adopted an intransigent attitude. On no account would he ever agree to any piece of machinery being transferred to Pakistan. The attitude was patently unreasonable, and Mountbatten, at first, tried to persuade Patel to relent, but when the combined efforts of the Pakistan leaders and Mountbatten failed to move Patel, Mountbatten came out with the proposal that he would ask the British government to give top priority to an order for a modern press which would be delivered to Pakistan within a few months. To any one who knew the critical condition of industrial production in Great Britain at this time, the offer meant nothing—it would take a few years for the printing press to reach Pakistan. But because Mountbatten made the proposal sound so convincing, he succeeded in creating an illusion of a solution, and the Partition Council was able to resume its work.

The Partition Council continued in its functions even after August 15. It was reconstituted to consist of two ministerial representatives of India and two representatives of Pakistan: one a minister, and the other either a minister or the High Commissioner for Pakistan in India.

Organizations similar to the Partition Council of the central government were set up in the partitioned provinces. They were presided over by the provincial governors and consisted of an equal number of representatives of the Congress (including those allied with the Congress, like the Sikhs) in the province and the Muslim League. Thus there was the Bengal Separation Council, the Assam Separation Council, and the Punjab Partition Committee.

In the event the Partition Council of the central government or the provincial partition committees failed to reach agreement, the question was to be referred to the Arbitral Tribunal for decision. The Arbitral Tribunal, to which Indian representatives were induced with great difficulty to agree, was presided over by an independent chairman, Sir Patrick Spens, the former Chief Justice of India. It had as its members one representative of India, Justice Sir Harilal J. Kania, and one representative of Pakistan, Justice M. Ismail. Disputes over the division of assets and liabilities and other related matters in the central government and the partitioned provinces could be referred to it for decision up to March 31, 1948; then it would cease to exist.

The Indian Independence Act, 1947, gave legal form to the decision for partition and to the establishment of two independent Dominions—India and Pakistan—as of August 15, 1947. The use of the name India, for only a part of what was formerly British India, was to cause a great deal of confusion in the outside world. The Congress leaders insisted on it in order to establish continuity of identity with British India, and to stake a claim as sole inheritor of the treaty obligations of undivided India and of its membership in the United Nations and other international bodies.

The Independence Act was shown to the Congress and Muslim League leaders in bill form before being introduced in England in the House of Commons on July 4. It defined the territories of the two Dominions, subject to final determination by a boundary commission to be appointed by the Governor-General. It provided that "for each of the new Dominions, there shall be a Governor-General who shall be appointed by His Majesty [but] the same person may be Governor-General of both the new Dominions." The Governor-General was to be a constitutional Governor-General "with full power to assent in His Majesty's name to any law of the Legislature of that Dominion" but with no power to disallow laws or to reserve them "for the signification of His Majesty's pleasure." The constituent assembly of each of the two Dominions was to function as the legislature and was to be entrusted with "full powers to make laws for that Dominion including laws having extraterritorial operation," even though such laws might be "repugnant to the law of England or to the provisions of this or any existing or future Act of Parliament of the United Kingdom." The words "Indiae Imperator" and the "Emperor of India" were omitted from the titles of the King of England. Each of the two Dominions was recognized as an independent state; and, as of August 15, 1947, the British government would have no control over the affairs of the new Dominions.

Under the Independence Act the suzerainty of the King of England over the Indian states lapsed, as did the treaties and agreements between His Majesty and the rulers of the Indian states. The British government's authority in the tribal areas was also relinquished.

However, the agreements with Indian states and tribal areas relating to customs, transit and communications, posts and telegraphs, or other like matters were to continue in force until they were denounced by the ruler of the Indian state or person having authority in the tribal areas on the one hand, or by the Dominion concerned on the other hand, or until they were superseded by subsequent agreements.

The Governor-General was given powers as of June 3 to make orders for bringing the Indian Independence Act into effective operation, for dividing assets and liabilities between the two Dominions, for amending and adapting the Government of India Act, 1935, and orders made thereunder, and for similar other purposes. These powers were to continue till March 31, 1948, unless either Dominion decided to terminate them earlier. With the powers given him, the Governor-General was to make "provision for the division of the Indian Armed Forces of His Majesty between the new Dominions and the command and governance of these forces until the division is completed." He was, in addition, to make provisions facilitating the withdrawal of British forces from the new Dominions. The British forces were to continue under the jurisdiction and authority of the British government. Those members of the Secretary of State's services who would continue to serve under the government of either of the new Dominions were guaranteed their existing conditions of service as far as remuneration, pension, etc., were concerned. Some other miscellaneous and transitional provisions completed the bill. It had a smooth passage through both Houses of Parliament and received the Royal Assent on July 18. The Indian Independence Act, which marked the end of British rule in India, was, according to Prime Minister Attlee, not an abdication, but the fulfillment of Britain's mission in India. India's and Pakistan's membership in the Commonwealth helped to soothe British sentiment. A former Viceroy, Lord Halifax, speaking in the House of Lords said, "In the long run influence is a very much finer and more durable and eternal thing than power."

Also to be resolved was the question of whether there should be one Governor-General or two. The deal between Mountbatten and the Congress leaders for a very early transfer of power in return for acceptance of Dominion Status by the Congress had one unforeseen consequence that was to leave its mark on the history of the partition of India. Since it was obvious to anyone with the slightest administrative experience that the processes of partition could not possibly be completed within two months, some provision for resolving unsettled problems had to be made. Mountbatten's solution was that he should continue as Governor-General of both the Dominions for eight or nine months from August 15, 1947, onward. He had won the trust of Congress and the Muslim League leaders and could, therefore, confidently expect that both would be agreeable to his staying on as common Governor-General. The Heads of Agreement, which he had presented to the Congress and the Muslim League on May 17, made a proposal to this effect. The Congress had no difficulty in accepting it, since by now Nehru and Sardar Patel were sure that Mountbatten would play their game. Moreover, they wanted to use his influence (as Viceroy and cousin of the King of England) over the princes to secure the accession of Indian states. Nehru wrote to Mountbatten: "We agree to the proposal that during this interim period the Governor General of the two Dominions should be common to both States. . . . For our part we should be happy if you would continue in this office and help us with your advice and experience." [12]

Jinnah did not mistrust Mountbatten at that time, but wanted him to continue after August 15 in the capacity of a super Governor-General, appointed by the Crown, and with powers to arbitrate between the claims of the two Dominions. Only thus could the division of assets and liabilities be carried out in a just manner. But this was the last thing the Congress wanted. Their deal with Mountbatten for an early transfer of power was made in order to deny Pakistan a fair chance of establishing itself. The British government, having decided to end their rule in India, were anxious to retain no responsibility for Indian affairs after August 15. Jinnah continued to press his proposal till the last, but it was not acceptable to the Congress or to the British government. That left only the proposal for a common Governor-General that was incorporated into the Indian Independence Act.

Jinnah, who by temperament and life-long training had a constitutional bent of mind, could not see how a common constitutional Governor-General faced with conflicting advice from two Dominion cabinets could discharge his responsibility properly. All he could do was try to persuade, but he would have no power to resolve the unsettled problems of partition. Although Jinnah himself was the undisputed leader of Muslims and enjoyed wide powers as President of the Muslim League, he never overstepped his authority and insisted on prior approval by the Working Committee or the Muslim League Council whenever this was constitutionally necessary. Mountbatten, and others, were often infuriated by what appeared to them as excessive formalism, and they suspected that it covered a deep strategy of noncommitment and was meant to gain time. In actual fact, it was wholly sincere. Jinnah was firmly convinced that one could act with responsibility only within the limits of powers constitutionally conferred. A common Governor-General for two independent governments with opposed interests was, to his mind, a constitutional absurdity.

Strong as the constitutional argument against a common Governor-General was, there was an even stronger political aspect. The powerful propaganda machine of the Congress concentrated on the theme that Pakistan was nothing but a temporary secession of certain territories from India that would soon be reabsorbed. A common head of state for India and Pakistan, who would inevitably be stationed most of the time in India, would strengthen this belief in India and Pakistan and throughout the world. What sort of independence have we got, the people of Pakistan might ask, when the Governor-General of India is our Governor-General, and the King of England is our King?

And this impression would be greatly reinforced when they saw that three out of four provincial governors were British, and that the Commanders-in-Chief of the army, navy, and air force were also British, not to speak of a large number of other civil and military British officials whom Pakistan would have to employ for want of experienced administrators and military officers. Pakistan would have a severe ordeal to face in its earlier years. Only a strong faith in their destiny as an independent nation could sustain the people through the trials and tribulations ahead of them. There must, therefore, be a visible act of cleavage between India and Pakistan. If the Quaid-i-Azam himself became the Governor-General of Pakistan, he would be a living symbol of Pakistan's independent status. His towering figure would overshadow everything else and cover up British governors and military and civilian officers. Perhaps Pakistan would lose some millions worth of assets, which the good offices of Mountbatten might have secured for it but, in the struggle for survival that lay ahead, moral factors would count far more than material losses. Such were the considerations the Quaid-i-Azam and his ministers had to weigh.

As June wore on, and Jinnah deliberated over this matter, Mountbatten's impatience was daily mounting. He had set his heart on going down in history, not only as the Viceroy who had been instrumental in granting independence to India and Pakistan, but also as the great statesman who had helped and guided the two new Dominions in their first faltering steps as independent states. The Congress leaders from whom difficulty might have been expected in accepting a Britisher as the first Governor-General of new India had given their warm assent; but here was this difficult man Jinnah, holding his own counsel, and putting off a decision from day to day. What could he possibly intend? Was it not obvious to him that, without Mountbatten's help, Pakistan as the weaker party would have a raw deal at the hands of the Congress, who were in possession of almost all the assets of India? There were, no doubt, advantages for Pakistan in having an impartial chairman to preside over the processes of partition till their completion. Mountbatten pointed them out to everyone he thought could influence Jinnah, and sent Ismay and Miéville two or three times to Jinnah, hoping that Jinnah would be persuaded. Ismay wrote:

> It was not until the end of June, that we learned that . . . Jinnah had decided to nominate himself as Governor-General, and to make Liaquat Ali Khan Prime Minister. In breaking the news to Mountbatten, Mr. Jinnah expressed the hope that it would make no difference to his acceptance of office as the first Governor-General of India, or to his being Chairman of a Joint Defence Council of the two countries. This unexpected turn of events was a blow. We had all felt that the best hope of an orderly transfer of power, an equitable partition of assets, and the establishment of friendly relations between the two new Dominions would be for them to start off with the same Governor-General.[13]

Mountbatten was wounded in his tenderest spot: his vanity was hurt and his pride affronted. He had lost face with the British government, who had been led to believe that Mountbatten was acceptable to both Dominions as common Governor-General. To make matters worse, he and his advisers totally misunderstood the motives behind Jinnah's decision. A meeting was called at Ismay's house on July 2, "to devise a formula whereby His Excellency the Viceroy could remain Governor General of both Dominions and at the same time satisfy Mr. Jinnah's vanity." [14] Vanity had nothing to do with the Quaid-i-Azam's decision, which was arrived at by a dispassionate consideration of Pakistan's interest.

I was made painfully aware of the intensity of Mountbatten's feeling when he one day burst into the room in the Viceroy's house where the Quaid-i-Azam was working on the Indian Independence Bill with Liaquat Ali Khan and me. He belabored the Quaid-i-Azam with arguments and appeals and bluster. He maintained that the proposal for a common Governor-General was inspired by the highest motives and was in the best interests of Pakistan. Without him as common Governor-General, Pakistan would put itself at the gravest disadvantage. It was with the greatest difficulty that he was securing for Pakistan what was due to her and, unless it was known that he would continue in this position even after partition, his power to help Pakistan would rapidly diminish. The responsibility for the immeasurable loss to Pakistan would rest on the shoulders of Jinnah. He threatened to make all this public and let the world judge. He was sure that the verdict of history would uphold him and go against Jinnah. He said again and again that he was most surprised that the objection to his continuance as common Governor-General should have come from Pakistan and not from the Congress. Jinnah bore this onslaught with great dignity and patience; he answered that in coming to this decision he had not been moved by any personal considerations but had objectively taken only the interests of his people into account. He assured Mountbatten that he fully trusted his sincerity and impartiality, and reiterated his proposal for making Mountbatten super Governor-General. But his protestations of faith in Mountbatten did nothing to assuage the latter's wounded vanity.

Ian Stephens, referring to the decision about the governor-generalship of Pakistan, wrote

> Lord Mountbatten himself seemed personally riled by it. Those brought in touch with him would doubtless agree that his weakness —perhaps the only one—was a curiously sensitive kind of vanity. Murphy's biography confirms this. That someone of his superb gifts should have had such a characteristic is odd; but evidently it was so. And it seemed noticeable at an editors' conference arranged the afternoon before Mr. Jinnah's decision was announced. Several of us inferred that the decision had not merely caused him political worry, but had hurt him. Perhaps he had set his heart on becoming dual Governor-General; the rebuff knocked against his most vulnerable point, his pride. [15]

From this stage on there was a noticeable change in Mountbatten's attitude toward the problems of partition and toward Pakistan. Mountbatten had barely tolerated Jinnah in the past; now there was active hostility. Jinnah, for his part, was still convinced of Mountbatten's essential fairness, and refused to see any change in him even when others pointed it out to him. The decision against a common Governor-General had far-reaching effects. The loss that Pakistan would incur in material assets was easy to foresee. But there were other intangible factors, such as the accession of the states, the Kashmir question, and the award of the Boundary Commission, in which the balance was tilted against Pakistan with far more momentous consequences.

Mountbatten's first reaction was to leave, but "nearly all his staff thought that the case for his remaining as Governor-General of India was overwhelmingly strong." If the Congress offer were turned down, they said, "the marked improvement in their [Congress] relations with the British might receive a severe setback; . . . animosity between the two Dominions would be increased . . . the British element, from the Commander-in-Chief downwards would probably refuse to continue to serve in India . . . and the Indian Princes would feel that they were losing their only chance of getting a square deal." [16] Finally, he agreed to serve as Governor-General of the Indian Dominion, provided the King, His Majesty's government and the opposition desired him to do so. Ismay was sent to London to find out and returned to Delhi in a few days, his mission successfully concluded—Mountbatten stayed on as the first Governor-General of the Indian Union after its independence.

Almost the first problem to be tackled by the Partition Council was the division of the former employees of the Government of India between the governments of the two new Dominions. Sardar Patel was emphatic in declaring that no Hindu official would consent to serve Pakistan, whether in the central government or in the provincial governments of East Bengal and West Punjab. Every government servant in the central government and in the partitioned provinces should, therefore, be given the option to serve India or Pakistan. The object was to deprive the governments of East Bengal and West Punjab of the services of experienced officials. Non-Muslims, being more advanced in education, filled the bulk of appointments in government service; their departure might bring about a break-down of administration. Hindu officials who had their ancestral homes in Muslim majority areas might, without such an option, have been content to stay on; and their presence would have had a reassuring effect on the minorities in these two provinces. But Patel was adamant. It was with considerable difficulty that he was persuaded to agree that a government servant should have the choice of making a final decision at once for one of the two Dominions or make a provisional choice with an opportunity to reconsider and indicate his final decision within six months. In actual fact, the disturbances that followed partition rendered this optional clause nugatory; and few, if any, availed themselves of it. All government servants were assured that their existing terms and conditions of service would be guaranteed by both the new governments. On the basis of replies received, separate cadres were drawn up, but actual transfers had necessarily to be arranged over a period of time. To enable the Pakistan government to function effectively, provisions were made, on an agreed basis, for the supply to Pakistan of office equipment, furniture, and stationery belonging to the undivided Government of India. It was also decided to give the Government of Pakistan such records and documents that exclusively concerned it, and duplicates of those of common interest.

Some idea of the magnitude of the task can be gained from the figures for the railways, which was the biggest employer. At this time about 925,000 employees worked for the Indian railways. Some 73,000 of the employees in the Pakistan portions of the North Western Railway and the Bengal-Assam Railway opted for India and about 83,500 employees on the remaining railways opted for Pakistan. Thus arrangements had to be made for an inter-Dominion transfer of 156,500 employees on the railways in such a manner as to cause no dislocation of railway services. The need for completing transfers within the shortest possible time was emphasized, but, even so, all transfers could not possibly be completed by August 15. Nor did the men who wished to go over to Pakistan, and vice versa, correspond exactly in each and every grade. It became necessary to retain certain personnel for running essential services, and releases had to be staggered. While these transfers were in progress, the Punjab, Delhi, and the northern districts of the United Provinces became the scene of extensive riots. Some government servants deserted their posts, and others found it difficult to reach their destination. Notwithstanding these tribulations, the work was carried to completion.

The question of compensating the members of the Secretary of State's services, which would come to an end on the transfer of power, had been under consideration for a number of months. The future governments of India and Pakistan both wished to retain the services of experienced officers and were prepared to guarantee existing terms as far as pay and pensions were concerned. Officers who did not desire to continue in service could retire on proportionate pensions. Since the transfer of power implied a more radical change for British than for Indian officers, the former were also paid compensation by the British government. Many of the British officers were offered service on a contract basis by the Dominion governments. Pakistan, which was short of senior administrative and technical officers, availed itself of the services of a fairly large number of British officers.

On the division of financial assets and liabilities, there were serious differences of opinion between the representatives of India and Pakistan. The most important of them related to the division of cash balances, sterling balances, and the public debt. The cash balances of the Government of India at the time of partition amounted to about Rs. 4 billion. Pakistan, which would have to incur heavy expenditures at the initial stage, asked for one fourth, or Rs. 1 billion, of the cash balances. In relation to population, resources, and requirements this was not an unreasonable demand. But the Indian representatives were prepared to allot Pakistan only Rs. 200 million, that is, one twentieth of the cash balances. They argued that the large cash balances were the result of anti-inflationary measures, and that the working cash balance was only Rs. 500 million, although they found it hard to explain why the benefit of anti-inflationary measures should accrue to the Indian Dominion alone. No agreement on the question could be reached even in the Partition Council where, as usual, Sardar Patel stuck doggedly to this unreasonable stand, which was plainly intended to deny Pakistan financial resources during the difficult interim period before it could establish its monetary authority and money market. The question was therefore left for the Arbitral

Tribunal to decide. The division of sterling balances was also left undecided.

In the division of liabilities, the main problem was the apportionment of the uncovered debt, which represented the excess of liabilities over the assets of the undivided Government of India. While Indian representatives were not prepared to allow more than 5 percent of the cash balances to Pakistan, they argued that, on the basis of population and other similar factors, Pakistan should assume liability for 20 percent of the uncovered debt. Pakistan representatives were of the view that the allocation of this liability should be in proportion to the contribution made by areas included in the Dominions of Pakistan and India to the revenues of the central government before partition. This had been the basis adopted by the Amery Tribunal at the separation of Burma from India. No agreement could be reached.

An even more serious difference of opinion arose over Pakistan's proposal that both Dominions should assume joint responsibility for the public debt of undivided India, and that a statutory commission, consisting of an equal number of Indian and Pakistan representatives, should be set up to administer the debt. Each government would from time to time pay its share of the amount due to this commission. This straightforward proposal met with strong resistance from the Indians. Since Hindus were far richer than Muslims, an overwhelming proportion of the securities was held by Hindu institutional and individual investors. The Congress leaders were convinced that Pakistan was economically and financially an unviable entity. They were advised by their financial experts that if the Pakistan proposal was accepted, the securities market in India would suffer a collapse with immense losses to Hindu banks and other investors. Therefore, the Indian representatives made the counterproposal that India should assume responsibility for the entire debt and that Pakistan should repay to the Indian Union its share of the debt. This meant that the Government of Pakistan should assume a liability not toward the individual holders of securities but toward the government of the Indian Dominion. I refused to accept this proposal, which was born of an unjustified distrust of Pakistan's credit. I explained that doubts about Pakistan's economic viability had little basis in fact and that Indian holders of securities need not fear default by Pakistan. But the more I explained, the worse grew their suspicion that there was in the Pakistan proposal a deep design to disrupt the financial structure of India.

Finally, in an effort to break the deadlock, I suggested that the Indian proposal could only merit consideration if it secured for Pakistan some of the objectives gained by our plan. For instance, there should be a period of grace in which there would be no repayment; the repayment should be spread over a period of fifty years or more; the rate of interest should be the average rate of interest for the Indian national debt. If a proposal of that kind were authoritatively put forward, it might be possible for me to submit it to the Quaid-i-Azam, but a final solution of the question must depend upon a fair allocation of the cash balances between India and Pakistan. I was, accordingly, given a proposal, signed by Sardar Patel, under which Pakistan was to repay its share in fifty annual installments, with the first installment falling due on August 15, 1952. By this time the Quaid-i-Azam had moved to Karachi. I went to Karachi on August 9, and returned with the Quaid-i-Azam's provisional approval, subject to a satisfactory solution of the cash balances issue. This was enough for the Viceroy to issue an order before August 15 transferring the initial liability for all loans to the Government of India. But Pakistan's liability had still to be determined and, until then, there was no formal commitment by Pakistan.

Before taking these and other disputed issues to the Arbitral Tribunal, I made a last effort at settlement by mutual discussion. In November, 1947, I suggested to H. M. Patel that if Sardar Patel agreed, I would ask our Finance Minister, Ghulam Muhammad, to go to Delhi with me to decide, if possible, all outstanding questions. If the effort failed, a reference would, of course, be made to the Arbitral Tribunal. Sardar Patel agreed and we went to Delhi. At lower-level meetings all the other issues were settled, leaving only the big questions of the division of cash balances, sterling balances, and the national debt for us to work out.

The meeting, held at the house of Sardar Patel, was attended also by the Indian Finance Minister, Shanmukham Chetty. Ghulam Muhammad was accompanied by Sir Archibald Rowlands, who had been Finance Member of the Viceroy's Executive Council in 1946, and was at this time Financial Adviser to the Governor-General of Pakistan. No agreement could be reached and it looked as if the meeting would end in failure. At this point Sardar Patel said: "H. M. Patel and Muhammad Ali have settled between themselves most of the problems. Let them go into the next room and not come out until they have settled this problem as well." We went into the next room as directed and in three quarters of an hour had reached agreement. Pakistan's share of the cash balances and of the disputed portion of sterling balances as well as of the uncovered national debt should be 17½ percent. We returned and announced our agreement. Sardar Patel, Ghulan Muhammad, and others signified their assent. A formal agreement was drawn up, which was signed by the representatives of India and Pakistan in the beginning of December, 1947. All references to the Arbitral Tribunal were withdrawn.

There is a sequel to this story. Under the agreement, Pakistan's share of the cash balances came to Rs. 750 million. Rs. 200 million had already been paid, and the remaining Rs. 550 million was to be paid immediately. The Government of India agreed to instruct the Reserve Bank of India to make this payment to Pakistan. When, however, we returned to Karachi we waited in vain for the transfer of this amount to our account. We discovered that the Government of India was holding it back on the pretext that Pakistan would use it in prosecuting the war which was going on in Kashmir. This was a monstrous pretext. Hostilities in Kashmir had been going on since the last week of October, 1947, and were in progress at the time when the agreement regarding cash balances was signed by Sardar Patel at the beginning of December, 1947. Since then, nothing new had happened that could provide an excuse for dishonoring an agreement freely arrived at between the Governments of India and Pakistan.

Accusations of bad faith against the new Government of India by the world at large disturbed Gandhi who, after studying the question, came to the conclusion that India's stand was morally untenable. He was at the time passing through the last and noblest phase of his life and was devoting all his energy to restoring communal peace and harmony. On January 13, 1948, he undertook an indefinite fast to bring peace to riot-stricken Delhi. To those who argued with him to give up the fast, he said that "the object should not be to save his life but to save India and her honour. He would feel happy and proud when he saw that India's place was not lowered as it had become by recent happenings." When Sardar Patel sent word that he would do anything that Gandhi wished, Gandhi replied that "the first priority should be given to the question of Pakistan's share of the cash assets withheld by the Union Government." [17] Thus, on January 15, 1948, the Government of India decided under pressure from Gandhi to implement the financial agreement with Pakistan immediately and released the withheld balances. Gandhi's biographer Tendulkar goes on to record that "the revocation of the Cabinet decision hurt Patel's feelings," [18] and that "it made those who were already angry with Gandhi for what they considered as his partiality towards the Musalmans angrier still." [19] This view is supported by Sardar Patel's biographer, who wrote that Gandhi's fast "created much discontent and ultimately led to tragic results. . . . The Hindu Mahasabha and its offshoot the R.S.S.S. were sore that Gandhiji should use the bludgeon of the fast to finance Pakistan for destruction of Indian soldiers and to secure unconditional protection to even rowdy Muslim elements." [20] "Tragic results" refers to Gandhi's assassination on January 30, 1948, at the hand of Godse, a member of the militant Hindu organization, the Rashtriya Swayam Sewak Sangh.

It would take far too much space to give even a brief account of discussions and decisions on the numerous other issues, such as valuation of assets; liability for returning stocks of lend-lease silver; division of revenues; avoidance of double taxation; responsibility for contracts; replacement of currency and coinage; arrangements with the Reserve Bank of India for ways and means advances and other similar matters; separation of foreign exchange earnings; policies regarding trade and economic controls, customs, foreign relations, treaties; and the determination of nationality and domicile.

Over many of these matters good sense prevailed in making decisions; over others, difficulties arose that had to be resolved as best as possible under the circumstances. When, for example, questions relating to trade and economic controls were examined, it was found that the long-term policies to be pursued by the two Dominions could only be discussed after the new governments had had time to examine their respective problems. Meanwhile it was agreed that until March 31, 1948, the status quo should be maintained as far as possible, and modifications in and removal of controls should not be effected except after consultation between the two Dominions. It was also decided that no restrictions on the movement of persons should be imposed and that no passports or visas should be required.

It was agreed that during the interim period no customs barriers should be raised between the two Dominions; no restrictions should be imposed on free movement of goods and remittances, including capital and capital equipment; existing import and export policies should be continued; and existing customs tariffs, and excise duties should be left unchanged. All this was eminently sensible; a customs cordon was not easy to maintain with frontiers of over a thousand miles between India and Pakistan in the East as well as in the West. But when, as a corollary to this, Pakistan proposed that customs revenue during the interim period should be pooled and shared on an equitable basis, the Indians refused and insisted on keeping what they collected. The reason was that practically the sole outlet for the jute crop, the bulk of which was produced in East Pakistan, was Calcutta. Chittagong was the only port that East Pakistan had. It was a minor port with a total capacity of half a million tons, and would take many years to develop. Pakistan jute would thus perforce move through Calcutta, and the Indians were determined to take full advantage of this situation. Faced with this attitude, Pakistan was forced to revise its policy toward free trade with India and had to levy export duty on jute exported to India.

The existing currency was to remain common to the two Dominions up to March 31, 1948. During the next six months, up to September 30, 1948, Indian notes and coins would be gradually replaced by Pakistan currency. The Reserve Bank was to continue as the common currency authority until October 1, 1948, when Pakistan would take over the management of its own currency. Later the date was changed to July 1, 1948.

Membership in all international organizations, together with the rights and obligations attaching to such membership, devolved upon the Indian Union, and Pakistan had to apply for membership. Both Dominions were successors to rights and obligations under international agreements to which undivided India was a party, but rights and obligations connected exclusively with territorial matters devolved only upon the government of the territory to which they related. Thus Pakistan had to negotiate agreements with the tribes on the northwest frontier.

Beside the assets in India, there were the assets of the India Office in London, which had been built at the expense of the Indian exchequer. These were investigated by a committee of representatives of the United Kingdom, India, and Pakistan. The most valuable of these assets was and is the India Office Library, consisting of 230,000 printed volumes and 20,000 manuscripts—perhaps the biggest collection of books relating to the subcontinent anywhere in the world. Protracted tripartite discussions are still going on.

The division of the armed forces was an exceptionally delicate and complicated operation, but it was necessitated by the very decision for partition and the establishment of two independent sovereign states. Without control of armed forces on whose loyalty it can depend, no state can protect its independence. But so great was the attachment of British officers to the Indian army, which they had built into a splendid war machine during a period extending over a century, that they found it difficult to reconcile themselves to its division even after the political decision for the partition of the subcontinent had been made. The prospect of this operation caught at their heartstrings and made many of them incapable of rational thought. Some idea of their sentiments can be gained from the remark of the usually calm and reasonable Lord Ismay, who called the partition of the armed forces "the biggest crime and the biggest headache." In his memoirs he relates how he did his utmost

> to persuade Mr. Jinnah to reconsider his decision. . . . I asked him to remember that an army was not merely a collection of men with rifles and bayonets and guns and tanks; it was a living entity with one brain, one heart and one set of organs. . . . But Jinnah was adamant. He said that he would refuse to take power on 15 August unless he had an army of appropriate strength and predominantly Moslem composition under his control.[21]

Actually Jinnah did not insist on a communal division of the armed forces. He was prepared to accept citizenship as the basis of division. On this, and every other appropriate occasion he affirmed that all who lived in Pakistan would, regardless of creed, enjoy equal rights. On the basis of citizenship the armed forces of Pakistan would be predominantly but not exclusively Muslim in composition. However, the decision of the Partition Council to allow government servants to elect the Dominion they wanted to serve was applied to the armed forces as well, subject to one exception. A Muslim from Pakistan did not have the option to join the armed forces of India, and non-Muslims from India could not elect to serve in the armed forces of Pakistan.

The strong feelings of the British military officers against the division of the armed forces were also shared by many of their Indian disciples. Great pains had been taken by the British to isolate Indian military officers from the currents of popular political opinion in the subcontinent as far as was possible. This isolation was never completely proof against strong environmental influences, yet Indian military officers lived largely in a world of their own, and their mental attitudes were shaped to an astonishing degree by their British superiors. I was not, therefore, altogether surprised when Brigadier K. M. Cariappa, who had the highest seniority among Indian military officers and who later became the first Indian Commander-in-Chief, came to see me during the partition days and argued strongly against the partitioning of the Indian armed forces. He was accompanied by a Muslim officer who was of the same mind as Cariappa. They thought that joint control of an undivided army by the political leaders of Hindustan and Pakistan was a practical proposition and hinted that if it was not, so much the worse for political leaders; it was better for the army to take charge of both Dominions than be divided. I tried to make them understand the political and military position that sovereign and independent states have to maintain, but I am not sure I succeeded in convincing them.

I have mentioned that Liaquat Ali Khan had proposed in April, 1947, that a plan for the partition of the armed forces be drawn up, and that this proposal had been opposed by Defence Minister Baldev Singh and by the Commander-in-Chief, Field Marshal Auchinleck. If that proposal had been accepted, valuable time would have been gained. As it was, when the decision for partition was taken in June, there was no plan—not even the outline of a plan. The very basis on which the partition of the armed forces was to be carried out had yet to be settled. It was not until the first week of July that work started in earnest. The process of division could not possibly be completed by August 15, and would have to be continued beyond that date, under the aegis of an impartial authority, in order to avoid the risk of armed conflict and to ensure a fair apportionment of military stores.

The Armed Forces Reconstitution Committee under the chairmanship of the Commander-in-Chief, Field Marshal Sir Claude Auchinleck, was set up. The other members of the Armed Forces Reconstitution Committee were three British officers—the Commanders-in-Chief of the air force and the navy, and the Chief of the General Staff of the army; and two civilians—G. S. Bhalja, Additional Secretary in the Defence Department, and I.

In spite of my preoccupation with the work of the Steering Committee, I was asked to serve on the Armed Forces Reconstitution Committee, in view of the importance of the work and the experience I had gained as Financial Adviser, War and Supply. The committee was assisted by four subcommittees—one each for the army, the navy, and the air force—and one to deal with the financial aspects of the division. Muslim and non-Muslim military officers as well as senior British officers were on these subcommittees.

Whatever plans for the division of the armed forces might be made had also to be executed. If this was to be accomplished without confusion and without loss of morale and efficiency, it was essential that all existing armed forces in India should be under a single administrative authority. This position was entrusted to Auchinleck, who was designated Supreme Commander, to distinguish him from the Commanders-in-Chief of India and Pakistan. The Supreme Commander worked under the direction of the Joint Defence Council, which consisted of Lord Mountbatten as chairman, the two Defence Ministers of India and Pakistan—Baldev Singh and Liaquat Ali Khan—and Auchinleck. The Joint Defence Council was the final authority making decisions on the division of the armed forces between the Dominions and their reconstitution as two separate Dominion forces. It regulated the allocation, transfer, and movement of officers and men as well as of plant, machinery, equipment, and stores; and handled the general administration and discipline of the armed forces of each of the two Dominions. But the Joint Defence Council exercised no operational control over the forces of each Dominion, except over the Boundary Force operating under joint command in disturbed areas.

The division and reconstitution of units was to be completed by April 1, 1948. By that date each Dominion would have its own administrative and maintenance services for its own armed forces. It was agreed that the Joint Defence Council and the organization under the Supreme Commander would also last till April 1, 1948. Through the Joint Defence Council, the Supreme Commander was responsible to the governments of India and Pakistan. But he was also directly responsible to the British government for the command and administration of all British forces staying in India after August 15. These forces were to be withdrawn within six months according to a phased program.

In order that Pakistan and the Union of India should each have, on August 15, within their own territories and under their own operational control, forces predominantly composed of Muslims and non-Muslims respectively, it was necessary to carry out the partition in two stages. The first stage was a more or less rough and ready division of the existing forces on a communal basis. Plans were made for the immediate movement to the Pakistan area of all Muslim majority units outside that area, and similarly for the movement to India of exclusively non-Muslim or non-Muslim majority units then in the Pakistan area. The next stage was to comb out the units themselves on the basis of voluntary transfers. Arrangements were also made for each Dominion to have its own administrative machinery to enable it to maintain its armed forces. At the beginning of August, new Commanders-in-Chief were appointed for the armed forces of the two Dominions.

Auchinleck had been opposed to partition. The Congress leaders were for that reason favorably inclined toward him. The Quaid-i-Azam and Liaquat Ali Khan were for the same reason mistrustful of him and wanted to replace him. But they accepted my view that whatever his personal opinion might have been, now that a political decision at the highest level had been taken, he would, as a loyal soldier, carry out faithfully and impartially the task entrusted to him.

On the basis of the relative strength of the two forces, Pakistan was to receive, according to the decision of the Joint Defence Council, one third of the military stores lying in India and Pakistan. The bulk of arms, ammunition, and other military stores was, however, lying in depots in the Indian Dominion. All the sixteen ordnance factories, many of which had been modernized during the Second World War, were also located in India. The Indians, who had possession of the goods and also had time in their favor, were determined to deny Pakistan forces their due share of equipment and stores. This was an important part of their scheme for undoing Pakistan; for without arms and ammunition, the Pakistan army would be but a feeble instrument. To achieve their purpose they employed two main weapons— intransigence in decision-making and obstruction in implementation. At the meetings of the Armed Forces Reconstitution Committee, the Indian representative Bhalja generally took a rigid and uncompromising attitude. In the few cases that came up before the Partition Council as, for example, the question of ordnance factories, Sardar Patel was even more stubborn. Never, never would he allow a single piece of machinery to leave India. Despite these obstacles, the reconstitution and movement of units as well as of unit equipment went ahead. But the transfer of the bulk of military stores lying in depots was still pending when the transfer of power took place on August 15.

Immediately on attaining independence, India felt free to throw off such restraint as it had exercised before the withdrawal of British authority. The Indian leaders had previously shown deference to the Supreme Commander; now they started a virulent campaign, in public and in private, against him. Auchinleck had no operational control. He had powers only in the administrative field, and that too only under the direction of the Joint Defence Council. His main function was to complete the reconstitution of the armed forces, so that both Pakistan and India should have balanced and well-equipped forces at their disposal; and he was trying, under very difficult circumstances, to carry out his task faithfully and impartially. The task would not be completed before April 1, 1948. The object of the attacks against the Supreme Commander was to force him to quit, so that there should be no independent authority to deliver to Pakistan its due share of military stores.

On September 26, 1947, Mountbatten wrote to Auchinleck that he was unable to avert the mounting Indian attacks on the Supreme Commander: "The Indian Ministers resent the fact that at the head of the Supreme Headquarters there should be a man of your very high rank and great personal prestige and reputation. . . . One of the most balanced and level-headed Ministers complained recently that you seemed to regard yourself as the champion of Pakistan's interests; such is the reward of strict impartiality!" The letter went on to say that Auchinleck should forestall the Indian move against him by himself proposing the winding up of Supreme Headquarters. Mountbatten also informed Auchinleck that he had already explained the position to Prime Minister Attlee and obtained "his contingent approval to my acting at my discretion if I felt the time had come." [22] In other words, Mountbatten had, under Indian pressure, decided that the Supreme Headquarters should be closed down and he was merely trying to save appearances for Auchinleck by asking him to resign of his own accord.

In a report to the British government on September 28, Auchinleck wrote:

I have no hesitation whatever in affirming that the present India Cabinet are implacably determined to do all in their power to prevent the establishment of the Dominion of Pakistan on a firm basis. . . . The Indian leaders, Cabinet Ministers, civil officials and others have persistently tried to obstruct the work of partition of the Armed Forces. I and my officers have been continuously and virulently accused of being pro-Pakistan and partial, whereas the truth is that we have merely tried to do our duty impartially and without fear, favour or affection. . . . It is becoming increasingly impossible for myself and my officers to continue with our task. If we are removed, there is no hope at all of any just division of assets in the shape of movable stores belonging to the former Indian Army. The attitude of Pakistan, on the other hand, has been reasonable and cooperative throughout. This is natural in the circumstances, as Pakistan has practically nothing of her own and must obtain most of what she wants from the reserves of stores etc. now lying in India.[23]

This episode is instructive in many respects. In the first place, it shows the disregard of Indian leaders for their solemn undertakings, and their readiness to adopt any means for gaining their ends. Secondly, it brings out their implacable hostility to Pakistan. Thirdly, it gives an insight into the character of Mountbatten's relationship with the Indian leaders. As long as he served their purposes, they made much of him; but when he pleaded justice and fair play, even toward a British Field Marshal, he soon reached the end of his influence with them. It also shows his willingness to sacrifice others to maintain his own position. He forced Auchinleck to resign for no fault except strict impartiality rather than tell the Indians that he himself would sooner resign than see "the greatest Commander-in-Chief that India has ever had," to use Mountbatten's own phrase about Auchinleck, driven out unjustly. Finally, it disposes, once and for all, of Mountbatten's claim that if he had been common Governor-General of India and Pakistan, he would have secured for Pakistan its just share of assets. Surely he carried far more weight with the Indian cabinet as their chosen and trusted Governor-General than he would have had as a constitutional Governor-General common to India and Pakistan. If he could not, in the former capacity, make India honor the agreement on the division of military stores, he would have been doubly powerless in the latter position.

Thus, barely six weeks after independence, the Indians had made it impossible for the Supreme Commander to continue till the completion of his task on April 1, 1948. On October 6, Auchinleck proposed, in a note for the Joint Defence Council, that the Supreme Commander and his headquarters should be liquidated by November 30. The note came up for consideration at a meeting of the Joint Defence Council in Lahore on October 16. Mountbatten was in the chair, and India was represented by Baldev Singh and Gopalaswami Ayyangar, Minister without portfolio. The Indians blandly supported the Supreme Commander's proposal, while Liaquat Ali Khan opposed it and insisted that the Supreme Headquarters should continue in existence until it had completed its task. Auchinleck explained that he had not made his proposal because he wanted to run away from the completion of his responsibilities, but because it had been made impossible for him and his officers to carry on their task. The Indian ministers pledged themselves on behalf of their government to deliver to Pakistan its due share of stores. Their pledges, of course, were worth nothing, since they had themselves created these circumstances in order to deny Pakistan its share of stores. No agreement could be reached, and the question was referred to the governments of India and Pakistan. As might be expected the two governments could not reach any agreement. The British government, on being consulted, decided to withdraw the British officers of the Supreme Headquarters in view of the disagreement between the governments of India and Pakistan. The Supreme Commander's headquarters was thus closed down in an atmosphere of great bitterness before any appreciable quantity of stores had been transferred. India had achieved its object. For some time, surplus and unwanted stores, such as outsized shoes, continued to reach Pakistan. Then even that trickle stopped.

Another major development in this critical period was the establishment of the Punjab Boundary Force in response to the threat of a Sikh rebellion. Ever since the first week of March, 1947, when Khizr Hayat Tiwana's coalition ministry in the Punjab resigned, and partition loomed on the horizon, the Sikhs had been planning to establish a Sikh state by force. "Their plans," wrote the Punjab Chief Secretary in his report in March, "embrace the whole community in the Punjab and it is said they also involve the Sikh States. The Sikhs are being regimented, they are being armed, if they are not armed already and they are being inflamed by propaganda both oral and written." [24] When the June 3 partition plan was announced, the Sikhs redoubled their efforts. The Chief Secretary's report for June said: "The [Shiromani Akali Dal] circular states that Pakistan means total death to the Sikh Panth [community] and that the Sikhs are determined on a free sovereign state with the Chenab and the Jamna as its borders, and it calls on all Sikhs to fight for their ideal under the flag of the Dal." [25]

The main Sikh organization—the Shiromani Akali Dal—controlled Sikh shrines and had ample financial resources. The Sikh community was organized on semi-military lines. There were *jathas,* or bands, under recognized leaders called *Jathedars.* To carry a sword was a religious duty. The Maharaja of Patiala and other Sikh rulers of states in the Punjab were in close touch with Akali leaders. They had their states' armed forces under their control and were prepared to support the Sikh plan with money and arms. The Hindus were in close alliance with the Sikhs and the Hindu militant organizations, such as the R.S.S. Sangh, cooperated with them in acts of organized violence.

In keeping with the temper of the Sikh leaders, the Sikh plan was brutal and ruthless. It had two aspects. The first, was to exert the utmost pressure (in collaboration with the Congress) upon the British authorities to move the boundary of East Punjab as far west as possible. The second, was to drive out the Muslim population of East Punjab by fire and sword and to replace them by a planned exodus of Sikhs from West Punjab. Few members of the Government of India believed this diabolical plan would succeed. Bloodshed and violence on a much larger scale than in previous communal riots was anticipated, but no one expected a systematic attempt at extermination and expulsion of Muslims from East Punjab and neighboring territories. A forcible exchange of population was, however, what the Sikhs had planned.

The Sikh leader Giani Kartar Singh told Sir Evan Jenkins, the Governor of the Punjab, that "in the Punjab there would have to be an exchange of population on a large scale. Were the British ready to enforce this? He doubted if they were, and if no regard was paid to Sikh solidarity a fight was inevitable." [26] Ismay records how Miéville and he "had two or three talks with their leaders, Master Tara Singh and Giani Kartar Singh. . . . We told them that if they resorted to violence, either before or after Partition, they would be very roughly handled; but we did not feel that our warnings had had the slightest effect." [27]

The Governor of the Punjab, Jenkins, kept on warning Mountbatten that the Sikhs were bent on creating serious trouble. Abell, who discussed the situation with Jenkins on July 10, reported to the Viceroy that "there is no doubt that the Sikhs are in a very dangerous mood." [28] On July 13, Jenkins again wrote a warning that the Sikhs threatened a violent uprising.[29] During this period the Quaid-i-Azam and Liaquat Ali Khan repeatedly drew Mountbatten's attention to the danger. The Quaid-i-Azam believed that unless the Sikh leaders involved in this vast conspiracy were arrested there could be no guarantee of peace. Mountbatten promised to take the sternest action against the Sikh leaders if they persisted in their designs. But what was needed, and what was demanded by the Quaid-i-Azam, was immediate action and not words. Mountbatten, although very forthcoming with words, was loath to take any effective action.

In April, 1947, Abul Kalam Azad had warned Mountbatten that, if the country was divided in an atmosphere of communal strife, "there would be rivers of blood flowing . . . and the British would be responsible for the carnage." Without a moment's hesitation Lord Mountbatten had replied, "At least on this one question I shall give you complete assurance. I shall see to it that there is no bloodshed and riot. . . . If there should be the slightest agitation, I shall adopt the sternest measures to nip the trouble in the bud." [30]

He continued to talk in this fashion but did nothing. In July he threatened the Maharaja of Patiala with dire consequences and lectured various Sikh delegations on the need for eschewing violence. In melodramatic fashion he declared he would use the whole might of the British Empire to crush any attempt at violence. But the Sikhs saw through the bluff and were not in the least moved by these outbursts. For Mountbatten's staff was all this time exuding sympathy for the "poor Sikhs," who had fared so badly under the partition plan. The Sikhs, therefore, felt reasonably certain of carrying through their plan without let or hindrance. One Sikh delegation tried to reassure Mountbatten by saying that there would be no disturbance while he was Viceroy, meaning that it was only after independence that they proposed to carry out their program of destruction.

At the height of the Punjab holocaust, while speaking to two Hindu journalists in New Delhi on August 27, Mountbatten gave a general account of what was happening in the Punjab. "The Sikhs . . . had launched an attack just as Giani Kartar Singh and Tara Singh before the 3rd June had told him they would. Mountbatten had expostulated with them at the time, stressing that the British would have gone. It would be Indian fighting Indian. But they were adamant, and had in fact observed that they were waiting for [the British] to go. The situation was now out of their control." [31] If the situation was then out of anybody's control it was because he, as Viceroy, did nothing to thwart the criminal plans of the Sikhs when he had the knowledge and the power and the responsibility. Mountbatten's failure to take action against Sikh leaders and to stop them from arming in this crucial period led to unprecedented carnage and the biggest mass migration in history.

On July 20, Mountbatten visited Lahore and discussed the situation in the Punjab with Jenkins and the Punjab Partition Committee. Two days later, on return to Delhi, he proposed to the Partition Council that a boundary force be formed to keep peace in the Punjab. The proposal was accepted, and a statement was issued by the Partition Council, which on this occasion included Baldev Singh on behalf of the Sikhs:

> The members of the Partition Council, on behalf of the future Governments, declare that they are determined to establish peaceful conditions in which the processes of partition may be completed and the many urgent tasks of administration and economic reconstruction taken in hand. Both the Congress and the Muslim League have given assurances of fair and equitable treatment to the minorities after the transfer of power. The two future Governments re-affirm these assurances. It is their intention to safeguard the legitimate interests of all citizens irrespective of religion, caste or sex. In the exercise of their normal civic rights all citizens will be regarded as equal, and both the Governments will assure to all people within their territories the exercise of liberties such as freedom of speech, the right to form associations, the right to worship in their own way and the protection of their language and culture. Both the Governments further undertake that there shall be no discrimination against those who before August 15 may have been political opponents. The guarantee of protection which both Governments give to the citizens of their respective countries implies that in no circumstances will violence be tolerated in any form in either territory. The two Governments wish to emphasise that they are united in this determination. To safeguard the peace in the Punjab during the period of change-over . . . both Governments have together agreed on the setting up of a special Military Command from August 1, covering the civil districts of Sialkot, Gujranwala, Sheikhupura, Lyallpur, Montgomery, Lahore, Amritsar, Gurdaspur, Hoshiarpur, Jullundur, Ferozepore and Ludhiana. With their concurrence Major-General Rees has been nominated as Military Commander for this purpose and Brigadier Digambar Singh (India) and Colonel Ayub Khan (Pakistan) have been attached to him in an

advisory capacity. After August 15, Major-General Rees will control operationally the forces of both the new States in this area and will be responsible through the Supreme Commander and the Joint Defence Council to the two Governments. The two Governments will not hesitate to set up a similar organization in Bengal should they consider it necessary.

The Punjab Boundary Force, consisting of some fifty thousand officers and men, took up its duties on August 1. It was mainly composed of mixed units not yet partitioned and had a high proportion of British officers. The majority of the force was non-Muslim; but whether Muslims or non-Muslims, there was a serious danger of their being affected by the surrounding atmosphere of communal passions. This inherent weakness in its structure grew until the Boundary Force became useless and had to be disbanded within a month.

British units whose impartiality could be relied upon were not included in the force. The reason for this omission is to be found in the anxiety of the British, in the last days of their raj, to disengage themselves from the affairs of the subcontinent without risking British lives, prestige, and popularity. Their responsibility for the safety and security of the millions over whom they had ruled so long, counted for little in their calculations. To shoot down rioters is a thankless task. Why undertake it and get the curses of both sides? The excuse that the Congress leaders would not have consented to the employment of British troops fails to carry conviction for no such proposal was made to them. They could not themselves be expected to ask for British troops. The judicious comments of a British writer on this question deserve careful thought. Lumby wrote: "When all is said, however, it is difficult to resist the conclusion that the British Government and Lord Mountbatten should have insisted to the utmost of their power that the two new Governments must accept a modicum of British control in the areas of worst danger until these had had time to adapt themselves to the new conditions of life." [32] A very different view would have been taken had it been British lives that were at stake. Although there was no anti-British feeling in the subcontinent at that time, the Supreme Commander and other British officers were greatly concerned with the safety of the British in India, and wanted to retain British troops, not for maintaining communal peace, but to safeguard British lives and interests.

The Punjab Boundary Force was thus neither properly constituted, nor was it strong enough to tackle the immense task confronting it. Moreover, it had to act in aid of civil authority and had no power of preventive action. It was in the position of a solitary fire brigade in a city full of dynamite—it could not remove the dynamite but had to struggle ineffectually to put out the fires after they had broken out. As in so many other matters, Mountbatten was concerned more to create the illusion of a solution than to find a real one. For a real solution of the problem in the Punjab he would have had to contend against Congress leaders, like Sardar Patel, who were backing the Sikhs; but for this he was not prepared.

By the time the Punjab Boundary Force was formed the situation had greatly deteriorated, because the Sikh leaders were still at large plotting and planning their criminal designs. The following entry of August 5, 1947, taken from Campbell-Johnson's book, gives a glimpse into the hideous reality and the total lack of readiness to act. Mountbatten, in closed discussion with Sardar Patel, Jinnah, and Liaquat Ali Khan, gave them a briefing on the Punjab situation.

> Intelligence . . . implicated the Sikh leaders in a number of sabotage plans, including a plot to assassinate Jinnah during the State drive at the Independence celebrations in Karachi next week. Jinnah and Liaquat immediately demanded the arrest of Tara Singh and other Sikh leaders. Patel, however, was strongly opposed to this course, arguing that it would only precipitate a crisis already beyond control. Mountbatten said he was prepared to support the arrests, but only if the authorities on the spot [that meant Jenkins] felt that this would be a wise step.[33]

On August 9, Jenkins rejected any suggestion that the Sikh leaders should be arrested before August 15, on the ground that any arrests were more likely to endanger than to improve the existing conditions. Because Mountbatten was to be at Jinnah's side in the state procession, he felt he could accept the decision made in the Punjab without personal reproach.[34]

Whatever the grounds, the result was always the same—no action against the Sikh leaders who, to Mountbatten's certain knowledge, were organizing a genocide campaign. Less than a week before the transfer of power it might really have been too late to arrest the Sikh leaders, for Sardar Patel would have released them on August 15. But if Mountbatten had taken action against them and against the Maharaja of Patiala in June or even in July, the effects would have been salutary. Any outbreak of trouble resulting from the arrests could have been put down with far greater ease than later, when preparations for organized violence had been completed.

One of the first decisions taken during partition days was the selection of Karachi as the capital of Pakistan. For strategic and other reasons, the capital could only be located in West Pakistan. Bengal was being partitioned and East Pakistan was faced with the problem of establishing a new provincial capital at Dacca. Karachi, which was the capital of Sind, was the obvious choice for a number of reasons. In West Pakistan the only province which had a Muslim League ministry was Sind; the Punjab was under governor's rule and the North-West Frontier Province had a Congress ministry. The Sind government came forward with the proposal to make Karachi the capital of Pakistan and offered to place the governor's house, the assembly building, and other necessary accommodation at the disposal of the central government.

Karachi had other advantages also. It was a clean modern town with a mild climate; it had a fine harbor and an airport which provided ready means of communication with East Pakistan and the outside world. It was also the birth place of the Quaid-i-Azam; though this was not the reason for the selection of Karachi.

Difficulties, however, soon appeared when a team was sent to Karachi to select and prepare office and residential accommodation for the central government. It appeared that the Sind government had exhausted its generosity by giving up the governor's house and the assembly building. The governor's house was to serve as the Governor-General's residence and the assembly building would house the constituent assembly and a small part of the central secretariat. But many more buildings were required for office and residential accommodation and now would have to be requisitioned. New buildings, even of a temporary kind, would not be ready by the beginning of August, when the staff would start arriving. Karachi was not a big town and had, at that time, a population of about 350,000. Serious inconvenience to its citizens would undoubtedly be caused by large-scale requisitioning, but there was no help for it. The officers and staff of the central government would also suffer considerable hardship and would have to make do with such housing as was available. A reception camp in tents was being put up for them, but they had to be provided with some accommodation, however inadequate, as soon as possible. The Sind government offered no help. Even for the ministers of the central government they could find no houses, and offered to receive them as guests in their own homes!

Time was pressing and immediate action was needed. I was in charge of all administrative work arising out of partition for Pakistan, including arrangements for the new capital. In desperation I sought the help of army general headquarters to prepare an alternative plan for moving to Rawalpindi, where army barracks could be made available. The need for the alternative plan did not, however, arise. When I explained the position to the Quaid-i-Azam, he said firmly that he would hold the Sind ministers to their promise. The most important consideration, he felt, was that Karachi, having an international airport, would be easy of access to the outside world and would help to put Pakistan on the map of the world. The Sind ministers were sent for and the Quaid-i-Azam ordered them to make all the necessary accommodation available. This eased difficulties considerably, and the work of making Karachi suitable for the reception of the Pakistan government went ahead. By August 15, somehow or other, shelter had been found for the thousands of families that poured into Karachi, and office accommodation for every ministry and department had been found or hastily constructed.

A transfer office in Delhi and a reception office in Karachi were set up to plan and arrange the movement of staff. About 25,000 persons and their personal effects had to be moved from Delhi together with government records and equipment. The move began on August 1, at the rate of one special train a day.

On August 8, the train was derailed after it had left Bhatinda junction in East Punjab. The railway line was blown up by means of a gun cotton slab detonated electrically. Three railway trucks were smashed and three derailed. A number of bombs connected by wire had been placed on the tracks to blow up the train completely, but, luckily, only one bomb exploded, and the casualties were slight. A woman and her four-year-old son were killed and about a dozen other passengers wounded. The attacks from hostile parties in hiding were averted by the prompt action of the military escort. Then there was another accident on August 14. By that time disturbances on a large scale had started in East Punjab, and it was decided to suspend the train service until the return of normal conditions. Arrangements

were made with the B.B. & C.I., a meter gauge railway that ran
through Marwar to Hyderabad, but even this service had to be dis-
continued within a week because disturbances occurred on that line
also. In all, 11,500 passengers were carried by rail.

The only other means of transport was by air. Tatas and Orient
Airways agreed to make planes available, but they had made only 18
flights when the Government of India requisitioned all their aircraft.
BOAC was approached, and placed 26 planes at our disposal.
"Operation Pakistan," as the BOAC flights were called, began on
September 4 and carried 7,000 persons. Because of the unrest that
prevailed in Delhi at that time, it was a problem to find transportation
to carry people to the airport. Muslims were attacked and murdered
in broad daylight. The civil authorities were not helpful and were not
prepared to provide gas or transport. With the help of army general
headquarters, military trucks were obtained and some Muslim soldiers guarded the passengers. In the middle of September, when train
services were started to evacuate Muslim refugees from Delhi to Pakistan, thousands of government servants also traveled by these trains.
Many of the trains were attacked by Sikhs and a great number of
passengers were killed.

A large number of government servants who had opted for Pakistan moved to Bombay from all over India. Most of them were railway
employees. A separate transfer office was set up in Bombay and
assisted in the evacuation of 17,000 Pakistan employees and their
families to Karachi. The work continued through October to the end
of the year.

Among the problems of partition was the drafting of an interim constitution for Pakistan. The Indian Independence Act, 1947, provided
that until the constituent assembly of each Dominion enacted otherwise, "each of the new Dominions and all Provinces and other parts
thereof shall be governed as nearly as may be in accordance with the
Government of India Act, 1935," subject to such omissions, addi-
tions, adaptations, and modifications (separately for each Dominion)
as may be made by order of the Governor-General. Though the
adapted Government of India Act was to be promulgated by the
Viceroy, there was an understanding that his approval was purely
formal, and that the interim constitution for Pakistan in the form recommended by the Quaid-i-Azam would be brought into force. Justice

Muhammad Sharif was entrusted with the task of amending the Government of India Act, 1935, and he worked for the most part directly under the guidance of the Quaid-i-Azam.

The interim constitution was a federal one based on the same pattern as those of the Indian Union, Canada, and Australia. The provinces of Pakistan were five in number: East Bengal, West Punjab, Sind, the North-West Frontier Province, and Baluchistan. The division of power between the central and provincial governments was the same as in the Government of India Act, 1935.

As in the other Dominions, the Governor-General of Pakistan was a constitutional head. Campbell-Johnson's allegation that the Quaid-i-Azam asked for and obtained "dictatorial powers unknown to any constitutional Governor General representing the King" [35] under the Ninth Schedule of the Government of India Act is without foundation. In actual fact, the Pakistan (Provisional Constitution) Order, 1947, conferred no special powers on the Governor-General and omitted the Ninth Schedule.

The Pakistan cabinet consisting of the Prime Minister and other ministers was responsible to the federal legislature. The Pakistan constituent assembly was to function in a dual capacity—as a constitution-making body and as the federal legislature. The strength of the constituent assembly was initially 69, but on the accession of states was later raised to 79.

On August 11, the Quaid-i-Azam was elected President of the Pakistan constituent assembly. In India the offices of the Governor-General and the President of the constituent assembly continued to be held by two separate persons. The Quaid-i-Azam agreed to take on the additional burden of the office of President of the assembly in order to guide and supervise the supremely important work of constitution-making. But the pressure of state business and of big events like the refugee and the Kashmir problems as well as failing health from May, 1948, on, prevented him from attending to it in his lifetime.

Also to be determined was the design of the Pakistan national flag, a matter which saw considerable discussion. Mountbatten, who claimed to be an authority on flags and emblems, took a great deal of interest in the subject. The green flag of the Muslim League, with the traditional Muslim symbol of the crescent and the star, could not be adopted without some change because it would identify the state with a particular political party. On the other hand, it had to provide the leading motif. It was decided, finally, to add a white stripe to represent the minorities. At Mountbatten's suggestion the crescent and the star were tilted forty-five degrees to give the crescent a more realistic resemblance to the rising moon.

CHAPTER 10

Radcliffe's Award

THE JUNE 3 partition plan provided that

> As soon as a decision involving partition has been taken for either province [the Punjab and Bengal], a Boundary Commission will be set up by the Governor-General, the membership and terms of reference of which will be settled in consultation with those concerned. It will be instructed to demarcate the boundaries of the two parts of the Punjab on the basis of ascertaining the contiguous majority areas of Muslims and non-Muslims. It will also be instructed to take into account other factors. Similar instructions will be given to the Bengal Boundary Commission. Until the report of a Boundary Commission has been put into effect, the provisional boundaries indicated in the Appendix will be used.

The Appendix gave a list of the Muslim majority districts of the Punjab and Bengal according to the 1941 census.

The boundary question bristled with difficulties and explosive possibilities. Nothing had aroused such passionate controversy as the partition of the Punjab and Bengal. The line of partition in each province would run across thickly populated areas and affect the fate of millions. It would cut in two an integrated economy and a single system of rail and road communication. In the Punjab, there was the added problem of an extensive irrigation and hydroelectric system. A line hastily and arbitrarily drawn might inflict immense economic injury and cause great hardship. Villagers might find themselves cut off from their fields by being placed on the opposite side of an international boundary. Innumerable problems of a similar kind might arise. A complicated and difficult task like this required many months of careful study. But, thanks to the deal between Mountbatten and the Congress leaders for a quick transfer of power, it had to be completed within a few weeks.

Each boundary commission was to consist of an equal number of representatives of India and Pakistan and of one or more impartial members. The claims of India and Pakistan were bound to conflict, and there was little chance that the representatives of India and Pakistan on the boundary commissions would reach agreement among themselves. The decision would thus rest with the impartial member, or members, of each boundary commission, who must have such high standing and established integrity as to inspire universal trust. There was a proposal "to put the vexed problem of boundary demarcation in the hands of the United Nations, but Nehru objected, on the grounds that this would involve cumbersome procedure and unacceptable delay." [1] The Quaid-i-Azam wanted three Law Lords from the United Kingdom to be appointed to the boundary commissions as impartial members. But he was told that the Law Lords were elderly persons who could not stand the sweltering heat of the Indian summer. Had it not been for the decision to transfer power within two months, the Quaid-i-Azam could have insisted that his suggestion be accepted. As it was, Mountbatten persuaded him to accept an English lawyer, Sir Cyril (now Lord) Radcliffe, as the chairman of both the boundary commissions who would have the power to make the award. The proposal was approved by the Partition Council. The members of the Punjab Boundary Commission were Din Muhammad and Muhammad Munir on behalf of Pakistan, and Mehr Chand Mahajan and Tej Singh on behalf of India. The members of the Bengal Boundary Commission were Abu Saleh Muhammad Akram and S. A. Rahman on behalf of Pakistan, and C. C. Biswas and B. K. Mukherji on behalf of India. All of them were High Court Judges.

The commissions were constituted toward the end of June, before the arrival of Radcliffe on July 8. Each commission was "instructed to demarcate the boundaries of the two parts of the Punjab/Bengal on the basis of ascertaining the contiguous majority areas of Muslims and non-Muslims. In doing so, it will also take into account other factors."

Both India and Pakistan agreed to accept the awards of the boundary commissions and to enforce them. The meeting of the Partition Council on July 22, which announced the formation of the Punjab Boundary Force and which on this occasion included Baldev Singh on behalf of the Sikhs, affirmed in an official communique:

> Both Governments have pledged themselves to accept the awards of the Boundary Commissions, whatever these may be. The Boundary Commissions are already in session; if they are to discharge their duties satisfactorily, it is essential that they should not be hampered by public speeches or writings threatening boycott or direct action or otherwise interfering with their work. Both Governments will take appropriate measures to secure this end; and as soon as the awards are announced, both Governments will enforce them impartially and at once.

Radcliffe did not take part in the public sittings of the commissions, in which arguments were presented by counsel on behalf of the Muslim League, the Congress, the Sikhs, and other interested parties. He studied the records of the proceedings and all material submitted for consideration, pored over maps and held discussions with the members of each commission. As expected, neither commission could reach agreement. The undefined and vague term "other factors" encouraged exaggerated claims and enhanced the inherent difficulties of the task. The awards for both the Punjab and Bengal were thus made by Radcliffe alone.

In Bengal (see Map II), by far the most important question related to the future of the great city of Calcutta. It was the capital of the province, its only major port, and its center of industry, commerce, communications, and education. It had sucked in the entire wealth of the countryside. For two hundred years the Muslim peasantry of Bengal had toiled and all the fruit of their labor had gone to Calcutta. East Bengal produced the bulk of raw jute in India and almost all its fine varieties, but all the jute mills were in or near Calcutta. Without Calcutta, East Bengal would be a "rural slum," to use the graphic phrase of Tyson, an Englishman who was Secretary to the Governor of Bengal. For Pakistan, separated into two parts by a thousand miles of Indian territory, the importance of sea communications and hence of the port of Calcutta could not be overemphasized. Calcutta would make all the difference between a Pakistan of uncertain economic

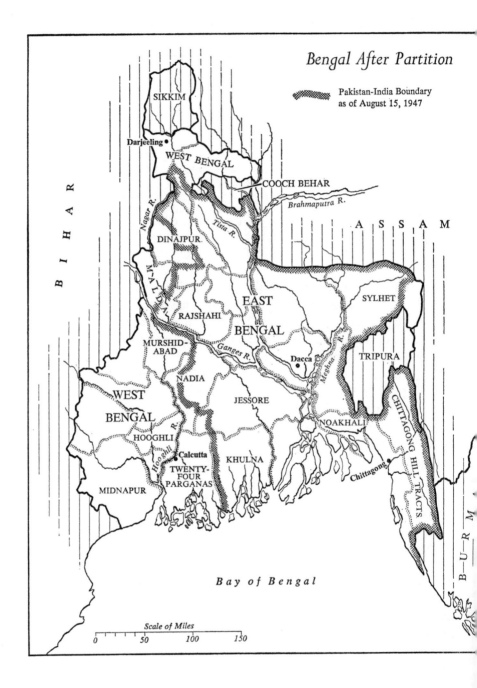

Bengal After Partition

Pakistan-India Boundary
as of August 15, 1947

SIKKIM

Darjeeling •

WEST BENGAL

COOCH BEHAR

Brahmaputra R.

A S S A M

B I H A R

Nagar R.

Tista R.

DINAJPUR

MALDA

EAST

BENGAL

RAJSHAHI

SYLHET

MURSHID-
ABAD

Ganges R.

Dacca •

Meghna R.

TRIPURA

NADIA

JESSORE

WEST

BENGAL

HOOGHLI

Hooghli R.

Calcutta

TWENTY-
FOUR
PARGANAS

KHULNA

NOAKHALI

CHITTAGONG HILL TRACTS

Chittagong •

MIDNAPUR

B – U – R – M

Bay of Bengal

Scale of Miles

0   50   100   150

viability and a Pakistan confidently striding into the future. For that very reason, the Congress leaders were determined to deny Calcutta to Pakistan and insisted on retaining it in India. Calcutta was thus the main bone of contention between the Congress and the Muslim League—the great prize both coveted and for which both were prepared to strive to the last. There was one way in which the clash of rival claims could have been avoided. Sir Frederick Burrows, the Governor of Bengal, was strongly in support of making Calcutta a free port whose facilities would be available to both East and West Bengal. But Mountbatten ruled this out.[2]

In the city of Calcutta itself, Muslims formed only a quarter of the population, but the hinterland, on which the life of Calcutta as a city and port depended and of which it formed an integral part, was a Muslim majority area. Calcutta had been built mainly by the resources of East Bengal, which also provided the bulk of its seamen and port workers. Pakistan had, therefore, a strong claim upon Calcutta and its environs, even on a demographic basis. There was also another important factor working in favor of the Muslim claim to Calcutta. A large section of Calcutta's population consisted of Scheduled Castes who were allied with the Muslim League, both in provincial and all-India politics. The Bengal Scheduled Caste leader, Mandal, had been nominated to the Viceroy's Executive Council by the Quaid-i-Azam in October, 1946, and was a member of the Muslim League bloc in the interim government. If a free plebiscite to determine whether Calcutta should go to India or Pakistan had been held in Calcutta, it was likely that the result would have been a victory for Pakistan.

Mountbatten was fully aware both of the importance the Muslim League attached to Calcutta and the strength of its claim to the city. Campbell-Johnson recorded that at the staff meeting on April 25, 1947, Mountbatten expressed "forebodings about the future of Calcutta. He felt that the Moslems would be bound to demand a plebiscite for it and that its fate would become a major issue. It would, however, be most undesirable to lay down the procedure of self-determination here which might well give the wrong answer."[3] By the wrong answer, Mountbatten obviously meant a verdict in favor of the Muslim League. If Mountbatten had been truly impartial, it should not have mattered to him, as Viceroy, what result was produced by a reference to the people of Calcutta. But he was far from being impartial. On the contrary, he had, as Sardar Patel later disclosed, entered into a secret agreement with the Congress leaders to have Calcutta assigned to India.

In a public speech in Calcutta on January 15, 1950, Patel declared: "We made a condition that we could only agree to partition if we did not lose Calcutta. If Calcutta is gone, then India is gone." [4] Obviously this condition could only have been made with Mountbatten. Ismay took Mountbatten's original plan of partition to London on July 2, 1947, to obtain the British government's approval. Under this plan, wrote Ismay, "Eastern Bengal and West Punjab were to go to Pakistan and Western Bengal (which was to include Calcutta) and the Eastern Punjab were to go to India. The frontiers would be demarcated by a Boundary Commission which would have a British chairman and one Hindu and one Moslem as members." [5] The Muslim League was kept completely in the dark regarding this crucially important part of Mountbatten's plan to hand Calcutta to India. Indeed, as Mountbatten knew very well, a partition plan, which openly incorporated the Congress condition about Calcutta going to India, had no chance of being accepted by the Muslim League. All that the Muslim League was told was that the issue of Calcutta was being left to the boundary commission to decide.

In the light of these facts, it is possible to see why Nehru opposed the proposal to entrust the United Nations with the demarcation of the boundary, and Mountbatten turned down the Quaid-i-Azam's suggestion for appointing three Law Lords from the United Kingdom to the boundary commission. These facts also serve to explain the otherwise inexplicable fact that the fate of Calcutta was publicly known many days before Radcliffe made his award. Ian Stephens, who was then editor of the *Statesman,* commenting on the timing of Radcliffe's Award, reported that there had been one leak, namely that Calcutta was to be assigned to India.[6] How did the leak occur? The India and Pakistan members of the Bengal Boundary Commission had disagreed and could have had no knowledge of Radcliffe's decision. And it is inconceivable that Radcliffe himself should have been responsible for the leak on so vital a point. Obviously some other party knew what the award was in advance; and that party, as Vallabhbhai Patel disclosed, was the Congress.

In dealing with Calcutta in his award, Radcliffe formulated two questions.

To which State was the City of Calcutta to be assigned or was it possible to adopt any method of dividing the City between the two States? If the City of Calcutta must be assigned as a whole to one or other of the States, what were its indispensable claims to the control of territory, such as all or part of the Nadia River System or the Kulti Rivers upon which the life of Calcutta as a city and port depended?

The questions were pertinent and showed that Radcliffe realized how important the city was and understood the foundation on which it had been built. But he raised questions only to answer them in a predetermined way without giving any reasons for the answer.

Radcliffe assigned Calcutta to India, and along with Calcutta, he also assigned to India the whole of the Muslim majority district of Murshidabad and the greater part of the Muslim majority district of Nadia. Nearly 6,000 square miles of territory with a population of 3.5 million Muslims that had been provisionally assigned to East Bengal were severed from it and transferred to West Bengal. The loss of Calcutta was irreparable. The loss of the Muslim majority districts in its hinterland was, however, compensated for to some extent by a gain in another area. One of the questions raised by Radcliffe related to the Chittagong Hill Tracts, "an area in which the Muslim population was only 3 per cent of the whole but which it was difficult to assign to a State different from that which controlled the district of Chittagong itself." The sparsely inhabited Chittagong Hill Tracts were almost wholly Buddhist; the district of Chittagong was predominantly Muslim. Radcliffe decided to assign the Chittagong Hill Tracts to Pakistan.

The Bengal Boundary Commission was also to "demarcate the Muslim majority areas of Sylhet District and the contiguous Muslim majority areas of the adjoining districts of Assam." The meaning of the term "adjoining districts of Assam" was disputed by the Pakistan and India members of the Bengal Boundary Commission. Radcliffe accepted the view of the latter that it referred only to those districts of Assam which adjoined Sylhet district. The distribution of population and the state of communications was such that Radcliffe came to the conclusion, that "some exchange of territory must be affected if a workable division is to result." Consequently, some non-Muslim areas were assigned to East Bengal and some Muslim territory was retained by Assam. Later there was a dispute over the demarcation of the boundary separating East Bengal from West Bengal and Assam.

In December, 1948, at an inter-Dominion conference held in Delhi, agreement was reached that a judicial tribunal should be set up to resolve the dispute. The award of the judicial tribunal has, however, not yet been fully implemented by India. In contravention of an agreed declaration by the prime ministers of India and Pakistan in 1958, the Government of India is still refusing to hand over the Berubari Union to Pakistan.

In the Punjab (see Map III), the Congress and the Sikhs based their demand for shifting the boundary as far west as the river Chenab mainly on the special position of the Sikhs. The Muslim majority districts of Gurdaspur, Sialkot, Gujranwala, Lahore, Sheikhupura, Montgomery, and Lyallpur were thus claimed for inclusion in East Punjab. Much importance was attached to Sikh shrines, such as Nankana Sahib, which was located in Sheikhupura. On the same grounds, Pakistan could have laid claim to Sirhind, Delhi, and Ajmer, which had Muslim shrines of great sanctity. The rich canal colony districts of Montgomery and Lyallpur were claimed by the Sikhs because of the contribution made by Sikh colonists to the development of these areas. In actual fact, the Muslim peasantry had played a much bigger part in bringing these newly irrigated areas under the plough. The British had no doubt allotted the choicest lands to the Sikhs as a reward for their services in the army; but, in any fair assessment, the contribution made by the Muslims, who outnumbered the Sikhs by four to one in the farming population of these districts, would have to outweigh that of the Sikhs. It is necessary to emphasize this fact, since the Sikh contribution to the development of canal colonies has often been grossly exaggerated. The Congress and the Sikhs also insisted on getting Lahore, which was the capital of the Punjab. Lahore was a Muslim majority town in a Muslim majority district contiguous to other Muslim majority areas. But so stubbornly did the Hindus and Sikhs cling to it that they refused to prepare an alternative capital for East Punjab until the fate of Lahore was known.

Sikh intransigence was reinforced by the attitude of the British who, from Mountbatten down to British officials in the Punjab, were anxious to save the Sikhs from the consequences of their own demand for the partition of the Punjab. At his press conference on June 4, Mountbatten, in answer to a question as to what provision had been

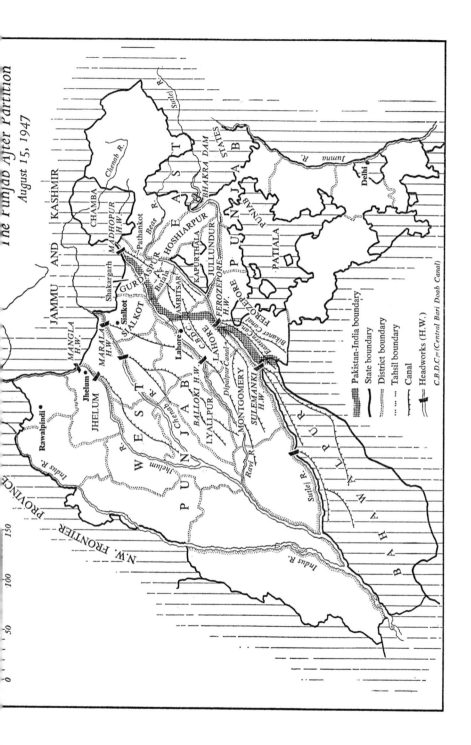

The Punjab After Partition
August 15, 1947

Pakistan-India boundary
State boundary
District boundary
Tahsil boundary
Canal
Headworks (H.W.)

C.B.D.C.=(Central Bari Doab Canal)

made in the partition plan "to keep the integrity of the Sikh people intact," said:

> They [the Sikhs] wanted the Punjab to be divided into predomi-
> nantly Muslim and non-Muslim areas. I have done exactly what the
> Sikhs requested me to do through the Congress. The request came
> to me as a tremendous shock, as I like the Sikhs am fond of them
> and I wish them well. I started thinking out a formula to help them
> but I am not a magician.[7]

Phrases like "The poor Sikhs! What can we do for them?" were continually used by Ismay and others on Mountbatten's staff. After the
boundary commissions had been set up, Arthur Henderson, Under
Secretary of State for India, in the course of a parliamentary debate
said that the Punjab Boundary Commission had been allowed to take
account of the location of Sikh religious shrines in the Punjab for the
purpose of determining the boundary between East and West Punjab.
The Quaid-i-Azam and Liaquat Ali Khan lodged a vigorous protest
against this unwarranted statement that was designed to influence the
boundary commission in favor of the Sikhs.

The Sikhs were preparing for a fight and were accusing the British
of breach of faith for not safeguarding Sikh solidarity. Jenkins, the
Governor of the Punjab, gave the Viceroy a summary of Sikh
demands as put to him by Giani Kartar Singh, one of the top-ranking
Sikh leaders.

> The Sikhs [are] entitled to their own land just as much as the
> Hindus or the Muslims. They must have their shrine at Nankana
> Sahib, at least one canal system, and finally arrangements must be
> made so as to bring at least three-quarters of the Sikh population
> from West to East Punjab. . . . Gianni said that unless it was rec-
> ognized . . . that the fate of the Sikhs was a vital issue, there
> would be trouble . . . they would be obliged to fight.[8]

That Jenkins himself was in sympathy with Sikh demands is clear
from his letter to the Viceroy. "I believe there is quite a lot in the
claims of the Sikhs, and, for that matter, of the other residents of the
East Punjab for a share in the canal colonies of the West," he wrote,
"and the Gianni's idea that the Montgomery district should be allotted to the East is by no means as ridiculous as it sounds." [9] Little
wonder that when Tara Singh undertook a fast unto death in 1961, to
secure the Sikh demand for a Punjabi-speaking province in which the
Sikhs would be in a majority, he offered to break it if Jenkins were

appointed arbitrator by the Government of India! And less wonder that the Government of India did not accept the offer!

The Muslim League naturally wanted to shift the boundary as far east as possible and claimed the whole of Lahore division and part of the Jullundur division. By and large, the Muslim League demand did not depart widely from the line separating contiguous Muslim majority areas from non-Muslim majority areas. Bahawalpur state, which was irrigated by the canals of the Sutlej Valley Project, was vitally interested in the boundary award, and made a representation to the Punjab Boundary Commission. Bahawalpur was a Muslim majority state under a Muslim ruler and its interests were identical with those of West Punjab. Bikaner state—a Hindu majority state ruled by a Hindu ruler—which was fed by a canal from the Sutlej River also made a representation to the Punjab Boundary Commission.

The award that Radcliffe gave in the Punjab lopped off a number of contiguous Muslim majority areas from Pakistan, but not a single non-Muslim majority area was taken away from India. If the justification for these decisions is sought in the phrase, "other factors," it is very strange that other factors should have worked consistently in favor of India and against Pakistan. In Gurdaspur district, two contiguous Muslim majority *tahsils,* or subdistricts, Gurdaspur and Batala, were given to India along with Pathankot tahsil to provide a link between India and the state of Jammu and Kashmir. The Muslim majority tahsil, Ajnala, in the Amritsar district was also handed over to India. In the Jullundur district the Muslim majority tahsils, Nakodar and Jullundur, which lie in the angle of the Sutlej and Beas rivers, were assigned to India. The Muslim majority tahsils, Zira and Ferozepore, in the Ferozepore district, which were east of the Sutlej River, were also transferred to India. All of these Muslim majority areas were contiguous to West Punjab.

For some of these transfers of territory from Pakistan Radcliffe offered no explanation. He merely said that he was "conscious that there are legitimate criticisms to be made [of his award] as there are I think, of any other line that might be chosen." But there were certain areas about which he felt it necessary to offer some sort of explanation. It is worth quoting his exact words.

I have hesitated long over those not inconsiderable areas east of the Sutlej River and in the angle of the Beas and Sutlej Rivers in which

Muslim majorities are found. But on the whole I have come to the conclusion that it would be in the true interests of neither State to extend the territories of the West Punjab to a strip on the far side of the Sutlej and that there are factors such as the disruption of railway communications and water systems that ought in this instance to displace the primary claims of contiguous majorities.

The explanation he has given is unconvincing in the extreme. Why should the true interests of Pakistan suffer because of a strip of territory east of the Sutlej River, and why was Radcliffe a better judge of the true interests of Pakistan than the representatives of Pakistan? The boundary line drawn by him was not following river courses but was cutting across them. As for railway communications, they would be cut, no matter how the boundary line was drawn.

The other reason for overriding the claims of contiguous majorities in order to avoid the disruption of water systems is even thinner. From the Ferozepore Headworks, which he awarded to India, not a single canal had been built to irrigate non-Muslim majority areas in East Punjab! Except for the Bikaner canal, which supplied water to a state outside the Indus Basin and outside Radcliffe's terms of reference, all the canals taking off from Ferozepore Headworks irrigated mostly Muslim majority areas in and contiguous to West Punjab. On the very grounds that Radcliffe advanced, these Muslim majority areas should have gone to Pakistan. By awarding them to India he disrupted a water system which he professedly sought to keep intact. He did a more damaging thing. He drew the boundary line in such a manner as to include Ferozepore Headworks in India, although the greater part of the water from the Headworks irrigated areas in Pakistan.

Similarly, by his award, Radcliffe aggravated the consequences of the severance of the Upper Bari Doab canal. This canal took off from Madhopur Headworks in the non-Muslim majority tahsil, Pathankot, in Gurdaspur district, but it irrigated mostly Muslim majority areas in and contiguous to West Punjab. Radcliffe awarded a number of these Muslim majority areas to India. Even so he could not avoid disrupting the Upper Bari Doab canal. In the report making the award he wrote: "I have not found it possible to preserve undivided the irrigation system of the Upper Bari Doab Canal which extends from Madhopur in the Pathankot tahsil to the western border of the district of Lahore, although I have made small adjustments of the Lahore-Amritsar district boundary to mitigate some of the consequences of this severance." But if he had not assigned the Muslim majority tahsils, Gurdaspur and Batala, in Gurdaspur district and the Ajnala tahsil in Amritsar district to India, the disruption in the irrigation system of the Upper Bari Doab canal would have been far less.

West Punjab depended far more than East Punjab upon the system of canal irrigation, which was among the most beneficent projects the British had undertaken in the subcontinent. The life-giving waters of the five rivers, which gave the Punjab its name (literally five waters), converted an arid area into the granary of India. Radcliffe's Award gave control of important canal headworks on the Sutlej and Ravi rivers to India, and thereby put the economic life of West Pakistan in jeopardy. That this was no theoretical possibility only is proved by India's action in cutting off canal water supplies in April, 1948, in contravention of solemn pledges.

An even more grievous injury was inflicted on Pakistan by the way in which Radcliffe divided the district of Gurdaspur. The district had four tahsils of which only one, Pathankot, had a non-Muslim majority; the other three—Gurdaspur, Batala, and Shakargarh had Muslim majorities. The district as a whole had a bare Muslim majority, but that was largely because of the high percentage of Hindus in Pathankot tahsil. Gurdaspur district was contiguous to the state of Jammu and Kashmir. For the Indian Union, rail and road communication with the state was only possible through the plains of this district that was flanked by high mountains in Indian territory to the east. If Radcliffe had awarded India only the non-Muslim majority tahsil, Pathankot, India would still not have gained access to Jammu and Kashmir, since the Muslim majority tahsils, Batala and Gurdaspur to the south would have blocked the way. By assigning these two Muslim majority tahsils also to India, Radcliffe provided India with a link to the state of Jammu and Kashmir and paved the way for the bitterest dispute between India and Pakistan.

At his press conference of June 4, 1947, Mountbatten was asked why he had, in his broadcast of the previous evening on the June 3 partition plan, categorically stated that "the ultimate boundaries will be settled by a Boundary Commission and will almost certainly not be identical with those which have been provisionally adopted." Mountbatten immediately replied, "I put that in for the simple reason that in the district of Gurdaspur in the Punjab the population is 50.4 per cent Muslims, I think, and 49.6 per cent non-Muslims. With a difference of 0.8 per cent you will see at once that it is unlikely that the Boundary Commission will throw the whole of the district into the Muslim majority areas." [10] Actually the Muslim population proportion was 51.14 percent, but that is immaterial. What is significant is that Mountbatten had made a particularly close study of the population statistics of Gurdaspur district and emphasized the need to divide it. Whichever way one looks at it, Mountbatten's statement was highly improper, by being designed to influence the judgment of the Punjab Boundary Commission on a crucial issue that was decisive for the fate of Kashmir.

Some days before the boundary commissions were set up, Mountbatten paid a visit to Kashmir (in June, 1947) to urge its Maharaja to take a decision on the accession of the state. V. P. Menon wrote, "[Mountbatten] assured the Maharaja that so long as he made up his mind to accede to one Dominion or the other before 15 August no trouble would ensue, for whichever Dominion he acceded to would take the State firmly under its protection as part of its territory." [11] But India and Pakistan were not equally well placed to undertake Kashmir's defense. Indeed, there was a world of difference between the two Dominions in this respect. All of Kashmir's lines of communications led into West Pakistan, whereas there was no link with India. Unless Gurdaspur district was divided in such a way as to provide India with access to Kashmir, India could not have taken the state under its protection or assumed responsibility for its defense. Lord Birdwood, an officer of the Indian army with great experience, expressed the view that "it was Radcliffe's Award to India of the Gurdaspur and Batala Tahsils with Muslim majorities which rendered possible the maintenance of an Indian force at Jammu based on Pathankot as railhead and which enabled India to consolidate her defences southwards all the way from Uri to the Pakistan border." [12] Surely, what was obvious to Lord Birdwood could not have been hidden from a great military commander like Lord Mountbatten. If, long before Radcliffe's Award, Mountbatten was assuring the Maharaja of Kashmir that India could safeguard the security of the state as well as Pakistan could, was it not likely that he had reached an understanding with Congress leaders in respect of Gurdaspur district similar to the one regarding Calcutta?

Radcliffe's Award in the Punjab was of such a character as to arouse immediate suspicions of outside interference. The only ones in a position to influence Radcliffe were Mountbatten and his staff. Mountbatten insisted that he and his staff were keeping aloof from Radcliffe. In his press conference on June 4, Mountbatten had said: "The Boundary Commission shall have representatives of all the parties. So far as it is humanly possible there will be no interference or dictation by the British Government." [13] Campbell-Johnson wrote that Mountbatten had given his staff the most explicit instructions to have no contact with Radcliffe.[14] Since, however, Radcliffe and his office were lodged in a wing of the Viceroy's house, it was possible to maintain discreet contact without any outsider coming to know about it. Conclusive evidence of such a contact was discovered by chance.

Among the papers that Jenkins, the Governor of the Punjab, left behind was a sketch-map of Radcliffe's Award in the Punjab, found accidentally by his successor Sir Francis Mudie. The sketch-map had been prepared by the Viceroy's Private Secretary George Abell on August 8, 1947, in response to a request from Jenkins, who was anxious to know the main outlines of the Punjab Boundary Award in order to make the necessary administrative and security arrangements. According to the sketch-map, prepared on the basis of information received from the Secretary of the Boundary Commission, the tahsils, Ferozepore and Zira, formed part of Pakistan. But in Radcliffe's report (dated August 12, 1947) making the award, these tahsils were included in India. Obviously between these two dates there had been a change at the expense of Pakistan.

Some writers have questioned the accuracy of the sketch-map on the grounds that it was based on a telephone conversation between George Abell and the Secretary of the Boundary Commission, and have tried to whittle down the significance of the discrepancy between it and the actual award. But the sketch-map was not intended to demarcate the boundary line with absolute accuracy down to individual villages and farms. It was required for an administrative purpose. For that object it was enough to indicate broad administrative areas, such as tahsils, which were to form part of one Dominion or the other. That it was based on a telephone conversation does not invalidate it in any way. But there is other corroborative evidence to show that Radcliffe had originally decided on the inclusion of the tahsils Ferozepore and Zira in Pakistan, but changed his mind as a result of outside interference. Justice Din Muhammad, a member of the Punjab Boundary Commission, informed the Pakistan government that when the question of these tahsils came up before the Punjab Boundary Commission, and the Pakistan members of the Commission started their arguments, Radcliffe stopped them with the remark that it was unnecessary to argue so obvious a case. In his award Radcliffe confessed that he "hesitated long over those not inconsiderable areas east of the Sutlej River and in the angle of the Beas and Sutlej Rivers in which Muslim majorities are found." How did these later hesitations arise over what Radcliffe had himself termed an obvious case? Who had intervened to cause these hesitations which led to a reversal of his previous judgment?

On August 9, 1947, I went from Delhi to Karachi for a day to consult the Quaid-i-Azam and Liaquat Ali Khan about the Indian proposals for the treatment of the national debt. Before I left Karachi to return to Delhi, Liaquat Ali Khan told me that the Quaid-i-Azam had received very disturbing reports about the likely decision on the Punjab boundary, particularly in the Gurdaspur district. In the Amritsar and Jullundur districts contiguous Muslim majority areas were also in danger of being assigned to India. He asked me, on my return to Delhi, to see Lord Ismay and convey to him, from the Quaid-i-Azam, that if the boundary actually turned out to be what these reports foreshadowed, this would have a most serious impact on the relations between Pakistan and the United Kingdom, whose good faith and honor were involved in this question. When I reached Delhi, I went straight from the airport to the Viceroy's house where Lord Ismay was working. I was told that Lord Ismay was closeted with Sir Cyril Radcliffe. I decided to wait until he was free. When, after about an hour, I saw him, I conveyed to him the Quaid-i-Azam's message. In reply, Ismay professed complete ignorance of Radcliffe's ideas about the boundary and stated categorically that neither Mountbatten nor he himself had ever discussed the question with him. It was entirely for Radcliffe to decide; and no suggestion of any kind had been or would ever be made to him. When I plied Ismay with details of what had been reported to us, he said he could not follow me. There was a map hanging in the room and I beckoned him to the map so that I could explain the position to him with its help. There was a pencil line drawn across the map of the Punjab. The line followed the boundary that had been reported to the Quaid-i-Azam. I said that it was unnecessary for me to explain further since the line, already drawn on the map, indicated the boundary I had been talking about.

Ismay turned pale and asked in confusion who had been fooling with his map. This line differed from the final boundary in only one respect—the Muslim majority tahsils of Ferozepore and Zira in the Ferozepore district were still on the side of Pakistan as in the sketch-map.

A word of explanation is necessary regarding the significance of these alterations. The tahsils Ferozepore and Zira had a considerable Sikh minority; the proportion of Sikhs in the population of this area was nearly double that of their average percentage of 13.2 in the Punjab. Mountbatten, Ismay, and others on the Viceroy's staff were anxious to appease the Sikhs, partly out of regard for their past services in the Indian army and partly to diminish the danger of the disturbances which the Sikhs were threatening to create. When Ismay went to London in July, 1947, he brought back with him Major Short who was devoted to the cause of the Sikhs. Penderel Moon, who met Major Short in Delhi toward the end of July, wrote that the latter

> realised at once that the time had passed for thinking of a Sikh-Muslim rapprochment. All he could do for the Sikhs was to plead for drawing the dividing line sufficiently far to the west to bring some of the colony lands within India. With all my sympathy with the Sikhs I did not think that on merits this could be done. . . . In various discussions in Delhi with Short and V. P. Menon I stuck to this view. Menon wanted to know whether by juggling with the line the danger of disturbances in the Punjab could be diminished. I did not think so.[15]

It is to be remembered that at the time Major Short was pleading for drawing the boundary line to the west and V.P. Menon was thinking of juggling with it, the issue of the boundary was solely in the hands of Radcliffe. And it was only by influencing Radcliffe that the Sikhs could be helped. How unfounded were these hopes of appeasing the Sikhs was shown by the holocaust in the Punjab that started even before the publication of the boundary award.

Many years later, while attending a Commonwealth Prime Ministers' Conference in London, Radcliffe was introduced to me at a social function at 10 Downing Street. He happened to ask me what place I came from. I could not help replying: "From that unfortunate Muslim majority area in the angle of the Beas and Sutlej Rivers over which you 'hesitated' before assigning it to India without any valid reason."

Mountbatten had promised that the awards of the boundary commissions would be published well before August 15, so as to allow time for administrative and security arrangements to be made on both sides of the border. If this promise had been kept, it might have mitigated the troubles about to break out in the Punjab even as, according to Ian Stephens, the leakage about Calcutta's final destination helped to avert riots in that turbulent city.[16] However, according to Campbell-Johnson, Mountbatten said on August 9, regarding the publication of the boundary awards, that "If he could exercise some discretion in the matter he would much prefer to postpone its appearance until after the Independence Day celebrations . . . [when its effects could not] mar Independence Day itself." [17] When Mountbatten said this, troubles in the Punjab had already started. The security of millions was at stake. It was a strange order of values that put the fleeting emotions of independence day celebrations above the lives and honor of the people. The dam was about to burst; and it was Mountbatten's responsibility as Viceroy to take whatever preventive and protective measures he could. Instead, in these last days of the British raj, he was anxious only that it should not burst while he was Viceroy and the British were still responsible.

Radcliffe signed his reports for the Punjab and Bengal on August 12, and for Sylhet on August 13; they were released by Mountbatten on the afternoon of August 16. On that day Liaquat Ali Khan and I had gone to Delhi to discuss the grim situation in the Punjab. It was then that we were handed Radcliffe's reports and read them with heavy hearts. That same evening there was a meeting at the Viceroy's house at which Nehru, Sardar Patel, Baldev Singh, Liaquat Ali Khan, I, and others were present. Mountbatten brought up the question of Radcliffe's Award for discussion. While Nehru and Patel kept quiet, Baldev Singh complained of the wrong done to Sikhs, whose sacred places were left in Pakistan. In reply I referred to the many large Muslim majority areas contiguous to Pakistan that had been assigned to India without any reason, and asked Baldev Singh to indicate even one non-Muslim majority area in the Punjab which had been allotted to Pakistan. To this question Baldev Singh could give no reply. I added that the boundary line could hardly be expected to follow the location of shrines. Many places sacred to the Muslims had been left in India.

Commenting on Radcliffe's Award in a broadcast speech, the Quaid-i-Azam said:

The division of India is now finally and irrevocably effected. No doubt we feel that the carving out of this great independent Muslim State has suffered injustices. We have been squeezed in as much as it was possible, and the latest blow that we have received was the Award of the Boundary Commission. It is an unjust, incomprehensible and even perverse award. It may be wrong, unjust and perverse; and it may not be a judicial but a political award, but we have agreed to abide by it and it is binding upon us. As honourable people we must abide by it. It may be our misfortune but we must bear up this one more blow with fortitude, courage and hope.[18]

CHAPTER 11

The Accession
of the States

THE INDIAN states, numbering 562, comprised roughly a third of India's territory and a quarter of the population. They were outside the administrative set-up of British India and were ruled by Indian princes who had accepted the United Kingdom as a paramount power. Most of them were small and exercised limited powers and jurisdiction, but there were 140 fully empowered states. The largest, such as Hyderabad, Mysore, and Kashmir, were, in extent of territory and population, comparable with British Indian provinces.

Their relations with the British government were established by treaties and agreements which had been negotiated or imposed during the gradual expansion of British rule in India, and varied from state to state. But in all cases the paramount power was responsible for foreign relations and external and internal security, and could exercise disciplinary authority over the princes in the event of misrule. In relation to the Indian states, the Viceroy functioned as Crown Representative and had directly under him a political department for administering their affairs. In the bigger states, officers of the political department were appointed as Residents; and the smaller states were grouped into zones for purposes of control by political agents. Railways, posts and telegraphs, and currency had integrated the states in many ways with British India and made them a part of the economic system controlled by the Government of India. But in the management of their internal affairs, the rulers of Indian states were free within the limits set by treaties and by the doctrine of paramountcy.

The rulers of the states recognized that as a class they had common interests in preserving their dynasties and their rights and privileges; but they were torn by jealousies over precedence, titles, and other ceremonial matters, which occupied their minds more than the welfare of their subjects. There was, however, a growing awareness that they could not remain unaffected by the march of events in British India.

The Chamber of Princes had been organized in 1921, but some of the largest states had not joined it. Representatives of the Indian states, including some rulers, had attended the Round Table conferences in London in 1930–32, and had expressed willingness to join the proposed Federation of India, though not on the same basis as the British Indian provinces. The accession of each state to the federation was to be the voluntary act of its ruler; the representatives of the acceding state in the Federal legislature were to be nominated by the ruler; and the instrument of accession, to be executed by the ruler, was to specify the matters with respect to which jurisdiction would be exercised by the federation. The Government of India Act, 1935, had provided for the establishment of the Federation of India, which included the states, but this provision was to come into force only when a specified number of states had acceded to the federation. Negotiations with individual states for executing instruments of accession had dragged on in a round of demands and partial concessions followed by further demands until the outbreak of the Second World War had put an end to them for the time being.

After the war a new situation developed that made the federal scheme envisaged in the Government of India Act, 1935, obsolete. Indian independence was in sight; the British government had made an unequivocal declaration for the transfer of power to Indian hands at an early date. With the attainment of independence by British India, there would be no British troops in India, and the British government would be unable to exercise paramountcy.

In a memorandum to the Chamber of Princes on May 12, 1946,

the Cabinet Mission advised the princes, in their own interests and in the interests of India as a whole, to make their contribution to the framing of the new constitution, and in suitable cases to "form or join administrative units large enough to enable them to be fitted into the constitutional structure." The rulers were also advised "to ensure that their administrations conform to the highest standards [and] to place themselves in close and constant touch with public opinion in their States by means of representative institutions." [1]

These exhortations to virtue came too late. By assuring protection to the princes against external aggression and internal subversion, the British had secured their undeviating loyalty to the Empire, but had weakened their moral fiber. Used to luxury and servile flattery from an early age, the princes were, on the whole, and apart from honorable exceptions, a decadent class. Interested more in their palaces than in their people, they paid scant attention to social and political reforms or economic development. Standards of administration and education in their territories were lower than in British India, except in some states with enlightened rulers. Civil liberties were virtually nonexistent; the will of the ruler, rather than the rule of law, was supreme. But the ferment of democratic ideas was slowly spreading from British India to the states.

In 1927 the All-India States' People's Conference had been organized with the object of attaining "responsible government for the people in the Indian States through representative institutions under the aegis of their rulers." [2] There had been serious political unrest in Kashmir and in some other states during the thirties, but despite much repression, some progress was made. Legislative assemblies with limited powers had been set up in a number of states, and though the states remained under a system of personal government, it was clear that the days of unfettered autocracy were numbered.

The composition of the population in the states was akin to that in the contiguous areas of British India. States in the northwest had a majority of Muslims; those in the rest of India had a Hindu majority. Accidents of history had placed Hindu rulers at the head of Muslim majority states like Jammu and Kashmir, and Muslim rulers in charge of Hindu majority states like Hyderabad. This complicated the process of establishing democratic institutions still further.

For a long time the activities of political parties in India had been confined to British India, and they had seldom interfered in the affairs of the states. But after the Government of India Act, 1935, was passed, this isolation tended to break down. The Act opened the way to a Federation of India which included the Indian states, and if its federal provisions had come into force, the states and their representatives in the central legislature would inevitably have been drawn into the arena of all-India politics. But before this could happen, the sweeping victory which the Congress had obtained in the majority of provinces in the elections of 1937 gave the Congress party an overweening sense of its importance. Now it felt strong enough to call itself the only successor to the British power over the whole of India including the Indian states.

In February, 1938, the Congress had passed a resolution that considered the states an integral part of India and demanded the same political, social, and economic freedom in the states as in the rest of India. "To-day," Jawaharlal Nehru had said "a remarkable awakening is taking place all over India including the Indian States. We on our part must try to nurse it, cherish it and we must organise ourselves." Thus an intimate connection was established between the Congress and the All-India States' People's Conference, which also came under Gandhi's leadership.[3]

In December, 1938, Gandhi had warned the states that the Congress policy of noninterference might be abandoned, and advised rulers to cultivate friendly relations "with an organisation which bids fair in the future, not very distant, to replace the Paramount Power." [4] In 1939 Nehru had been elected President of the All-India States' People's Conference, which became a satellite organization of the Congress. Leading members of the Congress had taken part in the agitation in the states. Gandhi himself had led a civil disobedience movement in Rajkot—the state of his birth.

By 1939 the struggle between the Congress and the Muslim League had assumed all-India proportions. The Muslim League could not ignore the efforts of the Congress to extend its sphere of activity and influence to the states. An All-India States Muslim League, which had been formed in 1939 on the pattern of the All-India Muslim League, aimed at the preservation and advancement of the rights and interests of Muslims in the Indian states.

When in 1940 the Muslim League put forward the demand for Pakistan in Muslim majority areas, the states were inevitably affected. The letter "k" in the word "Pakistan" stands for the state of Kashmir.

Muslims from all parts of India, including the states, had been drawn into the battle for the establishment of Pakistan. One of the most valiant of these fighters was Bahadur Yar Jung of Hyderabad, the President of the All-India States Muslim League. The untimely death, in 1944, of this noble man, who was one of the greatest orators Muslim India has produced, was a big loss to the movement for Pakistan.

In states in which the religion of the ruler was different from that of the majority of the people, the struggle between the people and the ruler had assumed a communal form, and had brought people from the neighboring areas of British India into the field. These circumstances had led the Muslim League to take an increasing interest in the affairs of the states. In general, the policy of the Muslim League toward the states was not as aggressive as that of the Congress, and the rulers were far more afraid of the Congress, particularly of its left wing.

This was the situation when the Cabinet Mission arrived in India after the end of the war. In their statement of May 16, 1946, the Cabinet Mission recommended that "there should be a Union of India embracing both British India and the States which should deal with the following subjects: foreign affairs, defence and communications." On the question of the relationship of Indian states with British India the statement said: "Paramountcy can neither be retained by the British Crown nor transferred to the new Government. . . . [We are assured that] the States are ready and willing to cooperate in the new development of India. The precise form which their cooperation will take must be a matter for negotiation during the building up of the new constitutional structure, and it by no means follows that it will be identical for all the States."

The reaction of the princes to the Cabinet Mission plan was given authoritatively by a conference of rulers held in Bombay. On January 29, 1947, the conference adopted a resolution which stated that the entry of the states into the Union of India should be on no other basis than that of negotiation. The final decision should rest with each state, and be taken after considering the complete picture of the new constitution. The states would retain all subjects and powers other than those ceded by them to the Union of India. The constituent assembly was not to deal with questions affecting the internal administration or constitutions of the states; nor should the existing boundaries of a state be altered except by free consent of each state.

The British government's statement of February 20, 1947, which announced June, 1948, as the date for the transfer of power to Indian hands, reiterated the position in regard to the Indian states, that paramountcy would not be transferred to any government of British India. With the lapse of paramountcy, every Indian state would become sovereign. The specter of the Balkanization of India was, therefore, haunting the imagination of Congress leaders, and they were anxious to bring as many states as possible into the constituent assembly. They appealed to the patriotism of the princes, and at the same time held over their heads the Damoclean sword of public agitation in the states. This was a serious threat, for the princes, by their pursuit of private pleasure and neglect of public welfare, no longer had a real hold over their subjects. Such attachment as their people felt for the princes was due more to tradition than to genuine sentiments of love and loyalty. In fact, this feudal order was ready to crumble at the first touch of reality; but neither the princes nor their opponents were quite aware of the extent of the decay.

Negotiating committees were appointed by the constituent assembly and the Chamber of Princes. They held joint meetings in February and March of 1947, but no decision was reached. The princes were by no means united. The Nawab of Bhopal, who was the Chancellor of the Chamber of Princes, was strongly of the view that the interests of the states would be best served by collective bargaining, and that they should not enter the constituent assembly individually but only after arriving at an agreement among themselves. Not all rulers, however, followed his lead. Some of the Hindu and Sikh rulers like Baroda, Bikaner, and Patiala felt that their safety lay in coming to terms with the Congress and strengthening its right wing. They looked upon the conservative Sardar Patel as their best friend. These rulers felt that by sitting on the fence and not joining the constituent assembly they might offend the Congress. This was not an imaginary fear. On April 18, 1947, Nehru, in a speech before the All-India States' People's Conference at Gwalior, publicly threatened that "any State which did not come into the Constituent Assembly would be treated by the country as a hostile State. Such a State . . . would have to bear the consequences of being so treated." [5] Although

Liaquat Ali Khan asked the states to disregard the threats of the Congress, which had no right to coerce them, a number of rulers succumbed to these threats. But the majority still held out, and even those who joined the constituent assembly did not commit themselves to accession. Thus on the eve of independence no one knew what shape the relationship between the Indian states and the successor governments of the Indian Union and Pakistan would take.

The June 3 partition plan for the transfer of power stated that the policy toward Indian states contained in the Cabinet Mission memorandum of May 12, 1947, remained unchanged. The operative part of this memorandum was contained in its concluding lines, which read: "All the rights surrendered by the States to the Paramount Power will return to the States. Political arrangements between the States on the one side and the British Crown and British India on the other will thus be brought to an end. The void will have to be filled either by the States entering into a federal relationship with the successor Government or Governments in British India, or failing this, entering into particular political arrangements with it or them." [6]

In keeping with this policy, there was a provision in the Indian Independence Act, 1947, which terminated all treaties and agreements between the British government and the rulers of Indian states as of August 15, 1947. Agreements relating to customs, transit and communications, posts and telegraphs, and other like matters, however, would continue in force until they were denounced either by the ruler of the Indian state or by the Dominion government concerned, or were superseded by subsequent agreements.

On June 3, Mountbatten explained the implications of the partition plan to the States Negotiating Committee. The next day at a press conference Mountbatten said that the Indian states had been independent states in treaty relations with the British. With the lapse of paramountcy they would assume an independent status, and were "absolutely free to choose" to join one constituent assembly or the other, or make some other arrangement.[7]

The problem of the Indian states was of far greater magnitude for the Indian Union than for Pakistan. Of the 562 states, Pakistan was contiguous with only fourteen, although these included a state of such overriding importance for Pakistan as Kashmir. The rest were geographically linked up with the Indian Union. But even so Pakistan could not be unconcerned about the fate of some of the other states.

In particular, the biggest state in India, the state of Hyderabad, which had been ruled by a Muslim dynasty from the days of the Mughul Empire, occupied a special place in the sentiments of Muslim India.

On June 13, the Viceroy discussed the question of the states at a meeting attended by Nehru, Sardar Patel, and Kripalani on behalf of the Congress; Jinnah, Liaquat Ali Khan, and Abdur Rab Nishtar on behalf of the Muslim League; and Baldev Singh on behalf of the Sikhs. Sir Conrad Corfield, the Political Adviser, was also present. It was decided at this meeting that each of the two new governments should set up a State department to deal with the problems of the states. The Political department would sort out records, and would hand over to the British High Commissioner those that concerned the private lives of rulers and the internal affairs of states.

On the question of whether the states could become independent, there was a difference of opinion. Nehru maintained that since the states did not have the means to establish international relations or declare war, they could not become sovereign independent states and should enter the political structure of one or the other Dominion government. Jinnah said that there should be no compulsion on them to do so. The states were free to decide for themselves, but it was in the mutual interest of the states and the Dominion governments to make the necessary adjustments. It was, therefore, agreed that there should be a meeting between the leaders of India and Pakistan and the representatives of the Indian states.

This difference in approach between the Congress and the Muslim League soon became public knowledge. On June 14, the All-India Congress Committee passed a resolution affirming that the lapse of paramountcy did not lead to the independence of the states because they could not live in isolation from the rest of India; and stating that the sovereign people would have the right to determine their own future. Gandhi said that declarations of independence by Indian princes "were tantamount to a declaration of war against the free millions of India." [8] Jinnah, on the other hand, declared in a statement issued on June 18, that, constitutionally and legally, the states would be independent sovereign states on the termination of paramountcy and would be free to adopt any course they liked.

It might at first sight appear that at least in the matter of states the interests of the Congress and the Muslim League pointed to the pursuit of a coordinated policy. It was to the advantage of both the

Indian Union and Pakistan to bring contiguous states into their respective folds; and they were more likely to gain their ends by concerted action. If both had agreed on a common policy with respect to accession and had based it on the principles underlying the partition of British India, many of the later troubles would have been avoided. Yet so deep had the cleavage between the Congress and the Muslim League become and so great was their mutual suspicion of each other's motives that a frank and fruitful exchange of views was not possible. Moreover, there was a real conflict of interests over the two biggest states—Kashmir and Hyderabad. Kashmir, contiguous to Pakistan, had a Muslim majority and a Hindu ruler. Hyderabad, contiguous to India, had a Hindu majority and a Muslim ruler. India wanted to grab both Kashmir and Hyderabad. Kashmir was an integral part of the Muslim concept of Pakistan; and the Muslim League leaders were in deep sympathy with Hyderabad's desire for independence.

On the question of tactics, too, there was a difference of approach. The Congress was prepared to use every means of pressure and coercion to secure the accession of states. The Muslim League strictly adhered to legal and constitutional methods. On a number of occasions in June and July of 1947 the Quaid-i-Azam said: "The legal position is that with the lapse of Paramountcy on the transfer of power by the British all Indian States would automatically regain their full sovereign and independent status. They are, therefore, free to join either of the two Dominions or to remain independent. The Muslim League recognises the right of each State to choose its destiny. It has no intention of coercing any State into adopting any particular course of action." [9] It was not merely the Quaid-i-Azam's penchant for constitutionalism that led him to make these pronouncements; they were also intended to safeguard Hyderabad's independence. By the same token they might jeopardize Kashmir's accession to Pakistan, but that was not considered a great risk.

In theory, there were three courses open to each state. It could join one or the other constituent assembly and accede either to India or to Pakistan; it could declare itself to be a sovereign independent state, but that was a feasible course of action only for the bigger states. Or, some of the states could join together to form an independent bloc. A number of states, such as Baroda, Bikaner, and Patiala, had already joined the Indian constituent assembly. Hyderabad and Travancore announced their decision to be independent. The Nawab of Bhopal was in favor of forming a separate bloc of states. He resigned his Chancellorship of the Chamber of Princes to work for this scheme. His place was taken by the Maharaja of Patiala, who had been the Pro-Chancellor.

Early in July the States departments of India and Pakistan were set up. For India, Sardar Patel was the Minister in charge, and V. P. Menon was appointed Secretary to the Department, in addition to his duties as Constitutional Adviser to the Governor-General. The corresponding portfolio for Pakistan was held by Abdur Rab Nishtar, and Ikramullah was the Secretary.

The Cabinet Mission plan had provided that the states would cede to the central government three subjects only, namely, defense, foreign affairs, and communications, and would retain all other subjects and powers. The Cabinet Mission had also proposed in their memorandum of May 12, 1946, that existing arrangements as to matters of common concern, especially in the economic and financial fields, should continue for the time being. Working on this basis, V. P. Menon drew up an instrument of accession for defense, external affairs, and communications, and a Standstill Agreement to cover existing arrangements for customs, currency, and similar matters. On July 5, Sardar Patel issued a statement which said in part: "We ask no more of them [States] than accession on these three subjects in which the common interests of the country are involved. In other matters we would scrupulously respect their autonomous existence." [10]

The scheme was simple and statesmanlike. Instead of entering into long and involved negotiations with individual states, every state was confronted with two standard documents from which no variation was allowed. It was in the obvious interest of most states to enter into the Standstill Agreement, but they were told that there could be no Standstill Agreement without an instrument of accession. Great credit is due to Sardar Patel and V. P. Menon for the firmness and skill with which they handled the princes. But it was Mountbatten's superb diplomacy which was really responsible for maneuvering the princes into signing the instrument of accession.

The greatest service that Mountbatten rendered to the Union of India was to contrive the accession of the states to India and to lay to rest forever the fear of a possible Balkanization of India. In the new and tumultuous world of democratic politics and cataclysmic change, the princes felt lost and bewildered. They looked to the Viceroy for guidance and protection. To the traditional loyalty the princes owed to the representative of the British Crown was added the reverence due to a scion of royalty. The Congress leaders turned these sentiments to their own advantage by entrusting Mountbatten with the task of bringing the states into the fold of the Union of India. Mountbatten spoke to the princes as one who was keenly solicitous of their welfare, and could perceive, with a superior wisdom, where their true interests lay. He dazzled them with the glitter of royalty and charmed them with the magic of his personality. By ceaseless persuasion and remorseless pressure, by friendly advice and viceregal admonition, he led them to accept what was the sure end of their power. For accession in defense, external affairs, and communications placed the rulers at the mercy of the Congress government. Between the nether stone of popular agitation, and the upper stone of intervention by the central government in the interest of internal security, the princes were squeezed out. Their states were merged with neighboring provinces or other states, and the map of India was redrawn. Not even their names were left to bear witness to their existence. The rulers were pensioned off with handsome allowances, which are in the process of being reduced by one means or another. Perhaps the princes were doomed to extinction anyhow, but that they should have been coaxed and driven to the slaughter house by the shepherd they trusted most is what adds poignancy to the scene.

On July 25, Mountbatten addressed the Chamber of Princes in his capacity as Crown Representative. He was "in full uniform with an array of orders and decorations calculated to astonish even these practitioners in princely pomp. . . . He used every weapon in his armoury of persuasion." [11] He emphasized that though the rulers were technically at liberty to link with either of the dominions, there were "certain geographical compulsions which cannot be evaded. Out of something like 565 States the vast majority are irretrievably linked up geographically with the Dominion of India. . . . In the case of Pakistan, the States although important are not so numerous and Mr. Jinnah the future Governor General of Pakistan is prepared to negotiate the case of each State separately and individually. But in the case of India where the overwhelming majority of the States are involved, clearly separate negotiations with each State is out of the question." The draft instrument of accession, he explained, provided for accession on the three subjects of defense, external affairs, and communications without any financial liability on the part of the states and had an "explicit provision that in no other matter has the Central Government any authority to encroach on the internal autonomy or the sovereignty of the State." After pointing out the advantages to the states of this arrangement, he added: "But I must make it clear to you that I have still to persuade the Government of India to accept it. If all of you will cooperate with me and are willing to accede, I am confident that I can succeed in my efforts." He reminded them that the transfer of power, after which he would no longer be Crown Representative, was close at hand and if they were prepared to come, they must come before August 15. "My scheme," concluded Lord Mountbatten, "leaves you with all practical independence you can possibly use and makes you free of all those subjects which you can not possibly manage on your own. You cannot run away from the Dominion Government which is your neighbour any more than you can run away from the subjects for whose welfare you are responsible." [12]

But this was not all. He canvassed individual rulers both before and after the meeting with the Chamber of Princes. Travancore state had declined to send a representative to the meeting on July 25, since it had decided to assume independence. In consequence, its Dewan (Prime Minister), Sir C. P. Ramaswamy Aiyer, had brought strong attacks on his head from Congress leaders. The Travancore State Congress had threatened a campaign of direct action from August 1. Mountbatten sent for the Dewan, who was at first "adamant but after a further interview with Lord Mountbatten he agreed that accession was inevitable." When the Dewan returned to Travancore, a personal attack was made on him and he was wounded. The Maharaja hastened to telegraph his accession. According to V. P. Menon, "This announcement had a distinct effect on other rulers who were still wavering." [13]

On July 28 Lord Mountbatten gave a reception for the princes which, V. P. Menon wrote, "was in the nature of a last-minute canvassing of voters near the polling booth. Those of the rulers who had not yet signified their intention of acceding were taken by the A.D.Cs. one by one for a friendly talk with Lord Mountbatten. When he had finished with them, he passed them on to me in the full view of the company and I, in my turn, conducted them across the room to

Sardar. This had a good psychological effect on the rulers who were present." [14]

In short, Mountbatten did everything in his power to secure the accession of states to the Indian Dominion. By contrast, he did nothing for Pakistan, although as Crown Representative he owed an equal duty to both Dominions. But worse than that, in every disputed case of accession, he threw his weight in favor of India. The clearest and most indefensible example is the part he played in the occupation by Indian forces of the Muslim majority state of Jammu and Kashmir. A less well-known instance is provided by the states of Jodhpur and Jaisalmere where he intervened to prevent their accession to Pakistan. These states were contiguous to Pakistan. Although the majority of their population was Hindu and their rulers were also Hindu, they wanted to accede to Pakistan where they felt their interests would be better safeguarded. V. P. Menon got wind of their approach to the Quaid-i-Azam and acted at once. He informed Lord Mountbatten, who made it clear to the Maharaja of Jodhpur that from a purely legal standpoint he could accede to Pakistan but that the consequences would be serious because he was a Hindu and the state was predominantly Hindu, as were the neighboring states. If the Maharaja acceded to Pakistan, his action would conflict with the principle underlying the partition of India, and serious communal trouble might break out in the state.[15] The upshot was that both Jodhpur and Jaisalmere acceded to India.

But Mountbatten paid little heed to "the principle underlying the partition of India" when he accepted the accession of Kapurthala to the Indian Dominion. This state was ruled by a Sikh, but had a Muslim majority of 64 percent and was contiguous to the Muslim majority area of West Punjab. Later, Radcliffe assigned these areas to India without any valid reason, but when Mountbatten accepted the accession of Kapurthala, he was not in possession of the Radcliffe Award.

Among the states that acceded to India were some—as, for example, Bhopal and Rampur—which were ruled by Muslim princes. Rampur had a high proportion of Muslims in the population. They rose against accession to India, but were suppressed by troops sent by the Government of India on the Nawab's appeal. General Tucker wrote:

> The Sirdar [Vallabhbhai Patel] was determined that no State, Muslim or otherwise, should secede from his Dominion, so before many

hours had passed we received direct and urgent orders to send troops into Rampur. We sent the 6th Jat Regiment. In this case the insurgents were Muslims who wished to carve out their own destiny. Later on we contrasted the speed in meeting the Nawab's request with the complete lack of response to our repeated appeal for troops to be sent to the help of the unlucky Muslims being obliterated in the Hindu States of Alwar and Bharatpur.[16]

By August 15 all the five hundred odd Hindu majority states had acceded to India except two—Hyderabad and Junagadh. One Muslim majority state—Kapurthala—had also acceded to India. The accession of other Muslim majority states including Kashmir was still undecided. The story of Junagadh, Hyderabad, and Kashmir will be related in Chapter XIV.

In marked contrast to the spate of accessions to the Indian Dominion, no state acceded to Pakistan before August 15. Ten states were contiguous to West Pakistan, had a Muslim majority in the population, and were ruled by Muslim princes. These were Bahawalpur, Khairpur, Kalat, Las Bela, Kharan, and Makran, and the four frontier states, Dir, Swat, Amb, and Chitral.

Bahawalpur had bigger resources in population and revenue than any of the other states, but even this state was too small to remain independent. Of its population of less than two million, 83 percent were Muslims. Its prosperity depended upon the Sutlej Valley Project, which was essentially an extension of the irrigation system of West Punjab. That the economic interests of West Pakistan and Bahawalpur were closely allied was shown by the fact that Pakistan's counsel Zafrullah Khan represented Bahawalpur also before the Punjab Boundary Commission. The North Western Railway, which linked the North-West Frontier Province and West Punjab with Karachi, passed for a considerable portion of its length through Bahawalpur. If there were any serious threat to its security, internal or external, Bahawalpur would have to turn to Pakistan for protection.

These ties pointed inevitably to the accession of the state to Pakistan. Nevertheless, there was hesitation and delay caused by the desire of the Nawab and his Chief Minister, Mushtaq Ahmad Gurmani, to "maintain a quasi-independent existence," [17] and a strong negotiating position. On August 15, the Nawab assumed the title of Jalalat-ul-Malik A'la Hazrat Amir of Bahawalpur, which signified an independent status. At the same time he decided to send representatives to the Pakistan constituent assembly to take part in its deliberations and, in due course, to arrive at a satisfactory constitutional arrangement between the state and Pakistan. But events were moving too fast for these dilatory methods. In the second half of August, 1947, the Punjab disturbances overflowed to Bahawalpur and although the state authorities took vigorous measures to protect the non-Muslim minority, a fairly complete evacuation of Hindus and Sikhs from more than half the state had taken place by the end of September. On October 3, Bahawalpur acceded to Pakistan.

Khairpur state followed Bahawalpur. The frontier states, Chitral Swat, Dir, and Amb also acceded to Pakistan during the next few months leaving only the four Baluchistan states, Kalat, Kharan, Makran, and Las Bela undecided.

The Baluchistan states, although extensive in area, were sparsely populated and poorly developed. Their combined population was about half a million, and their financial resources meager in the extreme. The Khan of Kalat wanted to stake a claim to independence. He employed an Englishman, Douglas Fell, as Foreign Minister. It was reported that Fell was negotiating with foreign companies for oil prospecting and was, possibly, seeking support through them. It was also alleged that the Khan's brother and uncle sought aid in Kabul. Negotiations for accession dragged on, although the Khan professed the highest veneration for the Quaid-i-Azam. Meanwhile the rulers of Las Bela, Makran, and Kharan, over whom the Khan of Kalat claimed some sort of suzerainty, got restive and decided early in March, 1948, to offer accession directly to Pakistan. The acceptance of their accession isolated Kalat, now entirely surrounded by Pakistan territory. Under these circumstances the Khan saw the path of wisdom and acceded to Pakistan before the end of March, 1948.

CHAPTER 12

The Birth of Pakistan

ON AUGUST 14, 1947, Lord Mountbatten, who had come to Karachi to convey His Majesty's and his own greetings to the new Dominion of Pakistan, addressed the constituent assembly. The previous evening at a state dinner given in honor of Lord and Lady Mountbatten, the Quaid-i-Azam had warmly praised the British government, whose decision to transfer complete power to the two sovereign independent Dominions "marked the fulfilment of the great ideal which was set forth by the formation of the Commonwealth with the avowed object to make all nations and countries which formed part of the British Empire self-governing and independent States, free from the dominion of any other nation."

In his address to the constituent assembly Lord Mountbatten, paying a tribute to the Quaid-i-Azam, said: "Our close personal contact and the mutual trust and understanding that have grown out of it are, I feel, the best of omens for future good relations." In a somewhat philosophic vein he remarked: "The birth of Pakistan is an event in history. We who are part of history and helping to make it are not well-placed even if we wished to moralise on the event, to look back and survey the sequence of the past that led to it. . . . There is no time to look back. There is time only to look forward." [1]

Pakistan

U.S.S.R.

CHINA

Boundary

Undefined

JAMMU AND

AFGHANISTAN

35

Kabul

Kabul R.

CEASE-FIRE LINE

Peshawar

Islamabad

Rawalpindi

KASHMIR
(Disputed Territory)

Srinagar

Indus R.

Jhelum

Kandahar

D.I. Khan

Jhelum R.

Chenab R.

Beas R.

Fort
Sandeman

Lahore

Ravi R.

Sutlej R.

30

Quetta

Montgomery

West Pakistan

D.G. Khan

Multan

75

Kalat

Bahawalpur

New
Delhi

Jacobabad

IRAN

INDIA

Indus R.

Bela

25

Turbat

Hyderabad

Karachi

65

Arabian Sea

Junagadh

Junagadh and Manavadar

70

Bombay

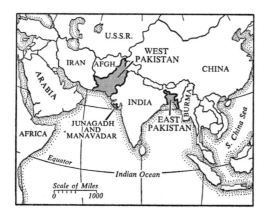

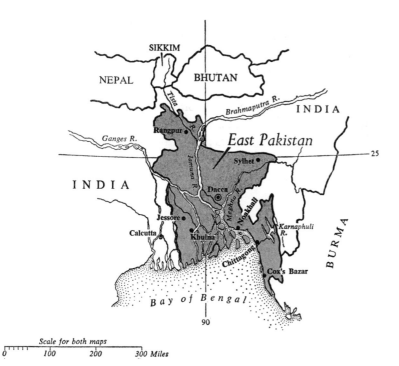

After the address to the constituent assembly the Quaid-i-Azam and Lord Mountbatten drove in state together to the Governor-General's house. The drive passed off safely without the feared Sikh attempt at assassination.

August 15, 1947, was the last Friday of the holy month of Ramazan—a day to which, traditionally, sanctity is attached among Muslims. On this august day, the Quaid-i-Azam assumed the office of Governor-General of Pakistan, and the cabinet was sworn in. The national flag with the crescent and the star was unfurled. Pakistan was born. The fifth most populous state in the world and the biggest Muslim state had come into existence (see Map IV).

The emergence of Pakistan was the triumph of a democratic idea. The faith of the people in Pakistan had made the idea possible, and their free acceptance of the leadership of the Quaid-i-Azam enabled them to achieve it. The Quaid-i-Azam had the resources of his own spirit and the trust of the people in his leadership, and with these intellectual and moral weapons he won Pakistan for his people. And the people were profoundly grateful. He was the Father of the Nation, the Quaid-i-Azam, the Great Leader. Formal recognition was given to this position when the constituent assembly resolved on August 12, that he should be addressed as "Quaid-i-Azam Muhammad Ali Jinnah, Governor-General of Pakistan" in all official acts, documents, letters, and correspondence from August 15, 1947, on.

The universal jubilation at the birth of Pakistan drowned for the moment the grief over the massacre of Muslims by Sikhs and Hindus in East Punjab. Whatever trials and tribulations the future might have in store for the people of Pakistan, the dream of a sovereign independent Muslim state had at last been realized. Now they had their own homeland in which to build a strong modern democratic state. The immensity of the undertaking did not daunt them; it aroused a powerful impulse to offer the state their dedicated service. The dire predictions of their enemies and others that Pakistan would soon collapse only spurred them on to further effort. They had abundant faith, and were resolved to overcome all obstacles to make Pakistan a worthy embodiment of Islamic ideals.

In this hour of fulfillment, there was no rancor or ill will toward the Hindus who had opposed Pakistan so stubbornly or toward anyone else; toward the British there was a feeling of gratitude and friendship. All thoughts and energies were now devoted to the great enterprise of building up Pakistan; and that needed, above all, peace and tranquillity and honest, hard, selfless work.

"At this supreme moment," said the Quaid-i-Azam in his message to the citizens of Pakistan on August 15, "my thoughts are with those valiant fighters in our cause who readily sacrificed all they had, including their lives, to make Pakistan possible." [2] There was also continuing concern for the forty million Muslims living in the Indian Dominion. As the Quaid-i-Azam said: "Those of our brethren who are minorities in Hindustan may rest assured that we shall never neglect or forget them . . . I recognize that it is the Muslim minority provinces in this sub-continent who were the pioneers and carried the banner aloft for the achievement of our cherished goal of Pakistan." [3] Now they would have to adjust themselves to new and difficult circumstances because the Hindus resented their having supported Pakistan. The Quaid-i-Azam's advice to them was to give unflinching loyalty to the state in which they happened to be.

It had always been known that partition would leave minorities on both sides. The best interests of both Dominions lay in peace and communal harmony. The Quaid-i-Azam had constantly reiterated that the non-Muslim minorities in Pakistan would have the same rights and privileges as the Muslims. He reaffirmed these sentiments in a characteristically vigorous fashion in his very first address to the constituent assembly on August 11.

> The first duty of a Government is to maintain law and order, so that the life, property and religious beliefs of its subjects are fully protected by the State. . . . In this division it was impossible to avoid the question of minorities being in one Dominion or the other. . . . We should wholly and solely concentrate on the well-being of the people, and especially of the masses and the poor. . . . You may belong to any religion or caste or creed—that has nothing to do with the business of the State. . . . We are starting with this fundamental principle that we are all citizens and equal citizens of one State. . . . Now, I think we should keep that in front of us as our ideal and you will find that in course of time Hindus would cease to be Hindus and Muslims would cease to be Muslims, not in the religious sense, because that is the personal faith of each individual, but in the political sense as citizens of the State.[4]

One would imagine that the import of these words is so clear as to leave little room for doubt. Questions of an ideological kind have, however, been raised, and a considerable controversy has been stirred up. Could it be, they ask, that as soon as Pakistan was won the Quaid-i-Azam abandoned the two-nation theory and invited all its citizens, Muslims and non-Muslims alike, to work together for the state on the basis of territorial nationalism? What then was its raison d'être, and what would be its distinguishing characteristic? Had the two-nation theory merely been the scaffolding that was to be discarded once the structure was built? Others have interpreted the Quaid-i-Azam's words as a long-term objective toward which the people of Pakistan would in course of time move.

What is overlooked is that Pakistan came into existence not by conquest but as the result of a negotiated agreement between the representatives of the Hindu and Muslim communities to partition the subcontinent. An explicit and integral part of the agreement was that the minorities in both states would have equal rights and equal protection of law. In that context the Quaid-i-Azam was wholly right in asserting the fundamental principle that "we are all citizens and equal citizens of one State." It follows that the state must give full protection to "the life, property and religious beliefs of its subjects [and] should wholly and solely concentrate on the well-being of the people and especially of the masses and the poor." These practical tasks of statesmanship can be fulfilled only by giving equal rights and equal responsibilities to all citizens. But this can neither negate the fact that the vast majority of the citizens of Pakistan are Muslims nor take away the responsibility for leadership from the Muslim community. The principles of governing the country will inevitably be based on Islam, if the leadership is sincere in its professions and if its perspective is truly Islamic. Such a leadership should work unremittingly to arouse the creative energies of the entire nation and direct them in building a strong and prosperous Pakistan on, as the Quaid-i-Azam put it, "the sure foundations of social justice and Islamic socialism which emphasises equality and brotherhood of man."

In this first address he also laid his finger unerringly on the evils that afflict underdeveloped countries like India and Pakistan. He said:

> One of the biggest curses from which India is suffering—I do not say that other countries are free from it, but, I think, our condition is much worse—is bribery and corruption. That really is a poison. . . . I want to make it quite clear that I shall never tolerate any kind of jobbery, nepotism or any influence directly or indirectly brought to bear upon me. Wherever I will find that such a practice is in vogue, or is continuing anywhere, low or high, I shall certainly not countenance it.[5]

The people and the administration responded to these lofty sentiments with sincere determination. Incidents of bribery and corruption were greatly reduced. Ticketless traveling, which had been endemic on Indian railways, was now denounced by the people themselves. A spirit of moral fervor and cooperation pervaded the atmosphere. The people felt themselves to be at one with authority. They were all comrades working together for the same goal.

The first cabinet of Pakistan, which was sworn in on August 15, consisted of the following: Liaquat Ali Khan, Prime Minister, also in charge of two ministries—Foreign Affairs and Commonwealth Relations and Defence; I. I. Chundrigar, Commerce, Industries, and Works; Ghulam Muhammad, Finance; Abdur Rab Nishtar, Communications; Ghazanfar Ali Khan, Food, Agriculture, and Health; Jogendra Nath Mandal, Law and Labour; Fazlur Rahman, Interior, Information, and Education. That Liaquat Ali Khan should become the first Prime Minister of Pakistan was natural and befitting. He had been General Secretary of the All-India Muslim League for many years, had been Deputy Leader of the Muslim League party in the central assembly, and had been Finance Minister and leader of the Muslim League bloc in the Viceroy's Executive Council. Chundrigar, Nishtar, Ghazanfar Ali Khan, and Mandal had been his colleagues in the Viceroy's Executive Council. Ghulam Muhammad had had a distinguished career in the Finance department of the Government of India, had been Finance Minister in Hyderabad state, and on retirement from government service had worked as director for Tatas, the great industrial house. Fazlur Rahman had been a minister in Bengal.

A little later, Muhammad Zafrullah Khan, who had gone to New York as the leader of the Pakistan Delegation to the U. N., was appointed Foreign Minister and took his seat in the cabinet next to the Prime Minister, who still retained the portfolio of Defence. Zafrullah Khan had been a member of the Viceroy's Executive Council, and later a judge of the Federal Court in British India.

In September, 1947, as the refugee problem grew to immense proportions, the Ministry of Refugee Rehabilitation was formed. H. S. Suhrawardy, former Chief Minister of Bengal, was offered the portfolio, but he declined it. The work was entrusted to Fazlur Rahman and later to Ghazanfar Ali Khan. When, in May, 1948, Chundrigar went to Kabul as Ambassador, Khwaja Shahabuddin from East Bengal joined the cabinet as Interior Minister, and Fazlur Rahman took charge of the Commerce portfolio. In July, 1948, Pirzada Abdul Sattar took the place of Ghazanfar Ali Khan who was appointed Ambassador in Iran. The new Ministry of States and Frontier Regions was created in July, 1948, and placed under the direct control of the Quaid-i-Azam. A separate Ministry of Kashmir Affairs was organized in January, 1949, and Mushtaq Ahmad Gurmani, then Chief Minister of Bahawalpur state, took charge of it.

In June and July of 1947 a number of officials prepared schemes for the organization of the Pakistan government. I also submitted a plan. According to it, eighteen administrative departments were to be grouped in eight ministries, and some of the ministries were divided into divisions. This plan (which was accepted) was, like other similar schemes, modeled on the Government of India, with some variations to suit conditions in Pakistan. But I also made a novel proposal. My knowledge of the Government of India, both in peace and in war, had convinced me that the higher administration in India suffered from lack of coordination. There was no single focal point except at the Viceroy's level. Toward the end of the Second World War, when the need could no longer be safely ignored, a post of Cabinet Secretary to the Viceroy's Executive Council had been created, which in some ways remedied the deficiency. In Whitehall also, though the First Secretary to the Treasury was the head of the Civil Service and as such responsible for a great deal of administrative coordination, the Cabinet Secretary, who was also concerned with important aspects of coordination among various ministries, was a separate official. In Pakistan we were aiming at a tightly knit, highly efficient, and relatively small, organization. The immensity of the tasks facing us in setting up a new administration in a new capital made rapidity in decision-making, execution, and providing information about action taken a matter of sheer survival. I proposed, therefore, that a post of Secretary-General with the duty of coordinating the work of the various ministries should be created, and that the Secretary-General should, in addition, be Cabinet Secretary and also be in charge of the establishment.

By entrusting these interrelated functions to one person, it would be possible to maintain effective liaison between the cabinet on the one hand and the administration on the other. By virtue of his responsibility for coordinating the work of the ministries, the Secretary-General would be able to remove conflicts and prevent the overlapping of functions and ensure that the administrative machine worked smoothly. By being in charge of the establishment, and thus of the posting and transfer of officers, he could prevent severe shortages of manpower from developing in any sector, central or provincial, and ensure an equitable distribution of the administrative talent available. It was no secret that Pakistan did not have enough qualified personnel to man adequately all the ministries and departments. A scramble for capable officers and a tendency not to part with a competent man, even though the need elsewhere might be much greater, was only to be expected. An official, whose primary duty was to see that the work of his department was properly done, could hardly be blamed for not surveying the entire national scene with an impartial eye.

The Secretary-General would be responsible to the Prime Minister. It was inherent in his functions that even as the Prime Minister is *primus inter pares,* the Secretary-General should be first among his equals—the other secretaries in the various ministries.

I made this proposal for the creation of the post of Secretary-General on the basis of general principles of government administration, with particular regard to the situation that existed at the time of the birth of Pakistan. I made no suggestion, directly or indirectly, as to who should be appointed to it. Both the decisions, whether such a post should be created and who should fill it, were to be made by the Quaid-i-Azam, advised by his ministers. The Quaid-i-Azam accepted the proposal and decided to appoint me to it. I can say in all sincerity that I would have been equally contented if someone else had been appointed to it.

I feel that it is necessary to state this because the post later came to be so closely identified with me that some thought it had been specially created for me. This impression was strengthened when the post of Secretary-General was not filled, but was allowed to lapse when I became Finance Minister in October, 1951.

In the national emergency created by the tragic assassination of the Prime Minister, Liaquat Ali Khan, the cabinet decided that the Governor-General, Khwaja Nazimuddin, should become Prime Minister and that the Finance Minister, Ghulam Muhammad, should be appointed Governor-General. I was then pressed both by Khwaja Nazimuddin and Ghulam Muhammad as well as by other ministers of the cabinet to accept the office of Finance Minister. My personal view, which I reiterated a number of times, that I should continue as

Secretary-General and that someone else should be appointed Finance Minister was not accepted, and the post of Secretary-General was not filled because a suitable person was not found.

During the four years that the post of Secretary-General lasted it amply justified itself. Since I was directly responsible to the Prime Minister and was daily and continuously in touch with him, I was in a position to take decisions rapidly and to obtain government approval without delay whenever necessary. I kept the closest watch over difficulties and bottlenecks. I held weekly meetings with the secretaries of various ministries at which many different problems were discussed and decided. In a sense, these weekly meetings corresponded to cabinet meetings held at the administrative level. Rarely is a single ministry solely responsible for the solution of a particular problem. In general, the business of government is so complex that two or more ministries are involved in any important matter. These weekly meetings, in which all the secretaries were present, helped the ministries whose problems were brought up appreciate each others' point of view, and kept other ministries not directly concerned in touch with current developments. New and difficult problems were continually arising, so much so that the Quaid-i-Azam often had to preside over the cabinet, and these weekly meetings provided a suitable forum for discussing those problems and rendering the best available advice to the cabinet. This facilitated the task of the cabinet, which invariably paid close attention to the reports I submitted and, in general, accepted the advice I tendered. Apart from these weekly meetings I would, whenever necessary, bring the various ministries together to discuss any important matter, resolve differences at the administrative level, and if needed, obtain orders from the Prime Minister directly or through the cabinet. I must here gratefully record that the trust the Quaid-i-Azam, the Prime Minister, the cabinet, and my colleagues accorded me enabled me to perform my primary duty of organizing and coordinating the administrative machine in a time of great stress and strain.

Since I accompanied the Prime Minister on many of his tours to the provinces, I was able to acquire direct knowledge of their problems and difficulties and could help resolve them, either on the spot or on return to Karachi. Coordination between the central government and the provinces was thus facilitated. Similarly, the personal relations I had formed with senior military officers, and the knowledge I had gained of the problems of defense during my years of service in the Government of India as Financial Adviser, War and Supply, enabled me to harmonize the work of the civil and military administration.

The office of the Secretary-General acted as a clearinghouse for information between the various ministries and also between the central government and the provinces. It was quicker and more convenient to find out how a certain matter stood or what decision had been taken from the Secretary-General than through the still somewhat uncertain channels of interdepartmental communication. This enabled me, in turn, to keep in touch with the progress of various projects and to locate bottlenecks. In those early days, events were happening thick and fast and the atmosphere was like that prevailing at times of war, not only in the sense that a struggle for survival was going on, but in a more literal sense, especially when the Kashmir dispute flared up. Rapidity of communication with the center of power, where decisions could be taken in time, was essential. In one way or another a variety of problems—administrative, economic, and in matters of defense and foreign policy—landed on my desk. Although my main responsibility and endeavor was to organize the structure of government—and that implied regular channels of communication and an established routine—the pressure of events kept on disrupting the routine. There was seldom time for elaborate minutes and memoranda. Decisions, which in normal times would have taken days and even weeks of consideration, had to be reached within the hour. My office was the center where the lines of communication from various sources met. There was at this time a voluminous correspondence, mostly telegraphic, with the Government of India, quite often from Prime Minister to Prime Minister. The correspondence dealt with all kinds of subjects—refugee movement, peace and order, problems arising out of Junagadh and Kashmir, and so on. It was not unusual for such telegrams to be handed straight to the cabinet, and for a reply to be drafted and approved before the cabinet meeting was over. It was within the sphere of my duty to see that these matters and the follow-up action to be taken by the ministries ran smoothly.

As new problems arose and the pressure of work in a particular direction increased, it became necessary to set up new administrative offices. It was my responsibility to foresee these developments and to submit recommendations accordingly. For example, the vast migration that was set in motion at the time of partition involved so much new work not falling within the scope of any of the existing ministries that the Ministry of Refugee Rehabilitation had to be formed early in September. Here a full-fledged ministry was formed at the very outset. In the case of the Kashmir problem, however, it took quite some time before a separate ministry was formed. Soon after the Kashmir dispute started and the movement of tribal *lashkars,* or irregular forces, and other volunteers to and from the area of conflict became a regular feature of the scene, a number of urgent questions arose that involved the provincial governments of the Punjab and the North-West Frontier Province. There was also the problem of relations with the recently formed Azad Kashmir government, including the provision of food and civil supplies for the population of Azad Kashmir. From one side or another, these questions were being brought to me, and I came to the conclusion that it was essential to post a trusted agent of the Pakistan government in Rawalpindi to handle these problems on the spot. The Prime Minister agreed with the proposal and asked me for suitable names. It occurred to me that Justice Din Muhammad, who had retired as judge of the Lahore High Court and was working as Chief Justice of Bahawalpur state, would be a good choice. The Prime Minister approved, and I was sent to obtain the consent of His Highness the Nawab of Bahawalpur. An air force plane took me to a landing strip near Bahawalpur. I knew His Highness of old; he readily agreed to make Justice Din Muhammad available for the work and was, in fact, relieved to find that nothing more serious had brought me to Bahawalpur.

In Karachi I set up an organization, consisting of a Deputy Secretary and an Under Secretary, to deal with the various aspects of the Kashmir problem. This organization worked directly under me, and it was only after more than a year that a separate ministry for Kashmir Affairs was formed.

I had to go off and on to Delhi for negotiations, or to the United Nations to discuss the Kashmir question. During my absence, Ikramullah the Foreign Secretary acted as Secretary-General. Similarly, when he went abroad, I handled the work of the Foreign Secretary. This kind of doubling up was a common practice at all levels, because of the paucity of officers who had sufficient experience. To make such an arrangement work, Ikramullah and I kept in touch constantly, even when both of us were in Karachi. It was also my responsibility to maintain relations with the heads of diplomatic missions at Karachi.

In July, 1947, a selection board was set up to select senior officers such as secretaries, joint secretaries, and deputy secretaries for the ministries, and to nominate heads of departments and other offices. Later, when the Pakistan government was established at Karachi, a reorganization committee was formed to make recommendations regarding the number and rank of employees needed in each ministry and its departments, and to determine surpluses and deficiencies. Large numbers of government employees with various skills had opted for Pakistan from all over India. Under these circumstances, it would have been a miracle if in the technical departments, such as Railways, the necessary number of trained men for each job had been available. The fact was that in some cases there was a surplus and in others a deficiency of manpower. Experienced administrators were needed most of all. Some of these gaps were filled by the appointment of British officers; five secretaries of the Pakistan government were retired British officers of the Indian Civil Service. They worked with zeal and devotion.

The governors of three provinces were also British. Sir Frederick Bourne was the Governor of East Bengal; Sir Francis Mudie, of West Punjab; and Sir George Cunningham, of the North-West Frontier Province. Only in Sind was there a Pakistani Governor, Ghulam Husain Hidayatullah. In the armed forces of Pakistan the number of British officers was much larger than in the civil administration. All the three commanders-in-chief were British. General Sir Frank Messervey was the first Commander-in-Chief of the Pakistan army; after some months he was succeeded by General Sir Douglas Gracey. Air Vice-Marshal Perry-Keane was the Commander-in-Chief of the Pakistan air force, and Rear (later Vice) Admiral Jefford was Commander-in-Chief of the Pakistan navy. For the technical services, British "other ranks" were also employed.

The initial difficulties arose mostly from deficiencies in staff, accommodation, records, office equipment, and communications. Hastily constructed tin sheds provided the bulk of office accommodations. It was not a rare sight to see five or six officers, including officers of very high rank, sitting in one small room. Housing difficulties were equally great and caused much inconvenience. Under the Government of India rules, civil servants were not entitled to houses, and had to make their own arrangements for billeting. In many stations, however, and particularly in New Delhi, the government had built houses for various categories of officials, and made this important amenity available at a modest rent. With the large population influx into Karachi, it was exceedingly difficult for most government employees to find a place to live in. There was no help for it but to requisition houses and to enlarge the supply by partitioning the houses wherever feasible. In the process, high officials as well as private citizens suffered considerable hardship.

The demand for stenographers and typists was far greater than the supply. Pakistan's share of office equipment and furniture could not be obtained from the Government of India by August 15, and even what was obtained could not all be moved to Karachi because of disturbances that disrupted communications. Local purchases were made, but still there were great shortages. Typewriters and telephones, and, at times, even the most ordinary supplies, like pens and pins, were not easily available. Also, not all the relevant files and records could be duplicated in Delhi and brought to Karachi. Not all the staff had reached Karachi from Delhi and other places in India. Members of the staff in a single office often did not know each other; and, of course, all had to adjust themselves to new surroundings and conditions. The lines of communication within the central government and with the provincial governments were not yet fully operative.

Yet, despite these multifarious difficulties, the work went steadily forward. The challenge which this start from scratch presented to the administration was met with a splendid display of energy. It aroused immense enthusiasm and a strong determination to overcome all difficulties. It evoked ingenuity and resourcefulness in improvising solutions to problems. Although some of the senior officers who were used to working in a set fashion and whose minds had become encrusted with a particular kind of routine felt themselves at sea, others were stimulated by the challenge. Outmoded methods of work were given up. Available manpower was put to the best use. A review was made of statistical returns, and it was found that a surprisingly large number of them served no purpose. No use had ever been made of them in arriving at decisions or in preparing forecasts. Even the lack of previous files turned out in some cases to be a blessing in disguise.

The dead weight of precedent was lifted and decisions were taken in the light of prevailing situations. So many decisions had to be taken that there was no time for elaborate procedures. Problems were, so to speak, jostling each other and competing for priority. Of necessity procedures were simplified. In the midst of these stresses some mistakes were, of course, made but, even in the light of hindsight, their proportion does not appear to have been higher than in quieter and more normal times.

The confident expectation of our enemies and many neutral observers that the administration in Pakistan would break down in a few months was proved false by the efficiency, fortitude, and devotion to duty of those in the service of Pakistan. The whole nation was imbued with a sense of mission to make Pakistan a going concern; and government servants as a class were deeply infused with this national spirit. They worked long hours ungrudgingly and put up with hardships of all kinds unflinchingly. There was no thought of self but only of how to serve the nation in order to strengthen and consolidate Pakistan. The whole administration worked as one team. Every government servant, from the highest to the lowest, placed all the resources of his knowledge and all the energy of his body and mind unreservedly at the service of Pakistan. Those who participated in the great task of establishing Pakistan were privileged beyond all others of later generations in sharing a unique experience.

Immediately on coming into existence, Pakistan applied for admission to the United Nations. The Security Council treated Pakistan's application as a special case and recommended that the General Assembly admit Pakistan so that it could take its seat at the next General Assembly session. Accordingly, Pakistan became a member of the United Nations in September, 1947. Pakistan also joined other international organizations and agencies such as the FAO, ILO, WHO, the World Bank, the International Monetary Fund. In the very first year of its establishment Pakistan took part in a number of important international conferences. A delegation was sent to Canberra to attend the conference considering the Japanese Peace Settlement. Pakistan was also represented at the FAO conference in Geneva. Pakistan representatives took part in an important trade and employment conference at Havana, the regional ILO conference, and the second session of the Economic Commission for Asia and the Far East.

Diplomatic relations with other Dominions and foreign countries were taken in hand immediately. High Commissions were exchanged with the United Kingdom and the Indian Union, and soon thereafter with Canada, Australia, New Zealand, and Ceylon. Embassies were set up in the United States, Egypt, Iran, Burma, Afghanistan, Turkey, the U.S.S.R., China, and other countries.

The constituent assembly of Pakistan was housed in the Sind assembly building in Karachi. The Federal Court was established at Lahore, where it could avail itself of the accommodation and library facilities of the High Court.

In East Bengal a new provincial government had to be organized at Dacca. H. S. Suhrawardy, who was Chief Minister of Bengal at the time of partition, was replaced by Khwaja Nazimuddin who became Chief Minister of East Bengal. Calcutta, which had been Suhrawardy's stronghold, had gone to India. Khwaja Nazimuddin came from Dacca and had a greater following among the members of the provincial assembly in East Bengal. Suhrawardy had wanted the Quaid-i-Azam to select one of them for the central cabinet and leave the other as uncontested Chief Minister of East Bengal. The Quaid-i-Azam, however, decided to let the members of the assembly exercise their democratic right of electing their leader. Khwaja Nazimuddin was elected leader and became the Chief Minister of East Bengal. On August 13, 1947, Suhrawardy accepted Gandhi's invitation to work with him in putting out the embers of communal discord in Calcutta. Their joint efforts met with success, and Calcutta and Bengal were spared the horrors perpetrated in the Punjab.

East Pakistan was faced with a number of serious problems. It had to establish a new capital at Dacca and to set up a new administration. During the first partition of Bengal in 1905, when Dacca became the capital of the newly created province of Eastern Bengal and Assam, a number of buildings for the provincial government, including a governor's house, had been built. These proved useful, but even so more construction was needed. The shortages of personnel presented even greater difficulties. The majority of officials were Hindus and they opted for West Bengal. Over 50 percent of the civil and criminal courts could not function, owing to the shortage of judicial and executive officers. The number of Muslims from Bengal in the Superior Services of government was negligible. Muslims from other provinces who had opted for the service of Pakistan were sent to East

Bengal to serve in the provincial administration. Similarly, a considerable number of Muslim railway employees from railways in India (who had opted for Pakistan) were sent to run the East Bengal Railway. Differences of language and manners were to create misunderstandings which later produced a crop of political controversies. But the task of establishing and running the administration was of overriding importance at that time and qualified men, if they could be found, were employed, no matter where they came from. The economic life of the province was affected by the partial withdrawal of Hindu businessmen who held a monopoly of commerce and banking; and for a time there was almost a total stoppage of consumer goods from West Bengal.

In West Punjab the Khan of Mamdot, who was the President of the provincial Muslim League, was unanimously elected Chief Minister. West Punjab had the advantage of inheriting Lahore, the capital of the undivided Punjab. But the mass influx of Muslim refugees from East Punjab, Delhi, and neighboring states, and the exodus of Hindus and Sikhs from West Punjab, created problems of such vast proportions and complexity that even a fully organized and well-established administration could not have coped with them. The Quaid-i-Azam and the central government had to devote much time and energy to these problems and to the even more serious Kashmir dispute that erupted soon after partition.

In the North-West Frontier Province, Dr. Khan Sahib's Congress ministry was still in office on August 15. The Quaid-i-Azam wanted the loyal cooperation of all citizens, regardless of political differences in the past, for the task of building up Pakistan. No one was to be victimized for having opposed the establishment of Pakistan. In keeping with this policy, Dr. Khan Sahib and his ministers would have been allowed to continue in office, but they refused to salute the Pakistan flag and showed no sign of a change in their previous attitude of antagonism to Pakistan. Therefore, on August 22, the Governor dismissed Dr. Khan Sahib's ministry on the Quaid-i-Azam's orders, and Abdul Qayyum Khan became Chief Minister.

Sind already had a Muslim League ministry. Some difficulty was experienced over the administration of Karachi, which was now the capital of Pakistan, but which continued to be a part of Sind province. It was essential that the central government should be in full control of the seat of its administration. In May, 1948, the constituent assembly, after a heated debate, adopted a resolution that "all executive and administrative authority in respect of Karachi and such neighbouring areas which in the opinion of the Central Government may be required for the purposes of the Capital of Pakistan shall vest in and shall be exercised by or on behalf of the Government of Pakistan and the legislative power shall vest in the Federal Legislature." The Sind Muslim League leaders who had been agitating against the separation of Karachi approached the Quaid-i-Azam. He advised them to accept willingly and gracefully the decision of the constituent assembly "the highest and supreme body in Pakistan," and the agitation came to an end. The Quaid-i-Azam himself was convinced that this decision was in the best interest of Pakistan and of Sind. Under the Pakistan (Establishment of the Federal Capital) Order issued on July 23, 1948, the Karachi capital area of 567 square miles was demarcated and placed under the administrative control of the central government. For a time the Sind government maintained its headquarters in Karachi but later shifted it to Hyderabad.

Baluchistan was not a full-fledged province and had no elected assembly or ministers. It was administered by the Governor-General "acting, to such extent as he thinks fit, through a Chief Commissioner to be appointed by him." The Quaid-i-Azam was keenly interested in the progress of Baluchistan, which in many ways was the most backward area of Pakistan, but which had great potentialities for development. He decided to make Baluchistan his special responsibility and care, and to constitute a Governor-General's advisory council, "a body which will enable the people to play their full part in the administration and governance of their province." [6]

Adjoining the North-West Frontier Province, the Punjab, and Baluchistan, are tribal areas. The relations of the Government of India with the tribes inhabiting these areas, although incapable of precise definition in international law, were governed by a large number of treaties and engagements, totaling nearly 150. Under these treaties the tribes agreed not to disturb the peace of the neighboring territories and in general, to be of good behavior, in return for which they received subsidies and grants for education and development. Section 7 of the Indian Independence Act laid down that all these treaties would lapse on August 15, 1947, subject to a standstill agreement on some matters until the provisions in question were denounced or superseded by subsequent agreements. The tribal bodies and Jirgas, or assemblies of headmen, were in no sense organized governments. The treaties of the British government with them did not have the character of international treaties and depended upon goodwill. Pakistan had no difficulty in winning the goodwill of the tribes and in maintaining previous agreements. The Pakistan government also took a wise and courageous decision of far-reaching importance. Much to the annoyance of the tribes, the British had maintained a number of forts and military outposts in the heart of the tribal territory. These fortifications and their lines of communications were periodically attacked by the freedom-loving tribes who resented the imposition of control by a non-Muslim power. A number of frontier wars had been fought by the British in their spasmodic return to the Forward Policy that aimed at extending full British administration right up to the Durand Line—the international boundary between British India and Afghanistan. This policy had no doubt provided the British with a live training ground for their army, but it had also produced constant friction with the tribes. Pakistan, as a Muslim state, had a fundamentally different attitude toward her Muslim brethren in the tribal area. There was no desire to interfere with their internal freedom, only a sincere wish to help them with schemes for economic development and advancement in education and health to the extent that they freely wanted to avail themselves of such services. It was, therefore, decided to withdraw military forces from Razmak and other places in Waziristan. The decision produced a most favorable impression on the minds of the tribes who repaid trust with trust and friendship. The efforts of Afghanistan to create disturbances through agents, like the Faqir of Ipi, failed completely to arouse the tribes against Pakistan. A slow and natural process of integration is going on in an atmosphere of peace and mutual confidence.

CHAPTER 13

The Great Holocaust and the Rehabilitation of Refugees

COMMUNAL RIOTS had disfigured the history of the subcontinent down the ages, but they had generally been local affairs that erupted for a few days and then died down leaving the composition of the population much the same as before. The 1946 massacre of Muslims in Bihar was the first organized effort at extermination of opponents over a wide area, but even that orgy of destruction had no long-term end in view and quickly exhausted itself. The Punjab massacres planned by the Sikhs were not only on a far larger scale, they differed in kind from all previous civil disorders. They had a defined political objective, and to gain it, uncontrolled violence and terror were used. The Sikhs organized a military campaign that would end only when its objective was attained. They had at their disposal the trained armed forces of Hindu and Sikh states and had planned to start the massacres at a time when the administrations in East and West Punjab would be in the throes of reorganization and, therefore, least capable of effective action. This last factor was decisive.

The secret deal between Mountbatten and the Congress for advancing the date for the transfer of power from June 1, 1948, to August

15, 1947, was deliberately intended by the Congress to deny Pakistan time to organize its administration and to establish itself on a sound basis. Its inevitable consequence was that the provincial governments of neither East Punjab nor West Punjab could reorganize themselves properly. The East Punjab administration was in an even worse condition since Hindus and Sikhs refused to set up an alternative capital in East Punjab for fear of weakening their untenable claim to Lahore. If the original date of June 1, 1948, had been allowed to stand, both East Punjab and West Punjab governments would have had eleven instead of two months in which to organize their administrative machinery for the maintenance of law and order, which is the first concern of every government. A British governor who had spent all his working life in India, commenting on the Punjab disturbances, wrote:

> This, again, was the result of Mountbatten's unwisdom in accelerating the date of Partition so suddenly. I am sure that if the Punjab had been given time (say eight or nine months) to sort out their services properly—Muhammadan and Hindu—the terrible massacres of Aug-Sept-Oct would never have happened in anything approaching the scale that they did assume.[1]

The provincial police and revenue services, which are responsible for law and order and which come directly in touch with the rural population, had a mixed communal composition in both East and West Punjab. Sardar Patel's insistence on giving the right of option to every government servant changed the character of these services. Hindu and Sikh district officials in East Punjab started disarming Muslim policemen in East Punjab some days before August 15 on the pretext that they might desert to Pakistan with their arms. That left only Hindus and Sikhs in the police force. According to a British officer of the Punjab Boundary Force, "There was no case on record of a Sikh or Hindu policeman having shot any one except a Muslim." [2]

The Hindu and Sikh rulers of states played a despicable part in this horrible tragedy. In the Punjab states of Patiala, Kapurthala, and others, as well as in Alwar and Bharatpur the story is the same. State troops joined with Hindu and Sikh bands in a systematic extermination of the Muslim population. The states of Alwar and Bharatpur were within the area of the Eastern Command; and there, writes Tuker, "State troops were employed in these ghastly massacres in conjunction with armed Hindu mobs who were allowed to kill and mutilate Muslim men, women and children," and he quotes from a report by an officer of the Punjab Boundary Force: "The States of Kapurthala and Patiala have provided sanctuary for raiding Sikh jathas, and also safe bases for them to operate from." [3]

In central Punjab, which was the epicenter of these disturbances, systematic attacks by Sikh jathas started toward the end of July and rapidly increased in frequency and intensity until by August 15 the whole area was ablaze.

Some idea of what was happening in East Punjab can be gained from a report sent by Ian Morrison, correspondent of the London *Times,* from Jullundur on August 24.

> "More horrible than anything we saw during the war," is the universal comment of experienced officers, British and Indian, on the present slaughter in East Punjab. The Sikhs are clearing East Punjab of Muslims, butchering hundreds daily, forcing thousands to flee westward, burning Muslim villages and homesteads, even in their frenzy burning their own. This violence has been organised from the highest levels of Sikh leadership, and it is being done systematically, sector by sector. [4]

Not only the countryside suffered; worse things were happening in the cities. "On 15 August the day of liberation was strangely celebrated in the Punjab. During the afternoon a Sikh mob paraded a number of Muslim women naked through the streets of Amritsar, raped them and then hacked some of them to pieces with kirpans and burned the others alive." [5] On September 18, the London *Times* wrote, "More Indian people have been killed during the short space of the past month than in all the civil broils of the past fifty years. Millions have been rendered homeless. A transfer of populations has been enforced on two administrations reluctant and ill-fitted to cope with it that already dwarfs in scale anything caused by war in Europe."

As Muslim refugees from East Punjab started pouring into Lahore and other places in West Punjab and told their tale of woe, there was instant retaliation against Hindus and Sikhs. So inflamed were the feelings of the people at the sight of the destitute, wounded, and maimed that the exhortations of the Quaid-i-Azam and other leaders to exercise restraint and eschew revenge fell, for the moment, on deaf ears. It was an instinctive reaction of blind rage. Unlike in East Punjab, there was neither plan nor organization behind these sporadic outbursts of violence. As often happens on such occasions, criminal elements saw their chance to loot and destroy property and joined in the fray. Sikhs were the main target of attacks, but the Hindus also suffered. Soon there was a stream of Hindu and Sikh refugees moving in the other direction.

On August 16 I had gone to Delhi with Liaquat Ali Khan to discuss the Punjab disturbances with Mountbatten and the Government of India. The situation, as reported by Auchinleck to the Joint Defence Council, was horrifying. The movement of refugees on both sides was yet in its early stages, but every day reports came that it was gathering momentum. It was decided to reinforce the Punjab Boundary Force, and also that the two prime ministers, Nehru and Liaquat Ali Khan, should visit both sides of the frontier in the Punjab and exert themselves to the utmost to restore law and order. I accompanied them. They held a conference at Ambala in East Punjab with the governors and ministers of East and West Punjab, the Deputy Supreme Commander, Major General Rees the Commander of the Punjab Boundary Force, and other officers. Already things had reached such a pass that when I asked Major General Rees for a candid appraisal, he did not at all feel confident of being able to stem the tide of violence. Both prime ministers emphasized the need for restoring peace and confidence, and the urgency of devising measures, administrative and psychological, for creating a proper atmosphere. The governments of East and West Punjab agreed to give the maximum assistance in evacuating the refugees from one province to the other, and the two central governments undertook to maintain train services. A committee of two ministers from each of the provincial governments was set up to coordinate measures in both territories. Both at Lahore and at Amritsar two officers, one from each government, were to be appointed to maintain liaison with the Punjab Boundary Force and the civil administration. The conference reached the conclusion that the area covered by the Punjab Boundary Force should be gradually reduced as the two Dominion governments assumed responsibility for the districts from which the Punjab Boundary Force withdrew.

On August 29, at a meeting of the Joint Defence Council in Lahore, which was attended by Mountbatten and the Quaid-i-Azam, it was decided to disband the Punjab Boundary Force and to let each Dominion government assume responsibility for law and order in its own territory. The Force was abolished on September 1, 1947.

Auchinleck in his farewell letter thanked Major General Rees for the excellent work done by him and his men "in the interests of humanity and security" and added:

> The massacres, arson and disorder which started in Amritsar before the Boundary Commission had made its award had nothing to do with the boundary or anything connected with it. The whole movement was undoubtedly planned long beforehand and soon gave rise to inevitable repercussions in the West Punjab. So that you and your troops were faced with a problem quite different from that which you had been asked to solve and far beyond your capacity.[6]

After the Lahore meeting, I accompanied the prime ministers Nehru and Liaquat Ali Khan on a joint four-day tour of the affected areas. Both prime ministers were firmly resolved to restore peace, and impressed everyone with their sincere desire to put an end to the disturbances. We visited a number of places, on both sides of the border, such as Amritsar, Batala, Hoshiarpur, Lahore, and Sheikhupura. In the so-called refugee camps men, women, and children were huddled together in conditions of the utmost misery. Food, water, shelter, sanitation, and medical care were grossly inadequate or totally lacking. It was the rainy season, yet some of the camps were under the open sky with only a few trees to give protection from sun and rain. Others, which were located in buildings, were terribly overcrowded. The one cry of the refugees was to be evacuated to the other side.

After the tour, the two prime ministers held a conference in Lahore, on September 3, and reiterated "the determination of the two Central and the two Provincial Governments that law and order should be immediately established and all lawlessness suppressed and punished." But within a day of the conference hell was let loose in Delhi, the capital of the Indian Union. Although Delhi had been the capital of India during centuries of Muslim rule, the population contained a minority of Muslims. Muslim houses in Delhi and its suburbs, such as Karol Bagh, were marked and systematically attacked by Sikhs and the Rashtriya Swayam Sewak Sangh.

By September 4 the situation in the capital was so serious that Mountbatten, who was in Simla at this time, was requested by the Indian cabinet to come down to Delhi immediately and take charge of it. He reached Delhi on September 6 and set to work at once. Gandhi, who arrived in Delhi on September 9, "strained every nerve to restore good feeling between the communities and to secure the life and property of Muslims." So did Nehru. But, as Abul Kalam Azad continues,

There was a difference of attitude between Sardar Patel on the one hand and Jawaharlal and me on the other. This was affecting local administration and it was becoming clear that the officers were divided into two groups. The larger group looked up to Sardar Patel as Home Minister and acted in a way which they thought would please him. A smaller group looked to Jawaharlal and me and tried to carry out Jawaharlal's orders. . . . Sardar Patel was the Home Minister, and as such the Delhi administration was directly under him. As the lists of murder and arson grew longer, Gandhiji sent for Patel and asked him what he was doing to stop the carnage. Sardar Patel tried to reassure him by saying that the reports which he was receiving were grossly exaggerated. In fact Patel went to the extent of saying that the Muslims had no cause for complaint or fear.[7]

Refugee camps for the Muslims were set up in Purana Qila, or old fort, Humayun's Tomb, and other places. Ismay who visited Purana Qila, where Muslim officials who had opted for Pakistan and their families were also sheltered, wrote that "thousands of Moslems were herded within its walls. There was no shelter, no doctor, no sanitary arrangements, no means of communication." [8]

The Government of India was obstructing the evacuation of Pakistan government servants, and BOAC planes had to be chartered to take them to Karachi. There was no relief in sight. The reports received from Zahid Husain, the Pakistan High Commissioner in Delhi, painted a most alarming picture of conditions in India. The refugees in their millions had to be evacuated to Pakistan as quickly as possible. In Jullundur division alone 1.8 million Muslim refugees were reported, on September 18, to be awaiting evacuation to Pakistan. Sikh attacks on convoys and trains were holding up the operation, and Tara Singh was declaring: "This is war." It looked, as Liaquat Ali Khan said, as if "To-day we in Pakistan are surrounded on all sides by forces which are out to destroy us."

On September 11, Ismay paid a visit to Karachi to apprise the Quaid-i-Azam of conditions in Delhi and to reassure him of the good intentions of the Government of India. Ismay reported,

He looked very dignified and very sad, and he spoke as a man without hope. "There is nothing for it but to fight it out." We went to his study, and he let himself go. How could anyone believe that the Government of India were doing their utmost to restore law and order and to protect minorities? On the contrary, the events of the past three weeks went to prove that they were determined to strangle Pakistan at birth.[9]

In truth, the outlook was grim in the extreme. In Pakistan the Quaid-i-Azam and the government were exerting themselves to the utmost to maintain law and order. There was no disturbance in Karachi, the capital of Pakistan, except one brief skirmish later, in January, 1948, which was quickly put down. It is true that Delhi was nearer the scene of the Punjab holocaust, but Karachi was as full of refugees as Delhi. All impartial witnesses are unanimous in their verdict that the troubles in West Punjab were a repercussion of the massacres in East Punjab. One of General Tuker's staff officers, who visited Pakistan on two occasions, reported in September that "there is no doubt whatsoever that the Sikhs of East Punjab are far more vindictive; they take every opportunity of derailing trains and attacking convoys with swords and spears which the civil authorities have not got the guts to confiscate. The attacks that are taking place on Sikh and Hindu convoys in West Punjab are more in the form of a reprisal for attacks taking place on Muslim convoys in East Punjab." [10]

The Indian press continued to pour out virulent propaganda against Pakistan. Even Gandhi was affected by the anti-Pakistan hysteria. On September 26, Sir Francis Tuker quotes him as saying at his prayer gathering that he had been an opponent of all warfare; but if there was no other way of securing justice from Pakistan, if Pakistan persistently refused to see its proved error and continued to minimize it, the Indian Union government would have to go to war against it.[11]

Thus, toward the end of September the threat of war between India and Pakistan was seen to be growing. In a report written on September 28 for the Prime Minister and chiefs of staff in London, Field Marshal Auchinleck, the Supreme Commander in India, recommended that

> in the event of open hostilities between the Armed Forces of the two Dominions, a by no means impossible contingency, it will be essential to order all British officers and other ranks serving with these Armed Forces to desist at once from any form of activity connected with their command and administration. Arrangements have been made to effect this at short notice and commanders concerned have been informed. Both Governments have been officially made aware of this position through the Joint Defence Council.[12]

During those anxious days, when genocide was in progress in East Punjab and Delhi, and war seemed imminent, the Pakistan government was making every effort to preserve law and order and to impress upon the people that duty and honor and the interests of Pakistan demanded peace and protection for the minorities. The atmosphere was so charged with emotion, and accusations and counter-accusations were being made so frequently, that the Pakistan government, though clear in its own conscience, sought outside help and advice in order to bring objectivity onto the scene. But for one reason or another the Government of India would not agree to a move of this kind. In the last week of September the Pakistan government asked the British government to communicate to the Dominion governments of Canada, Australia, New Zealand, and South Africa as well as India the Pakistan government's appreciation of the situation in the subcontinent, and suggested that consideration be given to ways and means of resolving the serious difficulties. This appeal for friendly help and advice evoked no response, because the Government of India was opposed to it.

By the middle of October violence in the Punjab was on the wane, even if only because the objects inciting violence were decreasing in numbers. But it was obvious that there would have to be an almost complete exchange of population between East and West Punjab and between some of the neighboring territories. The main problem was to secure as early and orderly an evacuation and settlement of refugees as possible.

The greatest mass migration in history was under way. Within a matter of weeks over twelve million people had left their homes and gone forth on foot, by bullock-cart, by railway, by car, and by plane to seek shelter and safety in the other Dominion. The London *Times* of September 4, 1947, reported a column of Muslim refugees 20 miles long, and estimated the number at twenty thousand; most of them were on foot, moving toward Pakistan. Footsore and weary, ill-nourished and exhausted, seven million refugees staggered across to Pakistan. They had no earthly possessions save the clothes they wore and, more often than not, these were in tatters. They had tasted misery to the dregs. They had seen babies killed, corpses mutilated, and women dishonored. Death had stalked them on the way. Tens of thousands had died on the road, of starvation and disease, or had been killed by Sikh murder gangs. Many others died as soon as they touched the frontier post.

During the four months up to December 10, 1947, 4.68 million refugees had arrived in West Punjab. Of these 3.92 millions were moved by the Military Evacuee Organization, which had been set up in Lahore on August 28. A similar organization was set up by India. To ensure close cooperation between the two MEO's, the Indian organization set up its tactical headquarters in Lahore alongside the Pakistan MEO; and the latter established its tactical headquarters in Jullundur.

Purely in administrative terms, the task of feeding, clothing, settling, and rehabilitating these millions was impossibly difficult. The violent upheavals that had taken place had shattered the economy, strained a yet hardly formed administration beyond breaking point, and disrupted communications. The Hindus who formed the bulk of the trading class had left. Shops lay empty. The Sikhs in their organized withdrawal had taken away cattle and grain. Fields and crops were untended. Chaos reigned supreme. What saved the situation was the spirit of the people and their faith in the leadership of the Quaid-i-Azam.

As refugees poured into Lahore and other places in West Punjab, the local residents went forth to share food and clothing with them, to render them assistance, and to alleviate their sufferings. They willingly made sacrifices and readily underwent hardships for the sake of rehabilitating refugees. There were, it is true, some selfish and hard-hearted inhabitants who took advantage of the prevailing conditions to misappropriate evacuee property for themselves. But by and large these were the exception in the first phase, when a generous impulse to help the refugees still pervaded all classes. Later there was a deterioration in public morals. The Quaid-i-Azam opened a relief fund which was liberally subscribed to, and which provided much needed succor for the refugees.

In the beginning of September, the Ministry of Refugees and Rehabilitation was formed in the Pakistan government and an emergency committee of the cabinet was set up. The following month, the Prime Minister shifted his headquarters to Lahore temporarily to help and supervise the provincial administration in the immense task of settling refugees. The Quaid-i-Azam himself paid frequent visits to Lahore. The strain and stress of the tragic events of those days, the colossal problems, and the ceaseless work impaired the health of both the Quaid-i-Azam and the Prime Minister. But with a grim determination which knew no relaxation they battled valiantly with every adverse circumstance.

By the middle of October the need was felt for a joint organization of the central government and West Punjab, the province most concerned with the refugee problem. The Pakistan Punjab Refugee Council was formed. It was presided over by the Prime Minister and included the Governor and Chief Minister of West Punjab and the central and provincial Refugee ministers. In the earlier stages I attended many meetings of the Council, which did extremely useful work in formulating the policy and coordinating the activities of the central and provincial governments. Later, similar joint refugee councils were set up for the North-West Frontier Province and for Sind.

The work of the Pakistan Punjab Refugee Council, which was served by a joint secretariat, covered a wide variety of subjects. Legislative measures had to be taken for the protection of evacuee property. Custodians of evacuee property and rehabilitation commissioners had to be appointed. Arrangements for the administration of camps and the evacuation, dispersal, and rehabilitation of refugees had to be made and supervised. Principles for the allocation of land, industries, shops, cinemas, houses, and for the fixation of rent had to be laid down. Measures for the restoration of the economic life of the province through the provision of consumer goods, normal functioning of rail and road services, revival of banking, trade, and agriculture had to be taken. Arrangements in concert with India had to be made for the recovery of abducted women and converts, for the transfer of prisoners, safe deposits, and provident funds, for the protection of sacred places, and for innumerable other matters incidental to the vast unplanned and involuntary exchange of populations that was taking place.

The Governor of West Punjab, Sir Francis Mudie, was an administrator of great experience. He worked devotedly day and night, and so did government servants of all ranks. But there were serious shortages in almost every department. Hindu officials had left. Their replacement by Muslims who had opted for Pakistan or refugees was not a mechanical task but required a thorough reorganization for which there was no time. The West Punjab ministry from the beginning showed signs of disunity and lack of cohesion. There were disputes regarding the delimitation of functions between the various ministers. The Minister in charge of Industries insisted upon dealing with everything that was connected with abandoned industrial undertakings. The Revenue Minister had to be consulted on all questions of abandoned land, and in many matters proposals for rehabilitation were initiated and final decisions were taken by him. The West Punjab Premier controlled the administrative machinery for the allocation of houses and shops. To complicate matters, abandoned evacuee property offered a temptation to which many of the leading figures in the districts succumbed, and these usurpers looked to one minister or another for political protection. It was partly as a protest against this division of authority and the constant conflict involved that the West Punjab Refugees Minister, Mian Iftikharuddin, resigned. The confusion regarding the functions of the various ministers had the disastrous result of making each deputy commissioner a law unto himself in his district. The Pakistan Punjab Refugee Council had to exert itself a great deal to bring order out of the administrative chaos produced by divided authority.

Camps were organized in a number of places to receive, feed, and clothe the refugees as they came in, and to nurse the sick and the wounded. Local volunteers as well as those sent from abroad by missionary societies, particularly from the United Kingdom and the United States of America, performed services of great value in these camps. Originally, the camps were regarded as transit camps only. The bulk of the refugees were agriculturists. By far the most pressing task was to allot them lands vacated by Hindu and Sikh refugees so that standing crops could be harvested in time and preparation made for sowing wheat.

However, the number of refugees West Punjab had to accommodate exceeded by some 1.7 million the number of evacuees who had left. As time passed, lands, factories, and shops available to new arrivals began to diminish. The great food shortage after January, 1948, which affected towns and villages alike, hampered efforts at resettlement. Thus the camps became more or less permanent with a population of about three quarters of a million in April, 1948. With strenuous efforts this number was brought down to half a million some months later. The prolonged stay in camps had a demoralizing effect on the people and bred a beggar's mentality. Special efforts had to be made to keep up the morale of the refugees. Schools for children and adults were opened and facilities for vocational training were provided. Nevertheless, it was essential to speed up the work of resettlement. Many of the refugees were keenly interested in being settled according to the district they came from, so that the social life and economic cooperation of village communities in East Punjab could be preserved intact. But this demanded resources in camps and organization far beyond the capacity of the West Punjab administration to provide. There was nothing for it but to settle the refugees as they came in.

There is a great divergence in the productivity of farm land in the various parts of West Punjab. Colony areas in Lyallpur and Montgomery, which are irrigated by canals, are far more productive than rainfed lands further to the west. Everyone wanted an allotment in the colony districts, but there was not enough land to go round. In Montgomery there was a serious clash between the police and a section of the refugees who wanted to settle forcibly on lands already allotted to earlier arrivals.

Trade in wheat, cotton, and other commodities had been almost entirely in the hands of Hindus, who had also provided the bulk of rural credit. Except for cooperative credit societies in Muslim villages and some cooperative banks, all other credit institutions, such as commercial banks, had been controlled and run by Hindus. Ginning factories and other industrial units were mostly owned by Hindus and Sikhs. When they left, there was a serious danger that the economy of West Pakistan might collapse. Before partition, when the whole subcontinent formed a single market, the channels of trade from West Punjab ran mostly in an eastern direction. Amritsar was a big commercial center. Wheat and cotton were the two main crops. Wheat was exported to East Punjab, Delhi, and other areas further south. Cotton went to the textile mills of Bombay and Allahabad by rail. In return, cloth and other manufactured goods flowed from these industrial centers to West Punjab. The upheavals in the Punjab disrupted these channels.

Karachi was the only major port of West Pakistan; and all exports and imports had now to be reoriented toward Karachi. The Karachi market was mostly in the hands of the Hindu merchants of Sind, who are noted for their business acumen. But for a few sporadic incidents here and there, which were quickly put down, nothing had happened to mar the peace of Sind. However, in a deliberate effort to paralyze the economy of Pakistan, the Hindus of Sind were prevailed upon to leave Pakistan. Hopes were held out that within a few months Pakistan would collapse and they could return to their homes. Acharya Kripalani, who was the Congress President at this time, originated from Sind and had considerable influence there. He was a strong believer in an Akhand Bharat, or undivided India. When the Congress accepted the partition plan, he called on the Congress party to make India a strong, happy, democratic, and socialist state, and declared, "Such an India can win back the seceding children to its lap . . . for the freedom we have achieved cannot be complete without the unity of India." [13] He came to Karachi in the third week of September, 1947, and saw the Quaid-i-Azam who assured him of the Pakistan government's firm intention to maintain peace and to give full protection and equal rights to the minorities. Nevertheless, Kripalani persisted in his efforts to spread panic among the Hindu community by painting a highly colored picture of their present hardships and making gloomy predictions about the future unless they pulled out of Pakistan soon. Despite the prevalence of peaceful conditions, and despite the Quaid-i-Azam's repeated assurances of equal rights and security for the minorities, an exodus of Hindus started which hurt both the migrants and Pakistan.

These designs against Pakistan were defeated by the indomitable will of the people to build a strong and prosperous Pakistan. Except for a few business communities of Muslim converts from Hinduism, the Hindus had from time immemorial a monopoly of trade in the subcontinent. For the Muslims in general, business was a closed field; and it was the common belief among Hindus and Muslims alike that Muslims lacked an aptitude for business. Now, with the departure of Hindus, these false inhibitions were swept away. With a display of enterprise that astonished even themselves, Muslims stepped forth into the field and filled the gap left by the exodus of Hindus. What might have been a crippling blow turned out to be a blessing in disguise. The spell of Muslim incompetence in trade and industry was broken forever, and the hold Hindus would have had over the economy of Pakistan was destroyed by their own miscalculations.

The government gave every possible support to the revival of trade, but it was private enterprise that did the job. As far as credit was concerned, a more direct effort by the government was necessary. Loans for agricultural operations were given to refugees settling on the land. To fill the void left by the closing of Hindu commercial banks, cooperative banks ventured into the profitable field of commercial credit. This was not an altogether happy development, since cooperative banks were intended to finance agriculture, which suffered in consequence. To aid refugee artisans, the Refugees Rehabilitation Finance Corporation, with a capital of Rs. 30 million, was set up by the Pakistan government. An endeavor was made to settle artisans in special colonies. Thus, the weavers of Panipat in East Punjab, who were skilled in manufacturing woolen goods, were settled together in Jhang.

The main burden of rehabilitating refugees was borne by West Punjab. This was inevitable since it lay straight in the path of the incoming refugees. But, as disturbances in India spread further afield and covered Delhi, the northern districts of the United Provinces, and neighboring states and territories, it soon became obvious that West Punjab alone could not possibly absorb the whole mass of refugees. Unless other provinces in West Pakistan were prepared to share the burden, a most serious situation would arise.

Almost all non-Muslims from the North-West Frontier Province had left for India, but their properties had in many places been taken over by locals, whom the provincial government, not wanting to court trouble, did not evict. Refugees who went to the province were turned back. In Sind the exodus of Hindus had not been so complete, but there were large areas of evacuee property and uncultivated land on which it was possible to settle refugees. But despite the Quaid-i-Azam's request, the Sind government refused to accept more than 150,000 refugees.

Under the circumstances, the central government felt compelled to assume powers for settling refugees; and to this end the Governor-General issued a proclamation under Section 102 of the adapted Government of India Act, 1935. The proclamation, which was issued on August 27, 1948, stated: "Whereas the economic life of Pakistan is threatened by circumstances arising out of the mass movement of population from and into Pakistan a State of Emergency is hereby declared." The next day the decision was made that out of the large number of refugees anxiously waiting in West Punjab's camps, Sind must absorb 200,000; the North-West Frontier Province, 100,000; Bahawalpur, Khairpur, and the Baluchistan Agency should rehabilitate 100,000; and West Punjab should make a renewed effort and settle 100,000 more. Even so, the efforts of the central government were only partially successful. According to the 1951 census, the number of refugees settled in Sind was 540,000 as against 900,000 evacuees. Though 269,000 non-Muslims had left the North-West Frontier Province only 51,000 refugees had been settled.

At the time the exchange of population began, many looked upon it as a temporary phenomenon. It was believed that when the passions excited by the civil war subsided and conditions returned to normal, evacuees would return to claim their properties. In the meantime, the governments of both Dominions were to take charge of the properties and look after them on behalf of their evacuee owners. At the meeting of the Joint Defence Council held in Lahore on August 29, 1947, under the chairmanship of Lord Mountbatten, it was agreed that each Dominion should appoint a custodian of evacuee property and that there should be close liaison between the two custodians. A joint statement by the prime ministers of India and Pakistan, which was issued on September 3, 1947, declared that "illegal seizure of property will not be recognized and both Governments will take steps to look after the property of refugees and restore it to its rightful owners." Accordingly, the West Punjab government appointed a custodian of evacuee property and issued an ordinance on September 9, 1947, stating: "Subject to the provisions of this Ordinance it shall be the duty of the Custodian within the area placed in his charge to take possession of the property and effects of evacuees and to take such measures as he considers necessary or expedient for preserving such property or effects." Similar measures were taken by the East Punjab government.

Certain types of property, such as the assets of joint stock companies and bank deposits, were exempted from the jurisdiction of the custodians. Settlement operations were regarded as temporary and interim measures until a permanent solution for the problem was found. But it soon became obvious that the exchange of population was irreversible. In July, 1948, the Government of India, alarmed by the return of some Muslim refugees to India, unilaterally introduced a permit system between India and West Pakistan. No person could go to India from West Pakistan without a permit from the Indian High Commission in Pakistan.

From that time on, the refugee's title to property he had left in the other Dominion became thin and shadowy and finally disappeared. All he could claim was compensation out of property left behind by the other side. But this was not an absolute claim that had to be satisfied in full—the amount of property left behind by evacuees, the number of refugees entering the Dominion, the state of the economy, and general policy considerations would play a part in determining how far refugees' claims could be met.

I was of the view that we should take advantage of this great upheaval to carry out a measure of land reform and that an upper and lower limit for the size of farms should be laid down. The proposal for an upper limit (varying from area to area on the basis of productivity) for the allotment of land to refugees was accepted, but not for the lower limit of 12½ acres of irrigated land, which would have formed an economic unit. Instead, permanent allotments were made on the basis of actual holdings, however low they might be. The prosperity of the Punjab depended upon its peasant proprietors, but the process of division and fragmentation of landed property had, in course of time, reduced individual holdings to an uneconomic size. By laying down a lower limit of 12½ acres for irrigated land, an economic unit would have been established and a sound basis laid for the rural economy of West Pakistan.

The agricultural land left by evacuees in West Pakistan was 9.6 million acres. Part of it was wasteland and part was in the possession of locals. The amount of land allocated to refugees—5.6 million acres—was grossly inadequate for the agriculturist refugee families, who numbered 1.5 million. For the proper settlement of refugees, further irrigation projects were needed as part of a comprehensive program of agricultural development.

In the cities the problem was in some ways even more acute. About 400,000 evacuee houses were available for nearly 600,000 refugee families in urban areas. Refugees tended to concentrate in big cities like Karachi, Lahore, and Lyallpur in the hope of finding employment. Karachi, in particular, as the capital and as an industrial center, attracted large numbers of refugees. Its population was about 350,000 at the time of partition. Within five years the population went up five times. The strain on the city's resources of housing, water supply, electricity, and other services was very great. A number of colonies like Lalukhet, Nazimabad, Landhi, and others were constructed, but the supply always lagged behind the demand. Apart from refugees, people from other parts of Pakistan came to Karachi looking for work and swelled its population.

To meet the big expense of resettling the refugees, the Pakistan government imposed rehabilitation taxes in various forms; their proceeds were partly used by the central government and partly distributed to the provinces.

A number of conferences between India and Pakistan were held during 1947 and 1948 to resolve problems, such as evaluation of property on each side, exchange of property records, settling the areas to which evacuee legislation was to apply, and making arrangements regarding movable property. Finally an inter-Dominion agreement was reached at a conference held in Karachi in January, 1949. The decisions taken related to agricultural property, urban immovable property, and movable property. The areas covered by the agreement on agricultural property were West Pakistan on one side and for the Dominion of India, East Punjab, Delhi, Himachal Pradesh, Patiala and the East Punjab States Union, and the states of Bharat, Alwar, and Bikaner. For urban immovable property the areas in India were extended to include Ajmer-Marwar, four northern districts of the United Provinces, the Rajasthan Union, and some states, such as Dholpur, Jaipur, and Jodhpur. These areas came to be known as "agreed areas." They were the areas where disturbances had led to mass migration. Revenue records of agricultural property were to be exchanged. Rents of agricultural and urban immovable property were to be collected by the Dominion in which the property was situated and an inter-Dominion adjustment made. Subject to some qualifications, the evacuee owner of urban immovable property was given the right to sell or exchange his property. As regards movable property, it could (except in certain specified cases) be sold or transported to the Dominion to which the displaced person had migrated.

The Indians were convinced that they had left behind in West Pakistan property of much greater value than that left by Muslim evacuees in the "agreed areas" in India. A pamphlet published in January, 1950, by the Indian Ministry of Rehabilitation concerning evacuee property admitted that "exact figures are extremely difficult to obtain," but went on to make the fantastic claim that "varying estimates have been made according to which the non-Muslim property is six to ten times the Muslim property left behind in India." The Indian belief was based on the most dubious statistics, but it led the Government of India to indubitably unethical conduct. In order to redress the balance and to have a bigger pool of Muslim evacuee property for distribution to Hindu refugees, evacuee legislation was unilaterally extended to the whole of India except West Bengal and Assam. In the Karachi conference of January, 1949 Indian representatives had suggested an extension of the area of evacuee legislation to the whole of India. Pakistan representatives opposed the proposal on the ground that no large-scale disturbances had taken place outside the "agreed areas" to justify such an extension, and the proposal was dropped. But within six months of the Karachi agreement, which clearly defined the "agreed areas," the Government of India asked various provincial governments in India to promulgate evacuee legislation. Under cover of this legislation, custodians of evacuee property were appointed all over India, except in West Bengal and Assam; and they proceeded to lay hold of the property of Muslim citizens.

In October, 1949, a new category of evacuees—"intending evacuees"—was introduced by India. Muslims declared to be "intending evacuees" were not only deprived of their property but of any possible means of livelihood in India, since they were officially declared to be potentially disloyal subjects. When a Muslim was thus driven out of his home to seek shelter in Pakistan, the Indian officials could triumphantly point to his departure in vindication of their unerring judgment in declaring him "an intending evacuee." These actions led to a fresh exodus of Muslims from India. They entered Pakistan mostly on foot through the Sind desert at the border station of Khokhropar. By this route 264,899 refugees entered Pakistan during 1950, and the number ultimately rose to nearly 600,000.

West Bengal and Assam were exempted from evacuee legislation by India in the interest of the twelve million Hindus of East Pakistan. For if this legislation had been extended to these two provinces, Muslims driven out of them under its operation would have had no option but to take shelter in East Pakistan. Similar legislation in East Pakistan would then have become inevitable, and the Hindus of East Pakistan would have suffered. According to the 1951 census, 700,000 Muslim refugees, mostly from Bihar, had been forced to take shelter in East Bengal. There was no evacuee property on which they could be settled. Nevertheless, the Pakistan government, out of consideration for its Hindu citizens, did not extend evacuee laws to East Pakistan.

In East Pakistan, Hindus formed one fourth of the population. The caste Hindus, although numerically smaller than the Scheduled Castes, were the dominant class in Hindu society and it was they who were most affected by the creation of Pakistan. In undivided Bengal they had enjoyed superior status and privileges throughout the period of British rule. They formed the landed gentry, the educated elite, and the moneyed class. When Pakistan came into existence, they felt politically powerless and economically insecure, and in general they found it difficult to adjust themselves to the new circumstances. A delegation of leading Hindus who met the Prime Minister on his visit to East Pakistan, in 1949, said to him in my hearing: "Our bodies are in Pakistan but our souls are in India." Most of the educated Hindu youth preferred not to enter government service in Pakistan. When quotas for recruitment to the various services of Pakistan were fixed by the central government on a provincial basis, I was struck by the fact that very few Hindus from East Bengal appeared to take the competitive examinations. I expostulated with Hindu leaders, pointing out that a larger proportion of Hindus in the public service would create a greater sense of security in the minds of the minority, but the response remained as poor as ever. Some of the richer Hindus took their money and migrated to West Bengal; others were attracted, as in the past, by the superior opportunities for education, employment, and trade in Calcutta. Thus, notwithstanding the prevalence of peaceful conditions in East Pakistan and the efforts of the government for fair and equal treatment of the minorities, there was an exodus of Hindus to West Bengal during 1948. Rajkumar Chakravarty, a prominent Hindu member of the Pakistan constituent assembly, remarked that the causes of the exodus of Hindus were psychological. But the Indian leaders were not satisfied, and the press in India was bellicose.

In April, 1948, an inter-Dominion conference held in Calcutta to discuss the position of minorities in East Bengal and West Bengal agreed on measures to protect the lives and property of minorities, to facilitate the return of evacuees to their homes, to set up provincial minority boards consisting of both Hindus and Muslims, and to discourage propaganda likely to inflame communal passion. In subsequent months there were lapses on both sides in observing the agreement. There was an exchange of lengthy telegrams between the prime ministers of India and Pakistan in October, 1948, on this subject. Sardar Patel, in his usual fashion, declared in a public speech in Nagpur on November 4, 1948: "If Pakistan was determined to drive away the Hindus from East Bengal, then Pakistan must agree to give us sufficient land so that we can rehabilitate them." [14] Despite their failure to protect the Muslim minority in India, the Indian leaders time and again threatened Pakistan for not giving adequate protection to Hindus in East Bengal. They felt far greater concern for the welfare of the Hindu minority in Pakistan than for the well-being of the Indian Muslims, whose loyalty was suspect in their eyes and who were being persecuted and denied opportunities of employment and economic advancement.

In December, 1948, another inter-Dominion conference was held in New Delhi, which was based largely on the Calcutta agreement but provided machinery for implementing it. Provincial minority boards were set up, as well as an inter-Dominion information consultation committee.

In the first quarter of 1950, tension between India and Pakistan mounted. This was partly a consequence of the economic war that India had started against Pakistan for not having followed India in devaluing its currency; but it was greatly accentuated by the communal disturbances that broke out in Calcutta, spread to East Pakistan and neighboring areas, and led to a two-way movement of refugees between East Bengal and West Bengal, Assam, and Tripura. Sardar Patel and other Indian leaders talked freely of war against Pakistan.[15]

A crisis was averted by Liaquat Ali Khan's statesmanlike act in going to Delhi to negotiate an agreement with Nehru. I accompanied the Prime Minister; and the actual negotiations were conducted between Girja Shankar Bajpai, the Secretary-General of the External Affairs Ministry of India, and myself. At the very outset, I put it to Bajpai that I would be prepared to accept any safeguards he proposed for the Hindu minority in East Bengal, or for that matter, for any minority anywhere in Pakistan, provided the same safeguards were extended to the Muslim minority in various provinces of India like West Bengal, Assam, the United Provinces, Bihar, and others. Bajpai, however, wanted to confine the problem to West Bengal and Assam. The matter was carried to the two prime ministers, who also failed to agree. I sought the help of Abul Kalam Azad, the Indian Education Minister, who was keenly interested in a just and equal treatment for the minorities on both sides. He still exercised considerable influence over Nehru, but in the face of Sardar Patel's opposition he failed to persuade Nehru. The deadlock lasted for a few days.

Finally, we had to be content with a general declaration of the responsibility of both governments for the protection of the rights of the minorities.

The agreement known as the Liaquat-Nehru Pact of April 8, 1950, opened with a solemn undertaking by the governments of India and Pakistan that "each shall ensure to the minorities throughout its territory complete equality of citizenship, irrespective of religion, a full sense of security in respect of life, culture, property and personal honour, freedom of movement within each country and freedom of occupation, speech and worship, subject to law and morality." There were detailed provisions for the protection of migrants from East Bengal, West Bengal, Assam, and Tripura; the restoration of normal conditions in these areas; and machinery for the implementation of the agreement.

An important part of the work of rehabilitation related to the recovery, restoration, and care of abducted women and children. An Indo-Pakistan agreement, reached in November, 1948, recognized the need for special legislation in both countries. The laws enacted under this agreement were so devised that by taking the victims away from the influence of their abductors, fear was eliminated, and by allowing them to resume contacts with their relatives and community they could make their own free decision regarding their future. Recovery offices and transit camps were set up in both India and Pakistan. Dedicated social workers helped greatly not only in the recovery but in the mental rehabilitation of abducted persons. By October, 1952, the number of non-Muslim women and children recovered from Pakistan was 8,326 and that of Muslim women and children recovered from India was 16,919.

The total number of refugees in West Pakistan ultimately rose to nearly nine million or one fourth of the population. Most of them have been rehabilitated, but the process of their integration into the social and economic life of the country is by no means complete. For a number of reasons the process of settlement and rehabilitation has been unduly slow and marred by inefficiency and corruption. Perhaps the main cause is to be found in the policy of staffing the organization almost wholly with temporary government employees whose personal interest is to prolong the period of their employment. Delay in the final settlement of claims has led to neglect of houses and factories allotted on a temporary basis, as well as to the sale of stocks of raw materials and spare parts to make a quick profit. It has provided greater opportunity for political pressures and for false claims and litigation. Yet the magnitude of the task performed must not be minimized. The problem was colossal and it threw, proportionately, a far greater burden on Pakistan than on India. Many predicted at the time that it would be beyond the economic and administrative resources of Pakistan to solve it and that Pakistan would be engulfed by the refugees. However, Pakistan not only surmounted these difficulties, but emerged stronger and more unified from this forced exchange of populations.

CHAPTER 14

Junagadh, Hyderabad, and Kashmir

THE STATES of Junagadh, Hyderabad, and Kashmir had not acceded to India or Pakistan by August 15, 1947. All of them were to fall victim to Indian aggression.

Junagadh was a small maritime state, 300 miles down the coast from Karachi. It had an area of 3,337 square miles, and a population of about 700,000. The majority of its population was Hindu and the ruler was a Muslim. Soon after independence, the state offered to accede to Pakistan with which it could maintain communication by sea. The Muslim ruler of Manavadar, a still smaller state contiguous to Junagadh, also acceded to Pakistan. These accessions were not accepted by the Quaid-i-Azam till September 5. The Government of India was also informed. The Indian reaction was immediate and sharp. The Governor-General of India telegraphed to the Governor-General of Pakistan: "Such acceptance of accession by Pakistan cannot but be regarded by Government of India as an encroachment on India's sovereignty and territory and inconsistent with friendly relations that should exist between the two Dominions. This action . . . is . . . in utter violation of principles on which partition was agreed upon and effected."

The "principles on which partition was agreed upon and effected" were that contiguous Muslim majority areas should be separated from contiguous non-Muslim majority areas to form the two Dominions, Pakistan and India, respectively. Junagadh, which had a Hindu majority and was contiguous to India, should not, it was argued, have acceded to Pakistan. The question of its accession should, the Government of India insisted, be decided by a plebiscite to be held under the joint supervision of the governments of India and Junagadh, but not of Pakistan.

Simultaneously with these formal protests, the Government of India took steps to solve the problem by other means. A Kathiawar defense force was organized. Junagadh was surrounded by Indian troops in conjunction with troops of the neighboring Hindu states of Kathiawar, which had acceded to India. The Jam Sahib of Nawanagar, a leading Hindu prince of the area, urged the Government of India to "take immediate and effective steps to assure continued protection of the Kathiawar States," [1] which were regarded as threatened by Junagadh's accession to Pakistan. An economic blockade of Junagadh was imposed. Rail communications with India were cut off. In consequence, Junagadh's sources of revenues from customs and railways dwindled, and there was a serious shortage of food. A provisional government of Junagadh with Gandhi's nephew, Shamaldas Gandhi, as President was formed at Bombay. The "provisional government" moved its headquarters to Rajkot, nearer Junagadh, recruited volunteers and organized raids into Junagadh.

During September and October, Junagadh formed a major subject of correspondence between the governments of India and Pakistan and was also discussed at various meetings of the Joint Defence Council. The situation was complicated by the presence, inside the Indian Union, of enclaves belonging to, or owing suzerainty to, Junagadh. Their exact status aroused much controversy, but Pakistan was prepared to refer this matter to independent legal opinion. Pakistan was also willing that, where the question of accession was in dispute, a plebiscite should be held. On October 23, the Prime Minister of Pakistan proposed to the Prime Minister of India that the two governments should discuss and settle the conditions for the holding of a plebiscite.

The Government of India was, however, bent on settling the matter by force. The blockade and raids had created such chaotic conditions

in Junagadh by the end of October, 1947, that the Nawab felt compelled to leave for Karachi with his family. On November 1, the enclaves of Babariawad and Mangrol were taken over by Indian forces.
Manavadar had already been occupied by India some days earlier.
On November 7, an *Azad Fauj,* or liberation army, of 20,000 men with
armored cars and other modern weapons entered Junagadh. The
Azad Fauj consisted largely of trained military personnel organized
and equipped by order of the Government of India. Two days later
control over the entire state was assumed by India. Pakistan, at that
time, was in no position to defend Junagadh. Her armed forces were
in the process of organization. The army was faced with innumerable
problems arising from refugee movements. There was only the nu-
cleus of a navy and an air force.

The Pakistan government received a telegram from the Prime Minister of India saying that the Government of India had taken control
of Junagadh state at the request of its Dewan, in order to avoid disorder and chaos, and that they intended to ascertain what the wishes
of the people were with regard to accession. In reply, the Prime Minister of Pakistan pointed out that since Junagadh had duly acceded to
Pakistan, the Dewan had no authority to negotiate a settlement with
India, and that India's action was a clear violation of Pakistan's territory and a breach of international law. He demanded that the Government of India immediately withdraw their forces from Junagadh
and restore the administration of the rightful ruler as a preliminary
for discussions between the two Dominions. Further correspondence
led nowhere. Some months later, the Government of India held a
referendum under its own supervision. The result of the referendum
was a foregone conclusion. A majority of votes were cast in favor of
accession to India. Pakistan, which was in no way associated with the
referendum, refused to recognize its validity. India is still in unlawful
occupation of Junagadh. A complaint lodged by Pakistan with the Security Council of the UN is still pending.

Hyderabad was the most important state of India. It had an area of
82,000 square miles, and a population of 16,000,000. Its annual
revenues were Rs. 260 million, and it had its own currency and
stamps. The majority of its people were Hindus, but its ruler, the
Nizam, was a Muslim. The dynasty was founded in the early years of
the eighteenth century by Nizamul Mulk, a grandee of the Mughul

Empire. The Nizam had the distinction of the title "His Exalted Highness," and was designated as the "faithful ally of the British Government." Hyderabad occupied a special place in the affections of Muslim India because of its association with the glory of the Mughul Empire. By virtue of its size, resources, importance, and prestige, Hyderabad felt entitled to the status of an independent sovereign state. On the announcement of the June 3 plan the Nizam declared that he would not accede to India or Pakistan. He hoped to secure Dominion Status for his state, and sent a delegation to the Viceroy on July 11, 1947. Mountbatten told the delegation that the British government would not agree to Dominion Status for Hyderabad. Instead, he pressed Hyderabad to accede to India. This, however, was not acceptable to the Nizam. When the delegation hinted that if India pressed the Nizam too hard he might consider joining Pakistan Mountbatten replied, "There was no doubt that the Nizam was legally entitled to do so, but . . . the mechanical difficulty presented by the facts of geography was very real. . . . Without implying any kind of threat, he foresaw disastrous results to the State in five or ten years if his advice were not taken." [2] The facts of geography to which Mountbatten was referring were that Hyderabad had no outlet to the sea and was surrounded on all sides by Indian territory.

No decision was reached by August 15. Further negotiations with the Nizam were entrusted by the Indian cabinet to the Governor-General, Lord Mountbatten; he strove to the utmost to bring Hyderabad within the Indian fold. The Nizam was reluctant to sign the standard instrument of accession, but expressed willingness to enter into a treaty of association with India in respect of defense, foreign affairs, and communications. Sir Walter (later Lord) Monckton, who was a friend of Mountbatten, was the Nizam's principal adviser in these negotiations with the Government of India. The Government of India, however, insisted on accession and would not agree to anything less.

In Hyderabad itself, the Muslim organization Ittehadul Muslimin and its leader Kasim Razvi were gaining strength. At the end of November, 1947, Mir Laik Ali, a leading Muslim industrialist of Hyderabad, became Prime Minister with their support, although the Quaid-i-Azam on being consulted by the Nizam had advised against the appointment.[3] The attitude of Pakistan leaders toward Hyderabad in its difficulties with India was one of sympathy, but it was felt that the decision as to its precise relationship with India must be left to the judgment of the Nizam and his government.

A standstill agreement between India and Hyderabad was concluded on November 29, 1947. The Nizam also gave a secret promise to Mountbatten not to accede to Pakistan.[4] The Government of India claimed that under the standstill agreement Hyderabad could not enter into any kind of relationship with any foreign country. Serious exception was taken to a loan of Rs. 200 million, which the Nizam's government had made to Pakistan, despite their protestation that it was a commercial transaction. The loan was in the form of Government of India securities. To deny its proceeds to Pakistan, the Government of India issued an ordinance freezing the securities.

K. M. Munshi, a former minister in Bombay and a staunch believer in Akhand Bharat, or undivided India, was selected by Sardar Patel to become the Agent-General of the Government of India under the standstill agreement. He took it as his patriotic duty to undermine the authority of the Nizam's government by inciting the Hindus and by other means. Allegations were made that Hyderabad had violated the standstill agreement, but when the Nizam's government offered to refer the matter to arbitration, as provided for by the standstill agreement, the Government of India did not agree. The Nizam was also asked to ban the Ittehadul Muslimin and to disband the Razakars, or volunteers. War was threatened. In a speech in Bombay on April 26, 1948, Nehru said: "If the safety of the people in Hyderabad was endangered by the activities of the Razakars, the Government [of India] would intervene in Hyderabad State."[5] Patel talked of Hyderabad going the way of Junagadh. In short, every kind of pressure was brought to bear on the Nizam by the Government of India to force him to accede to India.

Mountbatten and the Indian leaders believed that the entire Hindu population in Hyderabad was for accession to India. They stressed time and again that the issue of Hyderabad should be left to the people to decide. In August, 1947, Mountbatten had written to the Nizam offering "a referendum under the supervision of British officers," but the Nizam had not agreed.[6] In June, 1948, however, Mir Laik Ali accepted Mountbatten's proposal for the holding of a free plebiscite under impartial auspices "on the question whether the State should accede to India or remain independent." Much to Mir Laik

Ali's surprise and distress, the Government of India now insisted that the state should accede to India on defense, foreign affairs, and communications and "if the Government of Hyderabad so wished, they may have the matter further confirmed by a plebiscite." [7] The demand was also made for the immediate introduction of responsible government, since, as the Government of India stated in their *White Paper on Hyderabad,* "plebiscite without an interim Government representative of and satisfactory to the majority population in Hyderabad will only be a fraud on the people."

Lord Mountbatten left India on June 21, 1948, without having achieved his ambition of securing Hyderabad's accession. The pressures against Hyderabad increased in intensity. An economic blockade was imposed. Military preparations were begun. There were mutual charges of border raids and breaches of the standstill agreement. In a parliamentary debate on July 30, Winston Churchill referred to a speech made by Nehru four days earlier in which he was reported to have said, "If and when we consider it necessary we will start military operations against Hyderabad." Nehru went on to say that the regime of the Nizam's state was composed of gangsters, that the only alternative to its accession was its disappearance as a state, and that in the event of action against Hyderabad he would not confer upon it the designation of war. "It seems to me," commented Churchill, "that this is the sort of thing which might have been said by Hitler before the devouring of Austria."

On August 24, Hyderabad filed a complaint before the Security Council of the UN. But before the Security Council could arrange a hearing, India forced a military decision on Hyderabad. On September 13, 1948, less than two days after the Quaid-i-Azam's death, a full-scale invasion of Hyderabad state by the Indian armed forces was launched. After a brief resistance, the Hyderabad army surrendered on September 17. In due course the state was dismembered and incorporated into the different provinces of the Indian Union. The complaint before the Security Council is still pending.

Kashmir, or to give its full name, the state of Jammu and Kashmir, is the northernmost part of the Indo-Pakistan subcontinent. Its area of 84,471 square miles was the biggest of any state in India. Its international boundaries with Tibet, China, Afghanistan and, but for a small intervening strip, with Russia, gave it great strategic importance. Owing to its mountainous character the state was sparsely populated except in the beautiful valley of Kashmir. The total population of the state, according to the 1941 census, was about 4,000,000, of whom 77 percent were Muslims. The Muslims were in a majority in every province of the state; there was a 93 percent Muslim population in the Kashmir province; 61 percent, in Jammu province; and almost 100 percent, in the northern region of Gilgit. In Ladakh, which adjoins Tibet, there was a small Buddhist population.

Geographically the state is a continuation of the plains of West Pakistan into the mountains. The rivers Indus, Jhelum, and Chenab, which are the life-line of West Pakistan, flow from the state into the plains, making the whole a single geographical unit. All the rail and road communications of the state were with Pakistan. Its exports and imports moved through Pakistan. Timber, which was its most important source of revenue, was exported by being floated down the rivers into Pakistan. The cultural connections between the Muslims of the state and those of West Pakistan are so close as to make them virtually identical. The destiny of West Pakistan and Kashmir is linked together by nature and by all possible interests—economic, religious, cultural, and strategic.

Under the Treaty of Amritsar in 1846, the British had sold the state of Jammu and Kashmir to Gulab Singh, a petty Dogra chieftain, for the sum of 7.5 million rupees, or one and a half million dollars. Lord Lawrence, who negotiated the treaty, referred to this transaction as an "iniquitous arrangement." [8] The Maharaja and his Dogra kinsmen established and maintained for a century a despotic, reactionary, and oppressive regime in the state. No effort was made to develop the natural wealth of the state. The people were ruthlessly taxed and reduced to a condition of abject poverty. The Muslims suffered discrimination in every sphere. The Hindus had a more or less complete monopoly of state appointments. Since the cow is sacred to the Hindus, its slaughter was forbidden. If a Muslim killed his own cow to feed his family, the penalty was death—later mercifully reduced to a ten-year jail sentence. The Kashmiris are a highly gifted people, but their spirit was broken by repressive measures and arbitrary punishments.

With the spread of modern education, a demand for elementary political rights began in the early 1930s. The leaders of this movement were Sheikh Muhammad Abdullah and Chaudhry Ghulam Abbas. The former belonged to the valley of Kashmir and the latter to

Jammu. Together they organized the Jammu and Kashmir Muslim Conference. The Maharaja resorted to repressive measures of unusual severity. There were arrests and firings. To help their brethren, Muslims from the neighboring areas of the Punjab entered the state in large numbers. As many as 30,000 volunteers courted arrest. A Kashmir committee in support of the struggle in Kashmir was formed in Lahore under the chairmanship of the national poet, Iqbal, whose family had come from Kashmir to settle in the Punjab. The struggle led to the appointment of the Glancy Commission by the Government of India. On the recommendation of the commission, a measure of constitutional reform was introduced and a partly elected legislative assembly was formed.

In 1939, Sheikh Abdullah came under the spell of Gandhi and Nehru. The Congress leaders assured him of their support in the struggle against the Maharaja if the Muslim Conference was turned into a noncommunal organization. Accordingly, the Muslim Conference was converted into the National Conference. Soon, however, divergences between the interests of the Muslim and the Hindus came to the surface. The demand for an independent sovereign Pakistan, the very name and concept of which included Kashmir as an integral part, produced a new situation. The struggle between the Congress and the Muslim League over the partition of India had its repercussions in Kashmir. The Muslim Conference was revived under the leadership of Chaudhry Ghulam Abbas. Sheikh Abdullah continued with the National Conference as its leader. But as the idea of Pakistan gained ground, the National Conference, which was allied with the Hindu Congress, started losing its popularity. Sensing this, Sheikh Abdullah turned to the Quaid-i-Azam. In 1944, at the request of both the National Conference and the Muslim Conference, Quaid-i-Azam visited Kashmir and tried to bring the two organizations together, but without success. Sheikh Abdullah was too deeply committed to the Congress leaders. In particular, Nehru made much of him and professed attachment to him as a personal friend. In 1946, when Sheikh Abdullah was put in jail by the Maharaja for having started the "Quit Kashmir" movement in order to get rid of the Maharaja, Nehru, in the midst of negotiations with the Cabinet Mission, rushed to Kashmir to defend his friend. This dramatic gesture was intended to tie Sheikh Abdullah firmly to the side of the Congress.

When the Congress leaders accepted partition, they did so with the intent to truncate Pakistan and make it as unviable as possible. They tried their hardest to detach the North-West Frontier Province, but that province had no contiguity with India except through Kashmir. The desperate efforts of Gandhi and other Congress leaders to prevent the inclusion of the North-West Frontier Province in Pakistan make sense only as part of a broader strategy covering Kashmir as well as the Frontier Province. But entirely apart from the North-West Frontier Province, Kashmir had an intrinsic importance of its own. The occupation of Kashmir would give India control over all the rivers on which the economy of West Pakistan depends, and would make the most vital areas of Pakistan militarily vulnerable. Gandhi realized that Kashmir "had the greatest strategic value, perhaps, in all India." [9] Sheikh Abdullah in a statement to the press in Delhi on October 21, 1947, observed, "Due to the strategic position that the State [Kashmir] holds, if this State joins the Indian Dominion, Pakistan would be completely encircled." [10] By getting hold of Kashmir, India would gain a commanding position against Pakistan.

There was an important reason why the Congress leaders could not immediately come out in the open with their plans regarding Kashmir. The reason was provided by Hyderabad. Except for its far superior administration, Hyderabad was Kashmir in reverse. The former was a Hindu majority state ruled by a Muslim, and the latter a Muslim majority state under a Hindu ruler. Hyderabad occupied a pivotal position in the Deccan, or Southern India, and was nearly as important for the Indian Union as Kashmir was for Pakistan. If the Hindu Maharaja of the Muslim majority state of Kashmir had acceded to India before Hyderabad, the claim of the Congress to Hyderabad as a Hindu majority state would have been greatly weakened, and the Nizam of Hyderabad might have acceded to Pakistan. The Congress plan, therefore, was to reach a secret understanding with the Maharaja of Kashmir for accession to India, but not to accept that accession openly until Hyderabad had been brought within the fold of India. I received information of this "Hyderabad first and then Kashmir" plan of the Congress from a reliable source during the partition days, and the attitude and activities of the Indian leaders confirmed it.

Another reason for the seeming indifference of Indian leaders toward Kashmir during the partition days was the lack of communications between the Indian Dominion and the state of Jammu and

Kashmir. Their common border ran across high mountains through which no roads had been built. Although, as related earlier in Chapter 10, an understanding had been reached between Mountbatten and the Congress leaders regarding the partition of the Gurdaspur district, no overt action could be taken until Radcliffe actually awarded the Muslim majority tahsils of Gurdaspur and Batala in Gurdaspur district to India, and thus provided a link between India and Kashmir.

In the meantime every effort was being made by the Congress to win over the Hindu Maharaja. Acharya Kripalani, the Congress President at that time, was the first to pay a visit to Kashmir. Soon after the announcement of the June 3 plan, Nehru expressed a desire to go there. When the Maharaja objected, Gandhi said he would go in place of Nehru, if need be, in a private capacity. The Maharaja apprehended that visits by Gandhi or Nehru might lead to a visit by the Quaid-i-Azam; and he was strongly opposed to any Muslim League leader coming to Kashmir.[11] Mountbatten, through whom these negotiations for a visit by Nehru or Gandhi were conducted, decided to go first.

In the third week of June, 1947, Mountbatten spent four days in Kashmir discussing the situation with the Maharaja. Since both Nehru and Gandhi had been very anxious that the Maharaja should make no declaration of independence, Mountbatten urged the Maharaja and his Prime Minister "not to declare independence but to find out in one way or another the will of the people of Kashmir as soon as possible and to announce their intention by 14th August to send representatives accordingly to one Constituent Assembly or the other. He told them that the newly created States Department was prepared to give an assurance that if Kashmir went to Pakistan this would not be regarded as an unfriendly act by the Government of India. He went on to stress the dangerous situation in which Kashmir would find itself if it lacked the support of one of the two Dominions by the date of the transfer of power." [12] Actually the States department was created some days after Mountbatten's return from Kashmir, although the proposal for it had been made earlier. The above report of Mountbatten's talks with the Maharaja was, however, that given by Mountbatten to his Press-Attaché, Campbell-Johnson. It is confirmed by Mountbatten's speech before the Royal Empire Society in London on October 6, 1948, in which he described how he urged the Maharaja "to ascertain the will of his people on joining one Dominion or another. Had he joined with Pakistan the Government of India would have made no trouble. Had he joined with India, well, Pakistan did not exist, so again there would have been no trouble."

Mountbatten's attitude toward Kashmir's accession during these critical days of partition when he was Viceroy deserves careful study. At no stage did he tell the Maharaja, that, in view of the geographical and strategic factors and the overwhelmingly Muslim population of the state, it was his plain duty to accede to Pakistan. The arguments he so forcefully put before Hyderabad, Jaipur, and Jaisalmere for accession to India applied with equal strength to Kashmir's accession to Pakistan. But he never used them with the Maharaja. On the other hand, "He assured the Maharaja that [were] . . . he . . . to accede to one Dominion or the other before 15 August, no trouble would ensue, for whichever Dominion he acceded to would take the State firmly under its protection." [13] The assurance was given in June, 1947, when—assuming that an impartial boundary award were made—India would have had no means of communication with Kashmir, and the accession of the state to India in respect of defense, foreign affairs, and communications would have been meaningless.

Mountbatten could hardly ignore the Muslim majority in the population of the Kashmir state, but he did not draw the obvious conclusion and put it to the Maharaja. In Hyderabad and other Hindu majority states with Muslim rulers he had given forthright advice in favor of immediate accession to India. Only in Kashmir did he suggest that the Maharaja should not make a decision until he had somehow or other ascertained the will of the people.

Explaining his policy to Campbell-Johnson in October, 1947, Mountbatten said that he had "exerted his whole influence to prevent him [the Maharaja of Kashmir] from acceding to one Dominion or the other without first taking steps to ascertain the will of his people by referendum, plebiscite, election, or even, if these methods were impracticable, by representative public meetings." [14] Even in the matter of ascertaining the will of the people, there is a striking contrast between Mountbatten's methods in Hyderabad and Kashmir. In Hyderabad, Mountbatten insisted on a free plebiscite under impartial auspices and offered to hold it under the supervision of British officers. In Kashmir, he imposed no such condition and made no such offer, but left it to the Maharaja to sound the people in any manner he pleased. In a plebiscite or referendum held in Kashmir under impartial auspices the overwhelming majority of Muslims and some of the Hindus as well would have voted for Pakistan. For among the Hindus also there were leaders, like Pandit Prem Nath Bazaz, who were sincerely convinced that accession to Pakistan was in the best interest of Kashmir. But in the vague and indefinite method of public meetings held under a despotic regime, the Maharaja and his administration could proclaim any result they liked.

Thus, while maintaining an outward appearance of impartiality, Mountbatten was playing the Congress game in Kashmir and cannot be acquitted of complicity in the plans of Congress leaders to acquire Kashmir by hook or by crook. The way he equated the unequal claims of India and Pakistan, the assurance he gave of protection to the Maharaja if he decided on accession to India, the indefinite method he suggested for ascertaining the wishes of the people could only have left the impression on the mind of the Hindu Maharaja, that he could, with equal facility, accede to India if he so desired.

The Muslim League's attitude to the question of Kashmir's accession was stated by the Quaid-i-Azam in a talk with a delegation of the Jammu and Kashmir Muslim Conference workers in July, 1947. In the course of his talk he remarked: "I have already made it clear more than once that the Indian States are free to join either the Pakistan Constituent Assembly or the Hindustan Constituent Assembly or remain independent. I have no doubt that they, the Maharaja and the Kashmir Government, will give the closest attention and consideration to this matter and realise the interest not only of the ruler but also of his people." Actually he was convinced that a dispassionate consideration of the relevant facts of population and geography, the economic and cultural ties, and even the Maharaja's dynastic interest would inevitably point toward accession with Pakistan. He expressed a desire to go to Srinagar, but Mountbatten persuaded him to drop the idea in the face of objections made by the Kashmir government.

Although Mountbatten had dissuaded the Quaid-i-Azam from going to Kashmir or sending any Muslim League leader there, he arranged for Gandhi's visit there on August 1, 1947. This was Gandhi's first visit to the beautiful valley. He had not, needless to say, undertaken this long journey, at the age of seventy-seven, for aesthetic reasons. He saw the Maharaja and the Prime Minister, and had a series of interviews with the workers of the National Conference, among them Bakhshi Ghulam Muhammad. The Prime Minister of Kashmir at this time was Pandit Ram Chandra Kak; and although he was a Hindu he opposed the state's accession to India.

Gandhi's object was to oust Kak and to win over the Maharaja for accession to India. His approach was to play upon the religious sentiments of the Maharani through her spiritual guide. The reverence in which Gandhi was held by every pious Hindu helped him to gain his political ends. The Maharaja, who in his youth was easily black-mailed by a woman of easy virtue and her associates in London, was hardly of the caliber to withstand in his declining years pressures of a more exalted kind.

The measure of Gandhi's success can be judged from the report of his visit that he sent to Nehru and Patel. "I met [the Maharaja and the Maharani]. . . . However much they might wish to join the Union [of India], they would have to make the choice in accordance with the wishes of the people. . . . Bakhshi (Ghulam Mohammad) was most sanguine that the result of the free vote of the people, whether on the adult franchise or on the existing register, would be in favour of Kashmir joining the Union [of India] provided of course that Sheikh Abdullah and his co-prisoners were released, all bans were removed and the present Prime Minister was not in power." To Patel alone he wrote that the Maharaja wished "to remove Kak. . . . The only question (before him) is how. . . . In my opinion the Kashmir problem can be solved." [15]

Pandit Kak was removed from the office of prime minister within ten days after Gandhi's visit to Kashmir. A month later Sheikh Abdullah was released from jail, but Chaudhry Ghulam Abbas and other Muslim Conference leaders remained in prison. The Kashmir problem was on the way to being solved to Gandhi's satisfaction.

After independence was declared, a standstill agreement was signed between Pakistan and Kashmir. This was partly necessity, since postal communications and export and import trade via India would take time to organize, and partly camouflage. The Kashmir government also offered a standstill agreement to India, but the Government of India took no action on it. As already explained, it did not suit India to take overt action for taking over Kashmir until later.

The wishes of the Muslim population of Kashmir were demon-strated in an unmistakable fashion on independence day. August 15, 1947, was celebrated as "Pakistan Day" throughout the state. But August 15 was also the signal for the Maharaja to put into action his plan of liquidating the Muslim majority. To advise the Maharaja of Kashmir on this problem there were visits by the Sikh Maharajas of Kapurthala and Patiala. Kapurthala state had had a Muslim majority, but almost all the Muslims had been killed or driven out with the help of state forces. The Maharaja of Patiala was an even greater expert in genocide. If similar methods were followed in Kashmir, and the Muslim population was cut down and terrorized, accession to India might present no difficulty. To execute this plan, the Dogra General Janak Singh was appointed Prime Minister in place of Pandit Kak. The civilian population was ordered to deposit with the state authorities all arms in their possession. Sikhs and RSSS murder gangs started operations and were actively supported by state troops. Treachery was added to the methods adopted in East Punjab. Muslims were promised safe conduct if they left for Pakistan, and then were ambushed and slaughtered on the way. "In one area," reported the London *Times* of October 10, 1947, "237,000 Muslims were systematically exterminated, unless they escaped to Pakistan along the border, by the forces of the Dogra State, headed by the Maharajah in person." Ian Stephens, who was editor of the *Statesman* of Calcutta at that time, wrote:

> Within a period of about eleven weeks starting in August, systematic savageries, similar to those already launched in East Punjab and in Patiala and Kapurthala, practically eliminated the entire Muslim element in the population, amounting to 500,000 people. About 200,000 just disappeared, remaining untraceable, having presumably been butchered, or died from epidemics or exposure. The rest fled destitute to West Punjab.[16]

In Poonch, which is the western part of Jammu province, things did not go according to the Maharaja's plan. Poonch was one of the recruiting areas for the Indian army and was the home of 65,000 veterans of the Second World War. In August, 1947, there were demonstrations in many places in Poonch against the Maharaja's contemplated move to join India. State troops fired upon the meetings, inflicting heavy casualties. The people who had suffered so long rose against the Maharaja's rule. They obtained arms from tribal areas and fought back. The man who raised the standard of revolt was Abdul Qayyum, but "the folly of Dogras who burnt whole villages where only a single family was involved in the revolt," rallied the entire Muslim population to the popular cause.[17] In six weeks the districts of Poonch and Mirpur, except the town of Poonch, had been cleared of state troops. A little later, the Azad Kashmir government, under the presidency of Sardar Muhammad Ibrahim, a local barrister, was organized. Speaking in Delhi on October 21, 1947, Sheikh Abdullah, after referring to the fact that the Muslims of Kashmir were afraid that the state's accession to India portended danger to them, said:

> The present troubles in Poonch . . . were caused by the unwise policy adopted by the State. The people of Poonch . . . had started a people's movement for the redress of their grievances. It was not communal. Kashmir State sent its troops. . . . But most of the adult population of Poonch were . . . ex-servicemen in the Indian Army with close connections with the people in Jhelum and Rawalpindi [in Pakistan]. . . . They evacuated their women and children, crossed the frontier, and returned with arms supplied to them by willing people. The present position is that the Kashmir State forces have been forced to withdraw in certain areas.[18]

During this time the Pakistan government had its hands full; it had to deal with the task of establishing a new administration, the ordeal in the Punjab, and the mass migration that was under way. The people of Pakistan felt the most lively sympathy with their brethren in Jammu and Kashmir. The tragedy being enacted there appeared as part of a vast conspiracy to overwhelm Pakistan at its birth. As hundreds of thousands of Muslim refugees from Jammu and Kashmir moved into the neighboring areas of Pakistan, a new and grave threat to Pakistan took shape. These planned massacres signified evil. The Pakistan army authorities were greatly concerned as soldiers, who had been on leave to their homes in Poonch, reported that Muslim villagers there were being attacked by state troops. Vigorous protests to the Maharaja's government were made. But instead of putting its own house in order, the state government accused Pakistan of having deliberately cut off supplies of food, gas, and other essential commodities. There was no truth in these allegations. The movement and feeding of millions of refugees had put the utmost strain upon supplies and rail and road communications in the Punjab. If shortages occurred in the state, it was due to the wholly exceptional circumstances produced by the greatest migration in history. Nevertheless, the Pakistan government was anxious to do all it could.

The Quaid-i-Azam himself wanted to go to Kashmir about the middle of September; he hoped to have a friendly talk with the Maharaja, but the Maharaja did not want him to come. On October 2,

1947, Liaquat Ali Khan suggested that the question of civil supplies for Kashmir should be discussed by representatives of the two governments. The reply given by the Prime Minister of Kashmir was that at the moment he was too busy. Despite this, the Pakistan government sent a senior officer of the Ministry of Foreign Affairs, Colonel Shah, for discussion with the state authorities. The Prime Minister of Kashmir refused to discuss matters with him, and he had to return.

During September, 1947, significant moves had been made by the Government of India in collaboration with the Maharaja of Kashmir. Sheikh Abdullah was released but, as noted earlier, Chaudhry Ghulam Abbas, the leader of the Muslim Conference, was not. Gopalaswami Ayyangar, who had been Prime Minister of Kashmir from 1937 to 1943 and who was notoriously anti-Muslim, was appointed Minister without Portfolio in the Indian cabinet. On September 30, a provisional defense committee of the Indian cabinet was formed which included the Prime Minister, the Deputy Prime Minister, the Defence Minister, the Finance Minister and, significantly enough, the Minister without Portfolio. Although Gopalaswami Ayyangar was an expert on Kashmir, he could hardly be regarded as an expert on defense. To make up this deficiency, Mountbatten was made Chairman of the committee "in view of his knowledge and experience of high military matters." [19] Preparations for aggression in Kashmir had started. What moved the Government of India to start these preparations at this time was presumably the freedom movement in Poonch, which the Maharaja's forces had failed to put down, and which was spreading to other areas.

The next step immediately following the formation of the provisional defense committee was the appointment of a trusted Indian, Mehr Chand Mahajan, as Prime Minister of Kashmir in place of the Dogra General Janak Singh. From the very outset, Mahajan's attitude was aggressive. On the day he assumed office he held a press conference in which he denounced Pakistan. On the same day, October 15, 1947, he sent a telegram to the Pakistan government, suggesting an impartial enquiry into the complaints of the Maharaja's government and adding significantly: "If . . . this request is not heeded the Government much against its wishes will have no option but to ask for assistance to withstand the aggressive and unfriendly actions of the Pakistan people along our border." The reference was obviously to assistance from India. It was a clear pointer that Indian plans for a military occupation of Kashmir at the invitation of the Maharaja's government had reached a point where they could be openly avowed. The Pakistan government readily accepted the proposal for an impartial enquiry and suggested an immediate meeting between the representatives of the two governments. But the Kashmir government took no notice of this acceptance and made no further reference to the matter. Three days later, on October 18, another telegram came from the Prime Minister of Kashmir, this time to the Quaid-i-Azam, repeating all the previous allegations and again threatening to seek outside assistance. It was evident that a pretext for Indian military intervention in Kashmir was being sought. The Quaid-i-Azam in his telegraphic reply, on October 20, requested the Maharaja to send the Prime Minister of Kashmir to Karachi for discussions in order to smooth out difficulties and adjust matters in a friendly way. The Quaid-i-Azam stated:

> The threat to enlist outside assistance shows clearly that the real aim of your Government's policy is to seek an opportunity to join the Indian Dominion, as a coup d'état, by securing the intervention and assistance of that Dominion. This policy is naturally creating deep resentment and grave apprehension among your subjects, 85 per cent of whom are Moslems. The proposal made by my Government for a meeting with your accredited representative is now an urgent necessity.

No reply was sent by the Maharaja to this telegram despite a reminder by the Quaid-i-Azam.

About this time, unknown to the Pakistan government, a storm was brewing in the tribal areas. News of atrocities committed by the Maharaja's government on the Muslims of Kashmir had reached tribal areas from refugees and ex-soldiers from Poonch, who had gone there to purchase arms. Massacre of Muslims in East Punjab had already inflamed the feelings of the tribesmen. Now they felt a call for *jihad,* or holy war, in Kashmir. On October 21, Liaquat Ali Khan told me in a state of unusual excitement that a tribal lashkar, some thousands strong, was on the way to Kashmir. I asked him if he had informed the Quaid-i-Azam and he said, "Not yet," he had just received the report. There was nothing the Pakistan government could do about it. An attempt to prevent the tribesmen from performing what they conceived to be a religious duty would have set the whole frontier ablaze. The Pakistan army was neither fully organized nor adequately equipped. The demands made on it by the refugee problem were more than it could cope with. The tribal lashkar, which crossed the bridge on the river Jhelum into state territory on October 22, quickly overpowered the state forces, and by October 26 had reached the vicinity of Srinagar, the capital of Kashmir. The previous night the Maharaja fled from Srinagar to Jammu. Had the tribal lashkar been more disciplined, and had it not indulged in plunder on the way, it would have been in occupation of the Kashmir valley on October 26.

When the Indian cabinet received news of the tribal incursion into Kashmir, it wanted "to rush in arms and ammunitions already requested by the Kashmir Government," but Mountbatten urged that accession should first be obtained. "He considered that it would be the height of folly to send troops into a neutral State, where we had no right to send them, since Pakistan could do exactly the same thing, which could only result in a clash of armed forces and in war." [20] V. P. Menon was sent off to Srinagar to secure accession. Simultaneously Mountbatten, as one of his staff told me on my visit to Delhi a fortnight later, assumed direction of military operations—to use his dramatic language—"The mantle of the Governor-General fell from him and he assumed the garb of the Supreme Commander." To Mountbatten himself it might have appeared as only an extension of his functions as Chairman of the provisional defense committee. Anyhow, his great experience of combined operations during the Second World War was put at the service of Indian aggression in Kashmir. When, on the morning of October 27, 1947, he signed the instrument of accession V. P. Menon had brought back with him, the airlift of Indian troops to Srinagar had already started. As the formation of the provisional defense committee on September 30 and the threats of the Maharaja's government in mid-October to call in outside assistance clearly indicate, the Indians had been planning armed intervention in Kashmir for quite some time. But the credit for the improvisation of air-borne operations within a few days, and their success in halting the tribal lashkar outside Srinagar, must go to Mountbatten's military skill, even as the stratagem of obtaining the Maharaja's immediate accession is attributable to his diplomatic finesse. As Campbell-Johnson wrote, "Mountbatten's extraordinary vitality and canniness were well-adapted to the demands of the hour." [21] His was the brain that conceived the strategy and the hand that directed the operations.

Mountbatten's attitude toward Pakistan and Kashmir at this critical time in the history of Indo-Pakistan relations has been described
by Ian Stephens, who was called to dinner by Lord and Lady Mountbatten on the evening of October 26.

> I was startled by their one-sided verdicts on affairs. They seemed to
> have "become wholly pro-Hindu." The atmosphere at Government
> House that night was almost one of war. Pakistan, the Muslim
> League, and Mr. Jinnah were the enemy. . . . Because of the
> Pathan attack, the Maharajah's formal accession to India was at
> that moment being finalized. Subject to a plebiscite, this great State,
> its inhabitants mainly Muslim, would now be legally lost to Jinnah.
> The Pakistanis had been crazy to accept the accession of Junagadh.
> Indian troops were to be flown into Kashmir at once; arrangements
> had been made.

His memorandum records Mountbatten as "persuasive, confident,
charming, a successful commander on the eve of an important operation." [22]

Foreign writers reviewing the events of those days have questioned
Mountbatten's role and wondered why the Indian cabinet and, in particular, Mountbatten did not take the obvious course of consulting the
Pakistan government, with whom the Maharaja had entered into a
standstill agreement and who had the most vital interests at stake in
this issue. Lord Birdwood asks:

> How was it, then, that on 24 or 25 October no one in Delhi thought
> of getting on the telephone to the Pakistan Prime Minister and deal-
> ing with the crisis as a solemn responsibility to be shouldered by a
> display of joint statesmanship? If Mr. Nehru could not have risen to
> the occasion of his own free will, was there no one at his elbow of
> sufficient vision [the reference is to Mountbatten] to have influ-
> enced him to do so? Therein was the tragedy.[23]

Josef Korbel, who as the Indian nominee on the United Nations
Commission for India and Pakistan had an exceptional opportunity
to study the Kashmir problem, wrote:

> Why . . . did he [Mountbatten] advise that Indian military assis-
> tance to the Maharaja must be covered by the legal technicality of
> accession? How could he have reasoned that it would be illegal for
> Kashmir (which was at the time of invasion technically an inde-
> pendent country) to ask for military help from India without pre-
> ceding the request by accession? . . . . Why was there at this
> point no appeal made to the United Nations? . . . . Finally, it is
> most difficult to understand why no one, particularly Mountbatten,
> advanced the most obvious idea—that of immediately getting into
> contact with the Karachi government for consultation.[24]

The Quaid-i-Azam was at this time in Lahore, and not, as Mount-batten assured Ian Stephens, "waiting at Abbotabad ready to drive in triumph to Srinagar." When news of the Indian invasion of Kashmir reached him, he immediately ordered General Gracey, the acting Commander-in-Chief of the Pakistan army, to send troops into Kashmir. Gracey did not carry out the order but telephoned instead to the Supreme Commander, Field Marshal Auchinleck, in Delhi for instructions. The contrast with Delhi must be noted. There the British Commander-in-Chief of the Indian army did not question the orders emanating from the Governor-General Lord Mountbatten and the Indian cabinet to fly troops into Kashmir. Obedience to the Quaid-i-Azam's orders would, as Auchinleck reported to the Chiefs of Staff in London, have entailed the issuance of the "Stand Down Order," which called for the withdrawal of all British officers in the event of armed conflict between the two Dominions.[25]

Auchinleck flew to Lahore on October 28, the morning after the Indian invasion, to discuss the situation with the Quaid-i-Azam. As a result of the discussion, the Quaid-i-Azam agreed to withdraw his order to the Pakistan army to march into Kashmir and accepted Auchinleck's proposal for an immediate conference in Lahore between the Governors-General and the Prime Ministers of India and Pakistan. Mountbatten and the Indian cabinet also accepted Auchinleck's proposal but almost immediately afterward started resiling from it. Nehru took to bed from an indisposition; Patel, who had strongly opposed Nehru's going to Lahore, said he could not leave Delhi. The conference, which was due to be held on October 29, was postponed from day to day and finally Mountbatten alone reached Lahore on November 1.

The letter of October 27, 1947, through which the Governor-General of India accepted the Maharaja's request for accession stated: "Consistently with their policy that, in the case of any State where the issue of accession has been the subject of dispute, the question of accession should be decided in accordance with the wishes of the people of the State, it is my Government's wish that as soon as law and order have been restored in Kashmir and her soil cleared of the invader, the question of the State's accession should be settled by a reference to the people." [26]

In a telegram to the Prime Minister of Pakistan on the same day, the Prime Minister of India said: "I should like to make it clear that question of aiding Kashmir in this emergency is not designed in any way to influence the State to accede to India. Our view which we have repeatedly made public is that the question of accession in any disputed territory or State must be decided in accordance with wishes of people and we adhere to this view."

In a further telegram sent on October 31, Nehru gave this pledge: "Our assurance that we shall withdraw our troops from Kashmir as soon as peace and order are restored and leave the decision regarding the future of this State to the people of the State is not merely a promise to your Government but also to the people of Kashmir and to the world."

The Pakistan government saw through these assurances. A press communique issued in Lahore on October 30 stated that, "in the opinion of the Government of Pakistan the accession of Kashmir to the Indian Union is based on fraud and violence and as such can not be recognized." It could not be recognized since it was manifestly contrary to the wishes of the people. The Maharaja, having already entered into a standstill agreement with Pakistan, was debarred from entering into relations with any other power unilaterally. Furthermore, at the time he offered accession to India, the Maharaja had been divested of authority over large portions of the state by the people's rebellion. Only the people of Kashmir could decide the question of the accession of the state. The communique added: "The reference to a plebiscite for Kashmir is merely put forward to mislead as it ostensibly seems attractive but as a practical proposition it remains on paper. If the Indian Government are allowed to act freely and unfettered as they please by virtue of having already occupied Kashmir and landed their troops there, then this 'eldorado' of plebiscite will prove a mirage."

In the meeting with Mountbatten on November 1, the Quaid-i-Azam put forward the following proposals to settle the Kashmir dispute:

1. A proclamation should be made by the two Governors-General giving forty-eight hours' notice to the opposing forces to cease fire and warning the tribesmen that, if they did not comply, the forces of both countries would wage war on them.

2. Simultaneous withdrawal from Kashmir of the Indian troops and the tribesmen should be effected.

3. The two Governors-General should be vested with full powers

to restore peace, undertake the administration of the state, and arrange for a plebiscite under their joint control and supervision.

Mountbatten offered to refer these proposals to the Indian cabinet, but pleaded his inability as constitutional Governor-General to take a decision, or to conduct the plebiscite jointly with the Quaid-i-Azam. His position as constitutional Governor-General had not, however, debarred him from being the chief negotiator with Hyderabad or from directing military operations in Kashmir. When the proposals were referred to the Government of India, they did not accept them. But in a broadcast on November 2, Nehru declared that the Government of India "are prepared when peace and order have been established in Kashmir to have a referendum held under international auspices like the United Nations." [27]

The meeting on November 1 finally disillusioned the Quaid-i-Azam with Mountbatten. At this meeting Mountbatten gave the Quaid-i-Azam his word of honor that Nehru had really fallen ill and was unable to come to Lahore. But the very next day a high ranking British officer told the Quaid-i-Azam that he had seen Nehru as fit as ever the day before in Delhi.

The turn of events in Kashmir had an adverse effect on the Quaid-i-Azam's health. At the time of partition he had been confident of Kashmir's accession to Pakistan because of its Muslim population and geographical situation. "Kashmir," he would say, "will fall into our lap like a ripe fruit." Now he felt deceived, and his earlier optimism gave way to a deep disappointment. "We have been put on the wrong bus," he remarked.

While these discussions between the governments of India and Pakistan were proceeding, a local revolution occurred in Gilgit in the far north of Kashmir. The area is mountainous and its only communications with the rest of the state are two high passes that are snowbound in winter. The population is almost wholly Muslim. Although Gilgit formed part of the state of Jammu and Kashmir, it was administered by the British Government of India through a political agent. When independence was declared, the area was retroceded by the British government to the state, and the British political agent was replaced by a Dogra Governor. When the unexpected news of the Maharaja's accession to India reached Gilgit, the people were outraged and decided to throw off the Maharaja's yoke. On October 31, the Hindu Governor was taken into custody by the Gilgit Scouts, and on November 2, the Pakistan flag was hoisted amidst popular acclaim. In response to a request to take over the administration, the Pakistan government flew a representative to Gilgit on November 14. A little later, the rulers of Hunza and Nagir, which are comprised in the Gilgit Agency, requested accession to Pakistan. Since then, the whole area has been administered by the Pakistan government and has remained outside the arena of conflict in Kashmir.

On November 8, I accompanied Abdur Rab Nishtar to Delhi for a meeting of the Joint Defence Council. After the meeting, Nishtar had an exchange of views with Nehru about Kashmir and returned to Pakistan. Mountbatten asked me to stay on for further discussions. I worked with Ismay and V. P. Menon to find a solution for states whose accession was in dispute. In each of them the ruler of the state did not belong to the community to which the majority of his subjects belonged. The only manner in which the dispute over accession could be resolved was by a reference to the will of the people under conditions guaranteeing a free vote. In Kashmir it was essential that the tribal lashkar and the Indian troops should both withdraw. In the evening I was told that Mountbatten and Sardar Patel agreed to such a plan, but not Nehru, and I was advised to see him.

I had a long discussion with him and came away convinced that Nehru was resolved to hold Kashmir by force and had no intention of allowing the people of Kashmir the right to determine their future. My argument that a fair solution of the Kashmir dispute was the best guarantee of friendly relations between India and Pakistan, and was, therefore, in the best interests of both countries, left him cold. He talked only in terms of power politics, and said again and again that in matters of state no sovereign independent power could be trusted. If Pakistan had to be, it must never have the strength to be a possible threat to India. I pointed out that Kashmir's accession to Pakistan could not pose a threat to India because of the mountainous barrier between Kashmir and India. On the other hand, India would, by occupying Kashmir, be commanding the heights of Pakistan and controlling its life-line of rivers flowing from Kashmir. I found no trace in him of those sentiments of attachment to Kashmir with which he is often credited by virtue of his family's origins in Kashmir. The fact that in a prolonged struggle over Kashmir its people would be the worst sufferers did not move him in the least. What mattered to him was that Kashmir's accession to Pakistan would strengthen Pakistan.

Three weeks later, Liaquat Ali Khan came to Delhi for another meeting of the Joint Defence Council and there was a renewed effort at solving the Kashmir dispute. Again Ismay, V. P. Menon, and I worked together to produce a basis for discussion between the two Prime Ministers. The lines leading to a solution were clear. The fighting should stop, and both tribesmen and the Indian troops should withdraw. The governments of India and Pakistan should make a joint request to UN to hold a free and fair plebiscite in Kashmir under its auspices. Conditions of peace should be established so that citizens of the state who had been driven out could return to their homes. All political prisoners should be released. There should be no restriction on legitimate political activity. Similarly, a plebiscite should be held in Junagadh to decide its future. Had there been a will to abide by the decision of the people of Kashmir, there would have been no difficulty. But Nehru was neither prepared to withdraw Indian forces from Kashmir, nor to allow an impartial plebiscite to be held.

Sardar Patel, although a bitter enemy of Pakistan, was a greater realist than Nehru. In one of the discussions between the two Prime Ministers, at which Patel and I were also present, Liaquat Ali Khan dwelt at length on the inconsistency of the Indian stand with regard to Junagadh and Kashmir. If Junagadh, despite its Muslim ruler's accession to Pakistan, belonged to India because of its Hindu majority, how could Kashmir, with its Muslim majority, be a part of India simply by virtue of its Hindu ruler having signed a conditional instrument of accession to India? If the instrument of accession signed by the Muslim ruler of Junagadh was of no validity, the instrument of accession signed by the Hindu ruler of Kashmir was also invalid. If the will of the people was to prevail in Junagadh, it must prevail in Kashmir as well. India could not claim both Junagadh and Kashmir. When Liaquat Ali Khan made these incontrovertible points, Patel could not contain himself and burst out: "Why do you compare Junagadh with Kashmir? Talk of Hyderabad and Kashmir, and we could reach an agreement." Patel's view at this time and even later was that India's effort to retain Muslim majority areas against the will of the people was a source not of strength but of weakness to India. He felt that if India and Pakistan agreed to let Kashmir go to Pakistan and

Hyderabad to India, the problems of Kashmir and of Hyderabad could be solved peacefully and to the mutual advantage of India and Pakistan.

There was a second round of talks between the two Prime Ministers in Lahore on December 8, but they also produced no results. Nehru even backed out of the agreed proposal for a joint request to the UN to hold a plebiscite in Kashmir. During this time fighting was going on in Kashmir. The Azad Kashmir forces, ill-equipped and outnumbered as they were, bravely resisted the Indian army and succeeded in consolidating and strengthening their position. Mountbatten was afraid that without the intervention of a third party there was serious danger of war between the two Dominions, and he was most anxious to avert this. The British Prime Minister pleaded with Nehru for a peaceful and just solution, but to no avail. An appeal to the United Nations appeared to Mountbatten to be the only way of bringing in an outside mediator. Eventually, despite Gandhi's disapproval, Mountbatten succeeded in persuading Nehru to go to the United Nations with a complaint against Pakistan.

On January 1, 1948, the Government of India appealed to the Security Council to ask Pakistan to prevent its personnel, civil and military, from participating or assisting in the invasion of Jammu and Kashmir, to call upon other Pakistan nationals to desist from taking any part in the fighting in the state, and to deny to the invaders access to its territory, supplies, and other aid. The Government of India also stated that after the restoration of normal conditions the people of Kashmir would be free to decide their future by a plebiscite under international auspices.

Pakistan lodged a countercomplaint setting forth the attempts made by India to destroy Pakistan; the genocide of Muslims in East Punjab, Delhi, and other places in India, the forcible occupation of Junagadh, and the action taken by India to secure the accession of Kashmir by fraud and violence. The Security Council was requested by Pakistan to bring about a just and fair settlement of these disputes. For Kashmir, the request was for cessation of fighting, the withdrawal of all outsiders whether belonging to India or Pakistan, the return of Kashmir refugees, the establishment of an impartial administration, and the holding of a plebiscite "to ascertain the free and unfettered will of the people of Jammu and Kashmir as to whether the State shall accede to Pakistan or to India."

The Pakistan delegation to the Security Council was led by Foreign Minister Zafrullah Khan, and included M.A.H. Ispahani, Pakistan's Ambassaor in the USA and M. Wasim, the Advocate General. I was also made a member of the delegation on the Quaid-i-Azam's express orders. Golpalaswami Ayyangar was the leader of the Indian delegation, which included Sheikh Abdullah, who was first associated with the Maharaja's government and later appointed Prime Minister of Kashmir. Sheikh Abdullah was used by India in moral justification of her occupation of Kashmir. At that time, Sheikh Abdullah had been led by Nehru to believe that India fully respected the right of the people of Kashmir to self-determination, and that, after peace was restored, a plebiscite would be held. Sheikh Abdullah and I had been at college together. Now, after over two decades, we met in the corridors of the United Nations building at Lake Success. Although we were ranged on opposite sides, we arranged to have a private meeting in a New York hotel. We went over the whole problem of Kashmir in the context of Indo-Pakistan relations. I found Sheikh Abdullah firmly convinced that Nehru intended to grant virtual independence to Kashmir. I pointed out that Kashmir did not have the military potential to safeguard its independence and would have to depend upon a neighboring power for its security. If that power was India, and Indian armed forces were stationed in Kashmir, its so-called independence would be purely nominal and could be destroyed at any time. Could Muslim Kashmir safely entrust its destiny to predominantly non-Muslim India? But nothing I said could shake his faith in Nehru's personal assurances to him. At that time, Sheikh Abdullah had no inkling of how each undertaking would be violated by his friend Nehru and how he himself would suddenly be dismissed from the office of Prime Minister of Kashmir on August 9, 1953, and be thrown in prison along with his followers, to remain there for eleven years.

The Security Council started its hearing of India's complaint and Pakistan's reply on January 15, 1948. Zafrullah Khan's masterly exposition of the case convinced the Security Council that the problem was not simply one of expelling so-called raiders from Kashmir, as the Indian representative would have them believe, but of placing Indo-Pakistan relations on a just and peaceful basis and solving the Kashmir dispute in accordance with the will of the people of the state. Zafrullah Khan frankly admitted that volunteers from Pakistan had gone to the aid of their brethren in Kashmir, but, in the face of the universal sympathy in Pakistan for the just cause of the people of Kashmir, the Government of Pakistan could not have stopped them from going. On January 17, the Security Council adopted a resolution calling upon the two governments to take measures to improve the situation and requesting them to report to the Council any material change in it. By another resolution, made on January 20, the Council established the United Nations Commission for India and Pakistan, which was to be composed of three members, one to be nominated by India, one by Pakistan, and the third jointly by the two members. The number was later raised to five.

These first resolutions were followed by a debate in the Security Council which lasted for a fortnight, in which the representatives of India and Pakistan participated, and in which every aspect of the Kashmir question was brought under discussion. The consensus of opinion in the Security Council was crystallized in a draft resolution laid before the Council by its President, General McNaughton of Canada, on February 6. The draft resolution demanded an end to all acts of violence and hostility; the withdrawal of all irregular forces and armed individuals who had entered Jammu and Kashmir; the cooperation of the armed forces of India and Pakistan in the establishment of order and security; the withdrawal of regular armed forces on the reestablishment of law and order; the return of refugees to their homes, and the removal of restrictions on legitimate political activity; the release of political prisoners; the establishment of an interim administration commanding general confidence and respect of the people of the state; and the holding of an impartial plebiscite to be organized, held, and supervised under the authority of the Security Council at the earliest possible date to decide the question of whether the state of Jammu and Kashmir should accede to India or Pakistan.

To the surprise of the Security Council, the Indian representative strongly objected to the draft resolution and, in particular, to the withdrawal of the Indian army after the restoration of law and order, the establishment of an impartial administration, and the holding of a plebiscite under the authority of the Security Council. All he would agree to was "having the Security Council give advice and guidance to the Kashmir Government in the organization and holding of that plebiscite and to having the Security Council send observers to see how that plebiscite is conducted." [28] What India desired was that a plebiscite, held under the shadow of Indian bayonets, by a pro-Indian administration, should be accepted by the Security Council as the free vote of the people of Kashmir. The Security Council, on the other hand, wanted a plebiscite that would be really fair and recognized as such by the world. As Warren Austin, the United States representative on the Security Council, put it, "There is nothing, in my view of the matter, that will command that approbation as will a machinery that is free from suspicion and that gives to all the world the appearance of impartiality by actually being an impartial administration of the plebiscite." [29]

Although he had been stressing "the urgency and immediacy of the solution of this problem," the Indian representative now asked for a five or six weeks' adjournment of the debate. The Security Council was unhappy about an adjournment, but agreed to it despite Pakistan's strong plea against any postponement. We were convinced that India's only object in asking for an adjournment was to gain time in which to exert diplomatic pressure on the governments concerned, particularly the British government. The draft resolution before the Security Council had the support of the majority necessary for passing it. Russia and Ukraine were neutral, but the United States, the United Kingdom, Syria, Colombia, Argentina, and all the other countries represented on the Security Council had strongly supported the principles on which it was based. If the Security Council had pressed on with its business, the resolution would have been passed and the Security Council would have gained respect for its firmness.

The United Kingdom was represented in the Security Council by Philip Noel-Baker, the British Secretary of State for Commonwealth Relations. He had taken a leading part in the discussions that culminated in the draft resolution. His high idealism and sincere devotion to the cause of peace, which deservedly won him the Nobel Prize for Peace some years later, shone through every speech he made. But this was precisely the quality that made him disliked in India. "Mountbatten," wrote Campbell-Johnson, "is worried because he feels that Attlee and Noel-Baker do not seem to be showing themselves sufficiently alive to the psychological influences of this dispute and that their attempt to deal out even-handed justice is producing heavy-handed diplomacy." [30] Mountbatten had himself never made such a mistake in his conduct of Indian affairs. He was at this time engaged in working out a formula by which India could continue to be a member of the British Commonwealth, even after she became a republic under her new constitution. And he saw his whole diplomacy being wrecked by Noel-Baker's attempt to deal out even-handed justice in Kashmir. "Mountbatten says frankly," continued Campbell-Johnson, "that although individual Indian leaders are alive to the advantages of the continued Commonwealth connection, their political position has been weakened and the attitude of the Government adversely affected by the policy adopted towards Kashmir by the British delegation at the Security Council." [31] Once again, as in every conflict of interest between India and Pakistan, in particular at every critical moment in the Kashmir dispute, Mountbatten made himself the instrument of Indian ambitions. By exerting the full weight of his influence as the highest British official on the spot, he tilted the balance heavily in favor of India.

The threat that India would leave the Commonwealth unless the British government changed its policy toward Kashmir was enough to unnerve Attlee. Anticipating Indian pressure on the British government, Zafrullah Khan and I went to London. Zafrullah Khan's interview with Attlee confirmed our worst fears. Noel-Baker was overruled and a new line, in keeping with Indian wishes, was adopted. Because of their long connection with the Indo-Pakistan subcontinent, the views of the British government on its affairs commanded great respect in the counsels of Western nations. The United States, Canada, and other nations were easily induced to follow the United Kingdom's new line. As a further insurance to keep the Western powers on their own side, the Indians also threw out hints of turning to Russia to secure a Russian veto.

When the Security Council met again in March, 1948, McNaughton's draft resolution of February 6 was totally forgotten; and a vastly different resolution was moved by Tsiang, the Chinese representative, who was the President of the Security Council for the month. The new resolution, as Zafrullah Khan pointed out, made numerous concessions to India in violation of the principles which the members of the Security Council had themselves advocated before adjournment. The Indian representative was also critical of the new resolution which, although one-sided, was not sufficiently one-sided for him. However, the Security Council passed this resolution with a few amendments on April 21. The resolution provided for a plebiscite to be held after the restoration of peace; but the plebiscite administrator, although a nominee of the UN Secretary General, was to act as an officer of the state of Jammu and Kashmir. The weakness the Security Council displayed, first in agreeing to an adjournment and, later, in abandoning the draft resolution of February 6 was disastrous for the Kashmir case and for the prestige of the UN. Having taken the measure of the Security Council, India felt she could safely defy the UN. The resolution of April 21, despite its many concessions to the Indian point of view was not accepted by India. Pakistan while criticizing the resolution did not reject it.

While the debates in the Security Council were in progress, the Indian army in Kashmir was being strengthened. In the midst of winter rains and snowstorms, roads and airfields were being improved in preparation for a spring offensive. On March 15, 1948, the Indian Defence Minister announced in the Indian constituent assembly that the Indian army would clear out "the raiders" from Kashmir within the next two or three months. The Azad Kashmir forces and the tribesmen had put up a brave resistance against the onslaughts of the Indian army, but they had neither the strength, nor the equipment, to withstand a well-prepared offensive by far stronger regular troops.

On April 20, General Gracey, the Commander-in-Chief of the Pakistan army, submitted to the Pakistan government his appreciation of the military situation. After giving details of the build-up of the Indian army he concluded:

> It is obvious that a general offensive is about to start very soon now. . . . If Pakistan is not to face another serious refugee problem with about 2,750,000 people uprooted from their homes, if India is not to be allowed to sit on the doorsteps of Pakistan to the rear and on the flank at liberty to enter at its will and pleasure; if the civilian and military morale is not to be affected to a dangerous extent; and if subversive political forces are not to be encouraged and let loose within Pakistan itself, it is imperative that the Indian Army is not allowed to advance beyond the general line Uri-Poonch-Naoshera.

There was another vital consideration. Mangla Headworks from which the Upper Jhelum Canal took off to irrigate large areas in West Pakistan was in state territory. If the Indian offensive succeeded, Mangla Headworks, with its control of supplies from the river Jhelum, would fall into Indian hands. In an attempt to paralyze Pakistan's economy, India had on April 1, 1948, shut off water from the headworks on the rivers Sutlej and Ravi, which Radcliffe had unjustly awarded to India. By getting hold of Mangla Headworks as well, India would obtain a complete stranglehold over the economy of West Pakistan. An idea of the importance of Mangla can be gained from the fact that it is the only site at which a dam is being built for the replacement of water supplies from the three eastern rivers which are under India's control.

The Pakistan government accepted the recommendation of the Commander-in-Chief and sent limited forces to the state to hold certain defensive positions. The instructions to the army were, "Prevent India from obtaining a decision by force of arms." Only the army was engaged in this essentially defensive task; the air force was not used. The Indians had thus uncontested control of the air. Despite this and other handicaps, the Pakistan army succeeded in holding the Indian offensive.

The UN Commission for India and Pakistan, which had been established by the Security Council resolution of January 20 and had been instructed "to proceed to the spot as quickly as possible," took unduly long to form and arrived in Karachi on July 7, 1948. It was composed of five members: Argentina, nominated by Pakistan; Czechoslovakia, nominated by India; Colombia and Belgium, selected by the Security Council; and the United States, nominated by the Council's President. At the very first meeting with the commission, Zafrullah Khan notified it of the action taken by Pakistan in sending troops into the state. When the commission moved to Delhi, the Indians made much of what they alleged to be Pakistan's aggression. The members of the commission were new to the subcontinent and were only dimly aware of the historical forces behind the conflict in Kashmir. They were somewhat bewildered by the opposing points of views advanced with passionate advocacy by India and Pakistan. Eventually, they produced a plan of action and embodied it in the commission's resolution of August 13, 1948. The resolution provided for a cease-fire to be followed by a truce agreement under which the Pakistan troops, tribesmen, and volunteers on the one hand; and the bulk of the Indian army on the other hand, were to withdraw from the state. The last part of the resolution dealing with the plebiscite was extremely vague and provided only for negotiations between the two governments and the commission to determine fair and equitable conditions for a plebiscite. In the view of the Pakistan government, no real settlement was possible without a firm guarantee for a free plebiscite. The commission in its inexperience could not perceive this. Josef Korbel, a member of the commission, wrote: "Pakistan obviously was of the opinion that once the fighting had stopped, India would be satisfied with a de facto division of Kashmir (the better part of which was in her possession), the situation would subsequently become stabilized, and India would then obstruct a free plebiscite. The Commission was bitterly disappointed." [32]

Negotiations with the commission were resumed toward the end of the year in Paris, where the General Assembly of the United Nations met. The result was the resolution of January 5, 1949, that laid down the principles and procedures for a free and impartial plebiscite to be conducted under the auspices of the United Nations.

During these months, fighting was going on in Kashmir with varying fortunes. The Indian attacks on Uri and Titwal were halted and the line of battle stabilized in the south and west of the state. In the north, Zoji La, which was the gateway to the Valley of Kashmir, was threatened by the Gilgit Scouts, but the Indians succeeded in moving tanks up there. In November, 1948, the Indians were able to relieve Poonch town which had long been beleaguered, and to link up Naoshera with Poonch; the whole area east of that line, including Mendhar tahsil, the granary of Kashmir, was lost to them. There was a fresh influx of tens of thousands of Muslim refugees into Pakistan. Pakistan had not until then interfered with the Indian lines of communications though they were easily vulnerable. Now, however, the situation called for stronger measures. A sustained bombardment of the bridge at Beri Pattan shattered Indian ammunition dumps and threw the Indian lines into complete disorder. The Indians could have saved their forces in Kashmir only by an attack on and through Pakistan territory. Such an attack would have involved both Dominions in a general war. Though confronting each other in Kashmir, India and Pakistan had refrained from provoking unlimited warfare. Now, when they were on the brink of war, both shrank from it. With Nehru's consent, the Indian Commander-in-Chief, General Bucher, on December 30, approached the Pakistan Commander-in-Chief, General Gracey, for a cease-fire. General Gracey supported the proposal and the Pakistan government accepted it. The cease-fire became effective on January 1, 1949; Map V shows the cease-fire line.

The decision for a cease-fire has often been severely criticized in Pakistan as unwise. The Pakistan army, which had proved itself to be superior to the Indian army in the contest in Kashmir, could, it is argued, have won Kashmir before India could do much damage to Pakistan. Pakistan knew that India was determined to block a plebiscite and to maintain her military occupation of Kashmir. By placing a wholly undeserved trust in the ability of the United Nations to arrange a plebiscite, Pakistan committed a serious mistake of judgment. At this time I was lying ill in France, where I had gone with Zafrullah Khan for discussions with the UN commission, and cannot, therefore, speak from firsthand knowledge. But my impression is that the decisive consideration in the mind of Liaquat Ali Khan was the desire to avoid a general war between India and Pakistan, which, he was convinced, would lead to the destruction of both. India would not have taken its losses in Kashmir as a final defeat, but would have sought satisfaction by continuing the war with Pakistan. Neither Dominion had the military potential for a prolonged war. Both countries would soon have placed themselves at the mercy of outside powers in order to obtain needed war supplies, and would have put their new-won freedom in serious peril. In the last analysis, the decision was a political one based on wider considerations than the immediate prospects of gain on the Kashmir front.

As soon as the cease-fire was effected, tribesmen and Pakistan volunteers departed for their homes without waiting for the conclusion of the truce agreement. Indian propaganda has made much of the excesses committed by the tribesmen during the first few days of their incursion into Kashmir. Compared with the atrocities committed by the Maharaja's state force and the Indian army on the people of Kashmir, the plunder in which these undisciplined irregulars indulged for some days pales into insignificance. If plunder had been their only motive they would have evaporated as soon as they had to fight against the Indian army. But they continued to fight bravely against far superior forces for fourteen months, with no other end in view than the freedom of their brethren in Kashmir. The people of Kashmir and of Pakistan owe them a debt of gratitude for their gallant and, on the whole, selfless fight. The Azad Kashmir forces fought heroically in defense of their homes. The entire population of Azad Kashmir endured the privations of war and the bombings of the Indian air force with great courage and fortitude.

The two resolutions of the UN Commission for India and Pakistan, dated August 13, 1948, and January 5, 1949, were approved by the

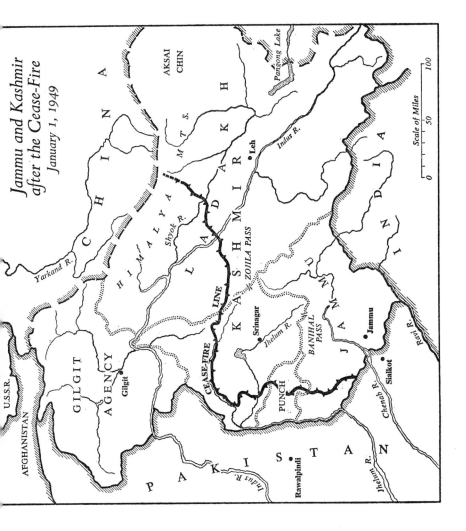

Jammu and Kashmir after the Cease-Fire
January 1, 1949

Security Council and accepted by both India and Pakistan. They constitute an international agreement that has still to be implemented. The essence of the agreement is that the people of Jammu and Kashmir should have the right to determine their future and decide in a free and impartial plebiscite held under UN auspices whether to accede to India or to Pakistan without coercion or intimidation by the state administration and the military of either country.

The many efforts made by the UN to secure compliance with the international agreement on Kashmir have produced no result. It is a sad commentary upon the anarchic state of world politics that the highest world organization has been powerless to break Indian intransigence, and to secure for the people of Kashmir their undoubted right to decide in a free vote whether they will join India or Pakistan. The detailed history of these events lies outside the scope of this book. Here it will suffice to indicate in broad outline their trend.

The UN Commission for India and Pakistan was soon to realize that Pakistan was right in having apprehensions about India's intentions to obstruct the plebiscite. The Indian tactics were essentially the same as they had adopted in dealing with the Cabinet Mission plan. They would misinterpret the plain words of the agreement to suit their own ends, and then refuse to accept any other interpretation, even that offered by the authors of the agreement. In keeping with this technique, the Indians insisted upon the disbandment of the Azad Kashmir forces, even though there was no mention of it in the agreement, and even though the commission stated specifically that "the Resolution [of August 13, 1948] does not contemplate the disarmament or disbanding of Azad Kashmir forces." Other points were raised on which again the Government of India would not accept the interpretation of the commission. Thereupon, the commission proposed that the differences be submitted to the arbitration of Admiral Chester W. Nimitz (of Second World War fame) who had been designated Plebiscite Administrator for Kashmir. President Truman and Prime Minister Attlee appealed to India and Pakistan to accept the proposal for arbitration. Pakistan accepted and India rejected the proposal.

This pattern of behavior was repeated on eleven subsequent occasions when eminent statesmen and mediators put forward proposals for a settlement of the Kashmir dispute—Pakistan accepted and India rejected. The distinguished Australian judge Sir Owen Dixon was appointed United Nations Representative in 1950; he replaced the UN commission and was to prepare and supervise a program of demilitarization and carry out its other functions. He reported to the Security Council:

> In the end I became convinced that India's agreement would never be obtained to demilitarization in any such form, or to provisions governing the period of the plebiscite of any such character, as would in my opinion permit of the plebiscite being conducted in conditions sufficiently guarding against intimidation and other forms of influence and abuse by which the freedom and fairness of the plebiscite might be imperilled.

In January, 1951, the Commonwealth Prime Ministers' Conference in London informally discussed every aspect of the Kashmir problem. To allow a plebiscite to be held under impartial conditions without jeopardizing the security of the state, three alternative methods were proposed by Prime Minister Menzies of Australia and endorsed by the other prime ministers including Prime Minister Attlee. They were a commonwealth force, a joint Indo-Pakistan force, or a local force to be raised by the Plebiscite Administrator. Each was accepted by Pakistan but rejected by India.

In April, 1951, former United States Senator Dr. Frank Graham was appointed UN Representative to make recommendations for implementing the resolutions (dated August 13, 1948, and January 5, 1949) of the UN Commission for India and Pakistan. He submitted a number of reports to the Security Council but because of Indian insistence on keeping a large force in Kashmir failed to bring about agreement on demilitarization.

In August, 1953, at a critical moment following the dismissal and arrest of Sheikh Abdullah, the Prime Ministers of India and Pakistan met and in their joint communiqué stated as their firm opinion that the Kashmir dispute "should be settled in accordance with the wishes of the people of that State with a view to promoting their well-being and causing the least disturbance to the life of the people of the State. The most feasible method of ascertaining the wishes of the people was by a fair and impartial plebiscite." The communiqué announced that the Plebiscite Administrator should be appointed by the end of April, 1954. But before the appointment could be made, Nehru backed out of his commitment on the specious grounds that the agreement between the United States and Pakistan under the Mutual

Security Act had upset the balance of power on the subcontinent and changed the entire context of the Kashmir negotiations. Just because Pakistan entered into an agreement for military aid to safeguard its security, why should the people of Kashmir be denied their right of self-determination?

In February, 1957, the Security Council deputed its Swedish President, Gunnar Jarring, to visit India and Pakistan and arrange a peaceful settlement, but the visit produced no results. Dr. Graham's subsequent efforts were equally fruitless.

Meanwhile, India set up a so-called constituent assembly in Kashmir that under Indian manipulation declared the state to be "an integral part of the Union of India." Thereupon the Security Council in its resolution of January 24, 1957, reaffirmed its earlier stand that any action by this assembly "would not constitute a disposition of the State," which could only be made "through the democratic method of a free and impartial plebiscite conducted under the auspices of the United Nations." Although India gave repeated assurances to the Security Council that any opinion expressed by the so-called constituent assembly on the question of accession would not bind the Government of India which would abide by its international commitments, Indian official spokesmen have, with the passage of time, become bolder and bolder in asserting that Kashmir is an integral part of India and have even denied the existence of the Kashmir dispute.

This pattern of behavior was changed for a short while following the serious Indian reverses against China in November, 1962. As a result of the efforts made by Averell Harriman, the United States Assistant Secretary of State and Duncan Sandys, the British Secretary of State for Commonwealth relations, the Prime Minister of India and the President of Pakistan in a joint communiqué agreed that "a renewed effort should be made to resolve the outstanding differences between their two countries on Kashmir and other related matters." Between December, 1962, and May, 1963, six rounds of talks were held between India and Pakistan on the Kashmir issue, but no agreement was reached. India reverted to its intransigent line.

For over eighteen years India has flouted her international undertakings and broken her pledges. She has subjected the people of Kashmir to a corrupt and vicious tyranny and denied them the right of self-determination. She has killed, imprisoned, and tortured the patriots of Kashmir. Sheikh Abdullah, whose support was paraded as the moral justification for India's provisional acceptance of the Maharaja's offer of accession, was kept in prison for eleven years, his only crime being his demand for self-determination by his people. This demand voices the innermost sentiments of the people of Kashmir that nothing can suppress.

The tremendous agitation that followed the desecration of the Hazrat Bal shrine in Srinagar in the winter of 1963–64 was an expression of these same sentiments that took the form of an insistent demand for the release of Sheikh Abdullah. Shortly before Pandit Jawaharlal Nehru's death in May, 1964, Sheikh Abdullah and his companions were released and it looked for a brief moment as if the great wrong that had been done to the people of Kashmir and their leader might be set right. With Nehru's consent, Sheikh Abdullah came to Pakistan in an endeavor to bring India and Pakistan together for a peaceful solution of the Kashmir question. In Pakistan he received a memorable welcome, but before he had completed his visit Pandit Nehru died. Nehru's successor, Lal Bahadur Shastri, at first appeared not to stand in the way of Sheikh Abdullah's peace initiative, but he soon moved in the opposite direction and started integrating Indian-occupied Kashmir into the Indian Union. Over the years the special status accorded to the state of Jammu and Kashmir in the Indian Constitution was eroded bit by bit, until practically nothing of it was left. In December, 1964, the Government of India decided to extend the scope of certain provisions in the Indian Constitution to Jammu and Kashmir so as to effect the integration of the state by decree. When Sheikh Abdullah returned to Delhi after a pilgrimage to Mecca in May, 1965, he was immediately arrested for speeches he had delivered abroad pleading for Kashmir's right of self-determination and was put in detention for an indefinite period.

These actions of the Indian government inevitably produced a strong reaction in Kashmir and worsened relations between India and Pakistan. During the border dispute between India and Pakistan in the Rann of Kutch area, India attacked and occupied three Pakistan posts at Kargil across the cease-fire line in May, 1965. This serious violation of the cease-fire line in Kashmir was only rectified after a strong protest was made by the UN Secretary General. On August 9, 1965, the anniversary of Sheikh Abdullah's dismissal and arrest in 1953, there were reports of a widespread revolt in Indian-occupied Kashmir, which led to clashes between the Indian armed forces and the patriots of Kashmir. The Government of India alleged that this was the work of armed personnel who had infiltrated from Azad Kashmir across the cease-fire line with the connivance of the Pakistan government. The allegation was denied by the Pakistan government who contended that a fight for freedom from the Indian yoke was being waged by the people of Kashmir aided by their brothers in Azad Kashmir. These accusations and counteraccusations brought bitterness between India and Pakistan to a new pitch of intensity. On August 15, Indian forces crossed the cease-fire line and reoccupied the three posts at Kargil. There was fierce fighting all along the cease-fire line. In a large-scale attack in the Uri-Poonch sector, the Indian forces captured Haji Pir Pass. A village in Gujrat district, West Pakistan was shelled on August 23. To forestall an attack in the vital southern sector, Azad Kashmir forces supported by the Pakistan army moved across the cease-fire line into the Chhamb area on September 1 and made a rapid thrust toward Akhnur, thus threatening Jammu and the Indian lines of communications. The Indians threw their air force into the attack and air battles began.

In the early hours of September 6, Indian forces crossed the international boundary between India and Pakistan and launched a three-pronged surprise attack on Lahore, the capital of West Pakistan. Against this naked aggression the President of Pakistan invoked the right of self-defense under the UN Charter and declared war between India and Pakistan. In the face of heavy odds, the Pakistan army and air force fought with superb courage and military skill and halted the attack on Lahore. Bigger and fiercer battles were fought in Sialkot district, West Pakistan, which the Indians attacked with a large force including an armored division. One of the biggest tank battles since the Second World War was fought in this area. The Pakistan army was outnumbered by three to one and yet succeeded in holding the Indian offensive and driving the enemy back. The small but highly efficient Pakistan air force took a heavy toll of the much bigger Indian air force and having gained command of the air, was able to give splendid support to the ground forces. The Pakistan navy also came into the action and in a daring raid demolished the Indian military base at Dwarka.

The Security Council was most seriously concerned. On September 4, the UN Secretary General made a fervent appeal for a cease-fire and withdrawal of armed personnel that was endorsed by the Security

Council in its resolutions of September 4 and 6. On September 9, the UN Secretary General flew to Pakistan and India to negotiate peace, but without success. There was danger of a wider conflagration, when China gave an ultimatum to India to vacate its aggression against Chinese territory across the Sikkim border.

On September 20, the Security Council passed a resolution demanding that a cease-fire should take effect on September 22 to be followed by a withdrawal of all armed personnel back to the positions held on August 5, 1965. The resolution went on to say that thereafter the Security Council would consider "what steps could be taken to assist towards a settlement of the political problem underlying the present conflict." That problem is none other than the Kashmir dispute, as the whole world knows. And it is because India is stubbornly resisting a plebiscite in Kashmir in defiance of the UN Commission for India and Pakistan resolutions of August 13, 1948, and January 5, 1949, that the dispute is still unresolved. The cease-fire became effective on the morning of September 23, 1965, and at the time of writing (October, 1965) there is an uneasy truce.

Every possible method of resolving the dispute has been tried. There has been international mediation. There have been proposals for arbitration. There have been direct negotiations between the governments of India and Pakistan at the highest level. Nothing has worked. World opinion has expressed itself unmistakably that India is in the wrong. The Kashmir dispute is the most vital and dangerous dispute between India and Pakistan. It is an ever present threat to the peace of the subcontinent and of the world. But ignoring every consideration of justice, morality, and international peace, India continues to hold Kashmir by force and to deny the people of Kashmir their right of self-determination. The people and the Government of Pakistan are resolved to persist in their endeavor to secure for the people of Kashmir their right to decide whether to accede to India or Pakistan. The people of Kashmir through all these long years of suffering have not reconciled themselves to Indian tyranny. Their brave struggle against Indian occupation will go on until they have won their cherished goal of self-determination.

CHAPTER 15

The Indus Basin
Water Dispute

THE INDUS BASIN water dispute had its origin in the partition of the Punjab. It broke into the open on April 1, 1948, when East Punjab in India cut off the flow of canal waters to West Punjab in Pakistan.

West Pakistan has fertile soil but a hot and dry climate. The rainfall is scanty and undependable. More than half of the area receives less than ten inches of rainfall a year and the rest, less than twenty inches. Agriculture, the mainstay of the economy, is dependent almost entirely upon irrigation by canals drawn from the Indus and its five tributaries. The three western rivers—the Indus, the Jhelum, and the Chenab—flow into Pakistan from the state of Jammu and Kashmir, and the three eastern rivers—the Ravi, the Beas, and the Sutlej—enter Pakistan from India. In a very real sense, the Indus river system is West Pakistan's source of life. Without its lifegiving waters, West Pakistan would be incapable of supporting more than a small fraction of its population of 43 million. By contrast, India has many river systems which flow to the sea virtually untapped, and much of its territory receives enough rain to support agriculture without irrigation.

From time immemorial the Indus Basin was irrigated from the overflow of rivers and by inundation canals. During the last hundred years, under the guidance of British engineers, irrigation was greatly extended through the construction of headwork weirs on the rivers and through a network of canals. Flourishing colonies were established. Cultivation of cotton, wheat, rice, and sugar cane was expanded. New towns sprang into existence. Orchards and well-tended farms covered the countryside. More land is irrigated from the Indus rivers than from any other river system in the world.

Before partition, approximately 37 million acres received irrigation from the Indus rivers. About 31 million acres are now in West Pakistan. In addition to this, there are in West Pakistan at least 55 million acres of desert that could be turned into farmland if there were enough water. The flow supplies (water available from the river flow without the construction of storage reservoirs) were almost wholly used up in the irrigation systems established and planned before partition. Throughout the winter and during the critical spring and autumn months, when the water requirements of the *Rabi* (spring) and *Kharif* (autumn) crops overlapped, the existing canals exhausted the available flow of water. As chief engineer A. M. R. Montague reported in 1946: "For the majority of the year every single drop of water available to the Punjab is extracted from its rivers for distribution to the crops." And since the variations from year to year in the river flow are considerable, there were, periodically, serious shortages in many canals.

During the monsoon season of July and August the rivers are, of course, in spate, and enormous quantities of water flow into the sea. But to harness these summer floods, big storage reservoirs are needed. Such projects are costly, take a long time to build, and need suitable sites. The only one planned before partition was the Bhakra Dam on the Sutlej River in East Punjab with a storage capacity of 4 million acre-feet. Before it was sanctioned, the downstream province of Sind complained that the operation of Bhakra Dam would adversely affect the functioning of its inundation canals.

To determine the rights of the various provinces and states to the waters of the Indus Basin, the Government of India appointed, in 1941, a commission under the chairmanship of Sir B. N. Rau, later a judge of the International Court of Justice. The Rau commission laid down, as the principle governing the respective rights of the parties, "equitable apportionment." This principle, which is internationally recognized as regulating the rights of states having a common river basin, includes the rule that an upper riparian can take no action that will interfere with existing irrigation of the lower riparian.

The partition of the Punjab cut across the rivers and canals of the Indus Basin irrigation system, making India the upper and Pakistan the lower riparian. Among the official committees appointed to deal with the various problems arising out of the partition of the Punjab was Committee B. This Committee consisted of an equal number of officials from East Punjab and from West Punjab, and was charged with settling questions of the future management of joint assets, the division of other physical assets and their valuation. In paragraph 15 of its report, Committee B, with the unanimous agreement of its members, stated: "The Committee is agreed that there is no question of varying the authorized shares of water to which the two Zones and the various canals are authorized." The Committee thus agreed on the maintenance of the prepartition division of the water resources, but it could not agree on the valuation of the canal systems through which the water was distributed, nor could it agree on the value of the crown wastelands brought under irrigation.

The report of Committee B came up before the Punjab Partition Committee, presided over by the Governor and consisting of ministerial representatives of East Punjab and West Punjab. The Partition Committee accepted the matters on which Committee B was in agreement, namely that the prepartition shares of West Punjab and East Punjab in the canal waters would be maintained. It appointed two members of Committee B to implement the provision in paragraph 15 with respect to the maintenance of supplies of water to each zone and canal. The Partition Committee, like Committee B, was, however, unable to agree on the valuation of the canal system and it was decided to refer this question, along with the related question of the valuation of crown wastelands, to the Arbitral Tribunal. All this happened during the partition days, before August 15, 1947.

The question of the apportionment of the irrigation waters of the rivers common to India and Pakistan was not referred to the Arbitral Tribunal because there was no dispute to refer.

When the Boundary Award was announced on August 17, 1947, it was seen that Radcliffe had not only given away large Muslim majority areas to India but had so drawn the boundary as to leave on the

Indian side of the border both the Madhopur Headworks on the Ravi River and the Ferozepore Headworks on the Sutlej River. The former controlled the Upper Bari Doab canals, of which the Central Bari Doab canals in West Punjab were only a continuation. The latter controlled the Dipalpur canal in West Punjab and the Eastern Grey canal, which irrigated part of Bahawalpur state. In his award on the Punjab boundary Radcliffe said:

> The fixing of a boundary in this area was further complicated by the existence of canal systems, so vital to the life of the Punjab but developed only under the conception of a single administration. . . . I think I am entitled to assume with confidence that any agreements . . . as to sharing of water from these canals or otherwise will be respected by whatever Government hereafter assumes jurisdiction over the headworks concerned.

Despite the fact that the Radcliffe Award had placed the control of headworks vital for Pakistan in the hands of India, the West Punjab government remained content because of the agreement reached by Committee B and the Punjab Partition Committee, that the prepartition shares of water would not be varied. No formal document specifying the precise shares of East Punjab and West Punjab in irrigation waters was drawn up and signed. The West Punjab ministers and officials felt assured by the repeated declarations of their counterparts in East Punjab that there was no question of any change in the prepartition arrangements for canal waters. The same declarations were also made by the East Punjab representatives before the Arbitral Tribunal, when the disputed question of the valuation of the canal system came up for a hearing. Actually, as events showed, the East Punjab ministers and officials were planning a deadly blow against Pakistan and were lulling the West Punjab government to sleep with sweet words. They were waiting for the day when the life of the Arbitral Tribunal would come to an end on March 31, 1948. On the side of East Punjab there was Machiavellian duplicity. On the part of West Punjab there was neglect of duty, complacency, and lack of common prudence—which had disastrous consequences for Pakistan.

On April 1, 1948, the day after the Arbitral Tribunal ceased to exist, the East Punjab government cut off the water supplies in every canal crossing into Pakistan. These consisted of the Central Bari Doab canal system, the Dipalpur canal system, and the Bahawalpur state distributary. Of this action, Sir Patrick Spens, Chairman of the

Arbitral Tribunal, said before the joint meeting in London of the East India Association and the Overseas League on February 23, 1955:

> I remember very well suggesting whether it was not desirable that some order should be made about the continued flow of water. . . . But we were invited by both the Attorney-Generals [of India and Pakistan] to come to our decision on the basis that there would be no interference whatsoever with the then existing flow of water, and the award which my colleagues made, in which I had no part, they made on that basis. Our awards were published at the end of March, 1948. I am going to say nothing more about it except that I was very much upset that almost within a day or two there was a grave interference with the flow of water on the basis of which our awards had been made.

The irony of the situation was that, in its award, the Arbitral Tribunal accepted, in principle, the contention of India that Pakistan should be accountable for a higher valuation of the canal system than its book value. It reached this decision on the premise that the existing allocation of water would be respected, for, without water, canals are dry ditches, a liability and not an asset. The Tribunal also required Pakistan to account to India for the crown wastelands at an appreciated value due to the advent of irrigation.

As soon as the Arbitral Tribunal ceased to exist, all promises made before it by the representative of India that "there would be no interference whatsoever with the then existing flow of water" were forgotten and water was shut off from Pakistan canals on which the irrigation of 1.66 million acres depended. East Punjab now contended that Pakistan had no right to any water and demanded seigniorage charges as a condition for reopening the canals. There was acute distress which, with every day that passed, became more and more intolerable. In large areas where the subsoil water is brackish there was no drinking water. Millions of people faced the ruin of their crops, the loss of their herds, and eventual starvation due to lack of water.

Under these distressful circumstances, a delegation was sent from Pakistan to Delhi in the beginning of May, 1948, to seek a solution to the problem. The delegation was led by Ghulam Muhammad, the Finance Minister of Pakistan, and included two ministers from West Punjab—Shaukat Hayat Khan and Mumtaz Daultana. At the meetings in Delhi, East Punjab representatives insisted that they would not restore the flow of water to the canals unless West Punjab acknowledged that it had no right to the water. To this the representatives of West Punjab could not agree. The Pakistan proposal that the two governments should submit their differences to the arbitration of the International Court of Justice was not acceptable to India. There was an impasse. Ghulam Muhammad appealed to Mountbatten who consulted with Nehru. A statement was then placed before Ghulam Muhammad, and he was asked to sign it without changing a word or a comma—a condition for restoring the flow of water.

On May 4, 1948, the statement was signed by Ghulam Muhammad and the two West Punjab ministers on the one hand and by Nehru and two East Punjab ministers on the other. The statement declared that, apart from the questions of law involved, the governments were anxious to approach the problem in a practical spirit. The East Punjab government would progressively diminish its supply to the Central Bari Doab and Dipalpur canals in West Punjab in order to give reasonable time to the West Punjab government to tap alternative sources. The statement announced that water was being restored to these canals, that West Punjab was to deposit in escrow such "ad hoc sum as may be specified by the Prime Minister of India" to cover certain disputed payments, and that, after an examination by each side of the legal and other issues involved, further meetings would take place. In conclusion, the Dominion governments expressed the hope that a friendly solution would be reached.

Though India restored the flow of water to the Dipalpur canal and the principal branches of the Central Bari Doab canals, water was still withheld from the Bahawalpur state distributary and nine lesser distributaries of the Central Bari Doab system. Eventually, considerable areas in Bahawalpur state reverted to desert. Notwithstanding the compulsion under which the arrangement was signed, Pakisan performed its part and deposited in escrow the sums specified by the Prime Minister of India. Later, Nehru, in an apparent fit of amnesia, denied that there had been any compulsion. In a letter to Liaquat Ali Khan in September, 1950, Nehru wrote: "Your Government's communication [states] that the agreement of 4 May 1948 was accepted by Pakistan 'under compulsion.' This has surprised and distressed me greatly. . . . I cannot imagine how any question of compulsion could possibly have arisen in these circumstances. There was then no kind of threat or even suggestion about stopping the flow of the water."

The further meeting between the two Dominion governments envisaged in the May 4 statement took place in Lahore in July, 1948.

At this meeting India reverted to the contention that "proprietary rights in the waters of the rivers in East Punjab vest wholly in the East Punjab Government"; and proposed that this should be embodied in a final agreement "which would take the place of all rights and liabilities which either side may have in law." Naturally no agreement could be reached on this basis. Nor could a settlement be brought nearer by correspondence between the two prime ministers. In a telegram sent on October 18, 1948, Nehru demanded that the May 4 arrangement be interpreted as recognizing "the right of the East Punjab Government to progressively diminish supply of water to the West Punjab," and stated that "any further meetings between representatives of the two Governments should be on the basis of this recognition by West Punjab." He warned that "If there was an unreasonable delay on the part of one side, it is open to the other party to put an end to the agreement by giving reasonable notice." In other words, unless Pakistan accepted the Indian contention quickly, India would end the arrangement and once again cut off the supplies of water. For Pakistan to accept the Indian interpretation would have been a permanent renunciation of Pakistan's legal rights. Pakistan offered to refer the legal issues in dispute to the International Court of Justice. India refused.

Direct negotiations between the two governments also produced no result. The only agreement reached in a conference in August, 1949, was to have another conference. Representatives of India and Pakistan met in Karachi toward the end of March, 1950. At this conference, which I attended as the leader of the Pakistan delegation, I tried to explore a purely practical basis for the settlement of the dispute. I proposed that existing uses be met from existing sources, and that new supplies be provided from flood waters now running to the sea, by building dams on the Sutlej, Beas, Ravi, and Chenab rivers, the costs involved to be shared in proportion to the benefits derived. An equitable division would be made of the new supplies in the light of relevant facts. The Indian delegation, which included A. N. Khosla, the Chairman of the Central Power, Irrigation, and Navigation Commission, suggested that the waters of the Sutlej, on which the Bhakra Dam was being built, be utilized wholly for areas in India, but that the waters of the Beas, the Ravi, and the Chenab be utilized for the maintenance of existing uses in Pakistan, subject to certain adjustments in favor of India. Any deficiencies in the supplies to Pakistan canals would be made good by building a link from the Chenab River, the entire flow of which would be available to Pakistan. If necessary, a dam on the Chenab could be built to make up for any deficiency that still remained and to provide supplies for an extension of irrigation. It was agreed that engineers on both sides should study the two plans, and put up the relevant engineering data before another meeting to be held in Delhi in May, 1950.

At the end of the meeting in March, I had been fairly hopeful of reaching a reasonable agreement. But when I arrived in Delhi two months later, I found the atmosphere completely changed. The Indians were unwilling to proceed along the lines discussed at Karachi. They announced that they proposed to appropriate the entire usable flow not only of the Sutlej, but also of the Beas and the Ravi, and besides, take 10,000 cusecs from the Chenab through a tunnel at Maru. In other words, India wanted to take all the water it could and leave Pakistan to fend for itself. The supplies from the Sutlej, Beas, and Ravi rivers had historically provided water for more than 5.6 million acres in West Pakistan and had supported a population of over 5 million people. India was now threatening these people with extinction. I had an interview with Nehru and placed before him the consequences of the attitude of his government. He was effusive in expressing those soulful sentiments that have appealed so much to foreigners and professed anxiety for a humane solution; but I could not change his mind on the point in question.

It was clear that no agreement on the sharing of water could be reached in bilateral negotiations. The question of legal rights was even more difficult to resolve. Pakistan had asked India many times to refer this issue to the World Court for adjudication. India had just as often refused. The interim arrangement of May 4, 1948, instead of paving the way toward an agreement had become an obstacle. When, in 1950, India filed it with the United Nations as Treaty No. 794, Pakistan explained the true nature of the statement to the UN and certified that it had been terminated.

The United Nations Charter provides that legal disputes should as a general rule be referred by the parties to the International Court of Justice. A word of explanation is needed to show why Pakistan did not take this dispute to the World Court. After the First World War, undivided India became a member of the League of Nations and, like the rest of the British Commonwealth, accepted the compulsory jurisdiction of the International Court of Justice, except in disputes between members of the Commonwealth. The assumption was that such disputes would be settled within the family of nations comprising the Commonwealth. When the subcontinent was partitioned into two sovereign states, the Dominion of India laid claim to being the successor of the old entity that was India. In consequence it inherited the international rights and obligations of undivided India, including compulsory jurisdiction of the International Court of Justice, except for disputes between members of the Commonwealth. Although the Commonwealth had shown itself powerless to resolve disputes between its members, yet, by virtue of the old proviso, the canal waters dispute could not be referred to the International Court of Justice by Pakistan unless India agreed. And India, knowing that its stand was invalid in international law, would not agree.

Finally, in September, 1950, the Government of India did offer to submit the legal issues to adjudication, but not before the World Court or any other impartial tribunal, but to a court of two Indian and two Pakistani judges. When the Prime Minister of Pakistan suggested an impartial chairman, Nehru replied: "To think ab initio of a third party will be . . . a confession of continued dependence on others. That would be hardly becoming for proud and self-respecting independent nations." Nor would he agree to refer to a further court with an impartial chairman issues on which the first court might be divided. It was clear that India's purpose was to prolong negotiations until the Bhakra Dam, the Rajasthan Canal, and other engineering works were completed, the effect of which would be to deprive Pakistan of vital water supplies.

Meanwhile, India was steadily increasing its forcible appropriation of water at the expense of Pakistan. Supplies to Pakistan canals were reduced at the critical times when crops were being sowed or were maturing. A headworks at Harike at the junction of the Sutlej and the Beas was under construction and was to bring additional areas in India under irrigation. New canals were being built. The height and storage capacity of the Bhakra Dam were greatly raised above the prepartition design so that it would be capable of storing the entire flow of the Sutlej River even during the monsoon season. The Bhakra Dam as actually constructed by India is the highest in the world. Its height of 740 feet is 14 feet more than that of the world-famous Hoover Dam in the United States. It can store 8 million acre-feet of water instead of the 4 million acre-feet originally planned.

To provide an insurance against continued Indian threats to cut off water supplies and, also, to provide a more uniform system of irrigation in the various colony areas some link canals such as the Balloki-Suleimanki link were built by Pakistan at its own expense. But these link canals could not wholly solve the problem. It was essential to find suitable sites for storage dams. Soon after the Indians stopped the flow of canal waters I asked West Punjab engineers to survey sites for storage dams on the Jhelum and Indus rivers. Of these sites Mangla, on the Jhelum, was the most promising. On the Indus River a site at Darband was at first favored, but later studies showed Tarbela to be more suitable. The Mangla Dam was sanctioned by the Pakistan government and work on its design and construction was started. No foreign aid was available so long as the dispute with India was not resolved.

In 1951, David Lilienthal, former head of the Tennessee Valley Authority in the United States, visited both India and Pakistan and recorded his observations in an article that appeared in *Collier's* magazine in August, 1951. He called the canal water dispute "pure dynamite, a Punjab powder keg" and warned that "peace in the Indo-Pakistan sub-continent is not in sight with these inflammables around." He continued:

> With no *water for irrigation* [West Pakistan] would be desert. 20,000,000 acres would dry up in a week, tens of millions would starve. No army, with bombs and shellfire, could devastate a land as thoroughly as Pakistan could be devastated by the simple expedient of India's permanently shutting off the sources of water that keep the fields and the people of Pakistan alive.

Lilienthal concluded by making a constructive proposal:

> The starting point should be, then to set to rest Pakistan's fears of deprivation and a return to desert. Her present use of water should be confirmed by India, *provided* she works together with India (as I believe she would) in a joint use of this truly international river basin on an engineering basis that would also (as the facts make clear it can) assure India's future as well. [He suggested that the new engineering works be jointly financed,] perhaps with World Bank help.

Eugene Black, President of the World Bank, felt attracted by the idea. He wrote to the prime ministers of India and Pakistan in September, 1951, offering the good offices of the Bank, if their governments were disposed to look with favor upon Lilienthal's proposal which contemplates meeting the requirements of both countries for expanded irrigation through the cooperative construction and operation of storage dams and other facilities to be financed in part perhaps by this Bank. It is the essence of the proposal, as I read it, that the development of the Indus water resources should be dealt with on an engineering basis and it appears to be Mr. Lilienthal's belief, after visiting both countries and talking with the highest personalities in the Governments, that it is within the realm of practicability to treat water development as a common project that is functional, and not political, in nature and that could therefore be undertaken separately from the political issues with which Pakistan and India are confronted.

Both governments accepted President Black's offer, and both sides agreed not to take any action to diminish the supplies available to the other side for existing uses, while the cooperative work continued with the participation of the World Bank. It was recognized that legal rights would not be affected.

India, notwithstanding its undertaking not to diminish supplies, continued to withhold water from Pakistan canals and to expand its own irrigation. In October and November, 1952, during the critical wheat sowing season in the Punjab, Pakistan received only 40 percent of its due share of these supplies. In February, 1953, it received only 8 percent. India used all of its share and, in addition, appropriated most of Pakistan's share. In 1952, India announced the opening of new distributaries from the Upper Bari Doab canal to bring under irrigation 108,000 acres not previously irrigated. In 1953, when supplies in the rivers were very low owing to drought, and crops in West Punjab were failing from lack of water, agriculture in East Punjab had one of its best years. While West Pakistan was facing a famine, the Governor of East Punjab, which before partition had been a deficit area in food, reported that "the food position is good," and gave figures of export of foodgrains.

When Pakistan brought the situation to the notice of the World Bank, President Black proposed that, in order to verify the data regarding the water supply, a commission be established consisting of an engineer from the World Bank, an engineer from India, and an engineer from Pakistan. Pakistan accepted; India refused. President Black proposed, as an alternative, that the World Bank designate engineers to work with Indian engineers in India, and Pakistan engineers in Pakistan, to the end that verified data might be available to both parties. Pakistan again accepted; India again refused. The pattern of behavior exhibited by India in the Kashmir dispute was being repeated in the Canal Waters dispute. In consistence with that pattern, Nehru declared on February 20, 1953: "We have not deliberately deprived them [Pakistan] of canal water nor do we propose to do so."

It would take us too far beyond the scope of this book to give a history of the long drawn-out negotiations between the World Bank and the governments of India and Pakistan. A brief outline of the three main stages in the mediatory efforts of the World Bank will suffice.

The Indus Basin working party, consisting of engineers appointed by India and Pakistan and their advisers, worked with the Bank representative and its consultants for almost two years to prepare a comprehensive plan for the utilization of the waters of the Indus system. No common approach was found. India claimed all of the supplies of the Sutlej, Beas, and Ravi rivers, and some of the supplies of the Chenab, and wanted to use these supplies for extending irrigation to large areas outside the Indus Basin. These new areas could well be irrigated from the Jumna River, but that would not serve the Indian objective of depriving Pakistan of vital water supplies. Pakistan proposed the maintenance of existing uses and the sharing of the uncommitted surplus on an equitable basis. Subsequent discussions produced some concessions, but no agreement was reached.

On February 5, 1954, the World Bank put forward its own proposal for the consideration of the two parties. The Bank frankly recognized that "water supplies and storage potentialities are inadequate to the needs of the basin." The proposal noted that "although the Working Party are planning on the basis of the development of the Indus Basin as an economic unit, two sovereign states are involved [and when] two sovereign authorities are concerned, it is difficult to use resources to the greatest advantage." But the most serious difficulty of all, in the Bank's view, was the "basic divergence of concept" between India and Pakistan.

The Bank plan provided that:

> The entire flow of the Western rivers (Indus, Jhelum and Chenab) would be available for the exclusive use and benefit of Pakistan, and for development by Pakistan, except for the insignificant volume of Jhelum flow presently used in Kashmir. The entire flow of the Eastern rivers (Ravi, Beas and Sutlej) would be available for the exclusive use and benefit of India and for development by India, except

that for a specified transitional period India would continue to supply from these rivers, in accordance with an agreed schedule, the historic withdrawals from these rivers in Pakistan.

The Bank plan allowed a

transition period [in which] to complete the link canals needed in Pakistan to make transfers for the purpose of replacing supplies from India [and stipulated that] India would bear the cost of such works to the extent of the benefits to be received by her therefrom.

The transition period was estimated to be about five years.

The Bank plan contemplated no storage dam, aside from the Bhakra Dam, which was already under construction in India to be used for Indian purposes only. It asserted that "even without further storage construction . . . Pakistan could supply her historic withdrawals and could bring most of the Sutlej Valley Canals up to allocation" from the flow supply of the western rivers.

The Bank plan was a complete departure from Lilienthal's proposal to develop the water resources of the Indus Basin as a single unit through the construction of storage dams and other facilities. It went in the opposite direction and proposed to divide the water resources of the Indus Basin into two on the basis of political boundaries; and it envisaged no cooperative development. The plan's justification, according to the World Bank, lay "in the fact that, after transfer works are completed, each country will be independent of the other in the operation of its supplies." It purported to avoid the complexities that would arise if the supplies from particular rivers were shared by the two countries.

India readily accepted the Bank plan, which conceded all that she had been asking for except the requirement that she should leave the flow of the Chenab undisturbed. According to the Bank plan, India was to bear part of the cost of link canals in Pakistan, but that was a small price to pay for precious water supplies. When an entire economy is dependent upon water, money can be no substitute for it.

The Bank plan confronted Pakistan with an intolerable situation. Vigorous representations were made to the Bank that the flow supply of the western rivers was totally inadequate to replace Pakistan's existing uses of the water from the eastern rivers. The construction of storage dams that would be necessary to make up for the shortage would be a costly and lengthy affair; and the Bank plan made no provision for them. Even with such a provision, Pakistan's limited storage capacity would be used merely to maintain her existing position and could not be utilized for the developing needs of her growing population. Like Alice in Wonderland, Pakistan would have to run as hard as she could in order to remain where she was.

An independent engineering appraisal of the Bank plan was undertaken for Pakistan by R. J. Tipton, a consulting engineer of Denver, Colorado. It revealed that the Bank proposal did not meet the standard of fairness required under international law, that it failed to apportion equitably the waters of the Indus system, and that it went contrary to the principle of using water resources in such a manner as to promote development most effectively. Tipton's studies disclosed that Pakistan would be very adversely affected by the Bank plan. Certain areas would be permanently deprived of water supplies; historic withdrawals would not be maintained; prepartition planned uses would be invaded; and Pakistan's future development potential would be seriously curtailed.

The next stage was reached when, after eighteen months of further studies by its own consultants, the Bank reached the conclusions contained in its aide memoire of May 21, 1956. The aide memoire conceded that "there would be consistent shortages in Rabi, occasionally beginning in late September or extending into early April . . . of a degree, duration and frequency which the Bank Group could not regard as 'tolerable.' " The Bank therefore felt "that an adjustment, in its Proposal of February 1954 [was] called for. This adjustment should, in the Bank's view, assure to Pakistan timely water sufficient to eliminate the shortage referred to."

The adjustment could take the form of continued deliveries of "timely" water from the eastern rivers, or construction of storage on the western rivers at India's cost. The Bank preferred the latter course, and suggested that for this purpose, the "flow of the Western rivers (Indus as well as Jhelum and Chenab) should be exploited to the maximum possible extent and that the minimum inroads should be made on Pakistan's limited storage capacity." In short, after nearly two years of argument and investigation, the Bank realized that the loss of water from the eastern rivers could not be made good by the flow supply of the western rivers. It is to the Bank's credit that it was prepared to rectify the mistaken assumption on which its original plan was based, if not by deliveries of water from the eastern rivers, at any rate by construction of storage on the western rivers at India's cost.

The World Bank therefore recommended in its letter of July 30, 1956, that both governments should be willing to continue the construction work with the assistance of the Bank on the basis of the Bank proposal of February 5, 1954, and of its aide memoire of May 21, 1956. Both governments agreed.

It took another four years of hard negotiating to work out a concrete solution. The difficulties did not arise merely from differences in approach between India and Pakistan. There were big problems of finance. It had become apparent that the cost of the constructions required for a settlement on the lines of the World Bank proposal was far beyond the capacity of India and Pakistan. The final agreement was made possible by the steadfast perseverance and "economic diplomacy," to use his own phrase, of President Black of the World Bank, and through the friendly assistance of the United States, the United Kingdom, Canada, Australia, New Zealand, and West Germany.

The Indus Waters Treaty was signed on September 19, 1960, in Karachi, by the representatives of India, Pakistan, and the World Bank. Simultaneously with the signing of the treaty, an international financial agreement was also executed by the representatives of the governments of Australia, Canada, West Germany, New Zealand, Pakistan, the United Kingdom, the United States, and the World Bank. This agreement created an Indus Basin development fund of almost 900 million dollars to finance the construction of irrigation and other works in Pakistan. The fund is made up of 640 million dollars to be provided by the participating governments, 174 million dollars payable by India under the Indus Waters Treaty and a loan of 80 million dollars by the World Bank to Pakistan. The program for construction work in Pakistan includes eight link canals nearly 400 miles long for transferring water from the western rivers to areas formerly irrigated by the eastern rivers; two storage dams, one on the Jhelum and the other on the Indus; power stations; 2,500 tubewells; and other works to integrate the whole river and canal system. The Indus settlement also envisages the construction of a storage dam on the Beas River in India which, together with the Bhakra Dam on the Sutlej and the Rajasthan canal, will irrigate large new areas in India.

The treaty provides for a transitional period of ten years, which may be extended by another three years, during which India will supply water to Pakistan from the eastern rivers. The treaty also provides, in case of need, for the services of a neutral expert to make a final decision on technical questions and for a court of arbitration to resort to under special circumstances.

Only time will show if the system of canals and reservoirs envisaged in the treaty will on completion fulfill its expectations. In the main, it is designed to maintain existing irrigation in Pakistan, but it also holds out hopes of development to meet the need for a higher standard of living by a growing population. There are those who seriously doubt its efficacy. They point out that dams on silt-laden rivers do not have a long life, and that the cost of maintaining the huge link canals and servicing the loans incurred by Pakistan will be beyond the productive capacity of the irrigation system. Far more serious concern is expressed over the hesitation to proceed with the storage dam on the Indus; without it all hopes of development would vanish and the liabilities would outweigh the advantages. It is too early yet to pass final judgment.

CHAPTER 16

Economic and Financial
Problems of the New State

E V E R S I N C E the idea of Pakistan was put forward, doubts had continually been thrown on its economic and financial viability. Hostile Hindu propaganda had concentrated on the theme, so much so that even those friendly to the concept were affected. When the British journalist Beverley Nichols interviewed the Quaid-i-Azam in December, 1943, the first question he asked after hearing an exposition of the concept of Pakistan was about the economic aspect of Pakistan: "Are the Muslims likely to be richer or poorer under Pakistan?" The Quaid-i-Azam's reply was characteristic: "The Muslims are a tough people, lean and hardy. If Pakistan means that they will have to be a little tougher, they will not complain. But why should it mean that? What conceivable reason is there to suppose that the gift of nationality is going to be an economic liability?" [1]

In September, 1945, Sir Homi Modi and Dr. John Matthai published their *Memorandum on the Economic and Financial Aspects of Pakistan*. It was a dispassionate study by two distinguished public men, one of them a prominent Parsi businessman and the other a leading economist who had been economic adviser to the Government of India and was subsequently its Finance Minister. They summed up their views in two propositions:

1. Judged solely by the test of ability to maintain existing standards of living and to meet budgetary requirements on a pre-war basis but excluding provision for defence, separation would appear to be workable on economic grounds.

2. If, however, provision is to be made for future economic development on a scale sufficient to raise the general standard of living to a reasonable level and for measures of defence which may be considered adequate under modern conditions, any scheme of political separation which may be contemplated should, as a necessary prerequisite, provide for means of effective and continuous cooperation between the separate States in matters affecting the safety of the country and its economic stability and development. If such cooperation did not exist, the position of both Pakistan and Hindustan might be seriously jeopardized.

Cooperation would have been to the advantage of both Dominions, but Congress hostility to Pakistan destroyed the basis for it. The Punjab massacres and the disputes over cash balances, defense stores, Kashmir, canal waters, and other questions arose from an aggressive spirit that would have liked to strangle Pakistan at its very birth. The Indian leaders were partly impelled by a blind rage that saw in the establishment of Pakistan the temporary defeat of their ambition to rule over the whole of the subcontinent. But in the main they reckoned that, since Pakistan was not economically viable while India was, they could, without serious injury to themselves, hasten Pakistan's collapse by an antagonistic policy.

The Union of India is not only five times bigger than Pakistan in area and population; it is a single geographical bloc separating the two parts of Pakistan. It is richly endowed with natural resources, particularly coal and iron, and has a strong industrial base. The British had administered the entire subcontinent as a single economic unit. Free trade within the whole area, a single tariff, a unified system of currency and credit, and a network of railways and telegraphs had helped to integrate the economy. But no regard had been paid by the British to the balanced development of various regions. In fact, the concept of planned development was foreign to British rule, concerned as it was primarily with defense and the maintenance of law and order. Its major achievement in the economic field was the development of the great ports of Calcutta, Bombay, and Madras and the lines of communications radiating from there to the remotest parts of the country; and even this owed more to strategic necessity than to planned economic welfare.

These major ports and the industrial centers that grew up near them or in other places were all located in the Indian Union. There was very little industry in the areas that were to become Pakistan. The agricultural products of these areas were transported to industrial centers in India to be used in manufacture or to be exported. The commercial houses and banks that controlled the integrated economy of the subcontinent had their headquarters in those centers. The trade and industry of the subcontinent was in Hindu or British hands. The entrepreneurs and investors, the industrial managers and the technicians were mostly Hindu. The Congress leaders, in the pride of superior strength, felt under no obligation to extend cooperation to Pakistan. On the contrary, they thought that by applying pressures and exploiting the structural weakness of Pakistan they would succeed in undermining its economy. Sardar Patel's view that the Indian Union "will be so powerful that the remaining portions will eventually come in" [2] was shared by almost all Hindu leaders.

Pakistan is unique in being composed of two equally important parts separated by a thousand miles of foreign territory. The population figures, according to the 1961 census, are 51 million for East Pakistan and 43 million for West Pakistan, making a total of 94 million. The population, which has been growing at an annual rate of over 2 percent was about 74 million at the time of independence. East Pakistan comprises an area of 55,000 square miles and West Pakistan has an area of 310,000 square miles. Thus East Pakistan, though its area is one sixth that of West Pakistan, has a population somewhat in excess of West Pakistan. The physical characteristics of the two regions are very different.

East Pakistan has a subtropical climate with an average rainfall of 88 inches a year. The land is mostly flat—in fact, a delta in the process of formation. The great river systems of the Ganges and the Brahmaputra, which flow into the Bay of Bengal, enrich the soil each year by spreading over it millions of tons of silt. There are thousands of streams that serve as channels of communication. Periodically, however, cyclones, torrential rains, and abnormal floods bring devastation to large areas. The fertile soil and the hot humid climate produce luxuriant vegetation. Rice and jute are the main crops. Tea is grown in the hilly areas to the north and east. Tropical fruits such as bananas, pineapples, and coconuts abound. East Pakistan is one of the most densely populated areas of the world. The average density of population is 922 persons per square mile; in some parts it rises to 1,500 per square mile.

West Pakistan lies north of the tropics. The rainfall averages 12 inches a year and hot summers are followed by severe winters. Large parts of the region are desert or barren hills incapable of supporting a large population. The average density of population is 138 persons per square mile. Agriculture depends for the most part upon artificial irrigation. The high mountains in the north give rise to a number of rivers that flow down to the Arabian Sea. In areas irrigated by canals from these rivers, there is a prosperous agriculture, but the area under cultivation could be doubled if water were available. The ravages of salinity and waterlogging reduce the area under cultivation by 75,000 acres every year and decrease the fertility of large tracts of land. Wheat and cotton are the main crops. Sugar cane, rice, maize, and tobacco are also grown. There are plenty of orange and mango orchards.

East Pakistan was dealt a staggering blow at the time of partition when Calcutta became part of India. Over 90 percent of the industrial units in undivided Bengal were located in Calcutta or nearby, in West Bengal. East Pakistan had only 5 percent of the total number of industrial workers of undivided Bengal at the time of partition. Industries, banks, insurance companies, commercial houses, import and export firms, communication centers, power stations, and educational institutions were all located in Calcutta, which had been the capital of undivided Bengal and its main port.

Undivided India had a virtual monopoly of raw jute in the world. The area which became East Pakistan produced nearly 75 percent of this golden fiber and all of its best varieties. But there was not a single jute mill in East Pakistan, and only a few modern baling presses. Almost all the jute produced in East Pakistan was sent to Calcutta, to be manufactured into hessian and other jute products in the numerous jute mills there, or to be baled and shipped for export. Jute is the most important cash crop of East Pakistan, and the prosperity of the farmers depends upon the price realized for it. But they were, to a large extent, at the mercy of conditions in the Calcutta market, where speculators and shippers made large fortunes at the expense of primary producers.

At partition, East Pakistan had only one port in Chittagong. It was a minor port with a capacity of half a million tons. It would take years before its capacity could be expanded and the lines of traffic oriented toward it. In the meantime there was no outlet for jute and other products from East Pakistan except Calcutta. There was an export duty on jute from which the Government of India and the provincial government of Bengal derived considerable revenue. As related earlier, in Chapter 9, the representatives of Pakistan suggested at the time of partition that, at least as an interim measure, the proceeds of customs and central excise duties should be pooled and distributed between the two Dominions on an equitable basis. The Indian representatives refused to agree and insisted that each Dominion should keep the revenue collected within its territory. Nor would they accept a special agreement for jute. The Pakistan government was therefore forced to levy an export duty on jute crossing the land frontier from East to West Bengal, and to face the difficulties that arise from maintaining a customs barrier along a long frontier. The difficulties were particularly great, since hundreds of waterways crossing the frontier provided many opportunities for smuggling.

In West Pakistan, the most important cash crop is cotton; it occupies a position similar to that of jute in East Pakistan. The area that became West Pakistan produced 40 percent of the raw cotton crop of undivided India including some of the best medium staple cotton of the American type. The cotton textile industry was by far the biggest industry in undivided India, but at partition 380 of its 394 cotton mills were located in the Indian Union and only 14 in Pakistan. The raw cotton produced in West Pakistan was moved, mostly by rail, to the centers of the textile industry in Ahmedabad and Bombay, which in return supplied cloth to Pakistan.

Thus, by and large, the relationship between Pakistan and India at the time of partition was that between a supplier of raw materials and an industrial producer. The pattern of trade between India and the two parts of Pakistan would inevitably have undergone a change in the course of time. But the Punjab disturbances and the wholesale exchange of population that took place between West Pakistan and northern India disrupted the normal channels of trade and traffic and violently forced them to flow in other directions. Cotton and other commodities that had moved by rail to industrial centers in India had to find an outlet to the outside world through Karachi. All exports and imports for West Pakistan moved through Karachi, which rapidly grew in importance. The growth of trade between East and West Pakistan enhanced the importance of Karachi at one end and of Chittagong at the other.

Both India and Pakistan were underdeveloped, but of the two, Pakistan was more underdeveloped and poorer. A primitive agriculture provided employment for the bulk of the population. Over 60 percent of the total national income of 18.6 billion rupees in 1949–50 was derived from agriculture. The per capita income stood at 237 rupees, slightly less than 50 dollars. Most people had barely enough on which to subsist. In years of drought or flood, famine threatened the land. Education and health services were inadequate. Most of the population—87 percent—lived in villages. Hardly 16 percent were literate.

The most pressing tasks confronting the country after independence were the establishment of an administration and the rehabilitation of refugees. How these problems were tackled has been described. But there were other urgent problems that also had to be solved.

At the time of partition, West Pakistan had a surplus of foodgrains. The colony areas of the Punjab exported wheat to deficit areas in India as far down as Madras. East Pakistan, however, had a deficit in rice, its staple food crop. In the summer of 1947 there were severe floods in the Chittagong and Noakhali districts of East Pakistan that damaged about 500 square miles. The *aus* crop of rice as well as the *aman* seedlings in the flood-affected area were destroyed. By the end of the year, 100,000 tons of foodgrains would be required; of that, 4,000 tons were needed immediately. Memories of the 1943 Bengal famine were still fresh in people's minds. The situation was so serious that the East Bengal Chief Minister, Khwaja Nazimuddin, came to Karachi on August 25, 1947, to ensure supplies. Fortunately West Pakistan had a surplus of rice, but there were difficulties of procurement and transport. On some branches of the railway system in West Pakistan, services had to be suspended because of the shortage of coal. Shipping was scarce. However, food shipments from West Pakistan were arranged in time. After January, 1948, there was a wheat shortage in West Pakistan caused by the vast upheaval of the refugee movement. In some districts scarcity conditions prevailed. No surpluses were available from the outside world. (Indeed, the Director

General of FAO had warned delegates in Geneva in August, 1947, that millions in Europe would be worse fed in the following winter and spring than during the war.) The year 1948 continued to be one of anxiety on the food front. In West Pakistan an area of 3.5 million acres was affected by floods and 600,000 tons of the Kharif, or autumn crop, were destroyed. The normal surplus of 400,000 tons was converted into a deficit. Even so, it was essential to send supplies of foodgrains to East Pakistan, where also considerable damage had been done by floods. Appeals were made to economize food consumption and legislation was introduced to check hoarding and dealings in the black market. There was a growing awareness of the precarious food position, of the need for increasing the output of foodgrains and taking protective measures against floods, as also of the pressure of a fast rising population. The change in the composition of population also had its effect on the food problem. The replacement of the vegetarian Hindus by Muslims greatly increased the consumption of meat. There was serious danger of the depletion of the cattle population on which agricultural operations and the supply of milk and milk products depended. Two days in the week were declared meatless.

The problem of communication was outstandingly important. East and West Pakistan are separated by 1,200 miles by air and 3,000 miles by sea. Telecommunication between East and West Pakistan was an urgent necessity. Work on the establishment of Radio Pakistan and the acquisition of a transmitter of sufficient power had started during the days of partition. Of no less importance was communication by air and sea. Karachi had an international airport that connected Pakistan with the outside world, but Dacca was not on the route of international airlines. It was essential to establish a domestic air service between East and West Pakistan. This need was met by a small company, Orient Airways; it shifted its headquarters from Calcutta to Karachi and improvised repair facilities. In 1948, another private company, Pak Air, was formed. The company owed its existence to the initiative of Ghulam Muhammad, the Finance Minister. Ghulam Muhammad, who had been Finance Minister of Hyderabad some years earlier, was very keen to have the Nizam transfer part, if not the whole, of his vast treasure of gold, precious stones, and cash by air to Karachi for safe custody. He paid a visit to Hyderabad but failed to persuade the Nizam, whose love of money was too great to let him send it out of his sight. Later, the Nizam lost all of it to the Indian government. Nevertheless, Ghulam Muhammad succeeded in getting a substantial contribution from Hyderabad to finance Pak Air. However, the company was ill-managed and went into liquidation after some serious crashes in which many valuable lives were lost, including two of the ablest officers of the Pakistan army, Major General Muhammad Iftikhar Khan and Brigadier Sher Khan.

Trade between East and West Pakistan was bound to grow but certain requirements, such as the shipment of food and salt from West to East Pakistan, were needed immediately. There was no mercantile fleet to speak of and even second-hand vessels were not easy to acquire. In the immediate postwar period, capital goods of all kinds were scarce. The reconstruction of the war-torn economies of the United Kingdom, Western Europe, Russia, and Japan took priority over all other demands. New and developing countries faced difficulties and delays in having their orders accepted and delivery dates were unduly long. It was against this background that Pakistan had to get its economy going.

With the loss of Calcutta and its facilities, the most important problem in East Pakistan was the creation of the basic framework of communications and power within which the economy could develop. This was in the nature of things and even more so in the conditions then prevailing in the world a slow and lengthy process. The foremost task was the modernization and expansion of the port of Chittagong. It was the first major project sanctioned by the central government, but, unfortunately, there is an inevitable interval between approval and execution. The appointment of competent consultants, the completion of surveys, the preparation of designs and estimates all take time. Railway tracks and rolling stock in East Pakistan had been worn out by the heavy movement of military supplies and personnel for the Burma front during the Second World War. Extensive replacements were needed. There were serious shortages of coal. Inland water transport, which plays a large part in the economy of East Pakistan, was disorganized. The headquarters of the Joint Steamship Company, which was by far the largest operator, were in Calcutta, and this produced a crop of difficulties.

In West Pakistan the position was better. Despite the disorganization caused by the vast disturbances in the Punjab and neighboring areas, the North Western Railway was able to cope with the mass movement of refugees. Karachi port, although needing repairs and expansion, was big enough for immediate needs.

In the matter of roads West Pakistan was also better off than East Pakistan. The network of roads in West Pakistan was one of the most developed in the subcontinent, partly for strategic reasons. In East Pakistan, on the other hand, the scarcity of stone and the character of the terrain, which has innumerable streams meandering through a flat plain, make the construction of roads a difficult and expensive business. Inland water traffic with its thousands of boats carries the main burden of transport.

Both in East and West Pakistan there was a shortage of electrical power. A large area in West Punjab was supplied by electricity from the Mandi Hydroelectric Works in East Punjab. With partition this became an undependable source. The total installed capacity in the country at the time of partition was 75,028 kw., but lack of repairs and of competent staff had greatly reduced effective capacity. In East Pakistan the capacity was only 15,600 kw. The Karnaphuli Hydroelectric Project held out prospects for the future, but it would take many years to translate the idea into reality. In West Pakistan also surveys were carried out for hydroelectric projects, and some years later Warsak Project in the North-West Frontier Province was taken in hand. Present needs could only be met by thermal stations, but the demands of postwar reconstruction in Europe were so great that orders for any kind of machinery took long to be fulfilled. West Pakistan produced some inferior coal and a small quantity of oil. East Pakistan, which had drawn its supplies of fuel from India in the past, faced continual difficulty in getting coal and oil. An industrial civilization rests upon a mineral base. Very little exploration of oil and mineral resources in Pakistan had been carried out before independence. The Geological Survey of India had barely scratched the surface.

Amidst these and numerous other difficulties and shortages, the work of development was taken in hand. The movement for Pakistan was inspired by the urge to develop the human and material resources of Muslim homelands so as to promote the moral and material welfare of the people, provide adequate living standards and social services, secure equality of opportunity, and achieve the widest and most equitable distribution of income and property. These social and economic objectives had their roots in the Islamic principles of social justice and the brotherhood of man. In furthering them, the government would be fulfilling the deepest aspirations of the people. And the work had to be done and brought to fruition as rapidly as possible. The neglect of centuries had to be made good in decades, if not in years. The financial and economic resources available were inadequate for the magnitude of the task. The country could not afford the waste of haphazard action. While the energies of the people had to be aroused and used to the maximum extent, the government itself had to play a positive and constructive role in the shaping of policy and the coordination of public and private enterprise. The railways, telegraphs and telephones, ports, defense installations, irrigation headworks, canals, and forests were owned by the government. There were also other fields of endeavor that private enterprise might feel shy to enter for want of capital or fear of loss. In Dacca, to give one example, even a hotel had to be built by the provincial government with a loan from the central government. The economy of Pakistan would inevitably be mixed and planned. But the deliberate policy of the government was strongly biased in favor of free enterprise.

Early in 1948, a development board was formed to coordinate plans, recommend priorities, and make periodic reports to the government on the progress of development projects. The Chairman of the Board was the Minister of Economic Affairs; I, the Secretary-General, was the Vice-Chairman; and the secretaries of the ministries concerned with development were its members. At the same time a planning advisory board, comprising officials of the central, provincial, and state governments and representatives of the private sector, was also set up to advise the government on planning, and to promote public cooperation with the development effort. The planning advisory board was assisted by a number of committees established by the central and provincial governments. In 1950, when a Six Year Development Program for Pakistan was formulated under the Colombo Plan, an economic council under the presidentship of the Prime Minister was set up. These early exercises in planned development were of considerable help at the time, but a properly integrated plan could only be prepared when a separate planning organization was set up in 1953.

Under the adapted Government of India Act, 1935, which formed the interim constitution, industry was a provincial subject, but rapid and planned development of the country demanded that key industries should be subject to the control of the central government. An industries conference, which was held by the central government in December, 1947, recommended the setting up of certain basic industries and laid down targets for them. In April, 1948, a statement of industrial policy was issued by the Pakistan government. The policy was kept under review and revised as occasion demanded. It laid down that Pakistan would seek, in the first place, to manufacture those goods made of its own raw materials for which there was an assured market at home or abroad. Of these jute and cotton were the most important and received the earliest attention. The jute industry would increase the country's earnings of foreign exchange; and the production of cotton textiles would meet an essential need of the people and save foreign exchange. At the same time the government would "develop any heavy industry . . . considered essential for the speedy achievement of a strong and balanced economy." Three groups of industries were reserved for public ownership: arms and munitions; generation of hydroelectric power; and the manufacture and operation of railway, telephone, telegraph, and wireless equipment. The rest of the field was open to private enterprise. It would, however, be the responsibility of the government to ensure that "employers of labour maintain fair labour standards especially in matters of hours of work, wages, conditions of work and employment."

Twenty-seven industries were to be subject to planning by the central government. These included iron and steel, heavy engineering, machine tools, heavy chemicals, cement, minerals and mineral oils, sugar, textiles, and tobacco. The government also reserved the right to take over or participate in any industry vital to the security or well-being of the state; and to set up a limited number of standard units if private capital was not forthcoming in adequate measure for the development of any particular industry of national importance.

The policy statement announced that "Pakistan would welcome foreign capital seeking investment from a purely industrial and economic objective and not claiming any special privileges." An assurance was given for the remittance of profits and for the repatriation of capital invested, including profits ploughed back. If any undertaking was nationalized, just and equitable compensation would be paid and allowed to be remitted. There was provision for participation of indigenous capital to the extent of 51 percent in thirteen specified industries and 30 percent in the rest, but if the requisite amount of indigenous capital was not forthcoming, the balance might, with government approval, be subscribed by foreign investors. Later, the requirement for local participation was reduced to 40 percent. In particular, foreign companies were encouraged to explore for oil and gas.

To stimulate industrial growth, the government gave every possible assistance through the provision of basic facilities, tariff protection, and fiscal incentives. The facilities included the survey of mineral resources, the development of electrical power, the improvement of communications, assistance in the procurement of machinery and essential raw materials as well as in the acquisition of land for industrial use, the promotion of technical education, scientific and industrial research, and the construction of industrial trading estates. The very first budget announced important tax concessions. For the first five years, profits up to 5 percent of the capital employed by new industrial undertakings were exempted from income tax as well as super tax and business profits tax. An initial depreciation allowance of 20 percent on new machinery and plant, and 15 percent on new buildings for industrial purposes, was granted. These depreciation allowances were like interest-free loans given to industrial enterprises by the government. The Industrial Finance Corporation was formed by the government in 1949 to give loans to industrial projects on a medium and long term basis. Fifty-one percent of its capital of Rs. 20 million was subscribed by the Pakistan government and the rest was offered to the public.

The response from entrepreneurs and the investing public was, however, disappointing. The reason for this was to be found partly in the lack of managerial ability and technical skill—a common failing in underdeveloped countries. But a more important cause was the lure of big and quick profits to be made in trade. The dislocation in business activity brought about by the departure of Hindu traders was being rapidly repaired. There was a good market for Pakistan's goods abroad. The severe controls on imports, which had been imposed during the Second World War, had built up a back-log of demand for consumer goods. When, in August, 1948, import policy was liberalized, imports jumped up from Rs. 115 million in the first half of the year to Rs. 310 million in the second half. Cotton textiles and yarn constituted over one third of the imports. Under these conditions, it is not surprising that the available capital flowed into trade rather than industry. The government appointed an investment enquiry committee to examine the causes and to suggest remedies. Frequent appeals to the patriotism of would-be industrialists were made. They had little effect until economic conditions were created that made industry as profitable as trade. As a result of the precipitous fall in commodity prices after the end of the Korean War, Pakistan's foreign exchange earnings were greatly reduced. Consequently, the unduly liberal import policy of earlier years, which had brought in far more consumer goods than capital goods, was drastically revised in 1952 and reoriented in favor of plant and machinery for new industries. The restrictions on the import of foreign cloth and other consumer goods stimulated and protected domestic industrial production. The result was a remarkable shift of capital and enterprise from trade to industry. At the same time, the Pakistan Industrial Development Corporation was established (January, 1952) to set up industries of national importance for which private capital was not forthcoming. The Corporation was wholly financed by the central government. Under the vigorous chairmanship of G. Faruque and with the help of the liberal resources placed at its disposal by the Pakistan government during a period of serious financial stringency, the Corporation made an outstanding contribution to the industrialization of the country. It promoted the jute industry on its own initiative and in collaboration with private enterprise. It set up the Karnaphuli Paper Mill and a number of sugar, cement, and chemical plants and also shipyards. The result of the combined efforts of private and public enterprise was that during the four years from 1952 to 1955 industrial production went up by over 100 percent—a remarkable rate of economic growth for any country at any time.

Agriculture, which provided raw materials for industry and food for the people, and which earned almost all the foreign exchange of the country and employed the great majority of workers, was a provincial subject. The central government helped by giving loans and grants for development projects. Irrigation projects, such as the Thal Project in West Pakistan and the Ganges Kabodak Project in East Pakistan were of great importance for the development of agriculture. To coordinate the work and provide technical assistance, the Pakistan government set up the Central Engineering Authority. An agricultural enquiry committee under Lord Boyd Orr was appointed by the Pakistan government. The central government also established the Agricultural Development Finance Corporation. But the primary responsibility for agriculture remained with the provincial governments, which unfortunately did not pay adequate attention to it.

Basically, the problem is how to transform existing methods of cultivation into those of scientific agriculture and thus increase productivity per acre and per man-hour. This requires a change in the social and economic conditions of rural life, reform in the system of land tenure, extension of cooperation into new fields, large investments in land improvement, provision of adequate credit facilities, opening up of communications, improved seeds, the use of scientific farming techniques, and the establishment of industries to produce fertilizers, pesticides, tractors, and other farming equipment. It also requires a reorientation of the attitude of farmers, so that they advance from a static economy, where they produce merely enough for themselves, to a more dynamic one, with emphasis on production for the market.

Small uneconomic holdings, which are becoming still smaller and more fragmented with the growth of populations, are the norm in East Pakistan and in most parts of West Pakistan. To consolidate holdings is an urgent need. In East Pakistan, where the population density is one of the highest in the world, the pressure on the land is particularly great. A fuller use of the land, for example, by raising an additional winter crop by artificial irrigation, is needed. In West Pakistan, water is the major problem and the use of land is limited by the amount of water available. A large and growing population can subsist upon limited land resources only by developing a highly intensive and scientific agriculture. This must be integrated with small and medium industries; for these the provision of electricity all over the countryside is essential. Uneconomic holdings and the low staying power and poor creditworthiness of individual peasants point the way towards cooperative action and collective endeavor.

In the first few years after independence, the magnitude and complexity of the problems involved in developing agriculture were not fully realized. The rainfall was normal. The country was self-sufficient in food—by how narrow a margin few cared to ponder. The prices of the main cash crops, jute and cotton, were reasonable with a tendency to rise. The much-feared depression after the end of the Second World War had not occurred. The departure of Hindu money-lenders from West Pakistan had almost wiped off the debt burden and given immediate relief to the cultivators, and the shortage of rural credit was not to make itself felt until later. Indian action in stopping canal supplies had given a jolt to West Punjab, but this was an external threat of a rather different kind from the challenge of internal problems, such as those of land tenure or floods and waterlogging.

In East Pakistan, the Permanent Settlement of Bengal by Lord Cornwallis in 1793 had created a class of *zamindars,* or landlords, mostly Hindus, who paid a fixed sum of land revenue to the government, but were free to extort what they could from the cultivator. The landlord rented out his interest to a subordinate tenure-holder who employed still another rent-receiver, and thus the cultivator supported by his toil a number of idle intermediaries. The cry for land reform had often been raised, but the political influence of the powerful landlord class made it ineffective. Despite the recommendations of the Land Revenue Commission of Bengal in 1940 to abolish the Permanent Settlement, the system remained unchanged until the end of the British rule. With the establishment of Pakistan, it became possible to carry out long needed reforms. The East Bengal State Acquisition and Tenancy Act of 1950 abolished the Permanent Settlement and established direct relations between the cultivator and the government. But other problems arose, such as the maintenance of embankments to secure protection from tidal waves and river erosion. With the abolition of zamindari these fell into disrepair, and the cultivators lacked the financial resources and power of organization to maintain them. Gradually, with government assistance and cooperative action, these problems are being overcome. But there remain still bigger problems relating to the control of abnormal floods and other natural calamities that periodically inflict severe damage on the economy. Huge works in cooperation with India are needed in order to train and contain the mighty rivers, Brahmaputra and Ganges, which flow from India into the flat delta areas of East Pakistan. Whether such cooperation will be forthcoming is open to question in view of the disregard shown by India to East Pakistan's interests in the construction of the Farakka barrage on the Ganges.

In West Pakistan, there was a large class of peasant proprietors who owned the land they tilled, but there were also big landlords, particularly in Sind and in some areas of the Punjab and North-West Frontier Province. The need for reforms was felt. In the Punjab, the Protection and Restoration of Tenancy Rights Act was passed in 1950, but it did not produce the desired results. The Tenancy Act of 1950 passed in the North-West Frontier Province worked somewhat better. Sind was the stronghold of big zamindars who owned 87 percent of the cultivated area. The Sind Tenancy Act of 1950 granted some meager rights to the *haris,* or cultivators. The states in West Pakistan had a feudal structure except where, as in the colony areas of Bahawalpur, newly irrigated lands had been developed by peasant proprietors.

Another big problem for West Pakistan is waterlogging and salinity, which has been spreading over the countryside like a cancerous growth. To reclaim the vast areas affected by this disease and to prevent its further ravages, an extensive system of pumping and drainage is needed, together with large volumes of fresh water with which to wash down the salts in the soil.

Education was also a provincial subject. One of the effects of independence was to stimulate the demand for education, but the provincial governments were not able to cope with it adequately. The departure of Hindu teachers had thinned the teaching cadres and temporarily set back education. The central government gave guidance and grants for universities and technical education. Karachi was a federal area, and the responsibility of education fell on the Pakistan government, which established the Karachi University. A council of scientific and industrial research was set up with a central laboratory in Karachi and regional laboratories in East and West Pakistan.

Similarly, health services were the responsibility of the provinces and the role of the central government was limited to advice, coordination, and assistance in such projects as malaria eradication. To relieve the housing shortage in the cities which were getting overcrowded, the Pakistan government set up the House Building Finance Corporation.

In addition to these problems of social and economic development, Pakistan also faced a heavy burden of defense. By its very structure, Pakistan is the guardian of the frontiers of the subcontinent in the northwest and the northeast. Until a few years ago, the high wall of the Himalayas to the north presented an impenetrable barrier. The great invasions, whether prehistoric as those by the Aryans, or historic as those by Alexander and others, had been from the northwest. The Japanese threat to the subcontinent during the Second World War had arisen in the northeast. But, in the immediate present, by far the biggest threat to the security of Pakistan was from the Indian Union. Indian aggression in Junagadh, Hyderabad, and Kashmir was a constant reminder of how precarious was peace in the subcontinent.

It is against this background that the Pakistan Finance Minister presented his first budget in March, 1948, for the financial year 1948–49. To the surprise of every one, friend and foe, it was a balanced budget. Following British practice, the budget in India and Pakistan was divided into a revenue budget and a capital budget.

For the seven and a half months, from August 15, 1947, to March 31, 1948, there had been a deficit; but the circumstances of that period were altogether exceptional. The establishment of a new administration and the vast influx of refugees had thrown a heavy financial burden on the government. The disruption of communications and trade had brought business activity and revenue receipts to a low level. Arrears of tax left behind by evacuees could not be recovered. The standstill arrangement with India under which each Dominion received only the revenue collected in its own territory operated unfavorably for Pakistan. Taxes were collected at the head offices of firms, most of which were located in India. Central excise duties were levied at points of manufacture, and India refused to give rebates of duty on excisable commodities exported to Pakistan.

The first budget presented for a full year was that for 1948–49; and it was balanced. In order to achieve this result, certain adjustments had to be made in the scheme of federal finance inherited from undivided India. The railway budget was included in the central budget. The North Western Railway, even after allowing for the loss from strategic lines in the North-West Frontier Province, was running at a substantial surplus while the East Bengal Railway showed a loss. The combined result, after making provision for depreciation, was a net surplus which was used in support of general revenues. After consultation with the provinces, sales tax, which was a provincial source of revenue under the Government of India Act, 1935, was temporarily taken over by the central government on the understanding that the provinces would be paid from the proceeds what they would have otherwise collected. The rest of the prepartition scheme of federal finance remained in force. Under the Niemeyer award of 1936, jute-growing provinces were entitled to 62.5 percent of the export duty on jute, and the central government had given an annual subvention of Rs. 10 million to the North-West Frontier Province. These payments continued to be made.

On the side of expenditure, there was a provision of Rs. 371 mil-

lion for defense services and Rs. 83 million on defense capital outlay. Economic development was not neglected. Apart from a capital
outlay of Rs. 100 million on railways, posts and telegraphs, and other
projects of the central government, provision was made for grants of
Rs. 15 million to provincial governments for development in addition
to loans of Rs. 120 million. This was not much, but a beginning had
been made. In subsequent years, as the revenue position improved,
far bigger amounts were allocated for development.

The provincial governments also managed to live within their
means, but not without serious difficulty. East Bengal had to establish
a new administration and a new capital in Dacca, and had thus to
incur extraordinary expenditures. Although East Bengal had double
the population of West Bengal, its revenue was only half that of West
Bengal at the time of partition. This was an inevitable consequence of
the loss of Calcutta and other industrially developed areas. To make
matters worse, East Bengal's share in the joint assets was not received from West Bengal. The Government of India also refused to
pay, on one pretext or another, the large sum of Rs. 120 million, due
for lands and buildings requisitioned during the Second World War.
All in all, East Pakistan faced very considerable financial difficulties.
The economy of West Punjab was shattered by the vast scale of the
disturbances and the mass exchange of population. Agriculture,
trade, industry, communications, in short every aspect of economic
life had suffered and had to be revived. Millions of refugees had to be
rehabilitated. Nevertheless, the recovery was remarkably rapid. Of all
the provinces, the position of Sind was the most comfortable. It had
ample resources in land and water in relation to its population. Large
areas had been brought under irrigation by the Sukkur barrage. Another barrage at Kotri on the lower Indus was nearing completion.

The overall position was that the provinces could maintain the existing administration, but they had insufficient means for nation-
building activities and felt that the revenue distribution between the
central government and the provincial governments needed to be
reappraised and revised. Such an appraisal was carried out in the winter of 1951–52 by Sir Jeremy Raisman, former Finance Member of
the Viceroy's Executive Council in undivided India, and his recommendations were accepted.

The first budget of Pakistan had a significance far greater than its
merely financial aspect. It showed that the Pakistan government had

sufficient resources to provide not only for the civil administration but also for defense and development. The dismal prophecies of its opponents were proved wrong. Pakistan was viable. The faith of the people in the economic stability of Pakistan was strengthened. In a speech on April 1, 1948, the Quaid-i-Azam said:

> When we first raised our demand for a sovereign and independent State of Pakistan there were not a few false prophets who tried to deflect us from our set purpose by saying that Pakistan was not economically feasible. . . . The very first budget must have caused a shock to those false prophets. It has already demonstrated the soundness of Pakistan's finances and the determination of its Government to make them more and more sound and strong.[3]

There was still another step which gave satisfaction and confidence to the nation. This was the opening of the State Bank of Pakistan on July 1, 1948. During the days of partition, I had pressed for the establishment of our own Central Bank and Monetary Authority at the earliest possible date, for, without it, we would be hampered in pursuing an independent policy. Ghulam Muhammad, the Finance Minister-designate, however, thought it more prudent to let the Reserve Bank of India manage our monetary affairs for about a year. Zahid Husain, a financial expert of great experience, was the obvious choice for Governor of the State Bank, but, in view of the decision to entrust the Reserve Bank of India with operations in Pakistan till October 1, 1948, he was temporarily appointed High Commissioner for Pakistan in India. When in December, 1947, under instructions from the Government of India, the Reserve Bank of India withheld Pakistan's agreed share of cash balances, the need for an early take-over became obvious, and the date was advanced by three months.

The State Bank of Pakistan was established on July 1, 1948, with a capital of Rs. 30 million, of which 51 percent was subscribed by the central government and the rest by the public. A Central Board of Directors, partly nominated by the government and partly elected by private shareholders is responsible for general direction and supervision. There are local boards at each of the three centers, in Karachi, Dacca, and Lahore.

In undivided India, banking had been a closed field reserved for non-Muslims, and only a few Muslims were trained in this profession. The difficulties which every department and institution in Pakistan faced from shortage of experienced personnel, confronted the State

Bank in an even greater measure. There was very little time for completing all the preliminaries. But under the able leadership of Zahid Husain, the Bank started functioning on the due date.

The opening ceremony on July 1, 1948, was performed by the Quaid-i-Azam, who defied ill-health to come down from Quetta to the heat of Karachi specially for this function. The occasion was made still more memorable by the fact that it was the last public appearance of the Quaid-i-Azam. "The opening of the State Bank of Pakistan," he said, "symbolizes the sovereignty of our State in the financial sphere." And he concluded his speech with some observations which show the deep concern he felt over the social and economic ills from which the world was suffering, and the direction in which a remedy was to be sought:

> The economic system of the West has created almost insoluble problems for humanity and to many of us it appears that only a miracle can save it from the disaster that is now facing the world. . . . The adoption of Western economic theory and practice will not help us in achieving our goal of creating a happy and contented people. We must work our destiny in our own way and present to the world an economic system based on true Islamic concepts of equality of manhood and social justice.[4]

Among the first tasks of the State Bank was the replacement of prepartition currency. From April 1, 1948, Indian notes superscribed with the words "Government of Pakistan" had been in circulation. These were gradually replaced by Pakistan notes. The Security Printing Corporation was set up in Karachi, by agreement with the British firm of Thomas De La Rue, for the production of currency notes and other security documents.

The main function of the State Bank was to ensure monetary stability and to promote the growth of the monetary and credit systems in the best national interest. In undivided India, banking had been a virtual monopoly of Hindus. During the partition days (from June 3 to August 15, 1947) most Hindu-managed banks transferred their headquarters and funds from Pakistan to India. The Punjab disturbances completed the process. Of 487 offices of scheduled banks in West Pakistan, only 69 were left after partition.[5] Only one bank —the Muslim-owned Habib Bank—moved its headquarters from India to Pakistan. Credit facilities were thus greatly curtailed and a special effort was needed in this field.

The State Bank was also entrusted with the control of foreign exchange and the management of the public debt. In view of the rudimentary state of the money market, it was decided to canalize all government borrowing through the central government, including loans to the provincial governments for their development projects. A series of loans were floated in 1948 and met with an enthusiastic response from the public. The total subscriptions during the year amounted to Rs. 705 million, which, considering the economic conditions in the country at that time, was a very remarkable result. It was another manifestation of the determination of all classes of people to build Pakistan into a strong modern state.

The foreign exchange position was comfortable. There was a good market for the commodities produced by Pakistan. In addition to current earnings, there was Pakistan's share of sterling balances accumulated during the Second World War, which amounted to £147 million. Releases from this blocked account for current spending were negotiated from time to time. The major exports were, on the average, 6 million bales of raw jute and 1.6 million bales of cotton per year. Jute contributed approximately half of the total export earnings and cotton about a third. The contribution of cotton rose to 47 percent during boom resulting from the Korean war, but declined substantially after the development of the domestic textile industry. Next in importance was the group of minor exports, tea, raw wool, and hides and skins. The principal imports were cotton cloth and yarn, machinery, vehicles, metals, oil, chemicals, and medicines.

The pattern of trade was that inherited from preindependence times. India was the chief purchaser of raw jute. On the import side, purchases from the United Kingdom led the rest. This was partly the result of Imperial preferences, under which British manufactured goods, including textiles and steel, were admitted at preferred rates of duty, and partly the effect of the long British connection with the subcontinent. There was a persistent trade deficit with the United Kingdom, which sold more to Pakistan than it purchased.

It was necessary to change this lopsided pattern in favor of a more balanced and diversified one, so that the economic fortunes of Pakistan were not tied to those of one or two countries. In pursuance of this policy, trade agreements were negotiated with a number of countries. These agreements laid down targets for mutual purchases which, although they were not invariably lived up to, served a useful purpose in opening up new avenues of trade and gave greater freedom and independence in the framing of policies.

A severe test of Pakistan's economic independence came in September, 1949, when the United Kingdom decided to devalue the sterling by nearly 30 percent. Both India and Pakistan were members of the sterling area. India followed the United Kingdom and devalued the Indian rupee. Pakistan decided not to devalue the Pakistan rupee. Pakistan's exports at this time consisted almost entirely of raw materials that found a ready market in the world at reasonable prices. Devaluation would not have promoted exports but would have raised the internal level of prices. When nine months later, fighting in Korea broke out and commodity prices soared, heavy export duties had to be levied on raw cotton and jute to avoid an inflationary rise in prices inside the country. On the other hand, devaluation would have raised the rupee prices of capital goods from outside the sterling area, and to that extent would have made industrialization more difficult. As against this, a decision not to devalue the Pakistan rupee would undoubtedly stimulate imports from the United Kingdom and the rest of the sterling area; and since a policy of free imports on open general license was being followed at this time, the market would be flooded with consumer goods from abroad. Such a state would hardly be conducive to the setting up of new industries.

Ghulam Muhammad, the Finance Minister, who happened to be away from Pakistan at this juncture sent a lengthy telegram to the Prime Minister strongly urging devaluation *pari passu* with the sterling. Fazlur Rahman, the Commerce Minister, however, insisted even more strongly that there should be no devaluation. There were lengthy debates in the cabinet. Zahid Husain, the Governor of the State Bank, was sent for to advise the cabinet. On the whole, he was in favor of devaluation but the advantages and disadvantages of either course of action appeared to him to be fairly evenly balanced. I was of the opinion that a devaluation was needed, not to stimulate exports—since these mainly consisted of primary commodities—but to stem the inflow of consumer goods; and for that purpose a partial devaluation, not so steep as that of sterling, would be enough. The situation might have been met by import restrictions, but the cabinet at this time was intent on maintaining a policy of open general license. After thoroughly discussing every aspect of the question for two days the cabinet finally decided not to devalue the Pakistan rupee. An important element in the final decision was the feeling that it would enhance Pakistan's prestige.

The decision to maintain the value of the Pakistan rupee was made after a careful weighing of pros and cons in the light of Pakistan's interests. It startled the world by its demonstration of Pakistan's economic strength and independence of judgment. The Indians were not only startled but felt humiliated into the bargain; they had to accept that 100 Pakistan rupees were worth 144 Indian rupees. Alone of all the countries of the world, India refused to recognize Pakistan's decision and started a trade war.

The jute crop was being harvested at this time. India which had 60 percent of the world jute loomage was the main purchaser. And Calcutta, with its many baling presses was the principal port for the export of raw jute from East Pakistan to outside markets. The Marwaris, who handled most of the trade, were Indian citizens with headquarters in Calcutta. Banking facilities for providing credit to the trade were also concentrated in Calcutta. So confident were the Indians of the strength of their position in regard to jute, that the leader of an Indian delegation remarked to me, during the course of negotiations for a trade agreement between the two countries: "What can you do with your jute except sell it to us? Burn it? Throw it into the Bay of Bengal?"

Now, suddenly, Pakistan was faced with a grave crisis. India's refusal to buy jute, and its blocking of the export and banking facilities of Calcutta meant a disastrous fall in jute prices and financial ruin for millions of farmers in East Pakistan. I accompanied the Prime Minister to East Pakistan where a number of emergency measures were taken. An ordinance was issued "to safeguard international trade in jute." Under it the central government could fix minimum support prices and appoint agents and brokers to purchase, store, and sell jute on its behalf. A Jute Board was formed to carry out these functions. Minimum prices for loose jute were announced. Agents were appointed throughout East Pakistan to buy at the minimum prices and Pakistanis were encouraged to enter the jute trade. To provide credit facilities it was decided to set up the National Bank of Pakistan. More orders were placed for modern baling presses. Work on the development of Chittagong port and the establishment of Chalna anchorage was accelerated. These vigorous measures, and the enthusiastic support of the people for government policies, enabled Pakistan to overcome the crisis created by India's hostile response to Pakistan's decision not to devalue its rupee. Ultimately, India realized the futility of its action and recognized the Pakistan rate of exchange in February, 1951. This rate of exchange was maintained till the middle of 1955. Imports of consumer goods were severely curtailed from 1952 onward, when the policy of open general licenses was belatedly abandoned. An intense drive was made for building up industries based on Pakistan's raw materials, particularly cotton and jute. When Pakistan's manufactured goods were ready for the world markets, devaluation was carried out in order to facilitate their export. An earlier devaluation would have served no purpose since it would have hampered the import of capital goods and made no difference to the offtake of primary commodities which were at that time Pakistan's main exports.

During the period 1947–48 the country was still suffering from the inflationary effects of the Second World War. Price controls with all their attendant evils of black-marketing and profiteering were in force. The production of food had suffered a decline following the dislocation caused by disturbances and migration. The availability of goods required from abroad for capital projects or essential consumer needs was limited. Measures had to be taken to offset the effect of these forces that were raising the general price level and the cost of living. Gradually the situation improved and prices were stabilized. The ground was prepared for economic growth. Pakistan had to win the right to exist before it could plan to develop. There was then no program of foreign aid and Pakistan had to rely on its own efforts. Even the extremely modest Point Four program of technical assistance announced by President Truman, and the Colombo Plan evolved by the Commonwealth, lie outside the period with which we are dealing. The record during the first years of Pakistan is thus one of severe handicaps and difficulties successfully overcome, and of financial and economic stability gained by courage, determination, and resourcefulness.

CHAPTER 17

Administrative and Political
Problems of the New State

THE BIGGEST administrative problem facing Pakistan was the shortage of competent and experienced personnel in the central and provincial governments. There were serious deficiencies in the cadres of general administrators as well as in the technical services. The administrative set-up inherited from prepartition days consisted of a number of classes: Superior and Class I Services filled the higher appointments; Class II were the junior executives; Class III, ministerial clerks; and Class IV, messengers and orderlies. The Indian Civil Service was the "steel frame" which empowered its administrators to maintain law and order, collect land revenue in the districts, and shape the government policies in the central and provincial secretariats. This was general service par excellence. Other services, such as the Indian Police Service, the Indian Audit and Accounts Service, and the Indian Service of Engineers, had specialized functions.

In Pakistan, the main structure of the services was preserved intact, together with the existing conditions of service, in keeping with the promise made at the time of partition to those who opted for the service of Pakistan. But significant modifications were made to suit conditions in Pakistan.

The Indian Civil Service was divided into a number of provincial cadres. Each officer was assigned to one province or the other where he spent all his service except for possible deputation to the central government for limited periods. The provincial cadres consisted for the most part of British officers; and since they had a fundamental unity of outlook, their allegiance to separate provinces did not affect the unity of the administrative structure in British India. With more than 15 major languages in India, it was in fact impossible for any British officer to master them all and thus be able to serve in any province of India.

With the establishment of Pakistan, the position was basically altered. The Civil Service of Pakistan, which replaced the Indian Civil Service, would now consist only of Pakistanis, and if they were to serve only in their own province, provincial loyalties might in the long run prevail over a national outlook. On my recommendation (in my capacity as Secretary-General) the central government decided to amalgamate the various provincial cadres into a single cadre that would meet the needs of the provinces and of the nation as a whole. An academy for the training of young civil service officers was set up at my instance. This was an innovation, for there had been no such institution for civil service probationers in prepartition India. Every officer was required to learn both Urdu and Bengali; his training was to be conducted in both East and West Pakistan; and he was to divide the first ten years of his service equally between East and West Pakistan. By these means an understanding of social and economic conditions in both wings of the country would be gained, friendships would be formed between East and West Pakistanis, and when, at a later stage in their careers, these officers would move to the central government, they would know the administrative problems of the whole country and be equipped to handle them. National unity would thus be forged through administrative integration. Partly to broaden the base of the Civil Service of Pakistan and partly to overcome shortages, a number of military officers and provincial service officers were appointed to it. This was also a departure from the previous rule according to which officers of the provincial civil service could be appointed to a specified list of posts, but could never be promoted to become members of the Indian Civil Service.

The decision to break up the provincial cadres and form a unified service was not reached without strong resistance from the conservative members of the Civil Service of Pakistan. There had also been passionate opposition to the suggestion that provincial civil service officers be promoted into the Civil Service of Pakistan. But the advantages of the new arrangement for Pakistan were so great that, finally, I was able to persuade them to agree to the change.

A few officers of the Indian Political Service (which was composed of officers drawn from the Indian Civil Service and from the Indian army for service in the Indian states and frontier areas) had opted for Pakistan. They were incorporated into the Civil Service of Pakistan. It was considered unnecessary to retain a separate political service for such a very small cadre. The specialized experience needed for frontier areas could well be gained by officers of the Civil Service of Pakistan in the course of their normal career.

I was of the view that the Pakistan Police Service also should be organized into a single national cadre. The reasons for amalgamating the provincial cadres into the Civil Service of Pakistan applied with equal force here. But during one of my absences as delegate to the United Nations it was decided to retain provincial cadres in the police service. The unfortunate effects of the decision were seen later when the central government found it had neither sufficient communication with nor adequate control over the operations of the provincial police force. The proposal to form a federal police force could not be accepted, on the grounds of expense, overlapping of functions, and likely friction with provincial authorities.

Again, at my instance all the accounts services—previously known as Indian Audit and Accounts Service, Military Accounts Service, and the Railway Accounts Service—were merged into a single Pakistan Accounts Service. The work of all these services was similar in nature, although different in detail. In a united service each officer would have a much larger range of experience. The number of officers in each service was not large, and many difficulties arise when working with small cadres. There may be unexpectedly rapid promotion followed by long periods of stagnation. However, this reform also met with strong internal resistance and after some time of experimenting with the new system, it was given up.

In the filling of higher appointments in the secretariat, a more elastic policy was followed than in undivided India, where higher appointments had been given only to Indian Civil Service officers. The only exception was a "pool" of higher appointments in the Finance and Commerce departments, which required expert knowledge. The Finance and Commerce "pool" was formed shortly before the Second World War and was filled with specially selected officers from the Indian Civil Service, the Indian Audit and Accounts Service, the Military Accounts Service, the Indian Customs Service, and the Income Tax Service. A similar "pool" was formed in the Pakistan government also. But apart from this specialized cadre, it was considered to be in the national interest to make use of talent wherever it was available. Suitable officers from services other than the Civil Service of Pakistan were, therefore, appointed to top posts. I, the Secretary-General, belonged to the audit and accounts service. An officer of the police service was appointed Secretary to the Ministry of the Interior, and so on.

There were severe shortages of administrators of middle rank in the secretariat. To remedy this deficiency, a general administrative reserve was formed. This was intended to be a temporary arrangement to tide over the first ten or twelve years until normal recruitment to the permanent services would have reached a level sufficient for filling all vacancies. The general administrative reserve was filled partly by promotion from the ministerial establishment of the secretariat and partly by recruitment through the public services commission from the open market. Those who proved themselves competent would have a chance of permanent absorption into one of the regular services. However, as often happens in expanding bureaucracies, temporary arrangements continue indefinitely.

An altogether new service, the Pakistan Foreign Service, had to be created for carrying out diplomatic and consular functions. In this field there was little experience among Pakistani officers. Ikramullah, a senior officer in the Civil Service of Pakistan was appointed Foreign Secretary; and he, with a handful of officers, some from the existing services and others newly recruited, strove bravely to set up the Foreign Office and to meet the ever increasing demands for diplomatic missions to be sent abroad.

The demands for administrators, from the provinces and the various ministries of the central government, were far greater than the available supply of officers with requisite experience. And as new and grave problems, like refugee rehabilitation and Kashmir and canal waters, continued to arise, the task of finding men to deal with them became harder and harder. An equitable distribution was the best that could be attempted, but this was far from easy when every ministry and department clung desperately to the few competent officers it had. An administrative collapse anywhere would have been disastrous. It was my responsibility as Secretary-General to keep every front supplied as well as I could and to maintain its morale. Notwithstanding these pressures, the easy and unreal solution of making unduly rapid promotions was avoided. Even when promotion to a higher grade was made, the full pay of the appointment was not given until the officer had completed a specified number of years of service. These and other measures for maintaining administrative standards were on the whole accepted in good spirit by the officers who at that time were filled with a patriotic fervor to build up Pakistan.

In February, 1948, the Pakistan government appointed a pay commission, presided over by Justice Muhammad Munir, to report on "the scales of pay and allowances and the standards of remuneration which should apply in Pakistan, keeping in view its financial resources and with the object of achieving rationalisation, simplification and uniformity therein in regard to services," for both the central and provincial governments.

At the time of partition two systems of pay scales existed. Those who had entered service before July 1, 1931, continued to draw pay on the old scale; new entrants recruited after this date received revised and substantially lower pay. This revision had been necessary because of the financial stringency that followed the great depression and was justified by the fall in prices and cost of living in the thirties. After the outbreak of the Second World War the general price index began a steep rise until, by the end of the war, it was more than three times as high. The fall in the purchasing power of the rupee brought acute distress to government servants with fixed incomes, particularly to those who received lower salaries. Cost-of-living allowances only partly alleviated the hardship: a systematic investigation was called for. A pay commission was appointed, and it submitted its report on April 30, 1947. After partition the question arose whether the recommendations made by the Indian pay commission to the undivided Government of India should be accepted by the Pakistan government. The financial circumstances of Pakistan were not the same as those of undivided India or even those of the Indian

Union. The grave disturbances and the vast population movement that immediately followed partition had placed a severe strain on the economy. But this was a transient phase that darkened the perspective; the time was not yet ripe for taking stock of long-range factors and visualizing the future shape of the economy.

Ghulam Muhammad, the Finance Minister, was a conservative financier and a strong believer in private enterprise. He was firmly possessed with the idea of a balanced budget and was ruthless in keeping down expenditure. At his instance there had been an appeal for a voluntary cut in salaries to which there had been a good response. Now, instead of finding a temporary or *ad hoc* solution to the problem posed by the findings of the Indian pay commission, he persuaded the cabinet to appoint a new pay commission. As the commission itself recognized, "We find ourselves engaged in an attempt to discharge our duty at a time when the only thing we can be sure of is that the whole thing, except that Pakistan has come to stay on the world map as an important State, is uncertain."

The appointment of the commission was a mistake. The circumstances under which it was appointed gave rise to a general impression that it had been commissioned merely to cut down salaries. It put avoidable work on departments which were already overburdened. It started with a bias imbibed from Ghulam Muhammad that public services need not be well paid since men with brains and energy were needed in trade and industry. The truth of the matter is that, in an underdeveloped country, it is impossible to achieve a high rate of economic growth except through a comprehensive plan, and this needs the best available administrative talent to produce and operate it. Only within such a framework can private enterprise function to the best advantage of the country.

I learned of the commission's views and advised the Prime Minister to send for its Chairman and put the problem in a balanced perspective. This was not simply a financial matter but one involving the purity, quality, and efficiency of public administration. Justice Muhammad Munir reported his conversation with the Prime Minister to Ghulam Muhammad who at once came to the conclusion that I had tried to interfere in his domain. The upshot of it all was that Ghulam Muhammad felt aggrieved and the pay commission stated flatly in their report that they "did not think it to be a right policy for the State to offer such salaries to its servants as to attract the best available talent. The correct place for our men of genius is in private enterprise and not in the humdrum career of public service where character and a desire to serve honestly for a living is more essential than outstanding intellect." One could hardly help wishing that the commission had the imagination to say instead that "the correct place for our men of genius is in our universities and research institutions." Instead of simplifying and rationalizing the pay structure, the commission's report left it still more complicated. The cabinet had to improve on the rather niggardly recommendations of the commission.

In the provinces, the severest shortages in personnel were to be found in East Bengal. East Pakistan had, at the time of independence, only one officer in the Indian Civil Service, a few in the Indian Police, and fewer in the other Superior Services. The rest of the Muslim officers came partly from West Pakistan and partly from Muslim minority provinces. Though Muslims from the minority provinces of India had an equal right to move to East or to West Pakistan, most of them settled in West Pakistan and were readily accepted as part of the general population. Throughout the ages, West Pakistan has been the gateway of the subcontinent. People from outside have poured into it and been absorbed into this melting-pot of races and cultures. East Pakistan being at the far eastern end has been more sheltered and consequently more insular. East Pakistan thus looked upon everyone—official or businessman—who came from areas outside Bengal as a West Pakistani. Officers from West Pakistan and from the minority provinces of India were lumped together in a single category.

Fundamentally, the imbalance between East and West Pakistan in the public services stemmed from the discrimination exercised against Muslims in undivided Bengal in every sphere, including education. Calcutta University was a closely guarded preserve of the Hindus. Hindu teachers dominated schools and colleges. Discrimination against Bengal Muslims so handicapped them that they could not compete successfully in all-India examinations for the Superior Services.

This state of affairs had to be remedied as rapidly as practicable so that East Pakistan could play an equal and effective part in the administration of the country. In the first competitive examination held by the Pakistan public service commission for recruitment to the Superior Services, forty-odd candidates qualified from East Pakistan.

Although we did not need so many, I recommended to the Prime Minister that all of them, including those who had barely qualified, should be appointed so as to redress the balance as rapidly as possible. Thus, in the very first recruitment of civil services candidates in Pakistan the number of East Pakistani officers was several times greater than at any time before partition. For future recruitment the cabinet approved a plan whereby 20 percent would be taken on merit from the whole of Pakistan, and 40 percent each from East and West Pakistan. The West Pakistan quota was further subdivided between various provinces so that the educationally backward provinces could secure their due share of appointments. The system worked to the disadvantage of candidates from the Punjab, but was in the best national interest. The effects of this policy can only make themselves felt over a period of time; it is impossible to redress the neglect of a century in a few years. All this was well recognized. Yet, voices of discontent soon began to be raised against the preponderance of West Pakistanis in the central government, and the entire blame for the existing imbalance was laid at the door of the central government. This unjust accusation was repeated endlessly until it became an article of faith with many in East Pakistan.

Another set of grievances arose from the posting of officers from other provinces to East Pakistan. There was a serious shortage of experienced officers in every province and in the central government. The overriding necessity of the time was to get the administration going. Since East Pakistani officers were not available, others had to be sent there to take care of the provincial administration and services under the control of the central government, such as railways and customs. Many of them had never been to East Pakistan before and were not familiar with the language, manners, and susceptibilities of the people. To the normal failings of bureaucratic behavior was added, in some cases at least, an attitude of supercilious superiority. With tact and sympathetic understanding the strains and stresses of establishing a new administration could have been eased. But not everyone is blessed with these virtues. Soon grievances multiplied and some people went so far as to suggest that the behavior of West Pakistan officers was the main cause of estrangement between East and West Pakistan. Though this is an exaggerated view, it has an element of truth in it.

The geographical separation of East and West Pakistan produced not only administrative but social, economic, and political problems as well. Distance made communication fitful and expensive. Misunderstandings arose easily and were difficult to dispel. Since the capital was in West Pakistan, East Pakistan felt neglected. The differences in language and background put obstacles in the way of national integration. Within West Pakistan there were a number of provinces and states, and four linguistic regions. The powerful binding forces of Islam—a common ideology, a common history as a single community in the Indo-Pakistan subcontinent, a common struggle for independence from British rule and Hindu domination, a common fear of Hindu designs, and the instinctive sense of a common destiny—had created a state of unique structure. The foreigner might feel entitled to doubt if these forces would successfully withstand the strains and stresses inherent in that structure. The nation in the first flush of independence won by unity, faith, and discipline felt certain of enduring as a single entity.

In a broadcast talk to the people of Australia, on February 19, 1948, the Quaid-i-Azam said:

> West Pakistan is separated from East Pakistan by about a thousand miles of the territory of India. The first question a student from abroad should ask himself is—how can this be? How can there be unity of government between areas so widely separated? I can answer this question in one word. It is "faith"; faith in Almighty God, in ourselves and in our destiny.[1]

A month later, he made an impassioned appeal for national consolidation. In a public speech in Dacca, East Pakistan, on March 21, 1948, he said:

> Let me warn you in the clearest terms of the dangers that still face Pakistan and your province in particular as I have done already. Having failed to prevent the establishment of Pakistan, thwarted and frustrated by their failure, the enemies of Pakistan have now turned their attention to disrupt the State by creating a split amongst the Muslims of Pakistan. These attempts have taken the shape principally of encouraging provincialism. As long as you do not throw off this poison in our body politic, you will never be able to weld yourself, mould yourself, galvanise yourself into a real true nation. . . . Islam has taught us this, and I think you will agree with me that whatever else you may be and whatever you are, you are a Muslim. You belong to a Nation now; you have now carved out a territory, vast territory, it is all yours; it does not belong to a Punjabi or a Sindhi, or a Pathan, or a Bengali; it is yours. You have

got your Central Government where several units are represented. Therefore, if you want to build up yourself into a Nation, for God's sake give up this provincialism.[2]

One sees clearly here the struggle between two forces: one making for unity, the other for disruption. It was the task of practical statesmanship to forge instruments of unity in every sphere of social and political action. The effort would, in the very nature of things, have to be a continuing one.

The background to the Quaid-i-Azam's warning against provincialism was provided by the language controversy that raised its head in East Bengal only a few months after the establishment of Pakistan. In spite of failing health, the Quaid-i-Azam undertook an arduous journey to East Pakistan in March, 1948 to still the controversy. During the Pakistan movement it had been universally accepted that Urdu would be the national language of Pakistan, and declarations to this effect had often been made. Urdu was the lingua franca of the Muslims of the subcontinent and the symbol of their unity. Differences between Muslims and Hindus over the language question have been noted earlier. These differences played a large part in shaping the demand for Pakistan. Urdu was not the mother tongue of the people in any of the provinces and states of Pakistan, East or West, but it enjoyed everywhere a unique position as the national language of the Muslims. It was never suggested that Urdu should replace any provincial language, least of all Bengali, which is a highly developed language with a fine literature.

The agitation against Urdu as the sole national language was started by a small group of politicians in East Pakistan, mainly to embarrass the Nazimuddin ministry; but it was soon taken up by the students. The powerful Hindu press of Calcutta fanned the flames of the controversy. In February, 1948, when the Pakistan constituent assembly was considering its rules of procedure, Dhirendra Nath Dutta, a member of the Congress party, moved an amendment that the proceedings of the assembly should be kept not merely in Urdu and English but also in Bengali, and suggested that the language spoken by the majority of people should become the state language. In a speech at the Dacca University convocation of March 24, 1948, the Quaid-i-Azam said:

> Is it not significant that the very persons who in the past have betrayed the Musalmans or fought against Pakistan, which is after all

merely the embodiment of your fundamental right of self-determination, should now suddenly pose as the saviours of your "just rights" and incite you to defy the Government on the question of language? I must warn you to beware of these fifth columnists. Let me restate my views on the question of a State language for Pakistan. For official use in this province, the people of the province can choose any language they wish. This question will be decided solely in accordance with the wishes of the people of this province alone, as freely expressed through their accredited representatives at the appropriate time and after full and dispassionate consideration. There can, however, be only one lingua franca, that is, the language for inter-communication between the various provinces of the State, and that language should be Urdu and cannot be any other. The State language, therefore, must obviously be Urdu, a language that has been nurtured by a hundred million Muslims of this subcontinent, a language understood throughout the length and breadth of Pakistan and above all, a language which, more than any other provincial language, embodies the best that is in Islamic culture and Muslim tradition and is nearest to the language used in other Islamic countries. It is not without significance that Urdu has been driven out of the Indian Union and that even the official use of the Urdu script has been disallowed.[3]

The tremendous weight of the Quaid-i-Azam's authority suppressed the agitation for the time being, but the issue remained alive. Some years later it assumed formidable proportions. Finally, the controversy was settled when the 1956 constitution recognized both Urdu and Bengali as the national languages of Pakistan.

But, as the Quaid-i-Azam said in his farewell message to East Pakistan on March 28,

This language controversy is really one aspect of a bigger problem —that of provincialism. I am sure you must realize that in a newly-formed State like Pakistan, consisting moreover as it does of two widely separated parts, cohesion and solidarity amongst all its citizens, from whatever part they may come, is essential for its progress, nay for its very survival. Pakistan is the embodiment of the unity of the Muslim nation and so it must remain. That unity we, as true Muslims, must jealously guard and preserve. If we begin to think of ourselves as Bengalis, Punjabis, Sindhis, etc., first and Muslims and Pakistanis only incidentally, then Pakistan is bound to disintegrate. Do not think that this is some abstruse proposition: our enemies are fully alive to its possibilities which I must warn you they are already busy exploiting.[4]

Another disease infecting the political life of Pakistan was factionalism; and this was at its worst in the Punjab. In the months following partition, the Punjab was threatened with one mortal peril after another. The rivers of blood flowing in East Punjab, the flood of refugees, the war across its borders in Kashmir, the devastation resulting from the closure of canals by India—all of these followed in rapid succession. But in the midst of these perils, the Punjab cabinet, instead of working as a united team, presented a spectacle of petty squabbles, sordid intrigues, and all the other accompaniments of an internecine war between factions. The highly ambitious Finance Minister, Mumtaz Daultana, was ranged against the slow and easy-going Chief Minister, the Khan of Mamdot. The Muslim League party in the legislature was split. High officials started taking sides. In April, 1948, the Quaid-i-Azam summoned Mamdot, Daultana, and Shaukat Hayat Khan, the Revenue Minister, to Karachi to sort out the ministerial tangle, but even he threw up his hands in disgust. Soon afterward Daultana and Shaukat Hayat Khan resigned and Mamdot formed his second ministry. After the Quaid-i-Azam's death, when there was a sense of national emergency, a move was made by the central government to bring about unity in the Punjab. Mamdot agreed to include Daultana and Feroze Khan Noon in the cabinet, but before they could be sworn in, a fresh dispute broke out. The quarrel was intensified when, in November, Daultana was elected President of the West Punjab provincial Muslim League. Finally, in the beginning of 1949, the ministry was dismissed; the Punjab legislative assembly was dissolved; and Governor's rule was imposed under section 92-A of the adapted Government of India Act, 1935. The communiqué issued by the central government stated:

> Public life has been demoralized by corruption and the discipline of the services destroyed by intrigue. The administration has been carried on for the benefit of the few and little or no heed has been paid to the hopes and needs of the people. Many causes have contributed to this state of affairs, but in the Governor-General's opinion the main cause is the failure of the Members of the Legislative Assembly elected in different circumstances to rise to the greater responsibility which Independence brings.

This was the first occasion on which normal constitutional processes had to be suspended in Pakistan.

In the North-West Frontier Province, Chief Minister Abdul Qayyum Khan had to face a difficult situation because of the opposition of Abdul Ghaffar Khan and his die-hard Red Shirt followers. After the arrest of Abdul Ghaffar Khan, the provincial government received reports that the Red Shirts were planning a civil disobedience movement in August, 1948. A large number collected at

Charsadda and there was a violent clash with the police in which some people were killed. Subsequently, however, peace was maintained. In the provincial assembly which had been elected in 1946, the Muslim League was in a minority, but public feeling in the province had since then undergone a profound change as was shown by the results of the referendum on the Pakistan question in July, 1947. In response to the state of public opinion, a number of legislators who had been aligned with the Congress in the past joined the Muslim League, and it became the majority party in the assembly.

Abdul Qayyum Khan's real trouble, however, lay outside the assembly. His autocratic ways and intolerance of any opposition alienated a number of Muslim League leaders, in particular, the influential Pir of Manki, who had rendered outstanding services in the referendum for Pakistan. The result was that the Pir of Manki and others were driven out of the Muslim League. In April, 1948, the Quaid-i-Azam toured the North-West Frontier Province. In a public speech in Peshawar, on April 20, he warned the people of a grave national emergency that existed both internally and externally, and adjured them "to avoid domestic controversies and provincialism." He continued:

> I know we have got men who are guilty of jobbery, bribery and nepotism. I do not say that the Government is perfect. Believe me, we are wide awake; we are watching your Government, your province, your ministry and your civil services. It is under our searchlight and there is no doubt we shall soon be able to X-ray it and throw out the poison from our body-politic. But you must have patience and give us a chance and a reasonable time.[5]

Before partition, Sind had been notorious for political instability produced by the shifting combinations of a number of groups. At the time of partition a Muslim League ministry under Muhammad Ayub Khuhro was firmly in the saddle. The Chief Minister was not, however, on good terms with the Governor, Ghulam Hussain Hidayatullah. In the beginning of April 1948, a public controversy started between Khuhro and two of his ministers, Pir Ilahi Bakhsh and Mir Ghulam Ali Talpur. Charges and countercharges appeared in the press. The Governor reallocated portfolios in the hope that this would lead to a more harmonious working of the cabinet, but Khuhro regarded this as undue interference by the Governor. The matter was reported to the Quaid-i-Azam. The Governor placed before him evidence of maladministration and corruption on the part of Khuhro.

Under the direction of the Quaid-i-Azam, who was determined to root out such evils in Pakistan, the Governor dismissed the Chief Minister on April 26, 1948, although he had the support of a majority of the Sind assembly. This action was taken under section 51 of the adapted Government of India Act, 1935. This section provided that the Governor's ministers "shall hold office during his pleasure," and that in the exercise of his functions under this section the Governor "shall be under the general control of, and comply with such particular directions, if any, as may from time to time be given to him by the Governor-General." The communiqué issued by the Governor stated that a prime facie case had been made out against Khuhro on charges of maladministration, gross misconduct in the discharge of his duty, and corruption. A judicial tribunal consisting of Justice Abdur Rashid, Chief Justice of the Lahore High Court, and Justice Shahabuddin of the Dacca High Court was constituted to try Khuhro on 62 charges. The tribunal found him guilty on a number of charges. But the curious position was that Khuhro was still the leader of the Muslim League party ruling in Sind and wielded great influence over the members of the Sind assembly. In December, 1948, while he was still being tried, he was formally elected President of the Sind Muslim League, although he decided to stand aside until the verdict of the tribunal was known. He had lost the responsibility of public office but not political power.

To deal with this anomalous situation, the constituent assembly passed, in 1949, the Public and Representative Offices (Disqualification) Act, or PARODA. The Act provided that any person found guilty of misconduct in any matter relating to his office as minister, deputy minister, or parliamentary secretary of the federal or provincial government, or as a member of the central or provincial legislature, might be disqualified from holding any public office for a period not exceeding ten years by an order of the Governor-General. "Misconduct" included bribery, corruption, nepotism, willful maladministration, and similar other offenses. The tribunal appointed to try cases under this Act was to consist of two or more High Court judges. The Governor-General was to exercise his powers under this Act not on the advice of the cabinet but in his personal judgment. Khuhro was disqualified under this Act for a period of two years by the Governor-General Khwaja Nazimuddin, although the Governor of Sind, Sheikh Din Muhammad, had recommended disqualification for seven years.

Khuhro's successor was Pir Ilahi Bakhsh. Within six months he was in serious trouble. Toward the end of October, 1948, the editors of five Karachi dailies simultaneously published an indictment against him headed "Pir Ilahi Bakhsh must go." The charges were the familiar ones of jobbery and nepotism. To these was added the charge of protecting criminals, of which a specific instance was that of the Chief Minister's Hindu confidential assistant who was arrested on the point of escaping to India, allegedly with state documents. At a meeting in the Governor-General's house attended by the Prime Minister, the Governor of Sind, and me, it was decided that the Governor should conduct an enquiry into these allegations. At the same time, there was a case against Pir Ilahi Bakhsh before the Sind election tribunal, which led to his disqualification. Pir Ilahi Bakhsh was followed by Yusuf Haroon. During these changes, Sind politics reverted to the old pattern of strife among the ministers and constantly shifting loyalties among the members of the assembly. Eventually the central government had to impose Governor's rule in Sind under section 92-A of the adapted Government of India Act, 1935.

In East Bengal, the difficulties encountered by Chief Minister Khwaja Nazimuddin from the activities of a small but active assembly group were considerably eased when at his request one of its prominent members was sent out as ambassador. When Khwaja Nazimuddin became Governor-General, in September, 1948, Nurul Amin succeeded him. During both regimes, East Pakistan maintained political stability. There was, however, a growing volume of opposition which played upon the people's sentiments by charges of neglect and stepmotherly treatment by the central government. A number of active political workers, including Maulana Bhashani who, as the President of the Assam Muslim League had campaigned vigorously for the success of the Sylhet referendum, joined the ranks of the opposition. Sensing a shift in the people's attitude, the provincial government fought shy of holding by-elections. This betrayed weakness and an inability to put the government's case before the people. There was a wholly inadequate appreciation of the staggering difficulties the central and provincial governments had to overcome in order to establish an administration and to stabilize the economy. The expectations of the people for a sudden transformation in the conditions of life after attaining independence could not possibly be fulfilled, but the disappointment would have been less acute if a true appraisal of the situation had been frankly and repeatedly put before them by the government. It was primarily the failure to establish public relations which (though understandable in the midst of the pressures of administrative work) had far-reaching effects on the political future of the country.

Suhrawardy, who found India inhospitable after Gandhi's assassination, returned to Pakistan to organize an opposition. At first he could make little headway, but as dissensions within the ruling party grew he was able to gather support. He joined hands with the Khan of Mamdot and Mian Abdul Bari, both former Presidents of the Punjab Muslim League, with Pir Manki Sharif in the North-West Frontier Province, and with Maulana Bhashani in East Bengal. All of them had rendered notable services in the cause of Pakistan, yet within a few years of the achievement of Pakistan they felt compelled to leave the Muslim League. Thus, within the space of a few years, the Muslim League was faced by an active opposition born from within itself.

These events threw into relief a structural weakness of the League. In the first thirty years of its life, the Muslim League had not been a mass organization. It voiced the aspirations of the Muslim intelligentsia, but was not actively at work among the masses. The pillars of society, the landlords, the well-to-do lawyers, the rich businessmen, and the titled gentry, were its main support. With some exceptions, they were not men noted for total commitment to any cause. Their willingness to sacrifice their personal interests or comfort for the sake of the nation was often in doubt, and not unjustly. They were, by and large, estimable men who served their country and their community within the limits dictated by discretion.

When the Quaid-i-Azam took the organization in hand in the middle thirties and started transforming it, its Hindu opponents and Muslim critics continued for a number of years to look down upon it as incapable of effective political action. But within a short period the character of the League had changed.

The striking successes that the Muslim League gained in the decade before partition were brought about by the political sagacity of the Quaid-i-Azam and the enthusiastic response to his leadership among the Muslim intelligentsia, the students, and the rising middle class, aided, of course, by the shortsighted folly and arrogance of Hindu leadership. Once the goal of Pakistan had been adopted by the Muslim League, it was not difficult for the middle classes to arouse the enthusiasm of the Muslim masses to whom the idea of an Islamic state with its just social order, its puritanical vigor, and its energy in looking after the interest of the common man has always had a profound appeal. The tradition of how the early Caliphs had nourished orphans and widows and had dealt out even-handed justice to high and low, the stern simplicity of their lives, and their ceaseless vigil over the welfare of the masses had passed into the common lore that was the heritage of every Muslim child. Despite the oppression and tyranny of intervening centuries, that distant ideal had not lost its force. The Muslim masses had never fully grasped the meaning of political safeguards in a united India. But a homeland for the Muslims in which an Islamic state could function was a simple and striking idea; it could be readily understood by the most ignorant and, by evoking memories of a heroic and just social order, could arouse mass enthusiasm as nothing else could. There was unison between the mass of the people, the middle classes who provided the bulk of the political workers, and the top leadership of the Quaid-i-Azam. For the first time in its history, the League was actively in touch with the Muslim masses, voiced their innermost aspirations, and drew its strength from them.

As public support for the idea of Pakistan gathered strength, Muslim politicians, who were in training under the British in the art of contesting elections and in capturing such crumbs of power as the British allowed to fall, turned more and more toward the Muslim League. They were shrewd and hard-headed men, capable of being infected temporarily by mass enthusiasm but never forgetful of their own advantage. As the decisive elections of 1946 drew near, they were the people who, for the most part, knew the electoral game and were, so to speak, the obvious candidates for the elections. The Quaid-i-Azam knew their quality, but he carried them along with him, and in that tide they were riding the wave of popular support. The masses also knew them for what they were, and looked to the Quaid-i-Azam to keep them disciplined. They, for their part, were mortally afraid of the Quaid-i-Azam, for they knew that their success in public life depended upon the trust he showed in them.

As long as Pakistan had not yet been established, the revolutionary mass movement led by the Quaid-i-Azam under the banner of the Muslim League was all that mattered. When Pakistan was achieved, the Quaid-i-Azam's attention was devoted almost wholly to the establishment of the state and the solution of the host of problems that rose thick and fast; he did not have enough time and energy to devote to the discipline and control of those politicians who needed it. If the social and economic objectives of the Pakistan movement had been kept more prominently before the leadership and the masses, the situation might have been different. However, with the establishment of Pakistan, some of the politicians felt free to revert to their old habits of a naked struggle for power through factions and cliques.

At the time of independence the All-India Muslim League, which had won Pakistan under the leadership of the Quaid-i-Azam, enjoyed universal support. It was the only political party of Muslims in Pakistan. The Congress party was confined to caste Hindus, and the Scheduled Caste Federation represented the Hindu Depressed Classes of East Pakistan. But Muslims, whether in East or West Pakistan, gave unstinted loyalty to the League. The small minorities of Christians, Buddhists, and Parsis also supported it.

On December 15, 1947, the All-India Muslim League meeting in Karachi resolved to split itself into two separate organizations, one for Pakistan and one for India. Although this decision came as a shock to the Muslims in India, who felt orphaned, it was an inevitable consequence of partition. The Pakistan Muslim League that came into existence was heir to the love and esteem in which the All-India Muslim League had been held. But from the very beginning it loosened its ties with the leadership that had made the All-India Muslim League so powerful and disciplined an organization. When the Council of the Pakistan Muslim League met in Karachi in February, 1948, to consider the constitution and rules of the League, an amendment to the draft constitution was moved and accepted, I was informed, against the wishes of the Quaid-i-Azam. The amendment provided that no minister or other officeholder in the government could become an office-bearer of the Pakistan Muslim League. It was proposed that the Quaid-i-Azam be exempt from this rule, but he declined the offer. Choudhry Khaliquzzaman, who was entrusted with the task of organizing the Pakistan Muslim League and later became its first President, had neither the authority nor the prestige to keep feuding factions within the League disciplined. Since the League was the only political organization, control over it was the key to political power. The struggle for power within the League was pursued by all sorts of dubious means. False returns of members, denial of membership forms to the opposing faction, and rigged elections of Council members and officeholders became common practices. The masses and the bulk of the intelligentsia began to lose interest in politics, which came to be regarded as a game pursued by professional politicians for self-interest. The failings of the politicians stood out all the more prominently against the prevailing atmosphere of Islamic zeal and patriotic fervor among the masses.

There was also another factor at work. Before partition, control was centralized in the All-India Muslim League organization. The provincial Leagues enjoyed limited power and had to obey the mandates of the central organization. The central organization drew its strength from the powerful personality of its President, the Quaid-i-Azam, and the support of the hundred million Muslims of the subcontinent. When the Pakistan Muslim League was formed in February, 1948, it was constituted on the federal pattern. Each province was allotted a fixed number of seats in the League Council. There were 180 for East Bengal, 150 for the Punjab, 50 for Sind, 40 for the North-West Frontier Province, 20 for Baluchistan, and 10 nominated by the President. The provincial League organizations were under the control of the Provincial Chief Ministers, who also controlled the election of the Pakistan Muslim League Councillors from their provinces. In some cases, the election to the League Council was nominal—the Chief Minister virtually appointed his loyal supporters. Thus the Pakistan Muslim League, instead of drawing its support directly from the masses, became dependent upon the provincial leaders.

Throughout this period, the stability and strength of the central government were in striking contrast to the state of the provincial governments. In the composition of the central cabinet, regard has always been paid to regional representation, particularly between East and West Pakistan. Under proper leadership this makes for unity and strength and not for weakness and division. Under the leadership of the Quaid-i-Azam and, after his death, of Liaquat Ali Khan, the central cabinet worked with a single will toward the solution of the grave problems facing the country. There were, it is true, differences of view which found vigorous expression but, in general, a consensus of opinion would emerge to which all gave willing consent. At times, as happens with every human group, misunderstandings would arise even over minor matters. On one occasion, a senior minister threatened to resign because the Prime Minister, who was also Defence Minister, ignored his recommendation for the promotion of an army officer and thus, in his view, failed to do justice. However, wiser counsels prevailed and I was able to bring about a reconciliation. A more persistent discord was that which developed, after the Quaid-i-Azam's death, between the Finance Minister, Ghulam Muhammad, and the Commerce Minister, Fazlur Rahman. In temperament they were poles apart—the one as quick and sharp as a rapier and the other as blunt and heavy as a bludgeon. I begged the Prime Minister a number of times to do something about this running quarrel, which unnecessarily hampered business, but he took a philosophic view of the matter. It is possible that he considered this conflict between two strong personalities not entirely disadvantageous. Anyhow, the differences never went beyond a certain limit, and remained more or less personal to the two ministers.

The only serious jolt to the cabinet came from the defection of the Labor Minister, Jogendra Nath Mandal, to India in 1950. As the leader of the Scheduled Caste Hindus in Bengal he had stood loyally with the Quaid-i-Azam in the struggle for Pakistan. After the Quaid-i-Azam's death a gradual change came over him, as the caste Hindus in the Pakistan constituent assembly started wooing him and urging him to assume leadership over them as well. At the same time links were being forged between him and the Indian High Commission in Karachi. Liaquat Ali Khan was aware of these developments, and I was taking precautionary measures not to let top secret documents fall into Mandal's hands. It appears that Mandal came to know he was being watched, took fright, and bolted to India.

Relations with India have played a pivotal part in determining Pakistan's defense needs and foreign policy. The leaders of India accepted partition in the hope of undoing it soon and establishing their hegemony over the whole subcontinent. "Most of the Congress leaders and Nehru among them," wrote Brecher, "subscribed to the view that Pakistan was not a viable state—politically, economically, geographically or militarily—and that sooner or later the areas which had seceded would be compelled by force of circumstances to return to the fold." [6] Pakistan was, for them, a transient phase, a tactical retreat that did not affect their strategic aims.

The events described in the earlier pages bear eloquent testimony to India's persistent hostility toward Pakistan: In the East Punjab massacres, the interference with canal waters, the withholding of military stores and other assets, the military occupation of Junagadh and Kashmir, and the trade war in 1949, every effort was made by India to truncate Pakistan territorially, to encircle it strategically, and to strangle it economically.

In order to safeguard the independence and territorial integrity of Pakistan, it was essential to build up and equip the armed forces. Resources that were urgently needed for economic reconstruction and development were diverted to defense, which used up half and, at times, even more of the central budget. The people bore these sacrifices willingly. Liaquat Ali Khan's remark "We can afford to be hungry for a day but we can not afford to be slaves even for a minute," reflected the will of the whole nation. The original plan for an army of 125,000 men was revised upward under the constant threat of aggression by India. Since India had withheld Pakistan's share of military stores, large sums had to be spent on defense equipment. In a broadcast to the nation on October 8, 1948, the Prime Minister said: "The defence of the State is our foremost consideration and has dominated all other governmental activities. We will not grudge any amount on the defence of our country."

Army, air, and naval headquarters had to be set up. The Indian air force and the Indian navy were not well developed. The number of Muslims serving in them was relatively small. The Pakistan navy and air force began in a modest way with headquarters in Karachi. The headquarters of the Northern Command in Rawalpindi became the general headquarters of the Pakistan army. Though Muslims had formed one third of the strength of the Indian army, there were no homogeneous Muslim units. The fragments left after the departure of non-Muslims had to be reorganized and brought up to strength. Shortages in technical arms, such as artillery, and in engineers, were very great, and even in the infantry the number of senior officers with staff and command experience was limited. The Pakistan army was, in consequence, far more dependent upon British officers than the Indian army. Nationalization of the armed forces could be carried out only gradually. A debt of gratitude is owed to the British officers who worked with zeal and devotion to build up the Pakistan army, navy, and air force.

For two centuries there had been a serious neglect of the military potential of Bengal. The result was that the Pakistan army, which was constituted out of the Indian army, had only a handful of men from East Pakistan. The importance of changing this state of affairs was realized from the very start. The false theory of "nonmartial" races was discarded and opportunities for recruitment from East Pakistan were opened up. The East Bengal Regiment was formed in February, 1948. To provide army accommodation in East Pakistan, cantonments were built.

Pakistan did not have a single ordnance factory. All the sixteen ordnance factories of British India were located in the Indian Union. They had been modernized and expanded during the Second World War; and new factories, such as the Hindustan Aircraft Factory at Bangalore, had been built. The Indian leaders were stubbornly opposed to the transfer of any factory or, indeed, any piece of machinery to Pakistan. They even refused to part with the machinery for a Bren-gun factory and a fuse-filling factory, which was lying packed and had not yet been installed.

In the face of this determined opposition, there were no means by which Pakistan could get its rightful share. The best that could be arranged was a financial settlement, and in the final agreement over the partition of assets, I negotiated a sum of Rs. 60 million in lieu of Pakistan's share of ordnance factories. With this money the establishment of a new ordnance factory at Wah near Rawalpindi was taken in hand. I had sponsored the project and I had to look after it. Finance Minister Ghulam Muhammad opposed it on the ground that private enterprise could do the job. Strangely enough, army headquarters did not take much interest in the project and was not prepared to spare any suitable officers for it. With great difficulty I persuaded the railway authorities to release a senior mechanical engineer for the job. For designing the factory, the services of an ordnance expert, Newton Booth, were obtained from England through the good offices of Sir Archibald Rowlands, who was Financial Adviser to the Governor-General of Pakistan and had been Permanent Under Secretary of the Ministry of Supply of the United Kingdom during the war. A scheme for the training of Pakistanis was started. When the Prime Minister of Hyderabad, Mir Laik Ali, escaped to Karachi after the occupation of Hyderabad, he was appointed Defense Adviser and was put in charge of the factory.

Apart from the Staff College at Quetta, which had an international reputation, Pakistan inherited no schools of instruction. A Military

Academy was set up at Kakul, and a number of training institutions for the army, navy, and air force were established.

In a broadcast talk to the United States, in February, 1948, the Quaid-i-Azam defined Pakistan's foreign policy in these terms:

> Our foreign policy is one of friendliness and goodwill towards all the nations of the world. We do not cherish aggressive designs against any country or nation. We believe in the principle of honesty and fairplay in national and international dealings and are prepared to make our utmost contribution to the promotion of peace and prosperity among the nations of the world. Pakistan will never be found lacking in extending its material and moral support to the oppressed and suppressed peoples of the world and in upholding the principles of the United Nations Charter.[7]

The concrete application of these principles can be seen in Pakistan's relations with the British Commonwealth and the West; its neighbors, including China and Russia; and the Muslim world of which it is an integral part.

On the eve of assuming office as Governor-General, the Quaid-i-Azam expressed his profound appreciation of "the high and noble ideals by which the Commonwealth has been and will be guided in future." The expectation that Pakistan's leaders had formed of the Commonwealth as a family of nations that looked after the interests of its members, composed their differences in a fair manner, and came to their aid in the event of aggression were belied by experience. When the Kashmir dispute went to the United Nations, the United Kindgom along with the United States, Canada, and the other members of the Security Council, at first took a just stand, but soon succumbed to Indian threats of leaving the Commonwealth and led the rest of the Security Council in an ignoble retreat. Within the Commonwealth there was an extreme reluctance to resolve the disputes that were dividing India and Pakistan. It was not until Liaquat Ali Khan refused to attend the Commonwealth Prime Ministers' Conference of January, 1951, unless the Kashmir question was discussed, that a discussion was arranged at an informal meeting. On this occasion, it was through the efforts of Prime Minister Menzies of Australia that a deadlock was averted. He stopped in Karachi on his way to London and after securing the agreement of the other Commonwealth Prime Ministers for a discussion of the Kashmir question, succeeded in persuading Liaquat Ali Khan to attend the Conference in London. As the true character of the Commonwealth became more apparent, there was disillusionment, but not to the point of wishing to break away from it.

Perhaps the main reason for this is to be found in an affinity with Western democratic institutions, which were the principal gift of the British to their former colonies. This was reinforced by cultural and economic ties. English was still the official language of the government and the higher courts, as well as the medium of instruction for university education. Pakistan was a member of the sterling area and held fairly large balances in London. Trade with the United Kingdom predominated. The Colombo Plan brought benefits of aid in economic development to members of the Commonwealth. As part of a worldwide community of nations, Pakistan could exercise some influence in the shaping of world policies.

The disillusionment with the British had, however, one marked effect in foreign relations. There was a tendency to turn toward the United States as the leader of the democratic world. In the Kashmir debate, the American representative in the Security Council of the United Nations, Warren Austin, had spoken in clear accents in support of a free and unfettered plebiscite in Kashmir. When the American hero of the Second World War, Admiral Nimitz, was designated as the plebiscite administrator, the people of Pakistan felt confident that he would carry out his task with strict impartiality. The ties with the United States were greatly strengthened when Liaquat Ali Khan paid an official visit to that country in May, 1950. The visit was a great success in promoting mutual understanding. Liaquat Ali Khan's speeches in the various parts of the United States emphasized the positive ideals for which Pakistan was working. In a speech in New York he said:

> We believe in democracy, that is, in fundamental human rights including the right of private ownership and the right of the people to be governed by their own freely chosen representatives. We believe in equal citizenship for all whether Muslims or non-Muslims, equality of opportunity, equality before law. We believe that each individual, man or woman, has the right to the fruit of his own labours. Lastly we believe that the fortunate amongst us whether in wealth or knowledge or physical fitness, have a moral responsibility towards those who have been unfortunate. These principles we call the Islamic way of life. You can call them by any name you like.[8]

Pakistan is an organic part of the Muslim world. Its *raison d'être* lies in Islam as the directive principle of social and political life.

Islamic doctrine and practice lay emphasis on the brotherhood of Muslims all over the world. Even during British rule the Muslim community of the subcontinent was noted for what others called its extraterritorial loyalty. "Having lost its own freedom," observed Ishtiaq Husain Qureshi, "the community developed a new consciousness of its ties with the other Muslim people." [9] With the establishment of Pakistan, this consciousness was heightened still further. Sentiment and interest pointed in the same direction. The geographical structure of Pakistan made it a part both of the Middle East and of South East Asia. To the west lie Afghanistan, Iran, Turkey, and the Arab countries; and in the southeast are the Muslim lands of Malaysia and Indonesia. In the north there are the Soviet Republics of Central Asia, peopled by Muslims and containing such ancient centers of Islamic civilization as Bokhara and Samarkand, which maintained active communication with the Muslims of the Indo-Pakistan subcontinent until modern times.

To strive for the freedom, strength, prosperity, and unity of the Muslim world has been a constant objective of Pakistan's foreign policy. Among the first acts of the Pakistan government was to send a mission of goodwill to the countries of the Middle East. Pakistan treated the Arab cause in Palestine as its own; and there was no more eloquent exponent of this cause in the United Nations than Pakistan's Foreign Minister, Zafrullah Khan. Pakistan has consistently refused to recognize Israel. Full support was given to independence for Indonesia, Malaya, Sudan, Libya, Tunisia, Morocco, Nigeria, and Algeria. On the West Irian issue, Pakistan stood by Indonesia. Treaties of friendship have been signed with a number of Muslim countries and cultural exchanges have been arranged. Motamar al-Alam al-Islami, or the World Muslim Congress, was organized. In 1949 the International Islamic Economic Conference representing eighteen Muslim countries was held in Karachi. It unanimously agreed to form the International Federation of Islamic Chambers of Commerce and Industry, but unfortunately the resolution has not been implemented.

The one Muslim country with which relations have been strained is Afghanistan. The border between Afghanistan and British India was settled in 1893 by Sir Mortimer Durand and is known as the Durand Line. Shortly before the transfer of power in India, Afghanistan raised untenable claims that were firmly rejected by the British government. The Durand Line is unquestionably the international boundary between Afghanistan and Pakistan; and the Afghan government has never openly challenged its validity. But aided and abetted by India, the Afghan government showed hostility to Pakistan from the very start, although Pakistan has made every endeavor to live on terms of friendship with its closest Muslim neighbor. The first diplomatic mission that Pakistan sent was to Afghanistan. Nevertheless, Afghanistan was the only country in the world to oppose Pakistan's entry into the United Nations. The cry for a "Pakhtoonistan," which originated with Gandhi and which was taken up by his disciple Abdul Ghaffar Khan, was adopted by the rulers of Afghanistan. Through malcontents, such as the Fakir of Ipi, and through the Kabul Radio, the Afghan government tried to subvert the loyalty of the tribes on Pakistan's side of the Durand Line. The Afghan consulates in Pakistan acted as centers of hostile propaganda. These efforts, however, failed. There has been peace and tranquillity on the frontier, such as the British were seldom able to attain.

Apart from ties of religion and culture, the economic interests of both countries, and particularly of Afghanistan, demand a policy of close cooperation. Afghanistan is land-locked and a major part of its import and export trade moves through the port of Karachi. Pakistan has readily made available free transit facilities for Afghan goods. The fruit grown in Afghanistan has a ready market in Pakistan in exchange for textiles and other manufactures. Even when Pakistan was faced with acute balance of payments difficulties, it did not impose exchange restrictions on Afghanistan, and goods imported from abroad for internal use in Pakistan found their way into Afghanistan. Despite these efforts, the rulers of Afghanistan have, for the most part, chosen to maintain tension for political ends. However, it is to be hoped that in the course of time the advantages of cooperation between two Muslim neighbors will be realized by the Afghan government.

Barring India and Afghanistan, Pakistan's relations with other neighboring countries have been cordial. The cultural association of Iran and Pakistan has a long history. Persian, which was for centuries the official language of the Muslim Empire in the subcontinent, has been the greatest single influence on Urdu. It is not uncommon for an Urdu poet to write Persian poetry, and two of the greatest Urdu poets, Ghalib and Iqbal, chose to express their profoundest thoughts in Persian. Turkey lies further afield, but is by long tradition close to the hearts of the people of Pakistan.

Pakistan was among the first countries to recognize Communist China, and exchanged embassies with it in 1950. When the Korean war broke out, Pakistan did not take part in it despite strong urgings by the United States, which offered to equip the brigade that Pakistan was asked to send to the scene of action. Liaquat Ali Khan said in an address at Los Angeles, in 1950: "Pakistan is resolved to throw all its weight to help the maintenance of stability in Asia. Stability in Asia is most important to us not only for our own freedom and progress but for the maintenance of world peace. As things appear to us in our part of the world we cannot imagine how world peace can be maintained unless Asia is stabilized." [10]

When almost immediately after independence Pakistan became a member of the United Nations, it shared the hopes that a war-weary humanity entertained of the world organization. Experience of its actual working, particularly in the Kashmir dispute, tempered that early optimism with a more realistic view. It has not, however, lessened Pakistan's faith in the principles of the UN Charter or in the need to support and strengthen the United Nations in every possible way.

For Pakistan, as for other newly independent countries of Asia and Africa, world peace is an essential condition for economic development and social progress. A world order based on law and justice, which would ensure peace and in which the weak could coexist with the strong without fear of being dominated or exploited, has, however, yet to evolve.

During the first year of Pakistan's existence, questions of such vital importance for the country had to be discussed that it was often necessary for the Quaid-i-Azam to preside over cabinet meetings. There was, it is true, a big gulf between the Quaid-i-Azam and his cabinet colleagues, including the Prime Minister, but that arose from the loftiness of his intellect and the greatness of his position as the Father of the Nation. But contrary to the general impression, he always permitted a full and free discussion. He would support his own view with compelling logic, but was prepared to listen to a contrary opinion, provided it was backed by facts and reason. It was only intellectual dishonesty or stupid obstinacy that aroused his ire. He was keen to persuade and would patiently explain at considerable length the pros and cons of a policy. He read carefully and conscientiously every paper submitted to him. His industry was as amazing as his inflexible pursuit of truth. No detail escaped him and no shoddy work could pass him. He gave of his best and expected from others the same high standards of integrity and devotion to duty. Not even in the most adverse circumstances did he lose the clarity of his vision and coolness of his nerve. His faith and courage sustained the country when it was passing through one dire peril after another. His motto of unity, faith, and discipline was not a mere slogan. It was the direct expression of a living experience shared by the Quaid-i-Azam with his people. He closed their ranks and composed their multifarious divisions. He gave them unity of command, restored their faith in their own destiny, and made them a disciplined force.

Overwork and the strain of exceptionally grave and pressing problems undermined his health, but he did not spare himself. In July, 1948, when it was discovered that he had serious lung trouble, he had perhaps a premonition that the end was not far off. In his message to the nation on the occasion of the first anniversary of Pakistan, on August 14, 1948, there is a hint to this effect. After recounting the achievements of the first year and reminding his listeners that "the establishment of Pakistan is a fact of which there is no parallel in the history of the world," he bade farewell to the nation with these words. "Nature had given you everything: you have got unlimited resources. The foundations of your State have been laid, and it is now for you to build, and build as quickly and as well as you can. So go ahead and I wish you God speed! Pakistan Zindabad." [11]

I saw him in Quetta a few days before his death. I had gone there to report to him the latest developments in the Kashmir dispute and to obtain his instructions on the policy to be followed in the future. He was lying in bed and his strength was ebbing, but there was the same clarity of intellect, the same vigor of will, the same spark in his eye, and the same faith in the destiny of his people that had always characterized him.

On September 11, 1948, he was brought down to Karachi and passed peacefully away the same evening at the age of seventy-two. An epoch passed away with him. His was a unique achievement in the history of Muslim India. He found a people dispirited by two centuries of foreign rule and led them to win the largest Muslim state in the face of overwhelming odds by peaceful and constitutional means. The people could hardly believe that the Quaid-i-Azam was dead. For years afterward, meetings would resound with the cry "Quaid-i-Azam Zindabad" (long live Quaid-i-Azam). On the day of his death and on the next, when funeral prayers were held before his burial, there was universal mourning. From India the sound of guns could be heard, for on the following day India invaded Hyderabad.

Great as was the shock of the Quaid-i-Azam's death, it did not stun or unnerve the nation. The best tribute to his memory, it was felt, was to carry on the task of national reconstruction with, if possible, greater determination and devotion. Khwaja Nazimuddin, the Chief Minister of East Bengal, was selected to succeed the Quaid-i-Azam as Governor-General. Moulvi Tamizuddin Khan, the Deputy President of the constituent assembly, became its President. The mantle of national leadership fell on Liaquat Ali Khan, the Prime Minister. The choice of Khwaja Nazimuddin as Governor-General was a happy one. He was from East Pakistan and was greatly respected for his sincerity and piety. All the papers and the information that used to go to the Quaid-i-Azam were submitted to him. The Prime Minister always sought his advice on important issues; and he performed his role as constitutional Governor-General with dignity and propriety.

Liaquat Ali Khan rose to unexpectedly great heights as the national leader. He had served with distinction as the General Secretary of the Muslim League and, as the Quaid-i-Azam's chief lieutenant in the central assembly and in the interim government in Delhi. For the last year he had carried the heavy burden of the office of Prime Minister. During the Quaid-i-Azam's illness he was forced to rely more and more upon his own judgment and initiative. His integrity and devotion to Pakistan was outstanding among the followers of the Quaid-i-Azam. He was shrewd of judgment, tenacious of purpose, steadfast, and tactful. He had remarkable self-control and his face gave no indication of the state of his feelings. The manner in which he consolidated the nation after the Quaid-i-Azam's death and carried on the task entrusted to him by the Quaid-i-Azam won national recognition. To this day, his memory is revered as the Quaid-i-Millat—the leader of the nation. But of course, he was not the Quaid-i-Azam, and he never pretended to be anything but a faithful follower of the Quaid-i-Azam. He had to work through provincial leaders who did not stand in the same awe of him as they had of the Quaid-i-Azam. He could guide, but not direct.

The only major criticism of him that is often voiced is that he did not press forward with the task of constitution-making at a time (1949–50) when the nation was united and the Muslim League party had an overwhelming majority in the constituent assembly. Only a handful of Congress Hindus out of a total membership of 79 were on the opposition side. Among the Muslims, Abdul Ghaffar Khan was opposed to the government, but since he was opposed to Pakistan his voice carried no weight. The only other persistent critic was Mian Iftikharuddin. The rest were solidly with the government.

The Quaid-i-Azam himself had been too absorbed in the problems of the establishment of Pakistan to have found time for constitution-making. There has been some speculation as to the type of constitution the Quaid-i-Azam had in mind for Pakistan. Though no one can say with certainty what precise form the constitutional structure would have taken under his guiding hand, certain aspects of his thought are clear beyond doubt. He envisaged a federal constitution for Pakistan but with a sufficiently strong central government to safeguard the integrity and security of Pakistan. He was keenly aware of the difficulties which the geographical separation of East and West Pakistan presented and wanted to forge every instrument of unity between the two wings of Pakistan.

His own position was unique. He was the Quaid-i-Azam, the Great Leader and the Father of the Nation. As Liaquat Ali Khan said, "Our freedom is the reward of the services and efforts of a single man and that you know is our most beloved Quaid-i-Azam." Even if he had not occupied any official position in Pakistan, those in authority would have turned to him for guidance. He was trusted by the people of Pakistan as no one else was. His judgment of men and affairs was beyond question. No one could dispute what he thought was right for Pakistan. If the cabinet decided, as it did a few months after the establishment of Pakistan, that the Quaid-i-Azam could overrule the cabinet, it was done for him as Quaid-i-Azam and not because he was the Governor-General. It was not an amendment of the constitution but a voluntary surrender of power on the part of the cabinet in favor of the Father of the Nation. It applied to him and to him alone. If the Quaid-i-Azam had so desired, the constituent assembly would have agreed to amend the interim constitution. The fact that there was not even a hint of such a procedure is sufficient indication that the Quaid-i-Azam did not desire to change the parliamentary form of government in any significant respect. However that may be, there cannot be the slightest doubt that the Quaid-i-Azam envisaged a democratic constitution for Pakistan. The ruling passion of his life was love of law and liberty. On innumerable occasions, before and after the establishment of Pakistan, he affirmed his faith in democracy, social justice, and the equality of man as taught by Islam. It will suffice to quote what he said on the subject in a broadcast talk to the people of the United States of America in February, 1948.

> The constitution of Pakistan has yet to be framed by the Pakistan Constituent Assembly. I do not know what the ultimate shape of this constitution is going to be, but I am sure that it will be of a democratic type, embodying the essential principles of Islam. Today, they are as applicable in actual life as they were 1,300 years ago. Islam and its idealism have taught us democracy. It has taught equality of man, justice and fairplay to everybody. We are the inheritors of these glorious traditions and are fully alive to our responsibilities and obligations as framers of the future constitution of Pakistan. In any case Pakistan is not going to be a theocratic State—to be ruled by priests with a divine mission. We have many non-Muslims—Hindus, Christians, and Parsis—but they are all Pakistanis. They will enjoy the same rights and privileges as any other citizens and will play their rightful part in the affairs of Pakistan.[12]

In the months immediately following the Quaid-i-Azam's death, the energies of the Prime Minister and the central government were devoted to national consolidation. By the beginning of 1949 it was possible for the Prime Minister to turn his attention to constitutional questions. On March 7, 1949, Liaquat Ali Khan moved the Objectives Resolution "embodying the main principles on which the constitution of Pakistan is to be based." It was adopted by the constituent assembly on March 12, after a stimulating debate that brought out the implications of the resolution. It envisaged a state in which the principles of democracy, freedom, equality, tolerance, and social justice as enunciated by Islam would be observed; where Muslims would be able to order their lives in accord with Islam, and minorities could practice their religion and develop their culture; a state which would guarantee fundamental rights including freedom of expression and association, which would secure the independence of the judiciary, and safeguard the integrity of the federation, "so that the people of

Pakistan may prosper and attain their rightful and honoured place among the nations of the World and make their full contribution towards international peace and progress and happiness of humanity."

The basic principles committee was set up on March 12, 1949, and the next year it presented a report. But when the report drew some adverse comments, the Prime Minister asked the constituent assembly to postpone consideration of the report and threw it open to suggestions from the public. Why, his critics ask, did he shelve constitution-making in this manner? India had completed the task by the end of 1949, and held its first general elections simultaneously for the central and provincial legislatures in 1951.

The reason is to be found in the plan that Liaquat Ali Khan formed at this time of holding elections, province by province, and finally for the central assembly, before grappling seriously with constitutional issues. He disclosed this plan to me and a few others. The interim constitution provided by the adapted Government of India Act, 1935, was, he felt, functioning satisfactorily. General elections on the basis of adult franchise were a surer guarantee of the establishment of democratic institutions, but to hold them simultaneously for the central and provincial legislative assemblies would throw excessive strain on the resources of the administration and the Muslim League party. They should, therefore, be staggered, beginning with the Punjab, and going on to North-West Frontier Province, then to Sind, East Bengal and, last of all, the center. Once newly elected governments with a fresh mandate from the people were in the saddle, the task of constitution-making could be taken in hand and completed. But an assassin's bullet, fired on October 16, 1951, put an end to Liaquat Ali Khan's life and to his plan. For Pakistan it was a terrible tragedy and an irreparable loss.

Constitution-making dragged on until the constituent assembly was dissolved in October, 1954. A new constituent assembly, elected the next year, tackled the task with vigor and completed it within six months. The Constitution of the Islamic Republic of Pakistan, which was based on the Objectives Resolution moved by Liaquat Ali Khan, was promulgated on March 23, 1956. The cornerstone of the Constitution, which I had the privilege of presenting to the country as Prime Minister, was equal partnership between East and West Pakistan in every sphere—administrative, economic, and political.

Notes

1. HISTORICAL BACKGROUND

1. J. H. Hutton, *Caste in India* (Bombay, Oxford University Press, 1961), p. 50.

2. *Ibid.,* p. 190.

3. For a critical review of the attitude of British historians, such as Sir Henry Elliot and Professor John Dowsen, see S. M. Ikram and Percival Spear, eds., *The Cultural Heritage of Pakistan* (London, Oxford University Press, 1955), pp. 97–99.

4. Percival Spear, *India: A Modern History* (Ann Arbor, Mich., The University of Michigan Press, 1961), p. 99.

5. Rajendra Prasad, *India Divided* (Bombay, Hind Kitabs, 1947), p. 85.

6. Sir Stanley Reed, *The India I Knew, 1897–1949* (London, Odhams Press, 1953), p. 176.

7. Philip Woodruff, *The Men Who Ruled India: The Founders* (London, Jonathan Cape, 1959), p. 93.

8. W. W. Hunter, *The Indian Musalmans* (Calcutta, Comrade Publishers, 1945; reprint of 3d ed.), p. 3.

9. Ram Gopal, *Indian Muslims: A Political History* (Bombay, Asia Publishing House, 1959), p. 16.

10. Hunter, *The Indian Musalmans,* pp. 144–45.

11. Gopal, p. 34.   12. Gopal, p. 35.

13. Quoted in Altaf Husain Hali, *Hayat-i-Javid* (Urdu), (Lahore, Aina-i-Adab, 1966; reprint of 2d ed. of 1902), p. 164; translation mine.

14. B. Pattabhai Sitaramayyah, *History of the Indian National Congress* (2 vols., Bombay, Padma Publications, 1946), I, 15.

15. Woodruff, pp. 165–66.   16. Quoted in Hali, p. 574.

17. Quoted in Hali, pp. 276–77. A fuller extract is given in Appendix II of Part I of *The Constitutional Problem in India* by R. Coupland (Madras, Oxford University Press, 1945).

18. *Struggle for Independence 1857–1947* (Karachi, Pakistan Publications, 1958), Appendix II, pp. 4–5.

19. Quoted in Coupland, Part I, p. 34.   20. Sitaramayyah, I, 27.

21. M. H. Saiyid, *Mohammad Ali Jinnah: A Political Study* (Lahore, Muhammad Ashraf, 1953), pp. 189–90.

22. D. G. Tendulkar, *Mahatma* (8 vols., New Delhi, Government of India, Publication Division, 1960), II, 82.

23. B. R. Ambedkar, *Pakistan or the Partition of India* (Bombay, Thacker, 1946), p. 304.

24. Quoted in Coupland, Part I, p. 111.

25. The full text of Iqbal's address is given in Appendix IV of *Struggle for Independence 1857–1947*.

26. Ishtaiq Husain Qureshi, *The Muslim Community of the Indo-Pakistan Sub-Continent* (The Hague, Mouton, 1962), p. 295.

27. Choudhry Khaliquzzaman, *Pathway to Pakistan* (London, Longmans Green, 1961), pp. 152–53.

28. Coupland, Part II, p. 111.   29. Gopal, p. 245.

30. Michael Brecher, *Nehru: A Political Biography* (London, Oxford University Press, 1959), p. 231.

31. Abul Kalam Azad, *India Wins Freedom* (Calcutta, Orient Longmans, 1959), pp. 15–16.

32. For details, see Sir Malcolm Darling, *The Punjab Peasant in Prosperity and Debt* (Bombay, Oxford University Press, 1947).

33. *Speeches by the Rt. Hon. John Bright, M.P.,* ed. by James E. Thorold Rogers (London, Macmillan, 1892), pp. 26–28.

2. *THE PAKISTAN RESOLUTION*

1. Quoted in Beverley Nichols, *Verdict on India* (London, Jonathan Cape, 1944), p. 31.

2. R. Coupland, *The Constitutional Problem in India* (3 parts, Madras, Oxford University Press, 1945), Part II, p. 180.

3. *Some Recent Speeches and Writings of Mr. Jinnah,* ed. by Jamil-ud-din Ahmad, 5th ed. (2 vols., Lahore, Muhammad Ashraf, 1952), I, 173–78.

4. Richard Symond, *The Making of Pakistan* (London, Faber and Faber, 1949), p. 59.

5. Nirad C. Chaudhuri, *The Autobiography of an Unknown Indian* (London, Macmillan, 1951), p. 231.

6. Quoted in Hector Bolitho, *Jinnah* (London, John Murray, 1954), p. 126.

7. *Speeches and Documents on the Indian Constitution, 1921–1947,*

ed. by Sir Maurice Gwyer and A. Appadorai (2 vols., London, Oxford University Press, 1957), I, 270.

8. In a letter to Jinnah dated June 21, 1937, reproduced in Appendix V to *Struggle for Independence 1857–1947* (Karachi, Pakistan Publications, 1958), p. 34.

9. *Speeches and Writings of Mr. Jinnah,* I, 76.

10. *Ibid.,* pp. 554–55.

11. *Documents and Speeches on British Commonwealth Affairs, 1931–1952,* ed. by Nicholas Mansergh (2 vols., London, Oxford University Press, 1953), II, 612–14.

12. Quoted in Coupland, Part II, p. 242.

13. *Documents and Speeches on British Commonwealth Affairs, 1931–1952,* II, 616–17.

14. Quoted in Coupland, Part II, p. 290.

15. Quoted in D. G. Tendulkar, *Mahatma* (8 vols., New Delhi, Government of India, Publication Division, 1960), VI, 263.

16. Quoted in Pyarelal, *Mahatma Gandhi: The Last Phase* (2 vols., Ahmedabad, Navajivan Publishing House, 1956), I, 91.

17. *Some Recent Speeches and Writings of Mr. Jinnah,* Vol. II, ed. by Jamil-ud-din Ahmad (Lahore, Muhammad Ashraf, 1947), pp. 180–83.

18. *Speeches and Documents on the Indian Constitution,* II, 550.

19. V. P. Menon, *The Transfer of Power in India* (Calcutta, Orient Longmans, 1957), p. 207.

20. Abul Kalam Azad, *India Wins Freedom* (Calcutta, Orient Longmans, 1959), p. 114.

21. *Ibid.,* p. 129.   22. *Ibid.,* p. 130.

3. THE CABINET MISSION PLAN

1. *Cabinet Mission and After,* ed. by Muhammad Ashraf (Lahore, Muhammad Ashraf, 1946), pp. 1–3.

2. *Speeches and Documents on the Indian Constitution, 1921–1947,* ed. by Sir Maurice Gwyer and A. Appadorai (2 vols., London, Oxford University Press, 1957), II, 574–75.

3. *Cabinet Mission and After,* pp. 127–29.

4. For the full text of the Cabinet Mission Plan, see *Speeches and Documents on the Indian Constitution,* II, 577–84.

5. Pyarelal, *Mahatma Gandhi: The Last Phase* (2 vols., Ahmedabad, Navajivan Publishing House, 1956), I, 214–15; and V. P. Menon, *The Transfer of Power in India* (Calcutta, Orient Longmans, 1957), pp. 268–69).

6. Quoted in Pyarelal, I, 222.

7. *Speeches and Documents on the Indian Constitution,* II, 589–90.

8. *Cabinet Mission and After,* p. 141.

9. *Speeches and Documents on the Indian Constitution,* II, 600–2.

10. *Ibid.,* pp. 595–96.   11. *Ibid.,* pp. 598–99.

12. *Ibid.,* p. 600.   13. Quoted in Pyarelal, I, 225.

14. *Speeches and Documents on the Indian Constitution,* II, 602–3.

15. Pyarelal, I, 234.   16. *Ibid.*, p. 233.
17. *Ibid.*, pp. 234–36.   18. *Ibid.*, pp. 236–37.
19. *Speeches and Documents on the Indian Constitution,* II, 606–9.
20. *Cabinet Mission and After,* pp. 181–82.
21. Pyarelal, I, 236–40.
22. Quoted in Michael Brecher, *Nehru: A Political Biography* (London, Oxford University Press, 1959), p. 392.
23. Percival Spear, *India: A Modern History* (Ann Arbor, Mich., The University of Michigan Press, 1961), p. 415.
24. Quoted in D. G. Tendulkar, *Mahatma* (8 vols., New Delhi, Government of India, Publication Division, 1960), VIII, 3.
25. Quoted in Abul Kalam Azad, *India Wins Freedom* (Calcutta, Orient Longmans, 1959), p. 155.
26. Quoted in Brecher, p. 316.   27. *Ibid.*, pp. 316–17.
28. *Speeches and Documents on the Indian Constitution,* II, 638.
29. See *ibid.*, p. 603.
30. *Some Recent Speeches and Writings of Mr. Jinnah,* Vol. II, ed. by Jamil-ud-din Ahmad (Lahore, Muhammad Ashraf, 1947), pp. 407–21.
31. *Cabinet Mission and After,* p. 309.   32. *Ibid.*, pp. 309–10.
33. *Ibid.*, pp. 311–19.   34. *Ibid.*, p. 325.
35. *Ibid.*, pp. 335–37.
36. In a letter dated August 28, 1946, to the *Statesman* of Calcutta, reproduced in *Cabinet Mission and After,* pp. 385–87.
37. *Cabinet Mission and After,* p. 323.
38. V. P. Menon, *The Transfer of Power in India* (Calcutta, Orient Longmans, 1957), p. 291.
39. The Urdu daily, *Nawai-Waqt,* of Lahore, July 1, 1961.
40. *Speeches and Documents on the Indian Constitution,* II, 640–41.
41. Azad, pp. 156–57.   42. *Cabinet Mission and After,* pp. 340–44.
43. *Ibid.*, p. 373.
44. Sir Francis Tuker, *While Memory Serves* (London, Cassell, 1950), pp. 154–57.
45. *Ibid.*, pp. 158, 160, 165.
46. Ian Stephens, *Pakistan* (London, Ernest Benn, 1963), p. 106.
47. Quoted in Pyarelal, I, 268.   48. Menon, p. 302.
49. Quoted in Pyarelal, I, 270–71.   50. Quoted in Menon, p. 303.
51. *Ibid.*, p. 308.   52. Pyarelal, I, 274–75.
53. Quoted in Menon, p. 313.   54. *Ibid.*
55. *Cabinet Mission and After,* p. 416.   56. *Ibid.*, pp. 415–16.

4. THE INTERIM GOVERNMENT

1. Michael Brecher, *Nehru: A Political Biography* (London, Oxford University Press, 1959), p. 324.
2. Abul Kalam Azad, *India Wins Freedom* (Calcutta, Orient Longmans, 1959), p. 166.
3. *Ibid.*, p. 166.   4. *Ibid.*, p. 167.
5. *Cabinet Mission and After,* ed. by Muhammad Ashraf (Lahore, Muhammad Ashraf, 1946), p. 430.

6. Quoted in E. W. R. Lumby, *The Transfer of Power in India, 1945–1947* (London, George Allen & Unwin, 1954), p. 120.

7. Sir Francis Tuker, *While Memory Serves* (London, Cassell, 1950), p. 176.

8. *Ibid.*, pp. 181–82. 9. Lumby, p. 121.

10. Quoted in Pyarelal, *Mahatma Gandhi: The Last Phase* (2 vols., Ahmedabad, Navajivan Publishing House, 1956), I, 650.

11. Tuker, p. 185. 12. Pyarelal, I, 641.

13. Tuker, pp. 196–201. 14. Azad, p. 170.

15. *Ibid.*, p. 171.

16. All the quotes in this paragraph are from *Speeches and Documents on the Indian Constitution, 1921–1947,* ed. by Sir Maurice Gwyer and A. Appadorai (2 vols., London, Oxford University Press, 1957), II, 655–57.

17. *Ibid.*, p. 657.

18. V. P. Menon, *The Transfer of Power in India* (Calcutta, Orient Longmans, 1957), p. 323.

19. *Speeches and Documents on the Indian Constitution,* II, 660.

20. *Ibid.*, p. 661.

21. *Some Recent Speeches and Writings of Mr. Jinnah,* Vol. II, ed. by Jamil-ud-din Ahmad (Lahore, Muhammad Ashraf, 1947), p. 492.

22. *Ibid.*, pp. 496–508. 23. Azad, pp. 167–68.

24. Quoted in Pyarelal, I, 489.

25. Quoted in Hector Bolitho, *Jinnah* (London, John Murray, 1954), p. 171.

26. *Speeches and Documents on the Indian Constitution,* II, 661–62.

27. Quoted in Menon, p. 332.

28. *Speeches and Documents on the Indian Constitution,* II, 662–66.

29. Paul Einzeg, "The Blocked Balances," in the weekly *Indian Finance* (Calcutta), March 1, 1947.

30. Quoted in *Indian Finance* (Budget Supplement), March 5, 1947.

31. Quoted in John W. Wheeler-Bennett, *King George VI* (London, Macmillan, 1959), p. 708.

32. *Speeches and Documents on the Indian Constitution,* II, 667–69.

33. Alan Campbell-Johnson, *Mission with Mountbatten* (London, Robert Hale, 1953), p. 44.

34. *Parliamentary Debates, House of Commons, 1946–1947,* Vol. CDXXXIV, cols. 503–5.

35. *Ibid.*, col. 678. 36. Quoted in Menon, p. 339.

37. Penderel Moon, *Divide and Quit* (London, Chatto & Windus, 1961), p. 72.

38. *Ibid.*, p. 74.

39. *Struggle for Independence 1857–1947* (Karachi, Pakistan Publications, 1958), p. 94.

40. Ian Stephens, *Pakistan* (London, Ernest Benn, 1963), p. 142.

41. The daily *Sind Observer* of Karachi, March 4, 1947.

42. Moon, p. 77.

43. Quoted in G. D. Khosla, *Stern Reckoning,* p. 100; cited in Kewal L. Panjabi, *The Indomitable Sardar* (Bombay, Bharatiya Vidya Bhavan, 1962), p. 122.

44. Moon, p. 77. 45. Stephens, p. 153.

5. POOR MAN'S BUDGET

1. Abul Kalam Azad, *India Wins Freedom* (Calcutta, Orient Longmans, 1959), pp. 175–76.

2. *Ibid.,* p. 176.

3. C. N. Vakil, "Some Reflections on the Budget," in the Bombay weekly *Commerce,* March 8, 1947, p. 417.

4. *Indian Finance* (Calcutta), March 22, 1947.   5. Azad, p. 207.

6. Quoted in Pyarelal, *Mahatma Gandhi: The Last Phase* (2 vols., Ahmedabad, Navajivan Publishing House, 1956), II, 83.

7. Kewal L. Panjabi, *The Indomitable Sardar* (Bombay, Bharatiya Vidya Bhavan, 1962), p. 123.

8. Quoted in *ibid.,* p. 123.

9. Quoted in Michael Brecher, *Nehru: A Political Biography* (London, Oxford University Press, 1959), p. 345.

10. Pyarelal, II, 3, 35.

11. *Speeches and Documents on the Indian Constitution, 1921–1947,* ed. by Sir Maurice Gwyer and A. Appadorai (2 vols., London, Oxford University Press, 1957), II, 669–70.

12. Quoted in V. P. Menon, *The Transfer of Power in India* (Calcutta, Orient Longmans, 1956), p. 348.

6. MOUNTBATTEN'S MISSION

1. The full text of this letter is given in John Connell, *Auchinleck* (London, Cassell, 1959), pp. 864–65.

2. Nicholas Mansergh, *Survey of British Commonwealth Affairs* (London, Oxford University Press, 1958), p. 211.

3. Alan Campbell-Johnson, *Mission with Mountbatten* (London, Robert Hale, 1953), p. 55.

4. Quoted in Pyarelal, *Mahatma Gandhi: The Last Phase* (2 vols., Ahmedabad, Navajivan Publishing House, 1956), II, 7.

5. E. W. R. Lumby, *The Transfer of Power in India, 1945–1947,* (London, George Allen & Unwin, 1954), p. 156.

6. Jawaharlal Nehru, *The Discovery of India* (Bombay, Asia Publishing House, 1961), pp. 569–70.

7. Sir Francis Tuker, *While Memory Serves* (London, Cassell, 1950), p. 257.

8. Quoted in Kewal L. Panjabi, *The Indomitable Sardar* (Bombay, Bharatiya Vidya Bhavan, 1962), p. 124.

9. Campbell-Johnson, p. 85.

10. Michael Brecher, *Nehru: A Political Biography* (London, Oxford University Press, 1959), pp. 410–12.

11. Campbell-Johnson, p. 56.   12. Quoted in Pyarelal, II, 85.

13. See *ibid.,* the second page of illustrations between pages 128 and 129.

14. Campbell-Johnson, p. 55.   15. *Ibid.,* p. 57.

16. *Ibid.*   17. *Ibid.,* p. 76.

18. Quoted in Lord Ismay, *Memoirs* (London, Heinemann, 1960), p. 420.

19. Campbell-Johnson, p. 60.   20. *Ibid.,* p. 71.

7. *THE MAKING OF THE*
PARTITION PLAN

1. Lord Ismay, *Memoirs* (London, Heinemann, 1960), p. 420.

2. Alan Campbell-Johnson, *Mission with Mountbatten* (London, Robert Hale, 1953), p. 66.

3. *Ibid.,* p. 65.

4. Pyarelal, *Mahatma Gandhi: The Last Phase* (2 vols., Ahmedabad, Navajivan Publishing House, 1956), II, 262.

5. Campbell-Johnson, p. 58.

6. Quoted in John Connell, *Auchinleck* (London, Cassell, 1959), pp. 874–75.

7. Quoted in *ibid.,* pp. 878–80.   8. Campbell-Johnson, p. 72.

9. Ismay, *Memoirs,* p. 420.   10. Quoted in Pyarelal, II, 158–59.

11. Campbell-Johnson, p. 50.   12. *Ibid.,* p. 72.

13. *Ibid.,* p. 81.   14. *Ibid.*   15. Pyarelal, II, 154.

16. *Ibid.,* p. 166.

17. Reproduced in Leonard Mosley, *The Last Days of the British Raj* (London, Weidenfeld and Nicolson, 1961), p. 127. Italics are mine.

18. Quoted in Campbell-Johnson, p. 86.

19. Quoted in *ibid.,* p. 88.

20. V. P. Menon, *The Transfer of Power in India* (Calcutta, Orient Longmans, 1957), p. 360.

21. Quoted in Campbell-Johnson, p. 87.   22. *Ibid.*

23. Ismay, pp. 417–18.   24. Menon, p. 363.

25. Campbell-Johnson, p. 89.   26. *Ibid.*   27. *Ibid.,* p. 90.

28. *Ibid.,* p. 76.   29. Menon, p. 365.

30. Campbell-Johnson, p. 94.   31. *Ibid.,* pp. 85–86.

32. Quoted in Kewal L. Panjabi, *The Indomitable Sardar* (Bombay, Bharatiya Vidya Bhavan, 1962), p. 126.

33. Quoted in John W. Wheeler-Bennett, *King George VI* (London, Macmillan, 1959), p. 708.

34. Menon, pp. 366–67.   35. Campbell-Johnson, p. 93.

36. Quoted in Pyarelal, II, 170.   37. Quoted in *ibid.,* p. 171.

38. *Ibid.,* p. 180.   39. *Ibid.,* p. 185. Italics are mine.

40. *Ibid.,* pp. 184–85.   41. *Ibid.,* p. 185.

42. Quoted in *ibid.,* p. 84.   43. *Ibid.,* p. 188.

44. Campbell-Johnson, p. 90.

45. Quoted in E. W. R. Lumby, *The Transfer of Power in India, 1945–1947* (London, George Allen & Unwin, 1954), p. 161.

8. THE PARTITION PLAN

1. *Speeches and Documents on the Indian Constitution, 1921–1947,* ed. by Sir Maurice Gwyer and A. Appadorai (2 vols., London, Oxford University Press, 1957), II, 670–75.

2. Alan Campbell-Johnson, *Mission with Mountbatten* (London, Robert Hale, 1953), pp. 99–100.

3. Abul Kalam Azad, *India Wins Freedom* (Calcutta, Orient Longmans, 1959), p. 193.

4. V. P. Menon, *The Transfer of Power in India* (Calcutta, Orient Longmans, 1956), p. 376.

5. Pyarelal, *Mahatma Gandhi: The Last Phase* (2 vols., Ahmedabad, Navajivan Publishing House, 1956), II, 277.

6. Government of India Records, quoted in Leonard Mosley, *The Last Days of the British Raj* (London, Weidenfeld and Nicolson, 1961), p. 132.

7. Menon, p. 376.

8. Government of India Records, quoted in Mosley, p. 133.

9. Lord Ismay, *Memoirs* (London, Heinemann, 1960), p. 424.

10. *Keesing's Contemporary Archives* (Bristol, Keesing's Publications, 1946–1948), VI, 8632–33.

11. Lord Mountbatten, *Time Only to Look Forward* (London, N. Kaye, 1949), pp. 10–12.

12. *Speeches and Documents on the Indian Constitution,* II, 681–84.

13. Quoted in the Delhi daily *Dawn,* June 5, 1947.

14. Lord Mountbatten, pp. 19–48.   15. Quoted in Menon, p. 382.

16. Azad, pp. 186–87.

17. Michael Brecher, *Nehru: A Political Biography* (London, Oxford University Press, 1959), p. 349.

18. Quoted in Menon, p. 384.   19. Quoted in *ibid.,* p. 382.

20. Azad, p. 198.   21. Menon, p. 386.

9. PROBLEMS OF PARTITION

1. Abul Kalam Azad, *India Wins Freedom* (Calcutta, Orient Longmans, 1959), pp. 193–94.

2. Government of India Records, quoted in Leonard Mosley, *The Last Days of the British Raj* (London, Weidenfeld and Nicolson, 1961), p. 132.

3. *Ibid.*

4. Pyarelal, *Mahatma Gandhi: The Last Phase* (2 vols., Ahmedabad, Navajivan Publishing House, 1956), II, 268–70.

5. Quoted in *ibid.,* pp. 267–68.   6. *Ibid.,* p. 273.

7. *Ibid.,* p. 275.

8. V. P. Menon, *The Transfer of Power in India* (Calcutta, Orient Longmans, 1957), p. 389.

9. Quoted in Pyarelal, II, 277.   10. *Ibid.,* p. 279.

11. *Ibid.,* p. 278.

12. Government of India Records, quoted in Mosley, p. 151.

13. Lord Ismay, *Memoirs* (London, Heinemann, 1960), p. 429.

14. Government of India Records, quoted in Mosley, p. 155.

15. Ian Stephens, *Pakistan* (London, Ernest Benn, 1963), p. 176.

16. Ismay, pp. 429–30.

17. D. G. Tendulkar, *Mahatma* (8 vols., New Delhi, Government of India, Publication Division, 1960–63), VIII, p. 252.

18. *Ibid.,* p. 260.   19. *Ibid.,* p. 252.

20. Kewal L. Panjabi, *The Indomitable Sardar* (Bombay, Bharatiya Vidya Bhavan, 1962), p. 139.

21. Ismay, p. 428.

22. Quoted in John Connell, *Auchinleck* (London, Cassell, 1959), pp. 915–18.

23. *Ibid.,* pp. 920–22.

24. *Notes on the Sikh Plan* (Lahore, West Punjab Government, 1948), p. 7.

25. *Ibid.,* p. 25.

26. Government of India Records, quoted in Mosley, pp. 205–6.

27. Ismay, p. 431.

28. Government of India Records, quoted in Mosley, p. 205.

29. *Ibid.,* p. 207.   30. Quoted in Azad, p. 190.

31. Alan Campbell-Johnson, *Mission with Mountbatten* (London, Robert Hale, 1953), pp. 174–75.

32. E. W. R. Lumby, *The Transfer of Power in India, 1945–1947* (London, George Allen & Unwin, 1954), p. 265.

33. Campbell-Johnson, pp. 148–49.   34. *Ibid.,* p. 152.

35. *Ibid.,* p. 156.

10. RADCLIFFE'S AWARD

1. Alan Campbell-Johnson, *Mission with Mountbatten* (London, Robert Hale, 1953), p. 124.

2. *Ibid.,* p. 100.   3. *Ibid.,* pp. 71–72.

4. Quoted in the Madras daily *Hindu,* January 16, 1950.

5. Lord Ismay, *Memoirs* (London, Heinemann, 1960), p. 420.

6. Ian Stephens, *Pakistan* (London, Ernest Benn, 1963), p. 180.

7. Lord Mountbatten, *Time Only to Look Forward* (London, N. Kaye, 1949), p. 33.

8. Government of India Records, quoted in Leonard Mosley, *The Last Days of the British Raj* (London, Weidenfeld and Nicolson, 1961), p. 206.

9. *Ibid.,* p. 212.   10. Mountbatten, p. 30.

11. V. P. Menon, *The Story of the Integration of the Indian States* (Calcutta, Orient Longmans, 1956), p. 394.

12. Lord Birdwood, *Two Nations and Kashmir* (London, Robert Hale, 1956), p. 74.

13. *Speeches and Documents on the Indian Constitution, 1921–1947,*

ed. by Sir Maurice Gwyer and A. Appadorai (2 vols., London, Oxford University Press, 1957), II, p. 679.

14. Campbell-Johnson, pp. 151–52.

15. Penderel Moon, *Divide and Quit* (London, Chatto & Windus, 1961), p. 96.

16. Stephens, p. 180.   17. Campbell-Johnson, p. 152.

18. Quaid-i-Azam Muhammad Ali Jinnah, *Speeches as Governor General* (Karachi, Pakistan Publications, 1963), pp. 32–33.

11. THE ACCESSION OF THE STATES

1. *Speeches and Documents on the Indian Constitution, 1921–1947*, ed. by Sir Maurice Gwyer and A. Appadorai (2 vols., London, Oxford University Press, 1957), II, pp. 767–69.

2. V. P. Menon, *The Story of the Integration of the Indian States* (Calcutta, Orient Longmans, 1956), p. 22.

3. B. Pattabhai Sitaramayya, *The History of the Indian National Congress* (2 vols., Bombay, Padme Publications, 1946), II, pp. 79–80.

4. Quoted in R. Coupland, *The Constitutional Problem in India* (3 parts, Madras, Oxford University Press, 1945), Part II, p. 173.

5. Quoted in Menon, p. 78.

6. *Speeches and Documents on the Indian Constitution*, II, pp. 767–69.

7. Lord Mountbatten, *Time Only to Look Forward* (London, N. Kaye, 1949), pp. 39–42.

8. Quoted in E. W. R. Lumby, *The Transfer of Power in India, 1945–1947*, (London, George Allen & Unwin, 1954), p. 233.

9. Quoted in the Delhi daily *Dawn*, August 1, 1947.

10. *Speeches and Documents on the Indian Constitution*, II, pp. 770–72.

11. Alan Campbell-Johnson, *Mission with Mountbatten* (London, Robert Hale, 1953), pp. 140–41.

12. Mountbatten, pp. 51–56.   13. Menon, p. 116.

14. *Ibid.*, p. 113.   15. *Ibid.*, p. 117.

16. Sir Francis Tuker, *While Memory Serves* (London, Cassell, 1950), p. 390.

17. Penderel Moon, *Divide and Quit* (London, Chatto & Windus, 1961), p. 157. Penderel Moon was Revenue Minister of Bahawalpur state at the time of partition.

12. THE BIRTH OF PAKISTAN

1. Quoted in the Karachi daily *Dawn*, August 16, 1947.

2. *Ibid.*

3. Quaid-i-Azam Muhammad Ali Jinnah, *Speeches as Governor General* (Karachi, Pakistan Publications, 1963), p. 17.

4. *Ibid.*, pp. 7–9.   5. *Ibid.*, p. 7.   6. *Ibid.*, p. 54.

13. THE GREAT HOLOCAUST
AND THE REHABILITATION
OF REFUGEES

1. Khalid Bin Sayeed, *Pakistan: The Formative Phase* (Karachi, Pakistan Publishing House, 1960), p. 181.

2. Sir Francis Tuker, *While Memory Serves* (London, Cassell, 1950), pp. 445–49.

3. *Ibid.*, pp. 329, 449.

4. Quoted in Ian Stephens, *Pakistan* (London, Ernest Benn, 1963), p. 183.

5. John Connell, *Auchinleck* (London, Cassell, 1959), p. 906.

6. *Ibid.*, p. 911.

7. Abul Kalam Azad, *India Wins Freedom* (Calcutta, Orient Longmans, 1959), pp. 213–14.

8. Lord Ismay, *Memoirs* (London, Heinemann, 1960), p. 438.

9. *Ibid.*, p. 439.   10. Quoted in Tuker, p. 489.

11. *Ibid.*, p. 455.   12. Quoted in Connell, p. 924.

13. Quoted in Michael Brecher, *Nehru: A Political Biography* (London, Oxford University Press, 1959), p. 378.

14. Quoted in the Karachi daily *Dawn*, November 5, 1948.

15. Kewal L. Panjabi, *The Indomitable Sardar* (Bombay, Bharatiya Vidya Bhavan, 1962), p. 190.

14. JUNAGADH, HYDERABAD,
AND KASHMIR

1. V. P. Menon, *The Story of the Integration of the Indian States* (Calcutta, Orient Longmans, 1956), p. 130.

2. Quoted in *ibid.*, p. 319.

3. Mir Laik Ali, *The Tragedy of Hyderabad* (Karachi, Pakistan Cooperative Book Society, 1962), pp. 89–90.

4. Menon, p. 335.

5. Quoted in K. M. Munshi, *The End of an Era* (Bombay, Bharatiya Vidya Bhavan, 1957), pp. 150–51.

6. Menon, p. 322.   7. Laik Ali, pp. 207–12.

8. K. Sarwar Hasan, *Pakistan and the United Nations* (New York, Manhattan Publishing Company, 1960), p. 87.

9. D. G. Tendulkar, *Mahatma* (8 vols., New Delhi, Government of India, Publication Division, 1960–63), VIII, 69.

10. Quoted in *Chronology of Pakistan, 1947–1957* (Karachi, Kamel Publications, 1957), p. 20.

11. Pyarelal, *Mahatma Gandhi: The Last Phase* (2 vols., Ahmedabad, Navajivan Publishing House, 1956), II, 352.

12. Alan Campbell-Johnson, *Mission with Mountbatten* (London, Robert Hale, 1953), p. 120.

13. Menon, p. 394.   14. Campbell-Johnson, p. 224.

15. Quoted in Pyarelal, II, 357–58.

16. Ian Stephens, *Pakistan* (London, Ernest Benn, 1963), p. 200.

17. Richard Symonds in the *Statesman* of Calcutta, February 4, 1948.

18. Quoted in Sarwar Hasan, p. 96.

19. Campbell-Johnson, pp. 212–13.   20. *Ibid.,* pp. 224–25.

21. *Ibid.,* p. 223.

22. Ian Stephens, *Horned Moon* (London, Chatto & Windus, 1953), pp. 109–10.

23. Lord Birdwood, *Two Nations and Kashmir* (London, Robert Hale, 1956), p. 64.

24. Josef Korbel, *Danger in Kashmir* (Princeton, N.J., Princeton University Press, 1954), pp. 79–80.

25. John Connell, *Auchinleck* (London, Cassell, 1959), pp. 931–32.

26. Quoted in Sarwar Hasan, p. 104.   27. Quoted in *ibid.,* p. 115.

28. Security Council Official Records, quoted in Sarwar Hasan, p. 128.

29. Quoted in Sarwar Hasan, p. 125.

30. Campbell-Johnson, p. 287.

31. *Ibid.,* p. 291.   32. Korbel, p. 144.

16. ECONOMIC AND FINANCIAL PROBLEMS OF THE NEW STATE

1. Beverley Nichols, *Verdict on India* (London, Jonathan Cape, 1944), pp. 189–91.

2. Quoted in Pyarelal, *Mahatma Gandhi: The Last Phase* (2 vols., Ahmedabad, Navajivan Publishing House, 1956), II, 83.

3. Quaid-i-Azam Muhammad Ali Jinnah, *Speeches as Governor General* (Karachi, Pakistan Publications, 1963), p. 106.

4. *Ibid.,* pp. 153–54.

5. J. Russell Andrus and Azizali F. Mohammad, *The Economy of Pakistan* (London, Oxford University Press, 1958), p. 376.

17. ADMINISTRATIVE AND POLITICAL PROBLEMS OF THE NEW STATE

1. Quaid-i-Azam Muhammad Ali Jinnah, *Speeches as Governor General* (Karachi, Pakistan Publications, 1963), p. 58.

2. *Ibid.,* p. 84.   3. *Ibid.,* p. 90.   4. *Ibid.,* p. 104.

5. Quoted in the Karachi daily *Dawn*, April 21, 1948.

6. Michael Brecher, *Nehru: A Political Biography* (London, Oxford University Press, 1959), p. 377.

7. Jinnah, p. 65.

8. Liaquat Ali Khan, *Pakistan: The Heart of Asia* (Cambridge, Mass., Harvard University Press, 1950), p. 33.

9. Ishtiaq Husain Qureshi, *The Muslim Community of the Indo-Pakistan Sub-Continent* (The Hague, Mouton, 1962), p. 255.

10. Liaquat Ali Khan, p. 82.   11. Jinnah, p. 159.

12. *Ibid.,* p. 65.

Index